EMPRESSES-IN-WAITING
Female Power and Performance
at the Late Roman Court

Women in Ancient Cultures

WOMEN IN ANCIENT CULTURES

Women in Ancient Cultures aims to unite ground-breaking research from all fields of ancient world studies, publishing scholarship that pertains to all aspects of women's lives in the ancient world, and the various levels of agency that they could, and could not, attain as well as the dynamics and modalities of female agency under, and against, oppressive conditions – patriarchal, heterosexist, and otherwise.

Series Editors
Marta Ameri, Colby College
Virginia Campbell, Independent Researcher
Amy Gansell, St John's University
Irene Salvo, University of Exeter
Rebecca Usherwood, Trinity College Dublin
Lewis Webb, University of Oxford

Editorial Board Members
Solange Ashby, UCLA
Erin Walcek Averett, Creighton University
Lea Beness, Macquarie University
Sandra Boehringer, Université de Strasbourg
Benjamin Cartlidge, University of Liverpool
Hsiao-wen Cheng, University of Pennsylvania
Eleri Cousins, Lancaster University
Walter Crist, Universiteit Leiden
Al Duncan, University of North Carolina, Chapel Hill
Paul du Plessis, University of Edinburgh
Abigail Graham, University of Warwick & Institute of Classical Studies
Judith P. Hallett, University of Maryland
Christina Halperin, Université de Montréal
Emily Hauser, University of Exeter
Emily Hemelrijk, University of Amsterdam
Tom Hillard, Macquarie University
Julia Hillner, Universität Bonn
Bret Hinsch, Fo Guang University
Owen Hodkinson, University of Leeds
Rosemary Joyce, University of California, Berkeley
Ariadne Konstantinou, Bar-Ilan University
Victoria Leonard, Royal Holloway,
University of London & Institute of Classical Studies
Lloyd Llewellyn-Jones, Cardiff University
Nandini Pandey, University of Wisconsin-Madison
Christine Plastow, The Open University
Christian Rollinger, Universität Trier
Kathryn Welch, The University of Sydney

EMPRESSES-IN-WAITING
Female Power and Performance at the
Late Roman Court

CHRISTIAN ROLLINGER AND
NADINE VIERMANN (EDS.)

LIVERPOOL UNIVERSITY PRESS

An Open Access version of Lewis Dagnall's chapter, 'The Empress Sophia and East Roman Foreign Policy', will be available on the Liverpool University Press website.

First published 2024 by
Liverpool University Press
4 Cambridge Street
Liverpool
L69 7ZU

Copyright © 2024 Liverpool University Press

Christian Rollinger and Nadine Viermann have asserted the right to be identified as the editors of this book in accordance with the Copyright, Designs and Patents Act 1988.

All rights reserved. No part of this book may be reproduced, stored in a retrieval system, or transmitted, in any form or by any means, electronic, mechanical, photocopying, recording, or otherwise, without the prior written permission of the publisher.

British Library Cataloguing-in-Publication data
A British Library CIP record is available

ISBN 978-1-80207-593-9 cased

Typeset by Carnegie Book Production, Lancaster

Contents

Acknowledgements vii

Contributors ix

Introduction

    Christian Rollinger and Nadine Viermann: Empresses-in-Waiting? An Introduction   1

    1. Anja Wieber: Towards a History of Scholarship on Late Antique Imperial Women: From *Theodora, the Tigress* to Matronage   15

Section 1: Political Agency and Power Brokerage

    2. Silvia Holm: Empress with Agency: Eusebia's Efforts to Consolidate the Constantinian Dynasty   43

    3. Belinda Washington: John Chrysostom's *Letter to a Young Widow*: Reflections on Imperial Women's Roles at Regime Change   67

    4. Silvio Roggo: The Empress Sophia Reconsidered   97

    5. Lewis Dagnall: The Empress Sophia and East Roman Foreign Policy   115

    6. Nadine Viermann: Dynasty, Endogamy, and Civil Strife: Martina Augusta and the Role of Imperial Women in the Early Seventh Century   137

Section 2: Performance and Representation

    7. Mads Ortving Lindholmer: Constructing Power through Rituals: The Case of Theodora   157

    8. Pavla Gkantzios Drápelová: Empresses on Early Byzantine Coins (Sixth to Seventh Centuries): Evidence of Power?   177

Section 3: Non- and Near-Imperial Women at the Imperial Court

  9. Geoffrey Nathan: Augusta Unrealized: Anicia Juliana and the Logistics of Place   205

  10. Christopher Lillington-Martin: Antonina *Patricia*: Theodora's Fixer at the Female Court and the Politics of Gender in Procopius   223

  11. Marco Cristini: Matasuintha: From Gothic Queen to Imperial Woman   243

Conclusion

  Julia Hillner: Imperial Women after Curtains   261

Bibliography   273

Figures   315

Indices   329

Acknowledgements

We would like to express our gratitude to a number of people who have contributed to turning an idea into the present volume. Greg Gilles launched the *Women in Ancient Cultures* series with Liverpool University Press and thus provided the first impetus to consider this publication. Rebecca Usherwood, as a member of the editorial board of the series, and the anonymous reviewers for the press have all significantly contributed to improving both the original proposal and the present book. Clare Litt at Liverpool University Press has been a steady guide and helpful ally in negotiations with the press and has shown great patience and enthusiasm in dealing with a project delayed by Covid and other difficulties. Marie Thielen, stud. phil., has gone over the manuscript and saved us from many errors; any that remain are, of course, solely our responsibility. We are also grateful to the institutions that have liberally and unbureaucratically granted image rights for objects in their possession, particularly the Museum am Dom, Trier; the Classical Numismatics Group; the Musée de Cluny – Musée national du Moyen Âge, Cluny; and the Opera di Religione della Diocesi di Ravenna.

Trier and Durham, All Hallows' Eve 2023
Christian Rollinger
Nadine Viermann

Contributors

Marco Cristini obtained his PhD in Classics at Scuola Normale Superiore (Pisa, Italy) in 2020. He subsequently held a fellowship at the University of Tübingen and at the Istituto Italiano di Storia Antica (Rome). He is currently Lecturer at the University of Florence. He is the author of *Baduila: Politics and Warfare at the End of Ostrogothic Italy* (2022), as well as several papers on sixth-century Italy, Cassiodorus, Procopius of Caesarea, and early medieval diplomacy. He is currently working on a book about African Latin Christianity from the Vandals to the Almohads.

Lewis Dagnall is a doctoral student and associate tutor at the University of Sheffield. His research concerns political economy, state formation, and foreign policy in Late Antiquity, with a focus on the sixth century. He contributed as a research assistant to the online prosopographical database, 'Clerical Exile in Late Antiquity'. His forthcoming thesis, *The Price of Empire? Justinian I's Use of Cash Subsidies in Foreign Policy, 527–565*, provides a synoptic account of the use of 'tribute' in the foreign policy of Justinian I.

Pavla Gkantzios Drápelová is a Byzantinist at the Institute of Slavonic Studies of the Czech Academy of Sciences (Department of Paleoslovenic and Byzantine Studies). She undertook her postgraduate studies at the Department of History and Archaeology of the National and Kapodistrian University of Athens. She completed numismatic courses organized by the Dumbarton Oaks Research Library and Collection, the British School of Athens, and the National Hellenic Research foundation. Her main interests are Byzantine numismatics, contacts between Byzantium and the Slavs, and Byzantine archaeology.

Julia Hillner is Professor of Dependency and Slavery Studies (Imperial Rome, Late Antiquity) at the University of Bonn, specializing in the history of the family and the household, of crime and punishment, and of the city of Rome at the end of antiquity. Her latest monograph is *Helena Augusta: Mother of the Empire* (2023).

Silvia Holm is a PhD candidate at the University of Rostock (Germany), where she completed her master's degree in Classical Studies in 2022 with a major in Ancient History. The primary focus of her research is the political history of the later Roman Empire, especially Roman imperial succession from the fifth to the seventh centuries.

Christopher Lillington-Martin is Associate Researcher at the University of Barcelona and Oxford Centre for Late Antiquity and a doctoral researcher at Coventry University. He is the editor of *Procopius of Caesarea: Literary and Historical Interpretations* (2018), co-author of 'Turning traitor: shifting loyalties in Procopius' Gothic Wars' in *Byzantina Symmeikta* with Michael Stewart (2021), and author of 'Procopius on the struggle for Dara and Rome' in *War and Warfare in Late Antiquity*, edited by Alexander Sarantis and Neil Christie (2013). He is currently working on historiography and characterization in Procopius.

Mads Ortving Lindholmer is vice-director at the Danish Institute in Rome. He is currently working on a monograph on the imperial admission (the so-called *salutatio* and *adoratio*), which explores the connection between this ritual and imperial power in the period from Augustus to Late Antiquity. Aside from this, he is currently completing (with Adrastos Omissi) the project *A New Map of the Fall of the Roman Empire, 270–480 AD*, and has published numerous articles and chapters on Cassius Dio. He is the co-editor of *Cassius Dio's Forgotten History of Early Rome: The Roman History, Books 1–21* (2019).

Geoffrey Nathan is Lecturer of History at San Diego State University and Honorary Senior Lecturer at the University of New South Wales, Sydney. He has published widely on the history of the family in Late Antiquity. He is currently writing a broader study on Anicia Juliana, as well as working on refugee crises in the fourth through sixth centuries.

Silvio Roggo holds a postdoctoral position at the University of Frankfurt, where he works as a collaborator on a DFG-funded project towards a new critical edition, translation, and commentary of the *Ecclesiastical History* of John of Ephesus. He obtained his PhD in History from the University of Cambridge in 2022 with a thesis on the Church of Constantinople in the late sixth century. Previously, he studied in Oxford, Heidelberg, and Freiburg/Switzerland; his main research interests include Late Antique Christianity, episcopal networks, prosopography, and the patriarchate of Constantinople.

Christian Rollinger is *Akademischer Rat* for Ancient History at the University of Trier. His research deals with Roman and Hellenistic monarchies and their performance of power, the social, economic, and cultural history of the late Republic and early Empire in general and of friendship in particular, and classical receptions in videogames. His most recent book is a study of the court rituals of the later Roman monarchy (*Zeremoniell und Herrschaft in der Spätantike. Die Rituale des Kaiserhofs in Konstantinopel*, 2024).

Nadine Viermann is Assistant Professor of Late Antique and Early Byzantine History at Durham University. Her first book, *Herakleios, der schwitzende Kaiser. Die oströmische Monarchie in der ausgehenden Spätantike* (2021), is a structural analysis of the reign of the emperor Heraclius in the context of Late Roman monarchy. She is currently working on the translation of relics in the Late Antique Mediterranean.

Belinda Washington is an independent scholar who lives in Scotland. Her research interests include imperial politics of the fourth and fifth centuries and the evolution of the roles of imperial women over the course of the Roman Empire. She previously contributed a chapter on Julian's Oration for Eusebia ('Playing with conventions in Julian's Encomium to Eusebia: does gender make a difference?') in *Imperial Panegyric from Diocletian to Honorius*, edited by Adrastos Omissi and Alan J. Ross (2020).

Anja Wieber is an independent scholar of ancient history and a member of the international research network *Imagines*. Her personal research interests include women's history and gender studies, with a focus on Late Antiquity and empresses, ancient and modern slavery, the history of education, and reception studies. In the last field she has specialized in the representation of antiquity in different filmic genres and has made a study of the variety of forms by which the Palmyrene queen Zenobia is portrayed. She is co-editor, with Filippo Carlà-Uhink, of *Orientalism and the Reception of Powerful Women from the Ancient World* (2020).

Empresses-in-Waiting? An Introduction

Christian Rollinger and Nadine Viermann

The late Roman imperial court was a busy place, buzzing with officeholders, courtiers, eunuchs, servants, and slaves; both as a physical space as well as a platform for social and political interaction, the court was centred around the emperor, who, in Christian Late Antiquity and in political discourse, was officially conceived as God's vice regent on earth. The emperors themselves, however, were surrounded by women: their wives, mothers, sisters, and daughters, as well as female members of aristocratic families and wives of the selfsame officeholders and courtiers that populated the palace. These imperial and near-imperial women had their own physical spaces, a 'female court' akin to the male one, bounded by social and cultural restrictions and possibly also physically delineated by doors, curtains, and palace staff. In some respects, this female court mirrored the male one, doubling the parts of the palace officials and staff, and including (female) courtiers. This is most famously depicted in the Justinianic mosaics of San Vitale in Ravenna, which feature on the cover of this collection (see also fig. 21), and show Theodora surrounded by *her* court. Collectively, the "Empresses-in-Waiting" of the title encompass both groups: imperial and near-imperial women. An admittedly frivolous pun on the multiple meanings of that expression, the title nevertheless serves to make a point: it alludes to the ladies-in-waiting that surround empresses, queens and (great-)duchesses of past and present monarchies, themselves members of their respective aristocracies and conceived of as female courtiers and companions. As Geoffrey Nathan considers the term in his contribution to the present volume, they were proximate to, but never *of* the ruling household. As depicted in the Ravenna mosaics, they were attendant ladies, to paraphrase T.S. Eliot, there to swell a progress, start a scene or two. More obliquely, however, the title is also intended to reference the complicated question of the formal and informal power of Late Antique empresses. As will become clear in the individual chapters as well as in the synthesis provided by Julia Hillner, in the Late Antique imperial court, female authority and power could hardly stand for itself, but was largely defined in relation to its male counterpart. Female members of the imperial house were very much '(co-)rulers-in-waiting', clustering around the husbands, sons, fathers, or other relatives whose hands clasped the imperial sceptres. Some of them seem to have tried to play the stage of the imperial palace in a more self-confident way; some used the means of female performance to support their families; some of them were successful in asserting a politically restricted, yet indubitably powerful position; others were kept down by patriarchal structures. Others still – female members of the highest nobility, such as Anicia Juliana, the proud and wealthy daughter and granddaughter of two individual western Augusti – may have felt themselves more suited to an imperial role than the actual rulers or might have held such aspirations for the male members of their family that never came to pass; they were, more literally, empresses-in-waiting, their potential and that of their house never to be fully realized. Such aspirations, but also the lives and existence, the roles and limitations of imperial and near-imperial women, are accessible to us as historians primarily through the lens of official imperial communications and the gaze of male authors. It is the aim of this volume to break through these barriers and assess the power and agency that imperial and near-imperial women could exert in a constrained setting and to explore their performance in a male-dominated environment.

This is not, in and of itself, a radically new ambition. It is a common trope in writing introductions to scholarly works to deplore the historiographical neglect attached to the chosen subject in order to justify writing (or editing) a book on that very subject. In some cases, this is true; often, the contention is questionable or only applies if one restricts scholarship to individual languages or academic contexts. In the case of Roman empresses – or, to use the preferred term employed in this volume, 'imperial women'[1] – perhaps surprisingly, allegations of scholarly neglect would be decidedly selective. As a matter of fact, Roman imperial women, their lives, roles, and actions across the centuries of imperial rule, have been the subject of extensive study in the past, albeit for the most part in the shape of temporary spurts of activity rather than sustained scholarly interest. This is particularly true for Late Antique and Byzantine imperial women. Charles Diehl, one of the founding fathers of modern Byzantine studies, devoted several early studies to empresses in the first decade of the twentieth century: his *Théodora, impératrice de Byzance* (1904) served as a companion volume of sorts to his *Justinien et la civilisation byzantine au VIe siècle* (1901) and a number of chapters in his two-volume *Figures byzantines* (1906–1908)

---

[1] Cf. Boatwright 2021, 2 ("those who shared marriage or immediate family with the emperor").

centred on Late Antique and Byzantine empresses.[2] His successors, on the other hand, seem to have lost interest for a while and it would be wrong to assume that this early work translated into a continuous scholarly inquiry into Roman imperial women of either the Principate or Late Antiquity during the middle decades of the century.

In fact, it was not until the 1970s and 1980s that a sustained effort to study the lives and roles of such women was undertaken, particularly with regard to imperial women of the Principate. Beginning with two early seminal works of the late 70s by Hildegard Temporini-Gräfin Vitzthum (*Die Frauen am Hofe Trajans. Ein Beitrag zur Stellung der Augustae im Principat*) and Erich Kettenhofen (*Die syrischen Augustae in der historischen Überlieferung. Ein Beitrag zum Problem der Orientalisierung*), imperial women of the 'classical' Principate have been the subject of continued and intensifying scholarly interest.[3] But whereas these two foundational studies were nuanced analyses of the roles and positions that imperial women occupied at court and in historiography, subsequent scholarship has often chosen a biographical approach, engaging with case studies of well-known figures or, rather, those for whom our sources are comparatively plentiful. By necessity, this included notorious figures such as Cleopatra or Theodora (to name but the two most egregious examples),[4] but generally this approach to the study of female figures of authority resembled what Gerda Lerner has termed "compensatory history", that is the history of "women of achievement", "the history of exceptional, even deviant women".[5] To a degree, this applies to more recent scholarship as well. Temporini-Gräfin Vitzthum's 2002 edited collection of biographical sketches of Roman empresses (*Die Kaiserinnen Roms. Von Livia bis Theodora*) remains an important starting point for students and researchers alike not least because it demonstrates in compact and accessible fashion the various roles that imperial women have played in the history of the Roman Empire.[6] Since the publication of this collection, attempts at biographical studies have been made for a number of imperial women of the Principate, such as Julia, daughter of Augustus, Livia, Messalina, Vibia Sabina, Faustina maior and minor, Julia Domna, and even Ulpia Severina, empress to Aurelian.[7] Work on Hellenistic royal

---

[2] Diehl 1901. 1904. 1906–1908. The chapters devoted to Byzantine empresses were later published in English translation as *Byzantine Empresses* (Diehl 1963).
[3] Temporini-Gräfin Vitzthum 1979. Kettenhofen 1979.
[4] For Cleopatra, see most recently Schäfer 2006. Roller 2012. For Theodora, see Cesaretti 2001. Evans 2002. Potter 2015.
[5] Lerner 1975, 5.
[6] Temporini-Gräfin Vitzthum 2002.
[7] Julia: Fantham 2006. Livia: Barrett 2002. Kunst 2008. Messalina: Cargill-Martin 2023. Vibia Sabina: Brennan 2018. Faustina maior and minor: Priwitzer 2009. Levick 2014. Julia Domna: Levick 2007. Ulpia Severina: Cassia 2023.

women has evolved in tandem, with important studies devoted both to individual figures – Eurydice, Arsinoe, Berenice II, Cleopatra Selene, and most recently Cleopatra Thea and Cleopatra III[8] – and to more systematic approaches to queenship.[9] In the field of Late Antiquity and Byzantine studies, the biographical approach has likewise flowered in the past decades. A number of important monographs appeared during the late 1990s and 2000s, studying female members of imperial dynasties such as the Constantinians[10] or Theodosians (again),[11] or focused on individual empresses such as Helena, Serena, Pulcheria and Eudocia, Galla Placidia, Ariadne, Anicia Juliana, Theodora, Amalasuintha, Gosvinta, and Anna Komnene.[12]

In parallel to these biographical endeavours, scholars have increasingly moved beyond individual figures in an attempt to better understand the roles, positions, and agency of imperial women. Kenneth Holum's 1982 *Theodosian Empresses* sparked a renewed interest in Late Antique and Byzantine imperial women and paved the way for a re-evaluation of Late Antique empressship (and hence, emperorship) in general. Holum not only convincingly argued that the position of empress gained in importance under the Theodosians, becoming more formalized and institutionalized than it had previously been, but also presented the female members of the Theodosian dynasty as political agents in their own right, with their own agency and resources. Influenced by Holum's work and particularly by the strides made in women's and gender history since the 1980s and 1990s, research into Roman imperial women has further proliferated and benefitted from the advances made into the research of ancient women's lives in general.[13] Four volumes published in short succession between 1999 and 2001 proved particularly influential for the following research: Lynda

---

[8] Eurydice: Carney 2019. Arsinoe: Carney 2013. Berenice II: Clayman 2014. Cleopatra Selena: Draycott 2022. Roller 2021, 27–48. Cleopatra Thea and Cleopatra III: Llewellyn-Jones and McAuley 2023.
[9] Aulbach 2015. Hämmerling 2019. Kunst 2021.
[10] Wieber-Scariot 1999.
[11] Busch 2015.
[12] Helena: Drijvers 1992a. Pohlsander 1995. Hillner 2023. Serena: Magnani 2002. Pulcheria and Eudocia: Sowers 2008. 2020. Angelidi 2008. Galla Placidia: Oost 1968. Sirago 1996. Sivan 2011. Salisbury 2015. Ariadne: Magliaro 2013. Anicia Juliana: Capizzi 1997. Theodora: Evans 2002. 2011. Potter 2015. Amalasuintha: Sirago 1999. Vitiello 2017. Gosvinta: Godoy 2004. Anna Komnene: Morelli and Saulle 1998. Neville 2016. In addition, there are a number of edited collections comprised of case studies of select imperial women, cf. Chiriatti and Villegas Marín 2021. Other recent publications, particularly the *Routledge Companion to Women and Monarchy in the Ancient World* edited by Elizabeth Carney and Sabine Müller (2020), focus on Hellenistic and Imperial (i.e., Principate) female rulers and elide the post-Severan empire.
[13] Cf., e.g., Laiou 1981. 1992a. 1992b. For a succinct review of the field's history, see Wieber-Scariot 1999, 39–55. Kolb 2010b, 12–14.

Garland's *Byzantine Empresses* and Judith Herrin's *Women in Purple: Rulers of Medieval Byzantium* take the shape of a series of analytical inquiries into the lives and biographies of select empresses, while Liz James' *Empresses and Power in Early Byzantium* and Barbara Hill's *Imperial Women in Byzantium 1025–1204* approach their subject from a more systematic perspective, centring on the exercise of actual political power.[14] Judith Herrin has more recently also published a study of empressship in Byzantium that takes a more systematic approach.[15] However, these studies all cover a considerable span of time, from 527 to 1204, and are thus mainly focused on properly Byzantine imperial women – with the exception of James, who also focuses on a long Late Antiquity (fourth to eighth centuries). Other edited collections focus on specific aspects of empressship, such as their representation on Late Antique coinage or their activities as founders and patronesses of religious institutions.[16] Brian Sowers has recently studied the imperial role of Aelia Eudocia through the medium of her own poetry, which survives to a remarkable degree: nearly 3500 lines, "about three times as many as Sappho, antiquity's most celebrated female poet".[17] Edited volumes by Anne Kolb (*Augustae. Machtbewusste Frauen am römischen Kaiserhof?*) and Christiane Kunst (*Matronage. Handlungsstrategien und soziale Netzwerke antiker Herrscherfrauen*) have attempted to sketch out specifically female forms of imperial authority and to better understand the foundations – and limitations – of female imperial power.[18] Building on a concept and terminology coined by Anja Wieber-Scariot in the context of her study of Constantinian imperial women, Kunst in particular has applied this to ancient monarchies, meaning specifically female modes and means of expressing and manifesting status, influence, and power in the absence of legal authority.[19]

Why then, one may ask, this book? We understand it as part of a rising chorus, not as a lonely voice in the wilderness: inspired by scholarship of the past decades and mindful of the gendered and indirect nature of our sources,[20] it intends to explore the lives and actions of imperial and near-im-

---

[14] Garland 1999. Hill 1999. Herrin 2001. James 2001b.
[15] Herrin 2013.
[16] For the latter, see Angelova 2015. Dirschlmayer 2015. For representations of empresses, see Longo 2009.
[17] Sowers 2020, 2.
[18] Kolb 2010a. Kunst 2013c.
[19] Cf. Wieber, this volume.
[20] With the exception of the above-mentioned poetry of Aelia Eudocia, almost all of our sources are male-authored and imbued with specific societal, cultural, and political norms. To a degree, the lives and deeds of empresses are depicted and used by ancient authors as cyphers of male authority. This applies equally to literary and non-literary sources, with very few, isolated exceptions. Thus, any attempt to grapple with female

perial women – some well-known, some underexplored – specifically in the context of the imperial court, which, in one way or another, delineated their agency. Most chapters centre on the court in Constantinople where the imperial household (or, for parts of the fifth century, one branch of the imperial household) resided permanently from the early fourth century onwards. It is here, in the urban context of the metropolis and the bustling maze of the Great Palace, that we encounter some rather familiar female protagonists such as Eusebia, Theodora, or Anicia Juliana. While these women certainly cannot be considered understudied, the chapters that discuss aspects of their lives and positions present original approaches to shed new light on their relations to, and exercise of, power. The analyses contribute to exploring specific aspects of the dynamics of the female court such as imperial (female) performance and ceremony (as in the case of Theodora, discussed by Mads Ortving Lindholmer) and the opportunities of women who were adjacent to the imperial sphere (as in the cases of Anicia Juliana and Antonina, discussed by Geoffrey Nathan and Christopher Lillington-Martin). Beyond these familiar presences, the book strives to include more 'neglected' (by academic scholarship and standards, that is) figures such as the sixth-century Augusta Sophia, who, despite significant early studies, has not been extensively treated in recent decades,[21] or the seventh-century empress Martina, whose scandalous marriage to Heraclius made her notorious in Byzantine sources, but who has not received much attention in the context of Late Antique studies (as opposed to Byzantine studies). Yet other figures, such as the Goth Amalasuintha, were drawn into the dynamics of the Constantinopolitan court and politics only later in life and occupy very specific sectors of Late Antique high society. These chapters seek to locate their protagonists within the mechanism of the imperial court, but also to sound out their appearances and echoes in the textual and material media of imperial and near-imperial communication.

The existence of the imperial court, both as an institution and as a physical space, and court society (in the sense coined by Norbert Elias, as a group of people regularly associated with and thus bound together by the court)[22] is an often-acknowledged fact in Late Antiquity, but one that has not yet produced a sustained and systematic analysis. It is strangely shadowy, even absent from most institutional or political histories, except in those cases where our sources recount court intrigues and gossip. What

---

imperial agency needs to question the representation of empresses in our sources and to address this problem, particularly in the context of traditional tropes such as adultery, 'female' intrigue, and intrusions into male-reserved areas of court life, such as Theodora's ceremonial privileges.

[21] E.g., Cameron 1975c.
[22] Elias 1969.

studies there are on issues connected to the courts were written mostly in the 1960s and 70s and are centred on legal or administrative questions. By contrast, the social system of the court as a place of power has been comparatively little studied, although individual groups within it – and particularly the notorious court eunuchs of the *cubiculum* – have been the subject of dedicated research monographs.[23] This is a striking omission, as the importance of the court institution is not disputed for other historical epochs. By contrast, scholarship has, for the longest time, ignored the Roman courts of the Principate or Late Antiquity, partly even going so far as to deny their existence. This has changed since the late 1990s, as Roman court studies have increased in significance and importance – though the Late Antique court, in particular, remains understudied.[24] It is still, to quote Andrew Wallace-Hadrill, "the skeleton in the cupboard of [late] Roman history", even though it was the centre of official, administrative, and political life in the late Roman world, a vast hub of patronage networks, an arena of political competition, and a stage for an extensive court life and a highly refined political ceremonial.[25] It is, in short, an institution that defies easy categorisation. Wallace-Hadrill proposed to define the court as "the space around the ruler within which access to imperial favour is negotiated. The aula is not a building, though it has its monumental expression in the Palatium. Nor is it a legal or constitutional institution, such as Mommsen could recognize [...]. Nor is it a bureaucracy, nor even the imperial household [...]. It is the space within which all these groups and institutions intersect in the pursuit of power."[26]

Imperial court and court society thus provide the admittedly still fuzzy bounds of female imperial agency and behaviour. Empresses, imperial and near-imperial females, like the male nobility of service and the palace

---

[23] Cf., e.g., Scholten 1995 for the *praepositus sacri cubiculi*, the highest eunuch courtier, and Tougher 2021 for different roles eunuchs occupied in the Roman Empire.

[24] Seminal works in Roman court studies of the Principate are Winterling 1997b. 1998. 1999. Wallace-Hadrill 1996. Paterson 2007. Recently, major new studies have been published: Kelly and Hug 2022 is a handbook-like systematic overview of the court, while the edited volume Davenport and McEvoy 2023 focuses on the changing nature of Roman courts from the early empire to Late Antiquity. For Late Antiquity, only a smaller number of short studies have so far appeared: see Spawforth 2007b and Smith 2011. For other ancient courts, particularly Hellenistic royal courts, see Strootman 2014. Erskine, Llewellyn-Jones, and Wallace 2017.

[25] Wallace-Hadrill 2011, 92–93. On the court as ceremonial stage, see Rollinger 2020. 2023. 2024.

[26] Wallace-Hadrill 2011, 94. Cf. Erskine, Llewellyn-Jones, and Wallace 2017, xxi: "a circle of elite people and attendants [...] in orbit around a monarch as well as [...] a larger environment of political, military, economic, and cultural structures [...] which converged within the monarch's household."

elite, derived their power, influence, and status from imperial proximity. As individual chapters of this collection will show, imperial female authority could take several shapes and derive from quite different sources and strategies. For instance, while imperial women often gained and defended positions of influence or power because of their role as bearers of imperial heirs or 'conductors' of dynastic policy (e.g., Eusebia, as discussed by Silvia Holm in her chapter), others did not. The women of the Theodosian dynasty – and emperors such as Arcadius and Theodosius II as well – derived at least part of their legitimacy and status from personal and official piety, up to and including public vows of chastity. Imperial women also regularly appear in our sources as mediators of access to the emperor himself. Theodora was notorious for holding receptions – holding 'court', really – by herself, without the emperor being present, as Mads Ortving Lindholmer discusses in his chapter.[27] But, Procopius' diatribes notwithstanding, this was neither singular nor even that remarkable. We know from our sources the previous (and later) empresses and imperial women had acted precisely in the same fashion: for instance, Marc the Deacon describes a private audience that Eudoxia granted to the saintly Porphyry of Gaza[28] and empresses were regularly accosted both in the palace and in public, in order to gain (or force) access to the emperor.[29]

The passage in Marc the Deacon is particularly important for its detailed description of the proceedings and for the information it contains regarding the 'female court'. The author mentions officials of the empress' household that mirrored the officials in the service of the emperor: the saint and his entourage are invited to the private quarters of the empress by porters (*decani*) sent by the *castrensis* of the empress. From a fifth-century constitution, we know that the *decani* and *cursores partis Augustae* were officials of *spectabilis* rank appointed by the *scrinium sacrorum libellorum*; they are mentioned in a list of other officials ranging from the emperor's ushers (*admissionales*) to administrative officials to the staffs of high-ranking military officers.[30] If the *decani* were subordinated to the *castrensis* (the administrator of the empress' quarters), the latter was subordinated to the empress' own *praepositus sacri cubiculi*, the supervisor of the empress' household.[31] In other words, the male and female imperial households were separate administrative entities that followed a precisely identical organisational model. Subtle nuances connoted the differences in status between emperor and empress. In particular, the number of attendants seems to have

---

[27] Cf. Procop. *Anecd.* 15.25–27.
[28] Marc. Deac. *v. Porph.* 39–40.
[29] E.g., Sozom. *Hist. eccl.* 2.28.5. Athan. *apol. sec.* 86. Nik. *Brev.* 4.
[30] *CJ* 12.59.10.5.
[31] *CJ* 12.5.3. Cf. Hillner, this volume, 264.

been the most significant marker of difference. Both emperor and empress were attended by *silentiarii*, ushers armed with a large rod of gilt silver and tasked with ensuring ritual silence during official appearances, but the empress had access only to four, while the emperor himself was served by the rest of the *schola* of silentiaries (twenty-six, for a total of thirty). From the fragments of Peter the Patrician, Master of Offices under Justinian, we are informed that the empress was allowed to choose 'her' silentiaries herself "from the regular complement, [...] men who are of good reputation and who have given evidence of an honourable way of life".[32] However, the quasi-institutionalized nature of the female imperial household does not indicate a separate source of authority: as with all things, female imperial authority was derived from the emperor. This is apparent not so much from the legal regulations of the Justinianic Code, but rather from performative context. In the case of the empress' silentiaries, the empress performs her own ceremony of appointment in her quarters, handing over the official rods of office to the new silentiary. This is in itself remarkable and a notable departure from the usual model of the emperor being the sole source of insignia and codicils.[33] In the end, however, it is but a repetition of the actual appointment ceremony performed by the emperor: she confirms the appointment of a silentiary to her personal service, "even though he already holds the office", as Peter the Patrician remarks.[34]

The (to a degree) institutionalised female court cannot be treated here in detail; neither can the ceremonial role of the empress, which is similarly understudied. Both of these topics deserve their own systematic and exhaustive analysis, as does the imperial court in general.[35] What this present edited volume intends to provide, by contrast, is a selection of case studies orientated along the threads outlined above in the hopes that they can stimulate and contribute to a larger study.

Although contributions span from the mid-fourth to the seventh century, the contingencies of academic editing have led to a slight imbalance in this book in favour of case studies from the 'late' Late Antiquity. But the book itself was never intended to be governed by chronological and biographical approaches, espoused for instance by Temporini-Gräfin Vitzthum in her fundamental collection; neither does it make any claim to completeness. Its authors and chapters are interested

---

[32] *De cer.* 1.86 (389–90 Reiske): ἐκ τοῦ κοινοῦ καταλόγου ... ἐξ ὑπολήμψεως χρηστῆς καί βίου μεμαρτυρημένοι σεμνοῦ.

[33] *De cer.* 1.86.

[34] *De cer.* 1.86 (390 Reiske): καίτοι ἔχοντι ἤδη τὴν στρατείαν.

[35] This applies not only to the social and political, but also to other contexts such as the question of the imperial *gynaikonitis*, i.e., the 'female quarters' mentioned by some of our sources; cf. Wieber, this volume, 20–25.

in a variety of imperial and near-imperial figures and in a broad range of questions, and neither this variety nor the undeniable focus on the later centuries are inherently pejorative. On the contrary, this clustering offers a combination of approaches to the later sixth and early seventh centuries, supplemented by individual case studies on the generally better-researched imperial women of the fourth and fifth. Likewise, these earlier chapters can serve as a counterpoint to the geographical focus on the imperial court at Constantinople, which is a fundamental feature of Late Antique emperorship from 395 onwards. The court environments navigated by Eusebia, wife of Constantius II (discussed by Silvia Holm), and the unnamed empresses in John Chrysostom's *Letter to a Young Widow* (discussed by Belinda Washington) were more fluid and multicentric, with mobile emperors and several courts across the empire. The chapters thus showcase a variety of methods in assessing female power and agency that can be applied to other periods and protagonists.

To this end, Anja Wieber's review chapter will first provide a critical analysis of existing scholarship on Late Antique imperial women and empresses, the concepts (such as 'matronage') associated with them, and changing attitudes in contemporary scholarship. It outlines recent trends in research and discusses the concepts briefly touched upon above: power and matronage, in particular.

The first section of this volume engages with the question of representation and performance in relation to imperial women. Mads Ortving Lindholmer's chapter takes its inspiration from ritual theory and anthropological studies into political and social rituals. Arguing that rituals construct narratives of power and cause participants to internalise these, Lindholmer investigates Procopius' account of ceremonial innovations at the court of Justinian, which saw Theodora as the addressee of the *adoratio purpurae*. He explores how Theodora's participation in the *adoratio*, which has largely been ignored in modern scholarship, constructed power for her and influenced the narrative about imperial rule.

Pavla Gkantzios Drápelová focuses on imperial coinage depicting empresses and imperial women in the sixth and seventh centuries. Her starting point is that in the late sixth century and beginning with Sophia, imperial consorts again started appearing on coinage after a hiatus of more than a century. Comparing iconographies and historical contexts of coinage under Justin II, Tiberius, Maurice, and Heraclius, Gkantzios Drápelová highlights the functions of numismatic representations and what they can tell us about empress' positions at court. She argues that imperial women figured on coinage mainly in moments when emperors needed to strengthen their political position and emphasise dynastic legitimacy. The coinage thus illustrates the function of the empress in imperial propaganda as guarantor of legitimacy and dynastic continuity.

The second section comprises five chapters focusing on the opportunities of and constraints placed upon female members of the imperial family within the dynamics of negotiating political hierarchies at court as well as in broader realms of imperial activity. The chapters investigate how imperial women attempted to secure or even expand their own positions of power, building up personal networks at court or beyond and fostering relationships with close allies and family members.

Silvia Holm's analysis of the political role of Eusebia, wife of Constantius II, centres on her involvement in imperial dynastic policy, arguing that Eusebia's interventions aimed at strengthening not her own position, but that of the imperial couple. By supporting Julian's rise to Caesarship, Holm maintains that Eusebia's objective was to commit him to the imperial line through marriage to the emperor's sister, Helena. Using the matronage concept as framework, Holm illustrates the possibilities and structural limitations of female imperial power, showing Eusebia as a political agent of her own.

Belinda Washington examines the (anonymous) imperial figures in John Chrysostom' *Letter to a Young Widow*, which relates the unhappy fates of fourth-century imperial women. Seeking to identify these nameless women, Washington argues that their fates, as described in the letter, were those of imperial women at moments of change. Through analysis of the letter itself and consideration of it in the broader shifting context of the imperial court, as well as Chrysostom's own career, she distils the evolution of the roles of imperial women over the course of the long fourth century through the prism of regime change.

Two consecutive chapters, by Silvio Roggo and Lewis Dagnall, approach the figure of Sophia, wife and empress of Justin II. Roggo aims to shed new light on an understudied episode of an empress' agency at a period of transition of imperial power by examining the machinations of Sophia, who, when the eventual demise of her incapacitated husband had become foreseeable, sought to ensure that she would maintain her central role at the imperial court after his death. Lewis Dagnall, by contrast, studies Sophia's possible influence over, or even domination of, imperial foreign policy during the period of Justin II's incapacitation. Dagnall argues that Sophia enjoyed greater policy flexibility than Justin because the latter felt obliged to emulate the ideal of the masculine, militarist 'imperial victor'. The empress, detached from these expectations, could employ a fuller range of imperialist stratagems in dealing with foreign powers.

Nadine Viermann's chapter engages with the scandalous figure of Martina, second wife (and niece) of emperor Heraclius. She explores the functions that Martina served as Heraclius' wife and her role at the Constantinopolitan court as guarantor of dynastic continuity. After Heraclius' death, Martina, in order to secure her and her son's position, aimed at establishing alliances with various actors from the religious and especially military sector, although these attempts ultimately failed. On the one hand, Martina's trajectory highlights that the authority and agency of imperial women was primarily based on dynastic connections; and on the other, her fate shows that in order to retain her position at court after her husband's death she had to negotiate and form alliances with actors from the military sector, which in the early seventh century achieved a dominating position in negotiating political hierarchies and imperial successions.

The third and final section of this volume takes a step back from imperial women and instead centres on female protagonists who themselves did not belong to the ruling imperial family, but – by virtue of their descent or through marriage – were situated in close proximity to the central nodes of power. A critical look at the careers of non- or near-imperial women can help establish a clearer understanding of those at the centre of the empire.

Geoffrey Nathan's chapter begins by investigating Anicia Juliana's public activities and persona, highlighting both similarities and divergences with her counterparts in the regimes of Zeno, Anastasius, and Justin. This includes exploring performative and symbolic events, the creation of vertical and horizontal social networks, and artistic and literary representations meant for public and private consumption. By focusing particularly on the differences between her life and that of women of the imperial household, Nathan shows how Anicia's life serves as an 'out-of-bounds' marker and defines more sharply the degree to which imperial women's agency and visibility might extend and to what degree it might be circumscribed.

Antonina, Belisarius' wife who so scandalized Procopius, is the subject of Christopher Lillington-Martin's chapter, which debates the extent to which Antonina acted as a political instrument of her friend, the empress Theodora, with whom she shared her background and socially scandalous origins. Depending by necessity on Procopius' highly biased account, Lillington-Martin examines Procopius' portrayal of Antonina's involvement in religious, political and dynastic affairs (from Constantinople to Rome), particularly with regard to her plans for herself and her daughter, Joannina.

The regional focus of Marco Cristini's chapter moves away from Constantinople to Ostrogothic Italy. Tracing the life of Matasuintha, granddaughter of Theoderic, Cristini shines a spotlight on her own agency (or lack thereof) in the dynastic policy of her kingdom, particularly with regard to her marriages, first to Vitigis, then to Germanus, who, as a cousin of Justinian, brought her from Italy into the imperial centre.

The studies collected in this volume are of course far from exhaustive; they cannot be. Individual readers may find themselves wishing that other (near-) imperial women had been chosen for study, or that other aspects of their lives and works had been highlighted. But such is the fate of all collective volumes and the present one is no exception: it can but offer spotlights into the lives and careers of selected imperial or near-imperial women. The individual case studies, however, address broader questions of how women acted within a confined space – be that the physical court or the gendered expectations imposed on them – to ascertain their own position or that of relatives or, indeed, that of actors who were beneficial to them. With sources that mainly represent the male gaze upon these protagonists, the analyses here have in common that they step away from gendered and, at times, misogynistic rhetoric and instead try to uncover the underlying mechanisms of female involvement in imperial politics and court procedure that are telling not only with regard to these women, but also with regard to the functioning of imperial rule at large. The picture that emerges is that, in fact, the ultimate source of an empress' agency was the emperor, but that this could allow sufficient room for manoeuvre for imperial women to capitalize on factors like dynastic roles, personal connections, and personal (or institutional) wealth. The imperial court provided a stage for these women to test the boundaries of what was possible for them – an endeavour which was sometimes rewarded with remarkable success, as in the case of Theodora, and which sometimes led ultimately to failure and loss of life, as in the case of Martina.

In short, then, this volume offers another piece in the great puzzle of female status, power, and agency in pre-modern societies; in this case the Roman one of Late Antiquity. Scholarship still awaits a study that synthesizes approaches to imperial women from the early ages of the Principate into the medieval Roman (or Byzantine) Empire – a study that connects Augustus' wife Livia to Anna Komnene, daughter of Emperor Alexios I – who, despite all the difference of individual fate and circumstances, navigated within an architecturally, socially, and ideologically defined space of remarkable permanence: the Roman imperial court – be it in Rome, Constantinople, or somewhere in between.

1

Towards a History of Scholarship on Late Antique Imperial Women: From *Theodora, the Tigress* to Matronage

Anja Wieber

Modern Biographical Studies about Ancient Empresses – a Genre with Limits?

In 1930, the Belgian classicist and connoisseur of Late Antique religious history, Joseph Bidez, wrote in his famous biography about Emperor Julian:

> Still, Julian's affair could have ended badly without that surprising as well as decisive intervening of a woman [i.e., empress Eusebia]: for the first time in his life appears on the horizon the lovable figure of a princess whom he adored and who cared for this unhappy young man with kindness. [...] Perhaps the empress felt for the unhappy prince a romantic affection that easily evolves from pity to a warmer feeling.[1]

At first sight this scenario is evocative of the formula for a classic fairy tale with typical ingredients: romantic love brings happiness to the less favoured among a cast marked by royal lineage. But Bidez referred here to a historical event of the fourth century CE: Empress Eusebia's intervention saved the future emperor Julian from being implicated in his half-brother Gallus' alleged high treason.[2] Her advocacy for Julian can be labelled as one of the strategies that belong to the field of *patronage-matronage*, widespread in antiquity. Actually, this re-interpretation of an empress in action demonstrates that a more prosaic approach to understanding Late

---

[1] Bidez 1956, 73–74; all following translations (from modern and ancient languages) are mine. Beside the editors, thanks are due to the following for their help during various stages of preparing this chapter: Filippo Carlà-Uhink, Christiane Kunst, Sigrid Mratschek, Enno Pape, Stefan Sandführ, Beate Wagner-Hasel.
[2] Wieber-Scariot 1999, 209–31.

Antique imperial women is needed.[3] In this article, I will therefore address how methods of a new historiography of Roman empresses have developed, in particular for the time of Late Antiquity.[4] Given the basic assumption that imperial women are to be regarded as an integral part of monarchic rule, my goal is to show how the scope of political action of these women can be redefined.

Writing the biography of Late Antique individuals may seem to be an impossible task because of the scarcity of the sources, their rhetorical topical character, and, in the case of women, also because of gender biases.[5] Yet empresses from Late Antiquity and into the Byzantine Middle Ages have long been a much favoured topic of biographies and character studies by popular as well as academic historians, initially around 1900 and again since the 1990s.[6] But at some points one can observe how their works shift between the genres of history and the romantic novel. Apart from Bidez's comments about Empress Eusebia, quoted above, Berthold Rubin's account of Empress Theodora may serve as another example in this regard. Rubin closes his chapter about her and the emperor with the following words: "Justinian and Theodora will go down in world history as lovers."[7] Following the Late Antique historian Procopius of Caesarea, who devotes much of his *Anekdota* to describing Theodora's machinations, Rubin adorns Theodora elsewhere in his text with the epithet "tigress".[8]

It has for some time now been common in the historical profession to deconstruct the image of the so-called 'bad' Roman emperors as politically motivated concoctions.[9] The same holds true for the treatment of 'ruthless' empresses. Their stereotypical depiction is often a reaction to the violation

---

[3] I follow Boatwright 2021, 2, in her use of "imperial women" for "those who shared marriage or immediate family with the emperor"; this inclusive model concurs with Opitz-Belakhal 2021, 22, who argues the case for paying attention to the importance of the female relatives in the premodern family-bound system of rule.

[4] Cf. Winterling 2011a, who called for a new historiography of Roman emperors ("neue römische Kaisergeschichte") grounded in a history of aristocratic communication and combining structural analysis with historical events. For recent works with a focus on earlier imperial times: Kunst and Riemer 2000. Kolb 2010b. For Theodosian empresses: Holum 1982. Busch 2015. For early Byzantium: James 2001b. McClanan 2002. For the Byzantine Middle Ages: Hill 1999. Herrin 2013.

[5] Hillner 2016.

[6] Academic history: Diehl 1906 = 1963. Garland 1999. Herrin 2001. Temporini-Gräfin Vitzthum 2002. Popular history: McCabe 1911. 1913. Günther 1995. For a wider audience, but with use of recent research: Freisenbruch 2010. For Byzantine empresses as heroines and villains in fiction: James 2000.

[7] Rubin 1960, 121; novelistic elements can also be found in Paolo Cesaretti's 2001 biography of Theodora.

[8] Rubin 1960, 116.

[9] Winterling 2009, 103–19: "Meaningful madness. The emperor Caligula".

1 Towards a History of Scholarship on Late Antique Imperial Women 17

of political boundaries by powerful women, as seen from the point of view of their contemporaries who do not have access to power, as the Byzantinist Hans-Georg Beck has demonstrated in the case of Empress Theodora, whom he described as a "victim" of the historian Procopius and his social envy.[10] On the other hand, noted Byzantinist Liz James has concluded in her structural analysis of the power bases of early Byzantine empresses that it was not so much the personality of the individual empress that was of relevance, but her official role as empress, for which she uses the term "office".[11]

Private Empress Vs. Public Emperor with an Office?

Critics of the terminology by which the empress is designated an office holder argue that no Roman empress held the position of a sole ruler and that even in Byzantine times there were only a few exceptions to that rule.[12] In contrast, the emperor is seen as the head of the state and of the administrative hierarchy. As an explanation of in what sense the positions of the emperor and the empress differ, Anja Busch[13] quotes the following law from the *Digest*:

> The emperor is above the law; whereas the Augusta is not. Yet the emperors may assign the same privileges to them as they have at their disposal.[14]

But as Hans Volkmann and recently Mary Boatwright have pointed out, this passage originally referred to specific provisions for bequests in the case of emperors or empresses being legatees (*Ulpianus 13 ad legem Iuliam et Papiam*) and thus it seems questionable whether this passus really can be used to characterise the place of the Augusta in general.[15] Besides, on

---

[10] Beck 1986; see also Leppin 2000a. McClanan 2002, 107–20. For a contrasting Late Antique image of Theodora: Ashbrook Harvey 2001. For stereotyping of powerful women: Garlick, Dixon and Allen 1992. Fischler 1994. Wieber-Scariot 1999, 44–45; 175–86. Hillner and MacCarron 2021, 20.
[11] James 2001b, 1–10 ("office": 6; 166).
[12] E.g., Holum 2003. Pfeilschifter 2013, 463.
[13] Busch 2015, 183; 198.
[14] *Dig.* 1.3.31 (Ulp.), (ed.) Mommsen 6: *Princeps legibus solutus est: Augusta autem licet legibus soluta non est, Principes tamen eadem illi privilegia tribuunt, quae ipsi habent.*
[15] Volkmann 1972, 1138. Boatwright 2021, 58–59. For the Greek version of that law (ninth century) in the *Basilica* (2.6.1): Bensammar 1976, 272. Bosch 1982 also rejects a connection between the law and the position of the Byzantine empress. Smith 2007, 230, draws an interesting conclusion about the position of empresses that might derive from this law without mentioning it: "Strictly speaking, their formal standing as Augustae was still a boon bestowed by the emperors, but *in practice* [my emphasis] the influence of a determined empress could by now determine particular imperial policies."

a more basic level, the power of the Roman emperor himself is also far from being precisely defined.[16] This applies all the more to Late Antique emperorship.[17] Imperial power in all phases of Roman history has recently been defined in terms of a system of acceptance and the emperor's successful communication with the aristocracy.[18] Therefore, the position of the Late Antique empress, too, should not be described in terms of constitutional law.[19] Instead, by applying a broader notion of the political, as proposed by cultural historians of political thought and by women's studies, one can redefine the role of imperial women.[20]

Classic sociological definitions in the tradition of Max Weber differentiate rule (*Herrschaft*) (with obedience guaranteed by law or tradition) from power (*Macht*), which may result in enforcing one's will, and mere influence. In traditional scholarship, rule was defined as a male prerogative, whereas possible female influence was often seen as only a derivative power. Instead of clinging to a gendered juxtaposition with institutional or formal structures as reference points, historians of gender propose a more comprehensive concept of power, e.g., "agency", which is based on access to resources and opportunities.[21] Furthermore, we should not treat every woman ruler – as Jörg Rogge has rightly pointed out for the medieval period – as an exceptional personality (*Ausnahmegestalt*); the same also applies to ancient imperial women.[22] As an alternative, it has proved useful to look into the functional mechanism of power and rule, even on a local scale.[23] In this way, it becomes clear that women who act on a municipal level do so often as part of family networks.[24] This also rings true for imperial women and their political actions. Finally, Max Weber's concept of "dynastic prestige" explains why women could carry out ruler's acts:[25] in

---

[16] Boatwright 2021, 60, alludes to the "lack of a Roman constitution, and the stress by Augustus and later emperors on a nebulous imperial *auctoritas* rather than on legally defined rights and privileges"; but see Millar 1977.

[17] Meier 2017, 512. Tougher 2020.

[18] Pfeilschifter 2013. Winterling 2011a, 10. Arguing against a constitutional interpretation of the ancient court system: Winterling 1999, 37–38; 90; 115. Flaig ²2019.

[19] Wieber 2006. Maslev 1966, 343, closed his article about the constitutional position of Byzantine empresses from the sixth century onwards with a reference to the "grown *dynastic attachment* of the Byzantines" [my emphasis].

[20] Opitz-Belakhal 2021, 13–16.

[21] Wieber-Scariot 1999, 47–53. Vuolanto 2019. Wagner-Hasel 2020a, 76: "Rulership [...] as a question of the disposal of labour and the control of resources". For the Middle Ages: Kelleher 2015.

[22] Rogge 2015, 441.

[23] Wieber 2006.

[24] Van Bremen 1996. Hemelrijk 2015.

[25] Weber ²1966, 107–109. Busch 2015 adopts the term "dynastic potential" for the Late Antiquity; it was originally coined by Priwitzer 2009 for earlier imperial times; see

1 *Towards a History of Scholarship on Late Antique Imperial Women* 19

350, Constantina Augusta,[26] daughter of Constantine the Great and sister of Constantius II, designated Vetranio as co-ruler with her brother in order to lead him to intervene against the usurper Magnentius.[27] Her affiliation with the ruling family obviously superseded her gender.

As the advances of women's and gender history since the 1980s clearly have shown, the dichotomy between private and public, as well as their definitions, must also be reassessed.[28] Pre-modern (or, indeed, even early modern) societies are not organized along such a rigid divide, nor do simple equations work (e.g., the private being exclusively the women's realm and inherently apolitical, whereas men preside over the political, i.e. public affairs).[29] Apart from gender issues, Aloys Winterling has underlined the terminological difficulties that arise from these dualistic terms in modern European languages. The words "private/public" differ between contemporary languages without corresponding to the ancient "social structures" and their "semantics".[30] As an alternative, he proposes to use a terminology based on ancient self-descriptions. In imperial times the ancient sources present a tripartite pattern of categories: private – public – imperial (*princeps*). The emperor as well as the empress and the other imperial women were not private persons at all and the court cannot be described as a private sphere.[31] Conversely, the Late Antique historian Ammianus Marcellinus uses the word *privatus* to denote a colleague of Emperor Julian in the consulship (!) as someone without any kinship connection to the imperial family or high nobility.[32]

Having said that, the dealings of imperial women were certainly a political, not a private, matter. Anja Busch has demonstrated that the

---

also Wieber-Scariot 1999, 49 n. 45. For blood-ties of a great many of the fifth-century empresses as daughters or relatives of emperors: McCormick 2001, 147; Smith 2007, 230. For a critical revaluation of the term "charisma" (now often used in the sense of "dynastic prestige") and its applicability to ancient history: Lendon 2006. Näf 2015. For a modern example ("the charisma of Sonia Gandhi"): Hellmann-Rajanayagam 2011.

[26] Her title is only corroborated by Philostorgios 3.22 and 28, but is accepted by Bleckmann 1994, 36–37, Wieber-Scariot 1999, 186–88, and Drinkwater 2000, 153.

[27] Wieber-Scariot 1999, 186. Omissi 2018, 153–92, referring to her as "Constantia".

[28] Reverby and Helly 1992.

[29] Wagner-Hasel 1988. Wieber-Scariot 1999, 43; 51; 67. James 2001b, 4; 76; 149. Cooper 2007a, with a figure demonstrating the overlapping of the spheres on 25. Scheer 2011, 53. Foxhall and Neher 2013 (*passim*). Milnor 2013, 107: "the gendered division of the spheres [...] was always a site of certain amount of ambiguity and contestation". Wagner-Hasel 2020b, 207. For the Middle Ages: Earenfight 2013, 7 and *passim*; for pre-modern times in general: Opitz-Belakhal 2021, 18–20.

[30] Winterling 2009, 61–69.

[31] Winterling 2009, 69–75; 94–100; 72 for his reference to Plin. *Pan.* 84.5, who argues that the two imperial women (Plotina and Marciana) are no longer private persons but keep up the appearance of a 'private' life; see also Schlinkert 1996, 479.

[32] Amm. Marc. 23.1.1. Wieber-Scariot 1999, 88. Cf. *PLRE* 1 (Sallustius 5), 797–98.

language of the Late Antique sources oscillates between the polysemous terms *basileia* and *arche*, whose meanings range from 'monarchical power', to 'majesty' and 'dignity' and finally to 'office', when describing Theodosian empresses and their power.[33] Looking further into the ancient terminology might be a point of departure for scrutinizing more closely the *office* of the Late Antique empress in the future – if such can be defined and that is not too constitutional an approach.[34] Furthermore, linguistic research not only sheds light on those women's titles but also on the question of where and how gender, power, and language of the ancient sources intersect.[35] To deconstruct the phenomenon of the generic masculine we must find out when the ancient source language could include women.[36] Feminist linguistics likewise assert that grammatical details such as introducing a male person as a husband of a certain woman (in contrast to the widespread use of referring to women as the wife of X) might indicate a role reversal in power.[37]

The Late Antique Palace – a Woman's Place?

The search for a segregated imperial women's court within the late ancient court architecture has turned out to be a tricky one. It is true that ancient sources mention different quarters[38] and separate imperial households

---

[33] Busch 2015, 19–21, among others.
[34] Interestingly, Mommsen ²1877 (764–65 and 795) sees no legal but only political hindrances for female participation in government during the Julio-Claudian dynasty in his constitutional analysis. For early modern times and the "office" of the empresses of the Holy Roman Empire: Keller 2021.
[35] Kolb 2010a, 23–35: a list of the empresses with the title of *Augusta* from Livia to Theodora. For the title *regina* in connection with Roman imperial women in literary sources: Wieber-Scariot 1999, 45; 103–104. For later Byzantine times: Bensammar 1976, 250–59, with tables of the use in official and in literary sources. James 2001b, 117–28.
[36] *Dig.* 50.16.195pr.: "expressions used in the masculine form generally refer to both sexes"; see also Evans Grubbs 2002, 16–17; James 2001b, 51; Ringrose 2008, 69, on the medieval use of *despotai* in the sense of royals for members of the royal family, the emperor as well as the empress and the children. Cf. Busch 2015, 131, for *fideles imperatores* as an acclamation addressed to Marcian and Pulcheria. For the abbreviation *AVGGG* on coins, indicating the ruling members of the dynasties in West and East (i.e. Valentinian III, Pulcheria, and Marcian): Angelova 2015, 199. Cf. also Kotsis 2012b, 203: empress Irene sometimes used the male title βασιλεύς for herself.
[37] Examples of linguistic analyses of the Late Antique sources under gender aspects (relational genitive; empathy) in Wieber-Scariot 1999: 34; 81–84; 106; 152; 186; 188; 333; 350; 353; 371. On the question of a female voice in the correspondence of empresses and queens, see Hillner 2019a.
[38] Procop. *Anecd.* 4.6.

in the palace area of Constantinople with an extra court of women (and sometimes in different locations.)[39] In modern reference literature, the term *gynaikonitis* is often used for the female quarters in the palace, although seldom specified or pinpointed.[40] But considering the current state of palace archaeology, we do not know where the separate personal chambers of the emperor and the empress were located,[41] not to mention the unclear situation in several western and eastern residences from the fourth century up to the sixth in general, and the housing for the extended imperial family in particular.[42] Besides, emperors of the fourth century were often rulers on the move with an itinerant court – and where does that leave the empress?[43]

As a matter of fact, scholars have observed that even given the likely existence of a form of gender segregation at the medieval Byzantine court, gendered spaces were not necessarily fixed in a physical way.[44] Moreover, using late medieval sources, Frouke Schrijver was able to show on the

---

[39] Lactant. *De mort. pers.* 7.9 informs us that Diocletian reconstructed Nicomedia by adding (palatial) architecture: *Hic basilicae, hic circus, hic moneta, hic armorum fabrica, hic uxori domus, hic filiae* – "here a court, here a circus, here a mint, here an arms factory, here a house for his wife, here one for his daughter". This could mean either separate households for Diocletian, Prisca, and (!) their daughter Valeria; alternatively, the domiciles could have been given as gifts to be used as temporary retreats, or were just meant to augment the means of the imperial women.

[40] E.g., Garland 1999, 242 (definition); in search of a topography of the *gynaeceum* in late ancient palaces and its connotations: Wieber-Scariot 1999, 137–42. Garland 2006a, 179–80 (private but not secluded). Herrin 2013, 268. Herrin 2014 (as a given entity in the palace and a place to rear children). Schrijver 2018 is a thorough study of the Byzantine Middle Ages, which discusses the private quarters. Kazhdan 1998 argues against a separate *gynaikonitis* in non-imperial dwellings of that period. The whole discourse about women's quarters in the palace should also be read in the context of the debate about Greek women and their so-called Oriental seclusion; cf. Wagner-Hasel 2020b.

[41] For reasons discussed above, I refrain from calling the quarters "private". For the Byzantine court of the Middle Ages, see the interesting remark by Kazhdan 1998, 6 (notwithstanding the description as "private"): "the private chambers of the empress did not differ much from the *kouboukleion* of the emperor, also secluded, also inaccessible to strangers, men and women alike". Regarding the site of the *koiton* of the empress, her personal bedchamber, see Featherstone 2005, 852, who offers a topographical reconstruction on the basis of the tenth-century *Book of Ceremonies*.

[42] Noethlichs 1998, 23; 25. McCormick 2001, 141. McClanan 2002, 181. Smith 2007, 188–95. Featherstone 2015, 587–88; 597: antiquarianism of the middle-aged literary sources about the palace buildings which might (or might not) give evidence for the palace buildings in Late Antiquity.

[43] Smith 2007, 189; 196; 231. For empresses on the move: Wieber-Scariot 1999, 226–27. Wieber 2013, 129. Kunst 2010, 153–54 (traveling with the emperor, the empress established contacts with client-kingdoms and provinces). Hillner 2017 (imperial women of Late Antiquity as visitors in the city of Rome).

[44] Ringrose 2008, 68–71: the presence of eunuchs defines the female space; see also

one hand that the *gynaikonitis* was defined as a gathering of women, the entourage of the empress, the ladies-in-waiting with whom the empress could consult.[45] On the other hand, the term could also refer to a separate space in the palace, even an impermanently separated one, as the historian and emperor's daughter of the twelfth century, Anna Komnene describes: during a reception of Emperor Alexios, a curtain served to separate the female space from the throne.[46] Such a flexibility and performativity of segregation might also apply to earlier centuries, and corresponds with findings about the function of curtains in Late Antiquity and Byzantine court ceremonies.[47] Tellingly, the eunuch in charge of palace curtains was singled out in official court hierarchy.[48] For Late Antiquity and especially for the Byzantine period, Kathryn M. Ringrose has argued that the presence of eunuchs as liminal figures and intermediaries between the sacred and the worldly, between the female and the male space, could be seen as "an extension of an empress's power", literally opening up her way to government.[49]

Imperial women belonged to what has been called the so-called narrow court and therefore had direct access to the emperor, which gave opportunities to influence the ruler in favour of others and guaranteed information power.[50] Closeness in personal relationship but also in space allowed the imperial women to take part in political decision making; even if decorum

---

78–79. On the overlapping of female and male spheres, and only occasional gender segregation in republican and early imperial Rome: Kunst 2005, 117–18.

[45] Schrijver 2018, 221. Cf. Smith 2007, 196, about the late ancient court in general: "The tendency of such locutions to continue to evoke a material object, a hall or courtyard, is noteworthy – but so is the fact that they are often manifestly being used to designate the court as a *human collectivity* [my emphasis] or a political institution, without reference to any particular topographical location at a given time."

[46] Anna Komnene, *Alexiad* 15.8.5.1–6. Can we assume that the use of space in the mediaeval palace resembles or has its roots in Roman architecture? Actually, the *tablinum* could be divided from the *atrium* during the ceremony of the *salutatio* by a curtain whereby the domina was enabled to receive guests separately (Kunst 2005, 113–14). For the wada-house structure (comparable to the atrium house) with outer rooms for meeting with strangers as the stage for *matronage* in modern India: Bedi 2016, 126.

[47] Veikou 2016, 150: "space is always in the process of becoming, always in the process of taking place" – the term *gynaikonitis* could therefore refer to a gathering of women. On curtains, see Wieber-Scariot 1999, 116–36, and 140 for the iconographical representation of ruling women (historical or mythical) or female allegories with curtains. Cf. Wieber 2019, 143. Parani 2018.

[48] Noethlichs 1998, 37.

[49] Ringrose 2008, 79.

[50] For the 'narrow court': Strootman 2014, 31. Winterling 2009, 79–90. Cf. Winterling 1997b, 15. Smith 2000, 563. McCormick 2001, 146–48. For the court as the centre of power: Smith 2007, 182.

1 Towards a History of Scholarship on Late Antique Imperial Women 23

forbade women to be present, they could play a part by hearing and watching from behind a curtain without being seen, and using that knowledge later. Ammianus Marcellinus describes Constantina Augusta's interference in court trials in Antiochia in precisely such a way.[51] To complement our understanding of female power in action and its role in Late Antique court society, comparisons with other societies, as well as cross-cultural studies have turned out to be extremely helpful.[52] In Chinese sources, for one, periods of female rule are referred to as "rule from behind a curtain" and equally show the important role of eunuchs as court figures sometimes in alliance with imperial women.[53] Comparative history tells us that courts are often centres of productive work, be it of a life-sustaining or cultural form.[54] Weaving seems to play an important part in the palace life of different times and cultures. We do not know whether there were specialised workshops within the palace district in Constantinople,[55] but Pulcheria Augusta, for one, owned workshops and bakeries within the urban area of Constantinople.[56] Recent research by Goran Nikšić has shown that Diocletian's palace in Split had originally been an imperial manufacturing centre for textiles (*gynaeceum*), which remained in operation when the emperor chose the building complex for his retirement.[57] Considering the importance of all sorts of textiles in Late Antiquity, I am bound to believe that textile production (even on a more modest level than the above-mentioned centre) was part of palace economics and that imperial women might have been involved in overseeing it, as did women of aristocratic mansions.[58] For the Byzantine Middle Ages, Béatrice Caseau-Chevallier has studied weaving in the women's quarter of the palace and points to the empress Zoe, who produced her own perfumes.[59] Could the *gynaikonitis* of the palace have been an 'economic wing'?[60]

---

[51] Amm. Marc. 14.9.3. Cf. Wieber-Scariot 1999, 115–50.
[52] Walthall 2008b. Woodacre 2018. 2021. For cross-cultural studies of courts, cf. Spawforth 2007a, 6–7, and generally Spawforth 2007b; McMahon 2016, xxix–xxxi.
[53] Wieber-Scariot 1999, 127; 300–301. McMahon 2016, xx; 11–13; 16; 20; 28; 38; 93; 139; 204, 240; 245–46.
[54] Walthall 2008a, 14–15; 17–18. For the late Roman court: McCormick 2001, 160–63. On how the contribution of Byzantine empresses to court culture should be re-evaluated with regard to Eudokia's and to Anna Komnene's literary production: Sowers 2020.
[55] McCormick 2001, 141.
[56] Holum 1982, 132.
[57] Nikšić 2011.
[58] Berdowski 2007, 290–91; Wieber 2019, 148–54.
[59] Caseau-Chevallier 2007, 39. For the possibility of imperial silk workshop locations in the palace district of Constantinople in the middle Byzantine period: Galliker 2014, 67–70.
[60] The Annunciation mosaic of Santa Maria Maggiore, Rome, presents a Maria in the attire of an empress seated on a throne with a casket by her side, spinning a purple thread (Taylor 2018, 215–17). At first sight this is the visualization of her work, also

As Antony Spawforth rightly remarks, for a long time a focus on institutional history has caused historians to ignore (or outsource to other fields, e.g., to art history or archaeology) the 'trappings' of power as ceremony, palace architecture, or dress.[61] There is now a consensus that court ceremony and political rituals provide means of communication between participants of the court society as well as between the court and other groups, from non-residential aristocrats and the populace at large to foreign visitors.[62] Although sometimes not explicitly mentioned (because of the generic masculine, especially when several royal family members were taking part in certain events) the empress played an integral role in court ceremonies, be it on special occasions such as coronations, weddings, the birth of an imperial heir, or the death of family members, but also during diplomatic events.[63] As Julian's account of Eusebia's adventus in Milan and in Rome makes clear, empresses on the move were granted an adventus ceremony, just as emperors.[64] Political rituals intersect with religious ceremony in the case of the cult of relics, in which the *basileia* of many a Byzantine empress was involved as Liz James has put it neatly.[65] Although this is not the place to resolve the scholarly debate about the Trier adventus ivory with a further suggestion of identifying the parties or a new dating,[66] one can say that this artwork (fig. 1) offers a good glimpse of a Late Antique or early medieval translation ceremony of relics in the style of an adventus with its attendees: emperor, bishops, court officials, civilians, and, last but not least, the empress herself, easily recognized as such by her imperial costume. Kenneth Holum has shown that by the late fourth century, core elements of female imperial iconography (mostly on coins) were the *paludamentum/chlamys* – originally a cloak of Roman generals and later on part of the emperor's official costume to which the

---

with a purple thread, in the apocryphal tradition (*Proto-Gospel of James* 11–12). But due to the overlapping of representations of Maria and imperial women (Wieber 2013, 126–27) there is also an imperial subtext to this: imperial women could be connected with textiles and their pre-production, but only with purple ones.

[61] Spawforth 2007a, 2.
[62] Winterling 1997b. McCormick 2001, 156–60. Spawforth 2007a. Smith 2007, 209–25. Duindam, Artan and Kunt 2011. Beihammer, Constantinou, and Parani 2013. Rollinger 2020. 2024.
[63] Ringrose 2008, 70–74; for pre-modern times see Opitz-Belakhal 2021, 19.
[64] Julian. *Or.* 3, 112A; 129B–C. Cf. Wieber 2010, 270–71. Adventus ceremonies for other empresses: Holum 1982, 25; 185–86; 189.
[65] Holum 1982, 107–108; 184–86; 189; 219. James 2001a, 123. Busch 2015, 70–71; 155–57; 223; 227.
[66] Holum 1982, 104–109. For a summary of the identifications with various historical personae, and four different empresses under discussion: James 2001a, 122. McClanan 2002, 24–26. Chatterjee, 2018, 29.

habit of the empress was adapted – closed by a fibula, the diadem, and pearl jewellery.[67] This sort of attire has been described by Gillian Clark (referring to Empress Theodora in the image of S. Vitale, Ravenna) as "power dressing".[68] The empress on the Trier adventus ivory can therefore be read as the powerful "lady of the house", as a guardian of the cross, i.e. orthodoxy, welcoming the relics into her home, the palace.[69]

Summing up with Claudia Opitz-Belakhal's statement about pre-modern courts – without women the Late Antique court was incapable of representation and of reproduction[70] – the latter leads us into the following discussion of the 'maternal' qualities of empresses and their matronage.

From Patronage to Matronage: The History of a Concept

In antiquity and generally in many pre-modern societies, the concept of patronage covers different forms of support between a person of high social ranking and less privileged persons or groups (which does not necessarily mean of low status). It also often denotes explicitly political action.[71] The term itself, as a modern neologism with roots in the Roman legal institution of *clientela* – the relationship between the freed slave and his former master (*patronus*) – has been widely used in anthropological studies since the 1960s. Its relevance to ancient history was established by Richard Saller nearly forty years ago, who applied this concept to the relationship between freeborn men of different status.[72] However, ancient epigraphical sources used *patrona* as an epithet to address benefactresses, and therefore scholars have for some time now been adding the adjective 'female' when women are involved in patronage.[73] By the end of the 1990s, in the light of advances in women's and gender history, I proposed the less patriarchal term 'matronage' when studying imperial women under the Constantinian dynasty, in order to make them more visible and to emphasize their agency.[74] At the same time, but unbeknownst to me, Leslie Brubaker had chosen the somewhat pleonastic combination "female matronage" in her article about memorial culture of Late Antique

---

[67] Holum 1982, 32–43; 65; 76; 130. Schade 2003, 109–15.
[68] Clark 1993, 109.
[69] Holum 1982, 107.
[70] Opitz-Belakhal 2021, 23.
[71] For patronage in the world of today, see Carswell and De Neve 2020.
[72] Saller 1982, vii. Cf. Mitchel 2010.
[73] Kurdock 2003 (not in the title but throughout the book). Bielman 2012. Meyers 2012. Theis, Mullett, and Grünbart 2014 (more than thirty times throughout the volume). For ample evidence of women as *patronae* of cities and guilds in the western hemisphere of the Roman Empire (empresses excluded), see Hemelrijk 2015, 233–40; 536–44.
[74] Wieber-Scariot 1998.

empresses.[75] Since then, the term has been well represented in the field of ancient history.[76] Furthermore, the word 'matronage' is used by art historians to denote female sponsorship in general and in particular for female artists.[77] As well as patronage, the concept of matronage is also widespread in the field of anthropology and ethnography.[78] Only recently have I discovered that the term had been in use in anglophone historical studies for quite a while, as Darlene Rebecca Roth addressed female networking in conservative women's organization in Atlanta, Georgia from 1890 to 1940 as "matronage" as early as 1978.[79]

'Matronage', just as 'patronage', is a neologism with roots in the Latin language. Critics of the term matronage have stressed that the ancient term *matrona* refers to the married woman and differs in its scope from its counterpart *patronus*.[80] In 2013, Christiane Kunst emphasized the necessity to define matronage as a distinct concept, separate from euergetism.[81] To a certain extent this is still relevant a decade later, especially as some authors refer now to matronage without further explanation.[82]

In the late 1970s, Roth offered the following definition, connecting female influence to marriage and motherhood: "A woman, a matron, a mother, a champion of a cause, with a place from which to champion it – such are the foundations of Matronage".[83] This is valid for Roman empresses, although they could also wield influence in the absence of children.[84] To

---

[75] Brubaker 1997. A 'female matronage' would imply that there is also a 'male matronage' with men acting like a mother; for a Late Antique example of that understanding: Mratschek 2007, 223. Greg. Naz. *Poemata de se ipso* = *carm. hist.* 2.1.50 vv. 35; 40 (*PG* 37, 1387–88) calls himself "father" and "mother" of his congregation.

[76] Wieber-Scariot 1998. 1999, 216–31. Biernath 2005. Kunst 2005. 2010. Wieber 2010.

[77] Strobel 2011. Modesti 2013. Bose 2016, 13. Capek 1987, 29, defines the lemma "art matronage" as a "feminist term for art support and influence by women".

[78] Schrijvers 1986. The anthropologist Tarini Bedi uses the term "matronage" for her study of women in political grass root movements in modern India (Bedi 2016, 110 and 123).

[79] Roth 1978/1994, based on a dissertation from 1978 but published in 1994 in the series *Scholarship in Women's History: Rediscovered and New* by Gerda Lerner, one of the leading figures of women's history in the US.

[80] *Matrona* does not refer to the relationship between the female owner and their ex-slaves. For its implications with marriage instead: Treggiari 1991, 35; 414. For the differences in the epigraphical evidence between a *patrona* of a city or a guild and a *mater* in the same context: Hemelrijk 2015, 267–69. For the Middle Ages: Caviness 1993.

[81] Kunst 2013b, 13.

[82] E.g., Taylor 2018, 1; 6; 9; 13; 16; 65; 83; 86; 89; 202.

[83] Roth 1978/1994, 16.

[84] E.g., the case of Pulcheria Augusta; on the contrary, for the fertility pressure on empresses see Wieber-Scariot 1999, 249–56.

interpret motherhood not only as biological but also as social and cultural reproduction is inherent in Roman law: a *mater* is first of all the legal wife of a *pater familias* (who also does not necessarily have to be a biological father), the latter mediating "power between the domestic and the political life. [...] The organisation of power within Roman society at large was thus grounded in the gender relationships which marriage enabled".[85] Against this background, matronage and patronage can be regarded as just as complementary and intertwined as the concepts of *matrimonium* and *patrimonium*, for it is marriage that is a prerequisite for transferring property to the next generation: only legitimate children or spouses had access to family resources via intestate inheritance.[86] In my opinion, the understanding of imperial couples as 'partners in power'[87] is in Late Antiquity still grounded in this now Christianized Roman institution of marriage, and in the personal character of rule as a family business. Along with this comes the perception of the emperor as the father of the people and the empress (or other imperial women, especially the 'empress dowager') as their mother – a notion that was furthered by imperial propaganda as well by the imperial subjects themselves.[88] The politics of the imperial couple were neatly represented in the Palace district of Thessalonica. The so-called 'small' arch of Galerius, now in the Archaeological Museum, originally included two portrait busts on either side: the likeness of the empress Galeria Valeria (reworked into a bust of Tyche after her execution), and a portrait of the emperor Galerius. As visitors originally had to pass this arch in order to enter the audience hall, it can be read as a sort of imperial business card, signalling that a couple is presiding over the palace.[89] The empress and emperor as a team were also addressed by the Late Antique poet, panegyrist, and military commander Merobaudes, who in a distich describes Valentian III and Licinia Eudoxia as the central part of an imperial family group – most probably in a painted ceiling: "The emperor in its full radiance has together with his wife taken possession of the centre of the ceiling, as if they were bright stars of the firmament."[90]

---

[85] Smith 2000, 559; see also Thomas 1994, 116–19.
[86] Kunst 2005, 125.
[87] Wieber-Scariot 1999, 65–66; 191; 267–68; 372. Angelova 2015, 183–202. Busch 2015, 227–30.
[88] Rufinus, *Hist. eccl.* 10.8: calls Helena *regina orbis ac mater imperii* ("queen of the world and mother of the Empire"). Cf. Angelova, 2015, 238. For the Byzantine Empresses Zoe and Theodora (eleventh century) as mothers of the empire: Kotsis 2012a.
[89] For the arch see Canepa 2009, 96–97. On the similarities between representations of Byzantine empresses with that of the pagan goddess of fortune for the city (Tyche): James 2016 = 2003.
[90] Merobaud. *carm.* 1.5–6 (Clover 1971, comm. 16–27, Latin text: 60): *ipse micans tecti medium cum coniuge princ<eps // lucida ceu s<u>mmi possidet astra poli.*

As early as the late 1970s, Géza Alföldy connected the title *pater patriae* with the emperor's function as a *patronus* for his people.[91] As this turned even members of the upper class, who were *paters* themselves, into clients, Thomas Späth has labelled the emperor "super-*pater*".[92] In reaction to that, Antonio Pistellato (who elsewhere in his article interprets the position of the empress from a constitutional angle) has coined the expression "super-*matrona*" for the Roman empress and explained her power, amongst other factors, by her broad networks of clients, instead of interpreting her position in terms of her involvement in rule.[93]

In general, matronage should then be understood as a wider sociological concept serving the purpose of ending the silencing of women's influence, which that was caused, among other things, by the use of the generic masculine and therefore the omission of women's agency as *dominae* and *patronae* in ancient legal texts or other genres, and by the uncritical reading of those sources as a mirror of social realities by modern historians.[94] With that in mind, given the ancient custom of coding political relationships in familial terms, I would argue that, whenever women are involved as benefactresses, regardless of the context or their social standing, the term matronage should be used instead of the gender-blind term euergetism.

Make-up and Mechanisms of Matronage

Diliana N. Angelova has rightly pointed to traces of Hellenistic monarchical ideology in the concepts of Late Antique and Byzantine rulership whereby the ruler was seen as a saviour, benefactor and founder.[95] Angelova's observations concerning the discourse of imperial founding from imperial Rome through early Byzantium offer a very helpful starting point for analysing the tripartite mechanisms of matronage in Late Antiquity: instances of rescuing, sponsoring, and founding can be analysed as facets of matronage that range from immaterial support to very materialistic deeds.

So far only a few scholars of ancient history have offered a systematic approach to the matronage of empresses. For the early imperial period, Christiane Kunst has stressed the importance of the greater financial independence the empress enjoyed compared to aristocratic women of Republican times (she was freed of *tutela*), and of her position at the narrow

---

[91] Alföldy ²1979, 89–90.
[92] Späth 1994, 339–46.
[93] Pistellato 2015, 416.
[94] Saller 1999. See Kunst 2013b, 12–13.
[95] Angelova 2015.

1 Towards a History of Scholarship on Late Antique Imperial Women 29

court as the basis of her matronage. The empress could wield matronage in acts of charity and by interceding in order to protect against injustice and to grant privileges or access to offices – this field of action corresponds to two of the aforementioned modules of matronage: rescuing and sponsoring.[96] Besides, Kunst provides another compelling argument for using the term: it marks more clearly both the woman in charge and her female protégés and it covers the fact that matronage goals could be connected to gender-specific issues (inter alia family affairs, female role patterns, and women's place in cult practices and religion).[97] In Late Antiquity, the matronage of the empress fits into a comparable, and to some extent, expanded framework; indeed, the parameters seem to remain valid up to the Byzantine Middle Ages as Barbara Hill has demonstrated when addressing the patronage (her terminology) of eleventh and twelfth century empresses.[98]

Legal matronage is an important field of action, referring to the matronage act of support and rescue. At court, the political and juridical scenes intersect (*court* stands for the court hall as well as for the palace where the highest judicial court is also located) and the empress as saviour can vouch for the accused and win their allegiance.[99] There are only a few epigraphical examples for the unspecific addressing of empresses as saviours (σώτειρα), but, from the beginning of imperial times, association of empresses with several deities symbolizing protection and nurturing qualities was part of the imperial cult.[100] Christianization did not bring this to a halt; the idea of the Virgin Mary as a heavenly empress offered another 'divine' prototype – again with protective qualities – for Late Antique empresses.[101] The empress could therefore not only intercede actively in worldly matters, but also spiritually through her own prayers or philanthropic deeds.[102]

---

[96] Kunst 2010. Hill 1999 = 2013, 177: the dowry and morning gifts as economic resources for empresses in the Middle Ages. Cf. Holm, this volume.

[97] Kunst 2010, 159. 2013b, 13–14.

[98] Hill 1999 = 2013, 152–80.

[99] For early imperial times: Kunst 2010, 157–58. For the legal matronage of Julia Domna: Tuori 2016; for the later period: Wieber-Scariot 1999, 216–22.

[100] Hahn 1994, 27; 224; 358; for the frequent addressing of empresses as Demeter (to name but one example) see the index, 434.

[101] Angelova 2015, 88; 234–40. James 2016 = 2003, 53–54, refers to Byzantine iconographic examples (counterweights, mosaics, and illuminated codices) oscillating between personifications, empresses, and pagan goddesses, especially Athena; also, representations of the Virgin Mary show similarities to pagan goddesses. For the merging of the visual cultures in Late Antiquity whereby Mary is represented as an Eastern empress (who could also stand for the personified *Ecclesia*) and for the inherent cultural transfer between West and East: Lidova 2016b; for merging of Mary with empresses in the eleventh century, cf. Kotsis 2012a.

[102] Hill 1999 = 2013, 159: empresses (in search of extra heavenly intercession) funding

It is true that epigraphical findings need more thorough contextualization and that many of the literary sources are critical or ambivalent in their rating of imperial matronage.[103] However, when reading the literary sources against the grain, one can find fragments supportive of imperial matronage. Julian, for example, having received legal matronage from the empress Eusebia, speaks of her intervention in terms of saving and active defence by using verbs like ἀποσῴζειν and ἀμύνειν and calls her his saviour (σώτειρα).[104] Expressing his gratitude for Eusebia's help, Julian employs female *exempla* such as the Phaeacian queen Arete and Penelope to characterize the empress in his panegyric, and introduces the goddess Athena as a female focalizer of the whole speech – thereby establishing a language of matronage.[105] Thinking of panegyrics as a genre of imperial self-promotion among other things, the imperial perspective on matronage might hereby become visible. Against this background Julian's use of prepositions is all the more meaningful: sometimes, Eusebia's help as a broker is referred to in unison with the emperor (δι' αὐτὴν παρὰ τοῦ [...] βασιλέως), whereas other *beneficia* are received from her alone (παρ' αὐτῆς).[106]

To invoke the helping hand of a member of the upper echelons of society, the petitioner, even if of aristocratic origin, had to abide by norms that structured these interactions. Being granted an audience, also with imperial women, was contingent upon gifts by the petitioner, which may be interpreted as 'entrance fees' or signs of gratitude for a future intervention.[107] Quite different from our modern understanding of bribery, this pattern of behaviour is to be read as the reverse side of patronage/matronage and highlights its reciprocity.[108] So far, I cannot account for gender differences concerning the gifts, but my impression is that women as petitioners approached powerful women, if possible (i.e. preferred gender-specific audiences). The rich patrician Melania,

---

the work of monks and holy men to ensure their prayers; in a way they were then donors and beneficiaries in one person, as it was also about their salvation.

[103] Kunst 2013a, 119.

[104] Julian. *Or.* 3, 121A and 120C. Julian lists further forms of Eusebia's matronage: she secured offices and honours for her relatives (116A) and arranged together with the emperor his marriage with Helena and supported his intellectual ambitions (123D; 118C; 120B–C); for Eusebia cf. also Holm, this volume.

[105] Wieber 2010, 259–64; for the genre panegyric under gender aspects, see 254–7, and for the narratological concept of focalization, the perspective through which a narrative is presented, see 260–61.

[106] Julian. *Or.* 3, 117B–C.

[107] Wieber-Scariot 1998, 102–104. Wieber 2013, 123–24.

[108] For the different motivations of gift-giving (partly overlapping with patronage/matronage), its typology, and the narrow boundary between gifts and bribery: Carlà and Gori 2014a, 27–31; see also: Wagner-Hasel 2020b.

for example, brought gifts with her and appealed to the imperial woman Serena (niece of Theodosius and daughter of Honorius) to achieve backing in her and her husband's decision to choose an ascetic lifestyle against the opposition of their families.[109]

An instructive description of an imperial Christian benefactress[110] (second module of matronage: sponsoring) is given by Eusebius in his *Vita Constantini*: Helena Augusta's journey to the East and her multiple good deeds, such as the distribution of gifts and *donativa* for soldiers and church foundations – so we learn – are made possible by her access to the imperial treasury (ἐξουσία βασιλικῶν θησαυρῶν).[111] The *Vita Constantini* does not offer any details,[112] but we have a later iconographical representation (sixth century) of the giving hand as an act of matronage. The mosaic of the so-called Lady Silthus/of Silt(h)o (from Kussufim) and the dedication miniature of the Vienna Dioskurides present a powerful female donor whose right hand offers a gift of money in form of coins. Karen C. Britt has interpreted the female donor of the Kussufim mosaic as a hybrid depiction of a local donor in the style of empress steelyard weights and consular diptychs (fig. 2). Besides, she has referred to the *mappa* in the woman's left hand as a sign of authority – after all the small piece of cloth is a politically charged symbol from representations of Late Antique consuls and emperors.[113] This interpretation can be corroborated by Liz James identifying a *mappa* in the hand of an empress bust as a steelyard weight.[114] There are other examples from the fifth and sixth century too: the personification of the Church, *Ecclesia*; Maria as a queen clad like an Late Antique empress; and one of Theodora's ladies-in-waiting on the mosaic in San Vitale, Ravenna, all are depicted holding a *mappa* as an attribute in their right hand.[115]

---

[109] Wieber-Scariot 1999, 103–104.
[110] Wieber 2013, 128–32. For empresses as religious patrons: James 2001b, 148–63.
[111] Euseb. *Vit. Const.* 3.41.2–47.3.
[112] Did Constantine give her access to his private fundings or the property of the crown (*res privata* or *patrimonium*); was this an exception for the time of her journey (for Euseb. *Vit. Const.* 3.47.3 see Cameron and Hall 1999, 296) or a general carte blanche?
[113] Britt 2008, 126–27. For the mosaic and the inscription, see also Ameling 2014a; others have interpreted the cloth as a handkerchief (e.g., Schade 2003, 115). The question is to what extent we tend to assume that an object is purely decorative when it is a woman holding it; for a comparable gender bias cf. Haines-Eitzen 2000, 41–48: female ancient scribes and calligraphers portrayed in ancient iconographic sources were routinely interpreted as secretaries or even cosmeticians by modern scholars.
[114] James 2016 = 2003, 52; 55.
[115] For the *mappa* and its further development into the ἀκακία (a cylindrically shaped object decorated with knobs on both ends filled with dust, a symbol of human mortality), an attribute typical for emperors: Dagron 2007; for *mappae* in female hands: Lidova 2016b, 114; 119. Zanichelli 2020, 173–75.

The dedication miniature in the Vienna Dioskurides (fig. 3) is likewise relevant for our topic, because it demonstrates how of the three modules of matronage, sponsoring and founding might intersect. The donor, the *patricia* Anicia Juliana (of imperial descent on both sides of her family), is represented in imperial attire, like an empress receiving *proskynesis*, accompanied by personifications of *Megalopsychia* – which is in the language of patronage/matronage connected with generosity – and Prudence.[116] The dedication of the manuscript is usually interpreted as an expression of thanks from the people of Honoratai, where Anicia Juliana had founded a church. Whereas some scholars only saw her as the recipient, others assumed that the manuscript itself was commissioned by her.[117] Notwithstanding the polyvalent readings of the image and Anicia Juliana's own political ambitions,[118] this scenario is a blueprint for imperial matronage, especially as Anicia Juliana is deemed one of the richest women of her time. Anne N. Kurdock has turned our attention to the inscription flanking the putto who holds the casket for the deposit of the coins: πόθος τῆς φιλοκτίστου – "Desire of the woman devoted to building".[119] She characterizes Anicia Juliana's work as a foundress as that of a "female Christian patron".[120]

Cándida Martínez López has argued that "the manifestation of autonomy of women in the construction or restoration of public buildings in ancient societies is one of the key elements of their matronage".[121] Although López's studies focus on the western hemisphere and on women of all strata, other research has provided promising evidence for the building matronage of Late Antique imperial women, ranging from residences over functional buildings (porticoes, baths, fortifications, and cisterns) to churches and monasteries.[122] Leslie Brubaker has described these activities

---

[116] Kiilerich 2001. Nathan 2011 points to an image-to-text-gap between the slightly more moderate text of the dedication and the very assertive, but not always consistent representation that combines aristocratic with imperial elements. Cf. Angelova 2015, 226–29. For Anicia's family history: *PLRE* 2 (Anicia Iuliana 3), 635–36, Kurdock 2003, 138–65, and cf. Nathan, this volume.

[117] Connor 1999, 508. For commissions in the context of patronage: Grünbart 2014, 22. Mullet 2014, 421, with general caveats: "Literary dedications are by no means prima facie evidence of commission or patronage either."

[118] Nathan 2006, and this volume.

[119] Kurdock 2003, 138 (trans. after Connor 1999, 507).

[120] Kurdock 2003, 139–40.

[121] Martínez López 2021, 19; cf. the project "Gender and Architecture in Ancient Roman Society. Civic Matronage in the Western provinces" (ArqGeAnt): https://www.ugr.es/~arqgeant/ (last accessed 3 November 2023).

[122] Brubaker 1997. James 2001b, 70–71. McClanan 2002, 98–100. On the Byzantine era: Theis, Mullett, and Grünbart 2014. On Eudokia's building matronage in Jerusalem

1 Towards a History of Scholarship on Late Antique Imperial Women 33

as "public discourse-through-monuments".[123] The act of (re-)founding is the third module of matronage. Apart from the cases were female sponsorship is undisputed, Angelova has pointed to the problem of family foundations that would not have borne the name of the imperial women in charge of the building project, but of male relatives.[124] Our ignorance of female founders might also be caused by biased ancient authors, who omit information (such as Procopius, who famously denigrated Theodora in his *Secret History*).[125] To untangle the driving force behind a building project in a married couple of founders poses another problem.[126] That being said, building matronage is overall better documented than that of other objects, such as donations of exclusive fabrics and textiles,[127] which possibly derived from household (i.e. palace) production. Even though very little is known about the context or the 'operating instructions' of such donations, we should keep them in mind when discussing matronage.

But what do the imperial woman gain from their matronage? These empresses were revered in dedicatory inscriptions and by statues, became eponyms of districts or cities, appeared in mosaics and ecclesiastical paintings, and their monograms were attached to walls and columns.[128] Prayers were read and hymns were sung to honour them.[129] They were also present in at least some of the many ceremonial appearances and were thus also exalted in performance. In short, they became visible and were heard, even after their death; they gained reputation and *memoria*.[130] Kurdock

---

with main focus on ecclesiastical buildings: Klein 2014. On Theodora's building matronage: Unterweger 2014 (maps of the locations: 100 and 105). Angelova 2015, 154–82; 219–33; 181: "women's partnering with the emperor in the re-founding of the capital city". Galla Placidia's possible plan to establish a type of Ravennatic emperorship: Busch 2015, 104–105. Dirschlmayer 2015. Carile 2021, 2–4. For the later Byzantine period: Talbot 2001.

[123] Brubaker 1997, 53.
[124] Angelova 2015, 155–56.
[125] Angelova 2015, 166–72; see also Unterweger 2014, 103–105; 108.
[126] Mullet 2014, 423. Klein 2019.
[127] Leatherbury 2017, 243 (on the loss of Late Antique textiles in general).
[128] Unterweger 2014, 101–106. Angelova 2015, 167–71.
[129] Catafygiotu Topping 1978. Unterweger 2014, 106–108. Romanos Melodos, *Kontakion* 54 (*On Earthquakes and Fires*), a hymn in twenty-five stanzas, is clearly panegyric and mentions Justinian and Theodora as a founding couple (four times pl. emperors = βασιλεῖς for both; once Justinian as the emperor with his consort = βασιλεύων and σύνευνος) who in their building patronage/matronage even surpass Constantine and Helena (22). Catafygiotu Topping 1978, 26 and 29, points to the divided structure of the *kontakion*, by which Christ is labelled as founder in the first part, whereas the emperor is addressed as such in the second part – this refers also to the building matronage of the empress.
[130] Grünbart 2014, 24. James 2014.

defined "female patronage" as the counterpart of the *cursus honorum* (an interesting idea considering the attire of empresses [*paludamentum*] and the use of a *mappa* in illustrations of powerful women) but has stressed its embeddedness in family politics.[131]

That imperial women aimed to propagate dynastic pride can be deduced from the information we have on the lost mosaic decoration of San Giovanni Evangelista, a church founded by the Augusta Galla Placidia after she and her children were rescued from a shipwreck. The reconstruction on the basis of ancient and early modern testimonies presents the empress, both on the textual and pictorial level, as near to Christ and as an important member of the Constantinian and Theodosian dynasty. On the triumphal arch in front of the apse the rescue is illustrated and the reason for the founding of the church is given in a short inscription, whereas the main dedicatory inscription inside the half dome of the apsis offers a more thorough description of the events: the church is dedicated by Galla Placidia and her children Valentinian and Grata Honoria to the apostle John the Evangelist as a thanksgiving for their survival.[132] On the soffit of the arch, the medallions of ten male imperial relatives going back to Constantine seem to shield Galla Placidia and her family. The bottom-most part of the wall decoration, the depiction of the eastern imperial couples, the psalm, and the clergy, appear almost to be the fundament of Galla Placidia's world (fig. 4).[133] With what seems to be the Christian imperial version of a Roman family tree (instead of ancestral wax masks), the empress symbolically gains access to precisely that part of the church which would have been denied to her due to her gender: the sanctuary.[134] This symbolic closeness to the

---

[131] Kurdock 2003, 189; for the interdependence of female patronage and family see 7–21.

[132] *CIL* 11.276 = *ILS* 818: *Sanctissimo ac beatissimo Apostolo Ioanni Evangelistae, Galla Placidia Augusta cum suo filio Placido Valentiniano Augusto et filia sua Iusta Grata Honoria Augusta liberationis maris votum solvent*; most scholars refer to the emendation *solvit* because of Galla Placidia being the grammatical subject of the sentence.

[133] Brubaker 1997, 54–55. Angelova 2015, 224–25. Carile 2021. Deliyannis 2010, 63–70, with the reconstruction diagram at 69. Malmberg 2014, 174–75.

[134] For the general ban of women from the sanctuary: Holum 1982, 140; see also Leatherbury 2017, 253–54 on textile donations (in the form of, e.g., altar cloths; for Pulcheria's robe as altar covering: Holum 1982, 144; 153) made by imperial and aristocratic women, "to connect themselves to the altar, the eucharistic ritual, and Christ himself". Lidova 2016a points to the identification of the altar space with the cave of nativity: in the famous Ravenna portrait, empress Theodora is shown in the sanctuary with gifts in her hands and an embroidered gift-giving scenery on her cloak. Therefore, access to the sanctuary (even a symbolical one by the donation of an altar cloth or other gifts) means access to Christ.

altar was of great significance to orthodox empresses who did not share the emperor's privilege of access to the sanctuary.[135]

Apart from the widespread reference to male family lines in late Roman and Byzantine times, imperial women invoked female lineage for their work, especially for their building matronage, a phenomenon aptly described by Leslie Brubaker as "matronage chains".[136] Examples are church foundations that became joint ventures over generations of imperial women as is the case with St. Euphemia in Constantinople having been founded by Licinia Eudoxia; thereafter her daughter Placidia decorated the church and the granddaughter Anicia Juliana, whom we already encountered as devotee to building projects, finished the embellishment.[137] By associating herself with the saint Euphemia, the guardian of Chalcedonian orthodoxy, Anicia Juliana also followed in the footsteps of her great-grand aunt Pulcheria's engagement with the councils of Ephesus and Chalcedon. Finally, another of Anicia Juliana's projects was to rebuild St. Polyeuktos in Constantinople, which had initially been constructed by her great-grandmother Eudocia.[138] This venture had an orthodox subtext, too. For our context, it will suffice to mention that the remains of that church (re-discovered in 1960), its sumptuous decoration, the dedicatory inscriptions,[139] and asides in contemporary sources give ample proof of Anicia Juliana's programme: the dedicatory poems connect her to Eudocia, repeatedly stress her imperial blood, and applaud her for surpassing the good works of her ancestors. The iconographic and architectural programme is centred on her own afterlife,[140] as well as on her ancestors and their immortalization. Archaeologists even

---

[135] Depending on time and place, the emperor's levels of access to the sanctuary differed from sharing the communion with the clergy to only leaving offerings there: McLynn 2019. For Pulcheria, who had convinced archbishop Sisinnius to let her receive the communion in the holy of holies, and her later conflict with archbishop Nestorius about that access: Holum 1982, 145 and 153. McLynn 2019, 331–32. Most probably it was also archbishop Sisinnius who was brought (by Pulcheria?) to paint an image of Pulcheria above the altar of the Great Church.

[136] Brubaker 1997, 55–56; 62.

[137] Dedicatory inscriptions: *Anth. Gr.* 1.12–17. Cf. Kurdock 2003, 145–50, and Dirschlmayer 2015, 167–69. By the ninth century, empress Irene draws legitimation by identifying herself with Licinia Eudoxia through sharing features with the numismatic portraits of her predecessor as well as through re-building St. Euphemia (Kotsis 2012b, 195; 198; 205; 206; 211).

[138] Kurdock 2003, 150–65. Dirschlmayer 2015, 169–77. Klein 2019, 110–14, believes that the church was originally planned to revere St. Stephanus.

[139] *Anth. Gr.* 1.10; for a detailed analysis see Connor 1999.

[140] For Anicia Juliana's plans to use the church as a burial site see Angelova 2015, 231, and Effenberger 2019, 180–81, who argues that the annex building was meant to serve as Anicia's burial chapel. By contrast, Bardill 2006, 345, argues that only emperors were allowed to be buried *intra muros*.

support the theory that she aimed at exceeding the temple of Salomon with her church.[141]

Whither Scholarship on Matronage?

The aforementioned quest for "memoria and mimesis"[142] has for a long time been connected to Helena, the Christian Augusta per se, as an *exemplum adhortativum* for later Byzantine empresses.[143] But Michaela Dirschlmayer, who has examined female imperial church foundations (fourth-to-sixth centuries), could not find enough substantial evidence for Helena's ecclesiastical building matronage.[144] Nonetheless, it is still worth looking more thoroughly into the question why Helena Augusta was turned into a model of matronage by the following generations; the concept of "lieu de mémoire" might be made fruitful to the study of this issue.[145]

Another way to indicate female lineage in Late Antiquity was the use of the *nomen* Aelia as a title for imperial women since the time of Theodosius I's first wife, Aelia Flavia Flacilla, and still in use even after the end of the Theodosian dynasty, until the end of the sixth century.[146] Frustratingly, we do not know whether imperial women had a say in the matter, i.e., could they choose to adopt it or not. Another possible way of empresses referencing their female predecessors might become visible by their representations on ivory leaflets. On both of the two so-called 'Ariadne' ivories (presently in the Kunsthistorisches Museum, Vienna, and the Bargello Museum, Florence, respectively; see figs. 5–7), we see an empress of the sixth century

---

[141] *Anth. Gr.* 1.10.58. Cf. Harrison 1989, 137–39. Bardill 2006.

[142] Kurdock 2003, 138.

[143] Kurdock 2003, 117–65. For Pulcheria and Marcian as the new Helena and new Constantine: Holum 1982, 215–16; for Empress Verina as the new Helena: James 2001b, 91 and 152; for Empress Sophia as the new Helena: McClanan 2002, 167–68. On Theodora, see n. 129 above. Klein 2014, 87 n. 11, believes that the description of Pulcheria finding the forty martyrs is modelled on Helena's finding of the holy cross (Sozom. *Hist. eccl.* 2.1. 9.2). For Empress Irene and her son as a new Helena and a new Constantine: Kotsis 2012b, 201.

[144] Dirschlmayer 2015, 38–52.

[145] Dirschlmayer 2015, 51–52, referring to the legend of the finding of the cross and to Helena's characterization as Maria by Ambrose to explain the tradition of the empress as a church foundress. For Pierre Nora's "lieux de mémoire" as a comparable framework to interpret the *vitae* of six Saints: Alwis 2011, 65–74.

[146] Holum 1982, 22: "a title of female distinction and dynastic exclusiveness", also: 32; 65; 123; 129–30. James 2001b, 128: Aelia as "not an official title […], but perhaps more of a traditional honorific, denoting continuity between empresses"; for a list of the empresses named *Aelia* (referred to as "title of empresses" on 40) see Garland 1999, 229. Busch 2015, 190–91: Aelia as "a dynastic name so-to-speak" and "'official' title" (German phrase with single quotes).

in her imperial attire with a *paludamentum/chlamys* and a *clavus/tablion*, a rectangular, elaborately decorated patch sewn onto the dress, typical for emperors and court officials.[147] In the case of the Viennese *tablion* (fig. 5), Angelova has speculated whether it could depict an empress.[148] If so, could the depiction be read as an example of an empress drawing her imperial identity from a reference to another empress? Unfortunately, the *tablion* of the Viennese ivory is too worn to be identified with any certainty.

But what about the *tablion* of the Florentine ivory (figs. 6–7)? It depicts the head of a person who is generally identified as an emperor, holding a *mappa* in his hand and wearing the *loros* and *pendilia*.[149] The *pendilia* are a sign of imperial authority; the *mappa* is typically male, but can (as discussed above) appear with female portraits. The *loros*, a long, narrow and embroidered cloth, which was wrapped around the torso was another part of the official male imperial attire. After already making a short-term appearance on the coinage of Licinia Eudoxia in the fifth century, it became part of the numismatic representations of female imperial dress during Empress Irene's time.[150] Perhaps, then, the gender of the person portrayed on the *tablion* of the Florentine Ariadne might also be questioned. But the sceptre in the left hand of the figure resembles the short-shafted sceptre (*scipio eburneus*), tipped with an eagle or an emperor bust, typical for consuls. Empresses are mostly shown with long-shafted sceptres.[151] Therefore, the idea of *tablia* with reference to an Augusta has (for now?) to be dismissed. The discussion has nonetheless made obvious that we need to find more evidence for 'insignia of power' in representations of imperial women and other agents of matronage; in some of the cases a reassessment of our source material might also be required.

For later Byzantine times, scholars have highlighted that the beneficiaries of matronage were often women in general and female relatives in particular;

---

[147] For an interpretation of the two ivories as representations of the empress Sophia see McClanan 2002, 168–78. James 2001b, 136–45, rejects the interpretation of two ivories as a depiction of a single particular empress, let alone of the same empress. Rubery 2013, 112, mentions princess Amalasuntha as a possible candidate, suggested by other scholars; she herself argues for an identification with the empress Ariadne, but at different times of her life.

[148] Angelova 2015, 190 and 192 (figs. 110 and 113). For the different interpretations of the Viennese *tablion* (patron goddess; son or husband of the empress Ariadne): Köhn 1999, 102–104, and Rubery 2013, 110, who proposes Augusta Verina as a possible female candidate for the *tablion*, although she herself favours Ariadne's son.

[149] For a thorough discussion of the *tablion* of the Florentine ivory and the different opinions about recognizing particular emperors: Angelova 2004, 12 n. 44.

[150] Kotsis 2012b.

[151] For the consular sceptre (that could be sometimes longer-shafted): Delbrueck 1929, Text: 61–62; for the sceptre of the empress: Angelova 2015, 180–95.

38 Empresses-in-Waiting

another finding in studies of medieval Byzantine times is that widows were more often the agents of matronage.[152] We need more precise data on Late Antique matronage, such as the family status of the parties of matronage, and the empresses' resources (properties, estates, etc., in the hand of imperial women) as well as the 'authorship' of buildings.[153] For the latter problem, Konstantin M. Klein has proposed the following questions as working tools: was the building commissioned by the empress herself or by the emperor, but under her name or by her suggestion?[154] To understand the matronage of imperial women we have to look into aristocratic matronage as well as into more modest forms of matronage in order to develop new research questions.[155] Still, modern biographical studies on imperial women other than the famous and notorious ones would be most welcome for the period of Late Antiquity and could give insight into mechanisms of matronage.[156]

Besides, future investigations should focus on network analysis[157] and on the question if and how far more nuanced gender-specific differences in acts of patronage vs. matronage can be accounted for. Flexibility is a core characteristic of matronage, since imperial women could act as brokers, forming their own power base, as donors, and as beneficiaries at the same time; hence, I propose to read matronage against the background

---

[152] Hill 1999 = 2013, 175: Eirene Doukaina decided to hand down a monastery only through the female line of her family. Talbot, 2001: matronage in form of foundation of nunneries, nursing home for laywoman, special privileges in a nunnery for female relatives, mausoleum for the family, etc. Both Hill and Talbot stress the connection between matronage and widowhood.

[153] Cf. the project *Patrimonium Geography and Economy of the Imperial Properties in the Roman World* – during the High Roman Empire: https://patrimonium.huma-num.fr/news/index.html; a comparable approach for Late Antiquity, hopefully gender-sensitive, would be of great use.

[154] Klein 2019, 89–92: *sub nomine alieno* (Suet. *Aug.* 29.4); *ex rogatu/ex suggestione* (*Lib. Pont.* 34.23; 34.21). On the other hand, it should not be forgotten that ancient foundresses have sometimes been ignored by scholarship, see Meyer 2014, 38–40, and by their contemporaries (see above); e.g., *Anth. Gr.* 1.12 offers the title: Εἰς τὴν ἁγίαν Εὐφημίαν τὴν Ὀλυβρίου – "At the church of St. Euphemia, founded by Olybrios", although all but one of the six poems (1.12–17) name Anicia Juliana as the foundress. Nathan 2006, 437, and Dirschlmayer 2015, 167, have interpreted "Olybrios" as a reference to the location of the church in the district of Constantinople named after Anicia's father; the title might as well be a later paratext; see generally Pelttari 2022.

[155] Mullett 2014, 428: "we need to focus more on what non-elite women we have access to".

[156] For earlier imperial times, see Joska 2019 (on the daughters of the Antonine family) and Moore 2021 (about Octavia minor).

[157] Cf. Grünbart 2014, 24. Bérat, Hardie and Dumitrescu 2021. Hillner and MacCarron 2021. See also: https://sites.google.com/sheffield.ac.uk/genderednetworks/; for the importance of family networks in the premodern politics, cf. Opitz-Belakhal 2021, 23 and 27.

of *heterarchy*, a model which is adapted from anthropology by the biblical scholar Carol Lyons Meyers. Instead of a static hierarchy she favours "the recognition that there were intersecting systems and multiple loci of power"; also, she points to the non-permanence and adjustability of social ranking.[158]

Then there are some topics that have not been addressed or only in passing, such as artistic matronage, matchmaking, and diplomacy as playgrounds for matronage, that deserve more attention. Most of all the approach should be interdisciplinary, covering the fields of Late Antique history and art history, archaeology, classics, and related disciplines such as religious history. No matter how important it is to deconstruct the sources because of their gender bias and hagiographical or panegyric character, we should not forget that even a concocted story about matronage provides insight into what a society deemed an important and plausible action for the persons involved.

Table 1: Matronage in Late Antiquity

Matronage by powerful women in late antiquity			
As brokerage or by own resources, be it immaterial as personal *auctoritas* or faith, or from personal assets	saviour	protection, support (also spiritual)	**Goals from the side of the powerful woman:** prestige; own networking and gaining loyalty; *memoria*; eventually gifts god's protection (for her, her family, the subjects)
	benefactress	networking for the recipient; brokerage of offices; matchmaking; gifts, donations, help for the needy; erection of public buildings	
	foundress	name giver (city, area, etc.); foundress of a city, cloister, church	
	immaterial ⟶ material		
Goals from the receiving side: every form of support			**Reciprocity, but also asymmetry of position**

---

[158] Meyers 2013, 163–67. Cf. Vukašinović 2017, 113–14, who adopts this model for a new approach to the role of medieval Byzantine empresses; see also Wagner-Hasel 2020a, 337.

Section 1

Political Agency and Power Brokerage

2

Empress with Agency: Eusebia's Efforts to Consolidate the Constantinian Dynasty

Silvia Holm*

Eusebia's term as empress was short yet significant.[1] The second wife of Constantius II is perhaps best known for being the mediator between that emperor and Julian, his estranged cousin and later successor. After Constantine's death, old and familiar problems of Roman emperorship resurfaced: rivalry for power between family members and usurpations by powerful extra-familial generals. As a result of his childlessness, Constantius included his cousins Gallus and later Julian in the line of succession as Caesars. By the time of Gallus' appointment as Caesar, the two brothers and Constantius himself were the only remaining male members of the Constantinian family, which had been depleted during the massacre of 337.[2] Constantius furthered the idea of shared rule with dynastic approaches to succession, as his father Constantine had done, and before him, Diocletian and Maximian.[3] Constantius tied both cousins, now Caesars, even closer to the imperial line by marriage to his sisters Constantina and Helena.[4]

---

* I would like to thank both editors, Nadine Viermann and Christian Rollinger, for their input and guidance, as well as Henning Börm and Anja Wieber for their valuable suggestions.
[1] *PLRE* 1 (Eusebia), 300–301. She married Constantius probably in 353 and died before 361, as Constantius remarried that year.
[2] See Burgess 2008, 5–51, for a detailed analysis.
[3] *PLRE* 1 (Hannibalianus 1), 407: Constantine married his eldest daughter Constantina to his nephew Hannibalianus, whom he then made *nobilissimus* to mark his dynastic status. Galerius Valerius Maximianus (*PLRE* 1 [Galerius Valerius Maximianus 9], 574–75) married Diocletian's daughter Valeria (*PLRE* 1 [Valeria], 937), and Constantius Chlorus (*PLRE* 1 [Constantius 12], 227–28) married Maximian's daughter Theodora (*PLRE* 1 [Theodora], 895), both upon becoming Caesar.
[4] Burgess 2013, 89–104, describes Constantine's plans for succession, binding senior advisors and dynastic members through marriage, stating why his plans ultimately failed and what remained of the tetrarchic principles afterwards.

Gallus, the older of the two brothers and the first to become Caesar, was removed from his post and executed shortly after his title was revoked. His wife Constantina, herself an influential figure whose possible rank of Augusta is nevertheless uncertain[5] and who was the link between the Caesar and the emperor, had died at the same time. After these events, Constantius was reluctant to admit another family member to power.[6] Eusebia, whom Constantius had married the year before, must have witnessed all of this.[7] But after another threat to Constantius' rule in the guise of an attempted usurpation by the *magister militum* Silvanus in Gaul and the concomitant pillaging of this province, it was necessary to install someone eligible to represent the emperor in the western provinces. The great privilege and responsibility of the post demanded a respected man of the highest connections who would not pose an immediate risk to the emperor's power. For Eusebia, the only suitable option was someone of dynastic descent; therefore, she advocated strongly on Julian's behalf.[8]

These political circumstances provide the necessary framework for understanding seemingly contradictory images of Eusebia. I propose that her aim was the consolidation of the Constantinian dynasty, which involves and necessitates a hierarchy of interest in the empress's agenda. The main focus of her actions, I argue, was to strengthen the position of the imperial couple by incorporating a broader scope of family members into affairs of state – first and foremost Julian, as designated successor. At the same time, she established a support network, which included Julian as Caesar, as well as her brothers Hypatius and Eusebius,[9] along with other family members and friends of her late father, whom Julian alludes to in his panegyric of the empress.[10] The objective of these actions was to strengthen and cement not only her husband's status but also her own, especially as she was to bear Constantius no children and thus no heirs to ensure the survival of the direct dynastic line. There is speculation in the sources as to why the couple had no children; probably, the empress was struggling with infertility.[11]

---

[5] Philostorgius is the only source for Constantina holding the title of Augusta (*Hist. eccl.* 3.22.3. 3.28.4). Bleckmann agrees with Holum 1982, 33–34, in assuming that the title is an anachronistic addition in his commentary on Philostorg. *Hist. eccl.* 3.22.3 (Bleckmann and Stein 2015, 253–54).

[6] Amm. Marc. 14.11.3 mentions Constantina's death. Cf. Barceló 1999, 23–24. Blockley 1972, 433–68.

[7] Julian himself (Julian. *Or.* 3.109B; 110D) alludes to a probable date of marriage before Magnentius' final defeat and his death in August 353.

[8] Tougher 1998b, 595–99.

[9] *PLRE* 1 (Flavius Hypatius 4), 448–49; *PLRE* 1 (Flavius Eusebius 40), 308–309. Both became consuls in 359 and were later given the title *patricius* (Amm. Marc. 29.2.9).

[10] Julian. *Or.* 3.116A–C.

[11] Philostorg. *Hist. eccl.* 4.7.1–2 describes her trying to treat her infertility with

Her support of Julian grew from this.[12] Conflicting depictions arise mainly in Ammianus Marcellinus' work but also in comparing the accounts of Julian and Libanius with Zosimus and the church historians Philostorgius, Sozomen, and Socrates.[13]

The role of Eusebia and other empresses in imperial dynastic power networks is particularly interesting. They are incorporated into the ruler's representation by acting in close proximity to the throne as wives and mothers. In turn, this potential of informal influence over the emperor and being part of his official public image enabled them to form their own factions at court and networks throughout the empire. From the moment of their marriage, they posed as powerful patrons who could petition the emperor in private. They could secure lucrative and influential posts at court, in the imperial household, in public office, and more. In the reciprocal system of matronage,[14] those who were benefitted by Eusebia would wield their power in accordance with the empress.

Thus, the gain of influence through Eusebia's imperial status and her matronage shows that a secure dynastic position equated to an undiminished position of authority for the empress in turn. Since empresses derived their authority from proximity to the emperor, by strengthening dynastic bonds they obtained positions of high rank for themselves, even as dowagers. If Eusebia had lived until Constantius' death in 361, her early support of Julian's career would likely have resulted in such a position for her with the new ruler.

The 'Stateswoman'

Julian's eulogy on Eusebia attests to her political involvement: "[Constantius] kept not one secret from her, but deemed her worthy of being a partner in his decisions and that she should reflect upon and help him ascertain what was to be done".[15] While her taking part in the imperial representation is shown throughout Julian's speech – but also, e.g., in Ammianus' account

---

medication, while Zonar. 13.11.29–30 claims Constantius was impotent – which is untrue, as he had a daughter, Constantia, with his next wife Faustina.

[12] Tougher 2020, 196–97, mentions the struggle of Constantine's sons to conceive heirs and his tendency to "keep marriages in the family".

[13] James 2012, 56–57, discusses the differing interests and motives of Christian historians in depicting the empress.

[14] Cf. Wieber-Scariot 1998, 109–112, and Kunst 2010, 145–62, for matronage as the female counterpart of patronage, which, due to the circumstances of women's access to power had to rely more heavily on informal means to support others in their careers. See Wieber, this volume.

[15] Julian. Or. 3.114B (trans. Wright): ἀπόρρητον δὲ ἐποιεῖτο πρὸς αὐτὴν οὐδὲ ἕν, ἀλλ᾽ ἠξίου κοινωνὸν γίγνεσθαι τῶν βουλευμάτων καὶ ὅτι πρακτέον εἴη συννοεῖν καὶ συνεξευρίσκειν.

of Constantius renaming the Pontic diocese after Eusebia (the new name, Pietas, was, of course, Latin for εὐσέβ[ε]ια)[16] – her *adventus*-like arrival in Rome and presence at a church synod established her as a politically active representative of imperial rule.[17] Her immense influence was met with conflicting responses by ancient historiographers: Libanius welcomed Eusebia's intervention on Julian's behalf and faulted Constantius for being easy to influence, thus criticizing him as weak for leaving space for female interference.[18] Ammianus regards the emperor in a similar fashion, but in his *Res Gestae*, the empress' actions function even more as a plot device: they are much appreciated while they benefit the later emperor Julian but are depicted in a negative light to account for him being childless.[19] Zosimus, on the other hand, describes Eusebia as a topically cunning female.[20] But there is more to Zosimus' portrait of Eusebia than just the trope of a "Machiavellian female".[21] In his portrayal of her advocating to elevate Julian, the matter-of-fact argumentation adopted by Eusebia's speech seems almost cynical and does not fit Julian's idealized picture.[22] This is partly a result of conventions imposed by the genre of panegyric on Julian's words but also partly due to the historical interpretation of the material.[23] Zosimus describes

---

[16] Amm. Marc. 17.7.6.

[17] Julian. *Or.* 3.129C: Ἐξῆν δὴ οὖν, ὡς εἰκός, διηγουμένῳ ταῦτα τοῦ δήμου μεμνῆσθαι καὶ τῆς γερουσίας, ὅπως αὐτὴν ὑπεδέχετο σὺν χαρμονῇ προθύμως ὑπαντῶντες καὶ δεξιούμενοι καθάπερ νόμος βασιλίδα – "I could indeed very properly have given an account of this visit, and described how the people and the senate welcomed her with rejoicings and went to meet her with enthusiasm, and received her as is their custom to receive an Empress" (trans. Wright). Cf. Noethlichs 1998, 17. Wieber 2010, 270–71. Hillner 2017, 77. On the synod Eusebia attended, see Philostorg. *Hist. eccl.* 7.6a.4 = *Suda* s.v. Leontius (L254); the synod mentioned may be identified with the 'Arian' Council of Seleucia of 359, relayed in Socrates, *Hist. eccl.* 2.40, or the synod of Sirmium in 358.

[18] Lib. *Or.* 18.26–27.

[19] Amm. Marc. 15.2.8. 16.10.18–19. Cf. James 2012, 55–56, who categorizes Ammianus' account of Helena's miscarriage as a mere story and compares it to Procopius' depiction of Theodora in his *Secret History*.

[20] Zos. 3.1.2–3. Amm. Marc. 16.11.13 also tells the story of Julian being appointed rather to be rid of him, than to secure the Gallic provinces, but does not link this to a specific person, instead relaying it like a rumour.

[21] A term used widely to describe Zosimus' picture of her by Aujoulat 1983, 430, and Tougher 1998b, 596. Cf. Wieber 2010, 274, questioning the label.

[22] Aujoulat 1983, 431; see also Tougher 1998a, 122, who argues that Julian's speech of praise should be read with caution because of its connection to his somewhat insincere panegyrics to Constantius II. Washington 2020, 113, and García Ruiz 2015, 157, on the other hand, read Julian's speech as a deliberate and sincere, albeit unorthodox, choice to express his gratitude to her publicly.

[23] Aujoulat 1983, 421–52. Tougher 2000, 94–101, discusses the seeming contradiction, while García Ruiz 2015, 171, argues for the possibility of Julian's panegyric being edited at a later stage.

the empress as a highly educated and intelligent woman before leading into her speech to Constantius, in which she favours Julian's accession.[24] He does not provide any interpretation. Still, it is implicit that the empress would undoubtedly be aware of her husband's hesitancy to appoint another Caesar after the disaster with Gallus.[25] Thus she would also have known that her plan, to do just that, would meet with the opposition of his advisors, as Ammianus (and, indeed, Julian himself) confirmed.[26] The picture emerging is neither that of a stereotypical selfless mediator nor of a power-hungry schemer. Instead, it is that of a person familiar with the workings of court and state with a determination to see her plan through. Ammianus also alludes to other possible motivations behind Eusebia's support of Julian and his detachment to Gaul, with selfish desires and a wish for the common good possibly coinciding. Both go hand in hand, as Julian's appointment would, in the eyes of the empress, strengthen the dynasty, and thus her position.[27] Eusebia makes her case for Julian in the only way Constantius may have accepted it: presenting him as a non-threatening option, even though she must have known Julian's appointment to be of similar risk to the emperor as the one of Gallus. Constantius' decision to surround Julian with loyal subordinates – the *magister equitum per Gallias* Marcellus and the *quaestor sacri palatii* Salutius[28] – speaks to this perception of risk. Julian's elevation to Caesar was regarded as necessary, but his sharing of imperial power was not ideal for the ruler.[29] So Eusebia had to reassure and convince

---

[24] Zos. 3.1.3: Νέος ἐστὶ' φησί 'καὶ τὸ ἦθος ἁπλοῦς καὶ λόγων ἀσκήσει τὸν ἅπαντα βίον ἐσχολακὼς καὶ πραγμάτων παντάπασιν ἄπειρος, ἀμείνων τε ἔσται παντὸς ἑτέρου περὶ ἡμᾶς· ἢ γὰρ τύχῃ δεξιᾷ περὶ τὰ πράγματα χρώμενος ἐπιγράφεσθαι τὸν βασιλέα ποιήσει τὰ αἰσίως ἐκβάντα, ἢ κατά τι πταίσας τεθνήξεται, καὶ οὐδένα ἕξει τοῦ λοιποῦ Κωνστάντιος ὡς ἐκ γένους βασιλείου πρὸς τὴν τῶν ὅλων ἀρχὴν κληθησόμενον – "He is a young man of simple character, who has spent his whole life as a student, and his complete lack of experience in worldly matters will make him more suitable than anyone else; for either he will be lucky and his successes will be ascribed to the emperor, or he will make a mistake and get killed and Constantius will be free of any imperial successors" (trans. Ridley).

[25] Zos. 3.1.2 describes him as ὑπόπτως, suspicious against all his relatives.

[26] Amm. Marc. 15.2.8: *nefando assentatorum coetu perisset urgente, ni adspiratione superni numinis Eusebia suffragante regina* – "[…] yet he would have perished at the instigation of the accursed crew of flatterers, had not, through the favour of divine power, Queen Eusebia befriended him" (trans. Rolfe). Cf. Julian. *Or.* 3.118B; 121A, for her defence and support of Julian.

[27] Amm. Marc. 15.8.3.

[28] *PLRE* 1 (Marcellus 3), 550–51; *PLRE* 1 (Saturninius Secundus Salutius 3), 814–17.

[29] Zos. 3.2.23. Salutis is identical with Salutius. Marcellus and Salutius oversaw the provincial administration, as Julian himself attests to; cf. Julian. *Ep. ad Ath.* 278B: οὔτε γὰρ ἀθροίζειν ἐξῆν μοι στρατόπεδον (ἕτερος γὰρ ἦν ὁ τούτου κύριος), αὐτός τε ξὺν ὀλίγοις ἀποκεκλεισμένος – "For I was not even allowed to assemble the troops; this power

her husband to put Julian fully in charge a second time, when he was sent to Gaul after his elevation, repeatedly advocating for the management of the empire through dynastic means rather than by close advisors to the emperor.[30]

Eusebia's pursuit of dynastic consolidation is very apparent during Julian's Caesarship and task of securing the western provinces. It was essential for her to furnish Julian with actual power, even against the opposition of Marcellus, an established *magister militum*. As he did not come to Julian's aid against an attack from Alamanni, Marcellus was relieved from his office by the emperor. And taking insult, the now discharged commander bore accusations against the Caesar towards the emperor, which were refuted and thus to no avail.[31] After Marcellus left Gaul, Julian received direct command of the subsequent campaign in 357.[32] Salutius, on the other hand, supported the Caesar as an advisor and continued his brilliant career, becoming *praefectus praetorio Orientis* under Julian in 361.[33]

In Ammianus' narrative around the elevation of Julian as the successor of Constantius especially, Eusebia is contrasted with an impulsive and easy-to-influence emperor and depicted as an element of moderation and balance. Her 'job' or, rather, her narrative function in Ammianus' account is clear: she is an example of an imperial woman, an empress, exercising power within the boundaries of her gender and status.[34] She works towards acquitting Julian through rebutting accusations against him, securing a meeting with Constantius to ensure that Julian may defend himself before the emperor against charges brought forward by Constantius' advisors and courtiers, who claimed that he had taken part in conspiring against the emperor with his brother Gallus.[35] This intervention of Eusebia secured Julian what can only be described as a fair trial, even though no official investigation had been initiated.[36] Ammianus emphasizes the need for Eusebia's *patrocinium* through context, as, in an earlier section, he stresses that

---

was entrusted to another, while I was quartered apart with only a few soldiers" (trans. Wright).

[30] Zos. 3.2.3. Wieber-Scariot 1999, 228–29.

[31] Amm. Marc. 16.7.1–3 shows Marcellus being discharged and the threat this could pose against Julian. Therefore Eutherius, *praepositus sacri cubiculi* and trustee of Julian, was sent after Marcellus to defend Caesar Julian before Constantius.

[32] Amm. Marc. 16.4.3 and 16.7.1. Julian. *Ep. ad Ath.* 278C–D. See also Stöcklin-Kaldewey 2015, 709 (*ad loc.* 278d).

[33] Amm. Marc. 22.3.1 and Lib. *Ep.* 740.

[34] Amm. Marc. 15.2.8. Julian. *Or.* 3.115A. Lib. *Or.* 18.27. Wieber-Scariot 1999, 107–108; 271–73; 311–12; Washington 2020, 72–73.

[35] Amm. Marc. 15.2.7.

[36] Julian. *Or.* 3.118B–C.

the killing of Ursicinus had been planned without trial.[37] The reasonings behind the empress' decision to defend Julian are also given in Ammianus, but not in an definitive way: often, when Ammianus alludes to something, the order in which pieces of information are given is significant, with the last one being the most important or probable. Thus, he ascribes three possible motives to Eusebia for her championing Julian:[38] firstly, a personal (and selfish) dread of the prospect of an arduous journey and prolonged stay in Gaul. This can be dismissed, as the imperial couple travelled extensively between Milan, Rome, and Constantinople.[39] Secondly, Ammianus states that her natural intelligence led her to a decision for the common good; this is in line with her positive portrayal in Libanius and Julian mentioned above. Finally, and most importantly, her advice was intended to remind the emperor that kinship was to be given precedence before all. This last remark emphasizes her thinking about the imperial rule as dynastic and bound by family ties.

Julian's oration confirms that Eusebia's motives were not only for the common good but also for her personal gain and the security of her and her imperial husband's position. He recalls being unable to refuse his elevation but showing his *modestia* in approaching Constantius and Eusebia on separate occasions. The reciprocal aspect of Eusebia's matronage is demonstrated by her demands on Julian when he comes to speak with her. She clarifies her expectations of Julian to be faithful and righteous (πιστὸς καὶ δίκαιος) towards herself and the emperor. She reminds him that his place and status require him to behave accordingly: with loyalty and respect for the superior authority of the Augustus. In this account, the emperor and empress appear as a tightly connected unit because Constantius sends Julian to his wife for reassurance and guidance to come to terms with his integration into the ruling house. Also, with Julian's new official position as Caesar, the roles of the couple reverse: before his elevation, Eusebia functions as Julian's informal but chief advisor, securing access to the emperor for Julian in order to set him up for his upcoming new dynastic role; now, as his position is made official, the emperor takes over the chief advising duty to his cousin.[40] Eusebia is portrayed as acting in accordance with her status as empress: not taking on official authority over either

---

[37] Amm. Marc. 15.2.5–6. Cf. *PLRE* 1 (Vrsicinus 2), 985–86. Szidat 1977, 35–36, emphasizes that he was Ammianus' former commanding officer.
[38] Amm. Marc. 15.8.3.
[39] Wieber-Scariot 1999, 226–27. At this time, the court was in Milan, i.e., close to Gaul. Cf. Hillner 2017, 90, for a visit to Rome in 357 with Constantius, and another one, probably alone, in 354; in 355 she was at court in Milan. Julian. *Or.* 3.112B recalls her visiting different palaces on her way from Macedonia to Constantinople before her marriage took place.
[40] Julian. *Or.* 3.121B–C; 123A–C.

emperor or Caesar, and giving precedence to the former.[41] Julian uses this depiction of her to present her actions as adhering to the most idealized and praiseworthy of female imperial virtues: temperance.[42]

Securing the Line: Eusebia Expanding her Status through Julian

Julian's detailed account of Eusebia's favour marks the relationship between supporter and supported. Her gifts to him, including a library befitting his interests, show their friendly relationship and emphasize Julian's new position.[43] His place within the hierarchy of the Constantinian family was further established through his marriage to Helena, Constantius' sister. It is another example of Eusebia's work towards consolidating dynastic rule, for the match was brought about with the empress' help.[44] Again, her depiction in Zosimus, where she casually accepts the possibility of Julian losing his life due to taking up his Caesarship and military command in Gaul, cannot express her true aim for solving Constantius' problems ruling the empire.[45]

The sources often single out Eusebia as the one person going against the court's opinion and tipping the scales in stalemate situations. Julian compares the empress' function to Athena, casting her vote in favour of the accused at trial.[46] She may have been privy to council meetings, albeit these were formally closed to her.[47] Eusebia was only in a position to buck

---

[41] Wieber 2010, 261–64, discusses how this is shown in Julian's speech via the image of Eusebia as Penelope, the ideal wife; see also Wieber's article in this volume on the dichotomy of private, public, and imperial spheres.

[42] Washington 2020, 103, traces this ideal back to Tacitus and the discrepancies between his depiction of Livia and the *senatus consultum Cn. Pisone patre*. James 2012, 51–53, and García Ruiz 2012, 84–85, also attest to this virtue, although the former draws the conclusion that it does not reflect Eusebia's real character because of genre and stereotypes.

[43] Julian. *Or.* 3.118D; 123D–124A. Wieber-Scariot 1998, 112. Kunst 2013b, 13–14. Wieber 2013, 123–24.

[44] Julian. *Or.* 3.123D.

[45] Aujoulat 1983, 432, adds that even from Constantius' point of view it would have been politically unwise to dispense with a potential rival by giving him a command and sending him to the defence of Gaul; if successful, he would have posed an even greater threat and, if defeated, the provincial unrest would still have had to be dealt with.

[46] Julian. *Or.* 3.114C–D. Vatsend 2000, 89.

[47] See Wieber-Scariot 1999, 214–15, for the presence of empresses and eunuchs at the imperial *consistorium*, and Wieber 2010, 266–67, for Eusebia as patroness in judicial cases. See also Harries 2013, 70–74; 88f., who identifies a lack of influence of Theodosian women (Pulcheria and Aelia Eudocia) on the imperial consistory, even though they could be asked to intercede, in the context of matronage. These failed

court opinion successfully and influence her imperial husband because her informal authority was not confined to, but surpassed, the private sphere and moved into the public and the imperial. The structure of informal influence and how it translates into real political power is best illustrated by the spreading of non-Nicene beliefs at court. At first, the eunuch of the empress' bedchamber and Eusebia herself came into contact with a favoured Arian presbyter. He influenced Eusebius, freshly appointed head of the imperial household (*praepositus sacri cubiculi*/προειστήκει τῆς βασιλικῆς οἰκίας), allowing non-Nicene beliefs to spread through the household, reaching even Constantius, and subsequently the palaces and provinces the emperor was residing in.[48] The combination of the empress' informal influence and formal status granted her considerable power. Still, having her protégé Julian fill the vacuum of power left after Gallus' and Constantina's deaths would have enhanced her position further. With the new Caesar and his marriage to Helena, the ruling of the empire and the imperial court were again firmly in the hands of the Constantinian family. Julian had friends to whom Eusebia became a beneficiary, too; thus, she 'networked', interconnecting, and expanding her own and Julian's spheres of influence.[49]

A specific example of the official means available to her as patroness and imperial mediator is given by Julian himself. Her protection extended to giving him safe passage via an escort when he travelled to Athens after being summoned to court in Italy after Gallus' death. Though the escort was given with permission of the emperor, it could have served different purposes at once: security and surveillance.[50] Julian later recalled that only through Eusebia's efforts did he feel safe then, which fits Ammianus' narrative of Julian's danger.[51] This perceived danger, seemingly emanating more from the emperor's advisors than from the Augustus himself, is, in

---

petitions are regarded as an outcome of roles changing for Theodosian imperial women, towards being public dynastic images, rather than being a reflection of the fairness and justness of the consistory – which Harries attests to.

[48] Socrates, *Hist. eccl.* 2.2.4–8. Sozom. *Hist. eccl.* 3.1.4. Julian's Letter to the Senate and People of Athens shows us how great the power of Eusebius was perceived to be; he accuses Eusebius of successfully plotting against his brother Gallus (Julian. *Ep. Ad Ath.* 272C). For the role of eunuchs at court, see n. 93 below.

[49] Julian. *Or.* 3.123D: ὁπόσους μὲν εὖ ἐποίησε τῶν ἐμοὶ γνωρίμων, ὅπως δὲ ἐμοὶ μετὰ τοῦ βασιλέως τὸν γάμον ἥρμοσεν – "Shall I tell how many of my friends she benefited, and how with the emperor's help she arranged my marriage?" (trans. Wright).

[50] Julian. *Or.* 3.118B: καὶ οἴκαδε ἐπιθυμοῦντι πάλιν ἀπιέναι πομπὴν ἀσφαλῆ παρέσχεν, ἐπιτρέψαι πρῶτον τὸν βασιλέα ξυμπείσασα – "and when I wished to return home, she first persuaded the emperor to give his permission, and then furnished me with a safe escort" (trans. Wright). Cf. Wieber 2010, 265.

[51] Amm. Marc. 15.2.7–8.

part, meant to justify Julian's later usurpation of full emperorship.[52] But a sufficiently large escort displayed not only imperial favour and the protection of the empress, it was also a testament to Julian's own imperial position as Constantius' successor. The connection of an emperor with his troops was regarded as vital to the stability of the state, e.g., by Synesius. It was a distinctive mark of the ruler himself.[53]

The mediating ability of Eusebia is evident: Julian was not at ease with an escort from the emperor after what had happened to his brother and the rest of his family. However, the relationship between him and the empress was unencumbered and therefore trusting. That Constantius took Eusebia's advice in providing such an escort indicates that he wanted to set the relationship with his cousin to rights for the sake of the empire's stability, although it should be noted that an escort was also a means for a mistrustful Constantius to control and surveil his kinsman. But his opinion of Julian seems to have changed in 355, as indicated by him expressing his wish for Julian's elevation to Caesar in front of his *proximi* later in the same year. As Ammianus recalls, Constantius was more and more troubled by reports of the province of Gaul being devastated.[54] In order to get Julian to be named successor, Eusebia had to exert all her official and informal influence. The resistance towards him felt by people close to the emperor shows the potential dynamic that another member of the Constantinian family would bring into the framework of court and state, especially in relation to other influential men such as Eusebius.[55] Julian's appointment must have been a welcome gain in leverage for the empress against the *proximi* at court.[56]

Dynastic and Court Conflict

During Julian's Caesarship, Eusebia appears at different points in Ammianus' account.[57] In particular, she plays a role in a much-discussed episode that shows a vastly different side of her as patroness and guardian of Julian. In 357, Julian's wife Helena was invited to stay in Rome with Eusebia and

---

[52] Julian. *Ep. Ad Ath.* 272D; 274D.
[53] Pfeilschifter 2013, 95–96. Syn. *De regn.* 16.2 paints an ideal picture of an emperor with military prowess, who travels extensively, implicitly criticizing Arcadius for his deficits in this regard.
[54] Amm. Marc. 15.8.1–2.
[55] Wieber-Scariot 1999, 213. *PLRE* 1 (Eusebius 11), 302–303.
[56] Julian. *Ep. Ad Ath.* 273C. Gaudentius (*PLRE* 1 [Gaudentius 3], 386) can be counted among this group of men who gained imperial favour by denouncing others; he was made *notarius* and spied on Julian in Gaul (Amm. Marc. 17.9.7). But in general, the *proximi* are an indistinct group of advisors or friends of Constantius, as in Julian. *Ep. Ad Ath.* 285A.
[57] Amm. Marc. 16.10.18–19.

Constantius, outwardly demonstrating the cordial relations between the dynasty's members. Ammianus, however, claims the actual reason was to ensure that Helena remained childless, as Eusebia herself struggled with infertility. Thus, the empress would coax her sister-in-law to drink what is to be interpreted as an abortive. Ammianus also alludes to Eusebia being responsible for the death of Helena's and Julian's infant son, probably in 356. Someone – Ammianus does not name the empress specifically – is said to have bribed a midwife who cut the umbilical cord too close, thus causing the baby's death. This happened when Helena was in Gaul with her husband before both women met in Rome.[58]

How do these allegations, if true, fit into Eusebia's aim to consolidate the Constantinian dynasty? What are we to make of them if we judge them to be malicious inventions? After all, Eusebia is not the first powerful woman to be accused of poisoning her political opponents: other famous Roman examples include Agrippina poisoning Claudius in 54 with mushrooms,[59] or Marcia, the mistress of Commodus, mixing poison into the emperor's drink or food.[60] Thus, Ammianus' account of Helena's maltreatment may well have been intentionally meant to not fit into his otherwise positive, even glowing, depiction of Eusebia, and to serve as a dramatic element in the narrative, with the first accusation being decidedly blunt and of immense cruelty, and the second only hinting at the empress' involvement.

In the matter of Helena's miscarriage(s) in Rome, Ammianus is straightforward in accusing Eusebia of poisoning. This passage has raised many questions about which poison could have been used, whether Ammianus had first-hand knowledge (probably not), and if this story is following a literary stereotype.[61] According to Anja Wieber, it is probable that Ammianus included this tale as a narrative element, a topos, to play out differences in rank and competition at court, while Otto Veh sees the accusation against Eusebia as a rumour developing from Eusebia's lack of children.[62] Maybe Ammianus relays this story with an intention to enthral his audience by putting Helena and Eusebia up against one another in an intrigue at court. On the other hand, it would be facile to ignore and reject the information in Ammianus as mere gossip or defamation. For one thing,

[58] Amm. Marc. 16.10.18–19.
[59] Tac. *Ann.* 12.67.
[60] Cass. Dio 73.22.4. Hdn. 1.16.8.
[61] Wieber-Scariot 1999, 238. See Barnes 1998, 192–93, for Ammianus knowledge' of Latin authors. Jonge 1972, 137–38, states that Amm. Marc. 16.10.18 and 19 both seem out of character for Eusebia without further commentary.
[62] Wieber-Scariot 1999, 239, concludes that such dramatic scenes are not uncommon, either in Ammianus or historical writing in general. Veh and Wirth ²1997, 802, surmise that the rumour's origins could be seen in Eusebia's attempts to help her own conception by ingesting different *pharmaka*.

this author often indicates to his audience when he is relaying gossip, which he does not do in either of these sections.[63] In the first section (16.10.18), Eusebia is the clear, explicitly named culprit in poisoning Helena in Rome. In the second (16.10.19), however, referring to the earlier incident in Gaul, her involvement is only alluded to by Ammianus.

From the previous arguments of this article, it has become clear that Eusebia was aware of the importance of her husband's position and of a stable dynasty as the basis of her own influence. And thus she sought to protect her and her husband's status.[64] From this basis, the conclusion arises that she may have tried to ensure her sister-in-law's infertility – because Julian providing a legitimate heir to the Constantinian throne before Constantius and Eusebia could do so could potentially disrupt the power structure in favour of Julian. In this regard, Eusebia could be said to have had a strong motive.

But Ammianus does not go into much detail on her involvement, and his account raises several questions, starting with the medical issues.[65] Barbara Scarfo discusses childbirth from the midwife's point of view, often referring to Soranus' *Gynaikeia*. She shows that the *obstetrix* had many responsibilities before, during, and after birth and was a person of special trust to the mother.[66] She was the one tasked with cutting the umbilical cord in a particular procedure (ἡ ὀμφαλοτομία), then with bathing and swaddling the baby before presenting it to the father.[67] Soranus gives specific instructions on all the above: the umbilical cord should be cut four fingers' width away from the baby's body and then tied off. We read nothing of a potential danger in cutting the cord too close, though he is specific about the length. He explicitly warns against cauterizing the cord because of the risk of infection and of the superstitious belief in using a shell, glass, or an *ostrakon* as cutting implements, recommending instead a sharp iron instrument to reduce the risk of excessive bleeding.[68] Both the

---

[63] According to Thompson 1947, 36, he refers to hearsay and gossip by inserting *ferunt* and *dicitur* numerous times.

[64] Amm. Marc. 16.10.19: *ne fortissimi viri soboles appareret*. Cf. Aujoulat 1983, 437.

[65] Wieber-Scariot 1999, 249–56, also discusses aspects of the medical issues in relation to this particular episode, referring to Julians physician Oribasius' recipes for contraceptives (*PLRE* I, 653f.; Oreibasios *RE* Suppl. VII (1940), 797–812). She concludes a probable natural cause of death for the infant and takes into account that Helena may have sought gynaecological procedures herself, as Eusebia is also reported to have done.

[66] Scarfo 2020, 77: the midwife attended to the needs of the mother throughout the whole pregnancy and women were often reluctant to be open about medical problems with male doctors.

[67] Scarfo 2020, 99; 105–106, specifically on Helena's pregnancies and *obstetrices* involved in differing legal cases.

[68] Sor. *Gyn.* 2.7.11 (80), in his chapter on cutting the umbilical cord.

superstition and authority of the midwife are perceived as possible dangers by Soranus and by other male physicians and men of senatorial rank. This can be concluded from laws concerning the administration of drugs by the midwife and the monitoring of the birth to prevent babies from being swapped by the midwife and/or the mother. Scarfo concludes that *obstetrices* were ambiguous figures, very much needed to provide healthcare for mother and child but, because of their responsibilities, also mistrusted.[69] So what happened to the midwife that may have caused the child's death? Ammianus does not say that the woman accused of being responsible for the death of an imperial heir (!) was prosecuted, which would have resulted in her death when found guilty. That he, or his source, does not provide the information is noteworthy. Because the unnamed, unprosecuted, and probably at the time of death, unblamed midwife appears as a figure easy to accuse. This makes it more reasonable that the bribery committed to harm Julian's heir was simply a rumour.

This is corroborated by Joachim Szidat, who was able to convincingly argue that Ammianus lacked information from the closest circle of the imperial court, especially around the time of Julian's accession, though he could well have heard rumours about what happened as he was himself in the province at the time.[70] The broader context of Julian's position at this early stage, being Caesar in Gaul without having been given full military command, lends more plausibility to rumours about Julian's infant son being murdered, but not necessarily on the orders of the empress. Ammianus himself, in his account, follows the accusations against Eusebia with Marcellus being relieved of his post as *magister militum* in Gaul because he did not come to Julian's aid. The Caesar was being mistreated by agents of the emperor, being set up for military defeat by Marcellus, and being spied on by Gaudentius, the emperor's *notarius*.[71] But Marcellus subsequently lost his military post, and Constantius would not credit Marcellus' accusations against Julian, so the emperor's involvement in any acts against Julian at this time seems unlikely. The same applies to Eusebia. After the troubles she had gone to have Julian installed as Caesar, her murdering his child so shortly after Julian's accession does not seem plausible.

A possible reconstruction of Ammianus's narrative, if it was not entirely made up, could be as follows: hearing of the death of Julian's and Helena's

---

[69] Scarfo 2020, 103–10. See *Dig.* 9.2.9.1 for medication and *Dig.* 25.4.1.pr. for swapped children.
[70] Wieber-Scariot 1999, 25. Sabbah 2010, 50, between the years 355 and 357. For this period of time, Ursicinus is a probable source of Ammianus: Szidat 1977, 33. See Matthews 1989, 38–39, for further discussion of Ammianus' experiences in Gaul.
[71] Julian. *Ep. Ad Ath.* 278B–C. Amm. Marc. 16.10.20–21. 16.4.3. 16.7.1. 17.9.7. Gaudentius was sent to Gaul as *notarius* to spy on Julian.

infant boy while in Gaul, Ammianus became aware of accusations against the midwife and rumours of her being bribed to kill the boy. Ammianus was seemingly confident in relating the account he heard, but evidently could not discern the real culprit. Thus, he used the passive voice to tell the story, not directly accusing anybody but the midwife, even though infant death was not uncommon and could have many different causes. Only the proximity of the events in Rome (the poisoning of pregnant Helena) and Gaul (bribing the midwife) in the narration leads him to regard Eusebia as the guilty party. Ammianus illustrates the perceived competition of the imperial couples through Eusebia's striving to keep power in the hands of herself and Constantius and concludes that great effort was taken to ensure Julian be without offspring – again in the passive voice, thus tying both stories together.[72] While Ammianus presents the murder of Julian's child as plausible, there is no evidence for Eusebia bribing Helena's midwife.

The poisoning in Rome in the spring of 357 is a different case, however.[73] The accusations against the empress cannot be deconstructed as mere rumours, although they may be less dramatic than the story makes them seem. That Helena became pregnant and bore Julian a son in 356 posed an imminent threat to Constantius' power. Because the emperor was without an heir, a healthy male child would have shifted the dynastic dynamic: Julian's son becoming heir presumptive after his father. This threatened especially Constantius' position and life since he was – being close to 40 – of no age to step back from ruling. Both Julian and Constantius had experienced what inner-dynastic competition and rivalry lead to: not only in the massacre of 337, where most of Julian's male family members were killed, but also in the power struggles among the sons of Constantine.[74]

As there were methods of contraception, it is possible that Constantius and Eusebia expected this from Julian and Helena for the time being. As drugs were often used for both contraceptive and abortive purposes, it is hard to ascertain what exactly happened, but since pregnancy and childbirth were considered mainly women's business, it is conceivable that Eusebia, as empress, sister-in-law, and constant mediator between Julian and Constantius, became the culprit of this story.[75] Helena becoming pregnant again, and quickly, can also be questioned, because Ammianus describes Julian as a very chaste man.[76] From this, Ammianus' remarks that

---

[72] Amm. Marc. 16.10.19: *tanta tamque diligens opera navabatur, ne fortissimi viri soboles appareret.*
[73] Amm. Marc. 16.10.20. Constantius left Rome after a month, on 29 May 357.
[74] See, e.g., Burgess 2008, Lewis 2020, and Humphries 2020.
[75] Scarfo 2020, 189–90; Sor. *Gyn.* 1.19.63.
[76] Amm. Marc. 24.4.27: he did not show interest in females, but (25.4.2–4) lived an altogether abstemious lifestyle.

a drink from the empress caused Helena to miscarry when she conceived seem rather like it was a contraceptive. But how could methods of contraception and abortion be misconstrued as poison (*venenum*)? The answer is that they often put the health of the mother at risk and often came with magical practices: they were combined with charms (e. g. specific amulets) and were administered as mixtures to drink, like a potion,[77] which is precisely what Ammianus is referring to in 16.10.18: *venenum bibere*. This type of treatment, involving some kind of magical component, continued well into the sixth century.[78]

Thus, what Ammianus interprets as poisoning by Eusebia to explain Julian's childlessness is more probably a misunderstanding of contraceptives and/or abortive drugs being taken by Helena and maybe as requested by the imperial couple.[79] It aligns with the proposed agenda of the empress to stabilize the dynasty while ensuring, above all, that the positions of herself and the emperor were protected. Of course, Helena remaining childless did not solve the problem of direct succession, but it bought the imperial couple time.[80] Furthermore, Constantius was believed to be protective of his sister and therefore unlikely to authorize or take part in deliberately inflicting serious harm on her. Libanius, a friend of Julian, attested to this in a speech in 365, where he refuted a rumour circulating in the eastern provinces that Julian bribed a doctor to poison his wife Helena, causing her death in 360:[81] Polycles accused Julian of this, but he bore a grudge against the late emperor for having been dismissed, for incompetence, as governor of Syria Phoenicia.[82] Polycles claimed that the prefect Helpidius[83] told him of a doctor receiving a jewel that Julian had inherited from his mother, as a payment for poisoning Helena.[84] To Libanius, the allegation against Julian is just slander. Too many doctors were present at court to let the specific symptoms go unnoticed. And it was simply inconceivable to Libanius that Helena's brother Constantius

---

[77] Jütte 2008, 49.
[78] See the works of Aëtius of Amida on medicine, where he describes in 16.17 what the amulet should contain and how it was to be worn.
[79] Wieber-Scariot 1999, 255.
[80] Wieber-Scariot 1999, 247, also suggests here that Julian having a son and securing the Constantinian line of succession may have relieved Eusebia of the pressure to conceive. I assume, from Julian's usurpation and struggles of later dynasties, that the opposite was the case: sons of other members of the dynasty were problematic to an emperor without male heir, e.g., Honorius and Theodosius II's relationship to their nephew and cousin Valentinian III; on this topic see Börm 2015a.
[81] Lib. *Or.* 37.3–11.
[82] *PLRE* 1 (Polycles), 712.
[83] *PLRE* 1 (Helpidius 4), 414: *praefectus praetorio Orientis* from 360 to late 361.
[84] Lib. *Or.* 37.3.

would have stood idly by.[85] In this way, Libanius gradually refutes the accusation, presenting his audience with facts so they would reject Polycles' well-fitting but sensational story.[86]

Thus, the seemingly contradictory images of Eusebia can be reconciled, especially in Ammianus. A prominent theme in his narrative of Julian's Caesarship is that Julian was in constant danger from Constantius and his friends; Ammianus may well have believed the rumours of Julian's son being murdered. Because he idealized Julian as ruler, his outrage at him being prevented from fatherhood is understandable, as are, on their own terms, the motives of Eusebia. Another argument against her committing one or multiple crimes is the absence of any other instances where she disposes of somebody in order to secure her position or misuses her influence. There is but one instance where she is described as seeking vengeance, after the bishop Leontius is disrespectful towards her, but even in this narrative, which is quite hostile towards her, she does not abuse her resources to harm the bishop.[87] Thus an argument for Eusebia deliberately harming Helena, Julian, or their late son cannot be made in a convincing way. With the episode in Rome, Ammianus illustrates the power dynamics that lie in favour of the ruling couple. But he imagines a resulting rivalry and victimhood that does not take into account the means that Julian, as Caesar, and Helena, as an emperor's daughter, possessed and their awareness of the requirements of their positions.

Building Networks

In Ammianus, Eusebia is shown as the sole fighter against Constantius' advisors, who aim to mainly please the emperor for their personal gain.[88] But the thorough investigation of charges that Constantius' advisors brought forward after the death of Julian's brother Gallus, mentioned by Julian in his panegyric, would not have been undertaken by her alone, rather she would have instigated it.[89] An episode shortly after Julian's elevation bears testament to the network surrounding him: when Marcellus was discharged as *magister militum* of Gaul and came to court to complain about Julian, Eutherius followed him to defend the Caesar before Constantius.[90] Julian tells us that Eusebia deliberately built a network for the new Caesar on his

---

[85] Lib. *Or.* 37.9–10.
[86] Gizewski 1997, 118.
[87] Philostorg. *Hist. eccl.* 7.6a.5.
[88] Amm. Marc. 15.8.3.
[89] Julian. *Or.* 3.118B.
[90] *PLRE* 1 (Eutherius), 314–15.

way to elevation, favouring his friends and furnishing him with an escort, her eunuchs being in attendance when Julian returned from Greece.[91]

Eunuchs could gain enormous influence, as the examples of Eusebius[92] and Eutherius, both heads of the imperial household, show.[93] But simultaneously, they were vilified and are regularly referred to by the sources in a biased way.[94] When Ammianus relays how highly Eutherius was respected for being intelligent and just, the introduction to the paragraph shows the extent of the systematic hostility that eunuchs faced: even Socrates would have been called a liar for reporting something good about an eunuch. Ammianus then goes on to compare eunuchs with wild animals and thorn bushes, with Eutherius styled as a surprising exception.[95]

Eusebius was a crucial figure in Gallus' death and probably in the accusations against Julian that were connected to his brother's downfall.[96] Even after Julian was cleared, members of the court kept him from returning and encountering Constantius in person, for fear of their importance being reduced.[97] This highlights Eusebius as a representative of ambitious court members in opposition to the dynastic expansion represented by Julian's summons to court and investiture as Caesar. The empress attempted to counter this influence with her own and that of her network.[98] Some elements of this network are visible in the sources. Two women that had a significant influence on the empress are known from the *Epitome*

---

[91] Julian. *Ep. Ad Ath*. 274B: Παραγενόμενον δή με τότε πρῶτον ἀπὸ τῆς Ἑλλάδος αὐτίκα διὰ τῶν περὶ τὴν θεραπείαν εὐνούχων ἡ μακαρῖτις Εὐσεβία καὶ λίαν ἐφιλοφρονεῖτο. – "Now from the first moment of my arrival from Greece, Eusebia of blessed memory kept showing me the utmost kindness through the eunuchs of her household" (trans. Wright).

[92] *PLRE* 1 (Eusebius 11), 302–303.

[93] Tougher 2020, 189–91, shows that Eusebius was the first significant example of a eunuch with profound influence at court; thus, accusations brought against him are hard to differentiate from the general discursive background against eunuchs and their alleged influence in the later Roman Empire.

[94] See Tougher 1999.

[95] Amm. Marc. 16.7.4.

[96] Amm. Marc. 15.3.2 accuses Arbetio and Eusebius of abuse of power and cruelty. Philostorg. *Hist. eccl.* 4.1.6f. describes Eusebius as the cause for delay of the imperial pardon, to ensure Gallus' death. In Julian. *Ep. Ad Ath*. 272D, Eusebius is surely meant by ἑνὸς ἀνδρογύνου, τοῦ κατακοιμιστοῦ. Wieber-Scariot 1998, 106–107, shows that Eusebius would have been present in the council with Ursicinus and Julian; see also Tougher 2020, 190.

[97] Amm. Marc. 15.2.7–8. Julian. *Ep. Ad Ath*. 274B, referring to Eusebius managing access to the emperor. Cf. Scholten 1998, 53–54, on unofficial access to the emperor; see also Scholten 1995.

[98] Kunst 2010, 149; 153, on the position of the empress in relation to the emperor and her power through matronage. Wieber 2010, 274, on Eusebia's networking.

de Caesaribus: Adamantia and Gorgonia;[99] but they are not mentioned anywhere else, and neither is their relationship with Eusebia. Possibly, they were members of her household. One potential connection is found in Ammianus, who mentions a eunuch called Gorgonius as the *praepositus sacri cubiculi* of the former Caesar Gallus in 354.[100] Besides him, six more persons of the same name are listed in the *PLRE*, mainly from the eastern provinces and especially Antioch. One was the father of a senator named Alexander in the 360s.[101] Thus, the mentioned Gorgonia might have been a friend of Eusebia or her servant; we cannot be certain.

As for Adamantia, the *PLRE* lists three men of similar name, likewise all from the eastern provinces: a lawyer from Antioch and a sophist in contact with Gregory of Nazianzus; these two lived in the reign of Constantius. There is also an imperial guard, Flavius Adamantius, *ex protectoribus*, probably from Lycaonia, with no reliable date.[102] If this Adamantia was connected to either, she was likely not of senatorial rank, but she may have served in the imperial household as the daughter of a clerk or guard. Or, the empress befriended her as the daughter of a well-educated man, since Eusebia's scholarly interests are widely known through Julian's eulogy.[103] But this is, of course, only conjecture, intended to illustrate what courtly networks may have looked like.

Julian also mentions that Eusebia greatly favoured friends and family, which was only to be expected of a person of her status.[104] Her family was exempt from paying taxes in 360, and in the year before, her brothers Eusebius and Hypatius had been made joint consuls.[105] Eusebius was governor of Hellespontus and later moved post to Bithynia in 355/56.[106] Both were powerful men, and after Eusebia's death, they were accused of reaching for the purple in 371/72 and subsequently were exiled, if only temporarily.[107]

Eusebia also sought to form relationships with clerical circles, as attested by Theodoret and Philostorgius. But in these instances, she was

---

[99] Ps.-Aur. Vict. *Epit.* 42.20.
[100] Amm. Marc. 15.2.10. *PLRE* 1 (Gorgonius 3), 399.
[101] *PLRE* 1 (Gorgonius 1–7), 398–99. Between them, one *comes*, one *assessor* in Armenia, and a *vir perfectissimus* from Arabia. Gorgonius 5 was the father of the senator Alexander (6, *PLRE* 1, 41) and may have been related to Gorgonia; both father and son are mentioned in Lib. *Ep.* 1167.
[102] *PLRE* 1 (Adamantius 1–3), 12.
[103] Julian. *Or.* 3.124A; her gifting Julian a library with books on philosophy, history, oratory, and poetry best illustrates this; cf. Wieber 2010, 275 on Eusebia's education.
[104] Julian. *Or.* 3.116A.
[105] Amm. Marc. 18.1.1. 21.6.4. The tax exemption is stated in *CTh* 11.1.1.
[106] *PLRE* 1 (Eusebius 40), 308f.
[107] Amm. Marc. 29.2.9–11. Tougher 2000, 99.

unable to achieve her aims, while the holy men are presented as good and just. Again, the interpretations of her motives here cannot be taken at face value as both sources were designed to show the clergymen in a good light.[108] The former tells us that she sent money to the exiled bishop of Rome, Liberius. Here, again, we can observe her in the position of the mediator, if an unsuccessful one, as the gift of money was not accepted. In the following chapter, Theodoret then relates how a network of noble women petitioned the Augustus successfully for Liberius' return when he and the empress visited Rome in 357.[109] Though he does not mention Eusebia, it is not far-fetched to presume her being present during the petition and deliberation, as the case of another bishop shows. Philostorgius relates the story of one Leontius, bishop of Tripolis (ad Maeandrum) in Lydia, who, at a synod with the empress in attendance, refused Eusebia the usual ceremonial courtesies, which angered her greatly.[110] Interestingly, and beyond the prima facie value of this passage, this scene offers insight into how Eusebia built her network, which included bishops and clerics, as she unsuccessfully tried to win Leontius over with promises of founding a church and gifts of money. She would not be the only Constantinian woman of her generation to make this promise, as Constantina founded the first basilica of the martyr Agnes in Rome.[111] Courtly and clerical networks were not distinct, but rather overlapping. This is evident in the appointment of the *vicarius* in the former *dioecesis Pontica*, then recently renamed *Pietas* in Eusebia's honour. While the man in question, Aristaenetus,[112] was appointed through the emperor Constantius, Eusebia might have taken part in bringing it about.[113] Firstly, it is conceivable that she had a say in this appointment, as the diocese was created in her honour. Secondly, there is the potential network of Aristaenetus to consider, who had previously declined other opportunities. The pagan rhetor Libanius, himself politically active and a friend of Julian, was closely connected to Aristaenetus and might have facilitated the contact between Aristaenetus and Julian, though this interpretation is again speculative.[114] This hypothetical network shows that Julian may have played a part in convincing Aristaenetus to take up this post or in recommending him for it to the imperial couple. Eusebia's

---

[108] For an overview of the motives for depicting holy men, see Brown 2001.
[109] Theod. *Hist. eccl.* 2.16.28. 2.17.
[110] Philostorg. *Hist. eccl.* 7.6a.5, for the synod, *vide supra* n. 18, probably in 358 or 359.
[111] *ICUR* 8.20752; cf. Trout 2015, 264–65, for a translation of the inscription.
[112] *PLRE* 1 (Aristaenetus), 104, sometimes referred to as Aristainetus.
[113] Amm. Marc. 17.7.6. Aristaenetus was killed shortly thereafter, when the earthquake of 24 August 358 left large parts of the city in ruins.
[114] Ruprecht 2021, 84–85, discusses the friendship of Libanius and Aristaenetus and how the latter declined a post of accessor of the praetorian prefect; Lib. *Ep.* 571.2 shows both as pagans.

brother Eusebius, the former governor of Hellespontus and Bithynia, also belonged to this network. He carried letters for Libanius on his way from Antioch to his new post in Nicomedia, including one to Aristaenetus himself.[115] Although the exact dynamics remain unknown, these examples suggest how Julian would strengthen and broaden Eusebia's network and how she may have influenced the appointment of offices.

Eusebia's sisters-in-law, Constantia and Helena, are further prime examples of Constantinian women protecting the dynastic line and informally exerting their power. Both were daughters and sisters to emperors and the granddaughters of the empress Helena, Constantine I's mother, who herself had great power as the *genetrix* of the dynasty. Like Eusebia did earlier, by providing an escort for Julian, Helena physically protected Julian with guards loyal to her: after his usurpation a guard in Helena's entourage, τις τῶν ἐπιτεταγμένων τῇ προόδῳ, thwarted an attack on the recently acclaimed Augustus in Gaul.[116] Constantina was even more powerful. As with Eusebia, she is often portrayed as stepping in when her husband Gallus was unsure of what to decide. Her intervention during the usurpation of Magnentius led to Vetranio's acclamation, showing a similar motivation: protecting the rule of the Constantinian family. Constantina is assessed much more negatively, but her power and influence cannot be disputed.[117]

The Means and Duties of an Empress

The power and influence of an empress were obtained through her status in the hierarchy of the dynasty. And the most prevalent duty of an empress in a dynasty was to ensure its continuation: it simply was a requirement to be met. Thus the role of being a mother was an essential source of authority for empresses as well, especially for Eusebia, who was no Constantinian by birth.[118] The degree of importance, and outright pressure, can be inferred from the different reports about Eusebia not being able to conceive: speculating about reasons as to why this was the case and how she

---

[115] Lib. *Ep.* 457–59. *Ep.* 459 is addressed to Aristaenetus, who was a friend to both Eusebius and Libanius, and begins with the words: "I asked the worthy Eusebius whether he counted you [sc. Aristaenetus] among his friends. 'Certainly!' he cried out. It was the shout of man revealing what value he placed on friendship" (trans. Bradbury 2011, 152–53).

[116] Julian. *Ep. ad Ath.* 285Bb.

[117] Amm. Marc. 14.1.2. 14.9.3. Wieber-Scariot 1999, 74–195. Hillner 2018. In protecting the dynastic line, Helena (mother of Constantine I) also was said to have been excluding Theodora's children from taking part in ruling the empire, of which Drijvers 1992a, 52–53, sees no proof in the sources.

[118] Kunst 2013b, 8. Wieber-Scariot 1999, 54f.; 246.

sought to be 'cured' but to no effect,[119] relating her childlessness to intrigue and dynastic competition,[120] and even attributing her death to fertility treatments.[121] The duty of continuing the imperial line directly would not only have cemented Constantius' power, but it would also have given Eusebia more security in case she outlived her husband. This was because in the case of Constantius dying before his wife, association with her would have given legitimacy to the next pretender for the position of Augustus. As examples from the fifth century show, this was no rarity: the empress Verina, wife to Leo I, and their daughter Ariadne both had legitimized claims to the throne: Verina as dowager empress supported her brother to usurp imperial power, while Ariadne – with more 'dynastic capital' – married Anastasius, who succeeded her husband Zeno as emperor.[122] Even for Eusebia there is an example in Ammianus. He strikingly mentions a contemporary letter written by Assyria, wife of the *magister peditum* Barbatio, who gives voice to her fear of just such a scenario: she is afraid that her husband will cast her aside to marry Eusebia.[123] Constantius' posthumous daughter Constantia, an issue of his last marriage to Faustina after Eusebia's death, likely in 360, is an excellent example of this: she and her mother were used by Procopius, Julian's cousin, to ensure the loyalty of his troops during his failed usurpation in 366. Later, Constantia was married to Gratian to establish a link between the new ruler Valentinian and the Constantinian house.[124]

While dynastic continuation was the primary role of the empress, the public image of the imperial power was also an important duty. Helena, the mother of Constantine I, who was an admired figure, set a strong precedent with her pious image of motherhood. Eusebia's piety is connected to this but also serves as a parallel with another tetrarchic empress: Diocletian's daughter, Valeria. As Eusebia, who gave her name, Greek for *pietas*, to the diocese of Pontus,[125] Valeria, who in addition held the title of Augusta, gave hers to a province (formerly part of Pannonia).[126] Like Eusebia, she and her husband Galerius had no children. After Galerius died in 311, Valeria refused to submit herself to the care of his co-emperor Licinius and fled to

---

[119] Philostorg. *Hist. eccl.* 4.7.1f.
[120] Amm. Marc. 16.10.18–19.
[121] Zonar. 13.11.29–30.
[122] *PLRE* 2 (Aelia Verina), 1156, and her brother (*PLRE* 2 [Basiliscus 2], 212–14); Verina's daughter Aelia Ariadne (*PLRE* 2 [Aelia Ariadne], 140–41), and Anastasius (*PLRE* 2 [Anastasius 4], 78–80).
[123] Amm. Marc. 18.3.2.
[124] Amm. Marc. 26.7.10. 16.9.3. McEvoy 2016a, 155; 159.
[125] Amm. Marc. 17.7.6.
[126] Harries 2014, 198. *PLRE* 1 (Valeria), 937. Amm. Marc. 19.11.4.

her husband's Caesar and new Augustus, Maximinus Daza.[127] But Daza did not help her, and instead seized Valeria's property and exiled her. As Lactantius relates it, Daza was prepared to put aside his wife and marry Valeria for his own gain, but she refused him.[128] Her 'dynastic capital' to a pretender or successor was obviously enormous, especially without a son to protect her or to make claims as Galerius' heir. However negatively Maximinus Daza is portrayed by Lactantius, his assessment of the situation was accurate: Valeria had either to be incorporated into the new regime or deprived of power, so as not to pose a threat to his rule.

Considering her concerns surrounding her own safety and for the fulfilment of her responsibility to continue the Constantinian line, it is evident that, for Eusebia, promoting Julian was a consciously chosen strategy. Beside Constantius, he was the last male representative of the dynasty and one who could pose a significant danger if he could not be made an ally. In the end, Eusebia's fears were proven right when Julian turned against Constantius after her death, but at the same time, he kept the empress in good memory.[129] In a way, her striving for consolidation ensured Julian was next in line to rule the Roman Empire. She remains a striking example of how vital dynastic preservation and consolidation were for imperial women, particularly when they were without direct descendants. Her actions resulted from the political motivation to build and maintain a strong dynasty that would secure her status and position in turn. She worked towards fulfilling her role as Constantius' wife and empress. This encompassed being responsible for maintaining the line of succession (hence her protection and mentoring of Julian), mediating between emperor and Caesar, and taking up to the role of advisor. This conclusion does not rule out her acting out of sympathy and kindness and as a friend towards Julian, but it is clear that she was, first and foremost, an active part of the ruling couple.[130] The negative reception of her actions, or rumours about them, is an expression of the continued expansion of female power during her short reign between 353 and 360, which was looked upon with suspicion by historians like Ammianus. He praised her support of his favourite Julian, while at the same time criticizing the emperor as weak for letting Eusebia exercise the same authority in other instances or in general.[131] Rather than

[127] *PLRE* 1 (Maximinus 12), 579.
[128] Lactant. *De mort. pers.* 39.1–5.
[129] Lib. *Or.* 18.27 describes her as Ino, daughter of Cadmus, who among other things, nursed Dionysus and helped Odysseus on his journey; Julian. *Ep. ad Ath.* 274B: ἡ μακαρῖτις Εὐσεβία – "the blessed Eusebia"; 273a: τὴν καλὴν καὶ ἀγαθὴν […] γαμετὴν Εὐσεβίαν – "the beautiful and good wife Eusebia".
[130] Cf. Lib. *Or.* 18.27. Julian himself (*Ep. ad Ath.* 273A) describes her as "kindly disposed to me" (τηνικαῦτά μοι παρέσχεν εὐμενῆ, […] Εὐσεβίαν, trans. Wright).
[131] Amm. Marc. 21.16.16.

interpreting the differing accounts in opposition towards each other, by striving for a holistic view of the source material, a more nuanced and well-rounded picture can be gained of the empress' agenda, actions, and motivations.

3

John Chrysostom's *Letter to a Young Widow*: Reflections on Imperial Women's Roles at Regime Change

Belinda Washington

John Chrysostom's *Letter to a Young Widow* was written before he became bishop of Constantinople in late 397, after which he regularly came into direct contact with the imperial court of Arcadius.[1] The *Letter* was written in Antioch to console a recently widowed woman and advise her against re-marrying and instead use her inherited wealth to benefit the Church. In it, Chrysostom refers to the fates of various recent imperial rulers and their wives. The passage on unnamed imperial women offers a rare collection of biographical details for fourth-century women. In particular, the women of the Valentinianic dynasty rarely feature in the extant literary sources, which increases the value of this letter as a historical record if these women can be identified.

In this chapter, I examine the information Chrysostom provides about imperial women and how his depictions were informed by the wider political climate. I first look at the passage in the context of the *Letter* itself and cautiously seek to identify the unnamed women and their husbands. I then consider appearances by fourth-century women at points of regime change, which provides the context for many of the female exempla in the *Letter*. I focus especially on the literary evidence for fourth-century usurpations in which imperial women were reportedly embroiled, including some of those cited in the *Letter*. Where possible, I also try to compare these

---

[1] I agree with Grillet's assessment (Grillet and Ettlinger 1968, 11–12), that the *Letter* was composed between 378 and 383. Grillet plausibly dates it to Theodosius' early Gothic campaign of 380–1. Liebeschuetz 2011, 152, suggests it was written between January 379 and October 382. I would like to thank the editors for their advice and support over the course of the drafting of this chapter; Ben Harriman and Alison John for looking at early drafts; and Victoria Leonard for her later advice. I first came across the *Letter* during my PhD research, which was facilitated by the generosity of the Kerr-Fry Bequest Fund.

women with their female counterparts across the broader imperial period to see how their roles were developing as the role of the emperor himself was changing from military leader to a figure whose court was permanently stationary. Finally, I consider Chrysostom's later fraught relationship with the empress Eudoxia (the wife of the emperor Arcadius) when he was bishop of Constantinople. Later portrayals by ecclesiastical historians suggested that Eudoxia was partly responsible for Chrysostom's exiles in reaction to his (alleged) criticism of her, specifically her public presentation. This later relationship showed how imperial women's roles had changed with the development of the emperor's own presentation, a process which was at an early stage when Chrysostom composed his *Letter* and had transformed by the time he became bishop of Constantinople. I hope to show the value such a perspective can bring to understanding the imperial politics of the late-fourth and early-fifth centuries.

The *Letter to a Young Widow*

The unnamed young addressee of the *Letter* has recently been widowed by the death of her husband Therasios.[2] The *Letter* is brief and strikes a personal tone, which suggests that Chrysostom was familiar with its subject.[3] In the first two chapters, Chrysostom outlines the subject's grief and the danger she is in from the petitions of parties after her wealth, especially in the form of marriage proposals. By the third chapter, Chrysostom turns his attention to Therasios and refers to the deceased's nascent political career. Mention of Therasios' career provides Chrysostom with the opportunity to turn to other examples of widows of those who had held high office. First, Chrysostom cites those who plotted against the emperor. Chrysostom starts his examples with Theodorus of Sicily, whose wife was enslaved upon his death.[4] Chrysostom then provides the second example of Artemisia, the only woman referred to directly by name in the *Letter*. Artemisia is

---

[2] Therasios is first mentioned by name in chapter 2 of the *Letter*: 2.143. *PLRE* 1 suggests this is the same Therasios who was governor of Cappadocia in 371 and who was the addressee in Basil. *Ep.* 77 (371).

[3] Chrysostom refers to the widow's uncle who has been in contact with him (1.29–34). Grillet and Ettlinger 1968, 9, think Chrysostom was possibly a family friend.

[4] *PLRE* 1 (Theodorus 13) argues that Chrysostom's association of this Theodorus with Sicily is an error. This Theodore served as an eastern *secundicerius notariorum* in 371: Amm. Marc. 29.1.8. He was executed by Valens for treason in Antioch, so Chrysostom and the young widow would have had local knowledge of the affair. The execution is mentioned by Amm. Marc. 29.1.8–9, 12, 14, 25; 33.5; 31.1.3, Eunap. *fr.* 38, and Libanius (another Antiochene local) *Or.* 1.225; 24.13.14. See *PLRE* 1 for further sources.

described in her widowhood as being reduced to poverty and becoming blind from her constant weeping.[5]

Chrysostom then progresses in his examples of wifely suffering to the widows of the rulers themselves (chapters 4–5). These imperial examples provide the conclusion of Chrysostom's comparisons of widows who have suffered more greatly than Therasios' widow, despite their higher social status. Therasios' widow, unlike these examples, was at least fortunate enough to be at her husband's bedside when he died (chapter 5). In the remaining two chapters (6 and 7), Chrysostom criticizes the accumulation of earthly wealth and the corrupting influence of high office, opinions which would not stand him in good stead once he became bishop of Constantinople.

Identifications of the Imperial Rulers in the *Letter*

Unlike the examples of other high-ranking men, all the imperial figures go unnamed, although Chrysostom lists the deaths of the emperors in enough detail that we may attempt to work out their identities. Within the timeframe of "our generation" (γενεά), Chrysostom refers to nine (ἐννέα) rulers (τῶν Βασιλευσάντων).[6] The vagueness of the term 'rulers' could mean that some are Caesars, rather than Augusti. Chrysostom provides specific details for the deaths of six rulers, which leaves three other rulers who can be accounted for as those currently reigning. Of these living rulers, Chrysostom only gives further details about two by referring to the two women who live with them. The deaths of the rulers are given a level of individual detail not afforded to deceased imperial women.[7] Chrysostom completes his exempla with imperial widows who are still alive and the wives of the two current emperors.[8]

There are three possibilities for the living Augusti which then determine the identities of the six rulers whose deaths are described. All three colleges of living Augusti offer some interesting biographical information for imperial wives who otherwise are relatively unknown, and so it is worthwhile to identify, however speculatively, the imperial figures mentioned. Below are the three possible combinations of Augusti.

---

[5] Artemisia's husband may have been Procopius, whose usurpation I discuss later. *PLRE* 1 tentatively makes her the wife of Procopius based on this letter. Zos. 4.3–5.1 refers to Procopius' wife and children but does not name them.

[6] 4.278–79. Grillet and Ettlinger 1968, 136–38 n. 2, examine Chrysostom's sometimes fluid application of the term γενεά.

[7] 4.283–85.

[8] 4.285–309.

70 *Empresses-in-Waiting*

Table 1: Chronology

Current Augusti	Period of their co-rule
1. Gratian and Valentinian II	9 August 378 to 18 January 379
2. Gratian, Theodosius I, and Valentinian II	19 January 379 to 24 August 383
3. Valentinian II, Theodosius I, and Arcadius	25 August 383 to 15 May 392

I take these current rulers to be included among the nine in total whom Chrysostom refers to as being in his generation. Chrysostom describes the deaths of six rulers before turning his attention to two who are ruling, which leaves one other ruler from the nine specified. The last two combinations in the list above allow for this remaining, peripheral figure to be a third unmarried member of the current imperial college of Augusti. The focus of Chrysostom's descriptions of the current rulers is the plight of their wives, which would allow for the third unmarried and much younger colleague to be ignored. The junior Augustus in the college of Gratian and Theodosius was Gratian's half-brother Valentinian II; and for Valentinian II and Theodosius it was Theodosius' young son Arcadius. Either of these combinations would account for the nine rulers Chrysostom specifies and so the first combination in the table above (Gratian and Valentinian II) can be discarded.

The six imperial deaths described in chapter 4 of the *Letter* are listed in the table below, along with the possible identities that are contingent upon the reigning imperial college. However, there are further options which could be considered, depending on Chrysostom's definition of the term 'ruler'.[9]

Table 2: Imperial Deaths

Cause of Death[10]	Imperial College of Gratian, Theodosius I, and Valentinian II	Imperial College of Valentinian II, Theodosius I, and Arcadius
Two who died natural deaths (δύο μόνοι κοινῷ θανάτῳ)	Constantius II and Valentinian I	Constantius II and Valentinian I

---

[9] Chrysostom uses βασιλευσάντων and γεγενημένων in relation to the deceased rulers.
[10] All the means of death agree with the phrase, "lost his life" (τὸν βίον κατέλυσαν) (280).

Cause of Death[10]	Imperial College of Gratian, Theodosius I, and Valentinian II	Imperial College of Valentinian II, Theodosius I, and Arcadius
One by a tyrant (ὁ ὑπὸ τυράννου)[11]	Constans[12]	Gratian
One in battle (ὁ ἐν πολέμῳ)	Valens	Valens
One by a palace guard conspiracy (ὁ ὑπὸ τῶν ἔνδον φυλαττόντων αὐτὸν ἐπιβουλευθείς)[13]	Julian[14]	Julian
One by he who appointed him and adorned him with the purple (ὁ ὑπ' αὐτοῦ τοῦ χειροτονήσαντος καὶ τὴν ἀλουργίδα περιθέντος αὐτῷ)	Jovian[15]	Jovian

As can be seen in the table above, in all cases Constantius II and Valentinian I are the rulers who died from natural deaths, leaving as widows Faustina and Justina respectively. Also, Valens is the only option for the ruler killed in battle (at Adrianople in August 378), who was survived by his wife Domnica.

The identities of the other rulers are harder to discern.[16] The one killed by a tyrant would depend on whether Gratian was one of the living emperors, as he was killed during Magnus Maximus' usurpation; otherwise the likeliest

---

[11] The definition of tyrant and, by extension, usurper was relative to the contemporary context and who was in power. Omissi 2018 offers extensive analysis of imperial legitimacy in the fourth century – see 34–39 for his analysis of the modern and ancient conception of usurpation. Omissi, 21–34, looks at the perception of a ruler as a tyrant.
[12] See Drinkwater 2022, 33–36, for a recent analysis of Constans' overthrow.
[13] There is ambiguity as to whether this is the deceased's palace guard.
[14] This could also refer to Constantine II if one of the current rulers is Gratian.
[15] Constantius II's Caesar, Gallus, who was resident in Antioch, should also be considered; see Grillet and Ettlinger 1968, 136–38 n. 2. It is more unlikely that usurpers should be included given there is a separate section relating to them in the *Letter*; 4.258–64. Magnus Maximus would be an important consideration since he was briefly recognized by Theodosius (Zos. 4.37.3 and Sozom. *Hist. eccl.* 5.12), but his usurpation was probably after the *Letter* was written. Lunn-Rockliffe 2010, 319–21, looks at Theodosius' recognition of Maximus.
[16] An interesting and, perhaps, informative text to read in tandem is Chrysostom's *Homily 15 to St. Paul on the Philippians*. In this other work, Chrysostom again summarizes violent deaths within the imperial household with a clear focus on the Constantinian dynasty (15.4), although again they are unnamed and the imagery used is more fantastical. For further analysis see Allen 2013, whose translation makes it Homily 16.

option is Constans who was killed following the usurpation of Magnentius (Justina's first husband).[17] The remaining two rulers are trickier to identify and the conjectures above are made extremely tentatively.[18] Julian seems the most likely identity of the one killed by a palace guard conspiracy, based on the rumour that he was killed by a spear thrown by his own soldier while on his Persian campaign.[19] However, Constans' death had also been precipitated by betrayal within his own administration.[20]

Given the specific reference to nine rulers, it seems that the last death can only refer to Jovian. Although Gallus, the Caesar who was executed on Constantius II's orders, seems more likely, it is odd that Jovian's more recent reign would be overlooked in the list of examples. The circumstances of Jovian's death are unclear, but if he is the one who was killed by the person who appointed him then that would refer to one of the military cabal who had him proclaimed Augustus.[21]

---

[17] Chrysostom appears to also refer to Constans' death by a tyrant in *Hom. Phil.* 15.4. For other sources for Constans' death, see *Cons. Const.* s.a. 350, Jer. *Chron.* s.a. 350, Zos. 2.42.5, Aur. Vict. *Caes.* 41.23–25, and Socrates, *Hist. eccl.* 2.25.

[18] Chrysostom seems to assume that his audience could infer the identity of each figure from the partial information provided, which reinforces the idea that he was being exact with the term 'generation'. Grillet and Ettlinger 1968, 138 n. 2, point out Chrysostom was often imprecise with such terms, but Chrysostom's mention of nine rulers suggests in this case he is being specific.

[19] There is no consensus as to how Julian died while on campaign: see Lib. *Or.* 18.275, 24.17–27, Sozom. *Hist. eccl.* 6.1.14, Greg. Naz. *Or.* 5.13, Amm. Marc. 25.3.6 and 6.6, and Socrates, *Hist. eccl.* 3.21.13. For discussion in modern scholarship see, for example Woods 2015 and Hahn 1960, 225–32; for earlier analysis see Büttner-Wobst 1892. There was also an Iranian/Islamic tradition relating Julian's death – for further discussion see Azarnoush 1991, 302–39.

[20] Drinkwater 2022, 34–36, and Omissi 2018, 163–64, draw attention to Constans' lack of support among his administration.

[21] The general consensus among the surviving sources is that Jovian died accidentally as a result of fumes either from coals burning in his tent or from the plaster in a building: Eutr. 10.18.2, Jer. *Chron.* s.a. 364, Aur. Vict. *Caes.* 44.4, Zos. 3.35.3, and Theod. *Hist. eccl.* 4.5. Amm. Marc. 25.10.12–13 relates the rumour that Jovian died as a result of accidental asphyxiation, but notes the suspicious circumstances were left un-investigated. Lenski 2000, 493–502 and 513, and Omissi 2018, 228–59, provide an overview of Jovian's election by a clique of Pannonian military figures who also influenced the subsequent elections of Valentinian I and Valens. A case could be made that Julian was excluded from Chrysostom's list as he was not a Christian, but it seems unlikely – Chrysostom referred to him as emperor (albeit unflatteringly) in *On St Babylas*. Shepardson 2009, discusses this work and draws attention to Chrysostom attributing Julian's death to his impiety (see esp. 107–10). Julian also looks likely to be the emperor described by Chrysostom in his *Hom. Phil.* 15.4, whose wife died of poisoning (see the next section for further discussion). In a footnote, Shepardson suggests Julian is not mentioned in the *Letter*: 2009, 110 n. 85.

It seems the most likely combination of living rulers are Gratian and Theodosius I, who are also the preference of both Liebeschuetz and Grillet, albeit for different reasons.[22] This cautious preference is due to the likely existence of a third Augustus, and the description of the women who 'live with' the current rulers (τῶν δὲ τοῖς νῦν βασιλεύουσι συνοικουσῶν). The two women described seem to be the Augusti's wives, which would allow for the third unmarried Augustus (likely Valentinian II) to not be mentioned in this section; his mother Justina is referred to as the widow of Valentinian I.

Identifications of the Rulers' Wives and Widows in the *Letter*

Chrysostom describes the deceased wives of emperors more vaguely than their husbands, categorizing them as dying either from despondency or poisoning.[23] Chrysostom himself permits the unfounded basis of these descriptions with the use of the phrase 'it is said' (ὥς φασι).[24] He provides more detail for those who are still alive, including both widows and the current consorts. The possible identities of these women are set out below, based on the assumption that Gratian and Theodosius I were reigning.

Turning first to the widows who are alive, Chrysostom outlines their concerns following the deaths of their husbands:

> Of those who are still around, one who has a fatherless child trembles in fear that one of those now ruling should kill him out of fear of what could happen. The other one, after being begged by many, has only just returned from foreign lands to which a ruler previously exiled her.[25]

The widow with an orphan son could either be Charito (widow of Jovian and mother of Varronianus), or Justina, whose son, Valentinian II, was

---

[22] Liebeschuetz 2011, 152 n. 71, and Grillet and Ettlinger 1968, 11.

[23] 4.283–85. Although not fatal, Ammianus describes Eusebia (wife of Constantius II) poisoning Helena (Julian's wife) in Rome, which caused Helena to later miscarry: 16.10.18–19. Tougher 2000 analyses the dual representation of Eusebia in the main account by Ammianus, as does Holm, this volume, who also specifically looks at the poisoning accusation. In *Hom. Phil.* 15.4, Chrysostom describes a wife of an emperor who was destroyed by pessaries, which seems to refer to Helena (although a case could be made for Eusebia as the vagueness of the description of the emperor could be Constantius). The text in Migne would suggest it was Helena (*PG* 62.294.48–295.46) but compare Allen 2013 whose translation is based on a different arrangement of the Greek.

[24] 4.284.

[25] 4.285–89: Τῶν δὲ ἔτι περιουσῶν ἡ μὲν παῖδα ἔχουσα ὀρφανὸν τρέμει καὶ δέδοικε μή τις αὐτὸν τῶν κρατούντων φόβῳ τῶν μελλόντων ἀνέλῃ. Ἡ δὲ μόλις πολλῶν δεηθέντων ἀπὸ τῆς ὑπερορίας ἐπανῆλθεν εἰς ἣν αὐτὴν ὁ κρατῶν ἐξέβαλε πρότερον. The translations of the *Letter* are my own.

proclaimed Augustus after the death of Valentinian I without the consent of the now senior Augustus Gratian, who was Valentinian II's half-brother.[26] The second option is more tempting, if the current Augusti are Gratian and Theodosius, since it fits with the image promoted by eastern panegyrists such as Themistius who referred to Valentinian II's marginalized role in the imperial college.[27]

Aside from Constantia, Justina, the wife of Valentinian I and mother of Valentinian II, is probably the best-known woman of the Valentinianic dynasty. While the information about Constantia, who died during Gratian's reign, is largely informed by her Constantinian descent, Justina is mainly defined by her conflict with the bishop Ambrose.[28] The largely negative portrayal of her in the literary sources, especially in the context of the Basilica Conflict, resonates with the later literary reception of Eudoxia, wife of Arcadius, who came into conflict with Chrysostom once he became bishop of Constantinople – a portrayal which I will turn to again later in this chapter.[29]

The other living widow, who has returned from exile, is surely Marina Severa, Valentinian I's first wife and mother of Gratian. It is likely that she left court by the time Justina married Valentinian I.[30] The term 'foreign

---

[26] Amm. Marc. 30.10.4–6. Errington 1996 and Omissi 2018, 255–90, provide useful examinations of Valentinian II's and Theodosius' elections. G. Kelly 2013 looks at Valentinian II's election specifically.

[27] Them. *Or.* 15.198B. Valentinian II's junior status is reflected by the coinage produced in this period, on which he has an unbroken obverse legend, e.g., *RIC* IX, 45b. Pearce 1934, 114–20, discusses the significance of such a legend with specific reference to Valentinian II and Arcadius.

[28] Most of the literary sources which describe this conflict follow on from Ambrose's account of the Basilica Conflict in *Ep.* 75, 75a, 76, and 77. See Paulin. *Vit. Ambr.* 13–14 and the ecclesiastical histories of Rufinus (*Hist. eccl.* 11.15–17), Socrates (*Hist. eccl.* 5.11), Sozomen (*Hist. eccl.* 7.13–14) and Theodoret (*Hist. eccl.* 5.13–14). On other occasions, Ambrose worked with the court: *Ep.* 30 mentions his embassies on their behalf to the usurper Magnus Maximus.

[29] The Basilica Conflict (385/86) was about two issues related to non-Nicene Christian worship, which Valentinian II and Justina observed, unlike Ambrose the bishop of Milan where Valentinian's court resided. For the primary accounts see previous footnote. The first issue was a law that legislated for freedom of religious assembly (*CTh* 16.1.4) and the imperial court's use of a basilica for Easter 386. Liebeschuetz 2005 provides the most comprehensive discussion of the conflict (based on Ambrose's account). For analysis of Justina's role specifically see Washington 2016, 173–85.

[30] Valentinian I divorced Marina Severa to marry Justina: Socrates, *Hist. eccl.* 4.31.10–18; Joh. Ant. *fr.* 187; Jord. *Rom.* 310; Theoph. Conf. AM 5860; Zonar. 13.15. Lenski 2002, 103, dates the divorce to 369. Amm. Marc. 28.1.57 mentions Marina Severa at Gratian's court. Her recall by Gratian is mentioned in *Chron. Pasch.* s.a. 378, Joh. Malal. 13.32. For discussion of her recall, see Al. Cameron 2012, 349–50, and Whitby and Whitby 1989, 49 n. 153. Woods 2006, 181–82, argues Valentinian

lands' (τῆς ὑπερορίας) which Chrysostom uses could in fact refer to the eastern part of the empire which was ruled by Valens.[31] Her return would therefore be to the western empire once Valentinian I died. However, if Chrysostom implies a formal exile, then Marina Severa would be an unusual fourth-century example.[32]

Chrysostom reserves his most vivid depictions for the wives of the current rulers, who I take to be Constantia, the first wife of Gratian, and Aelia Flaccilla, the first wife of Theodosius I:

> Of those who live together with those now ruling, one who recovered from earlier misfortunes has a great deal of pain mingled with her pleasure on account of the ruler still being very young and inexperienced and having many plots formed against him from many places; the other one is dead from fear[33] and lives more wretchedly on account of her own husband who, from the moment he was crowned with the diadem until today, is embroiled in wars and battles and besides he is consumed by shame of the calamities and calumnies that come from everywhere. For that which has never happened is now coming to pass, and the barbarians, having left their own country, have so often overrun so many thousands of stades of ours.[34]

I banished Justina based on the information in the *Letter*. This seems unlikely since Valentinian II was with his mother when Valentinian I died: Amm. Marc. 30.10.4.

[31] This term can simply refer to the land beyond one's frontiers, which would be the case here if Marina Severa moved to Valens' territory. Woods 2006, 180–81, discusses the use of the term for exile. The second entry for the term in *LSJ* notes the term indicates exile.

[32] In the early Principate, more imperial women were exiled than were deified: see Varner 2001, 43, and Kienast, Eck, and Heil ⁶2017. Exiles in the Julio-Claudian dynasty tended to be to islands: see Cohen 2008, 217. Boatwright 2021, 47–82, traces the evolution of punishments given to imperial women in the first three centuries. There was a marked change in the late fourth and fifth centuries where the general pattern was for (allegedly disgraced) imperial women to remove themselves voluntarily from the emperor's court to their own property. For example, compare Eudocia's residence in the Holy Land where she was involved with building patronage (Lenski 2004, 117–18, Burgess 1993–1994, 50, and Holum 1982, 177) with Julia the Elder and Younger who were placed under armed guard on an island: Tac. *Ann.* 1.53. Galla Placidia and her children left Honorius' court to live in Constantinople after the death of her husband Constantius III: Olymp. *fr.* 38. Hillner 2020 traces the development of punishment of imperial women in the fourth and fifth centuries.

[33] This is an allusion to Arist. [*Mag. Mor.*] 1191a23–36; ἀποτέθνηκε (293) is translated as the perfect tense with present meaning to describe Flaccilla's state, which is worse than those who know that they are going to die. I thank Jennifer Nimmo Smith for their assistance on this point. The passage also echoes Chrysostom's earlier quote of 1 Tim. 5.6 in the *Letter* (2.127–31).

[34] 4.289–300: τῶν δὲ τοῖς νῦν βασιλεύουσι συνοικουσῶν ἡ μὲν ὑπὸ τῶν προτέρων

If my identification is correct, then Constantia's 'earlier misfortunes' include: the death of her father, Constantius II, before she was born; Procopius' use of both Constantia and her mother, Faustina, in Constantinople to promote his own ties with the Constantinian dynasty when he usurped; and her near abduction when en route to marry Gratian.[35] Although Gratian was technically Theodosius I's senior colleague, he was about fifteen years younger and without military experience. The election of Valentinian II, without the authorisation of Gratian, could even have been one of the plots referred to in the passage above (as could the election of Theodosius I).[36]

If Constantia is the first wife, then Aelia Flaccilla is the only option for the second consort, since she outlived her western counterpart (Gratian married a second time to Laeta).[37] Aelia Flaccilla being in a state of 'dead from fear' would reflect the unstable situation following the battle of Adrianople and the continuing Gothic War when a conglomeration of Gothic tribes established themselves as a permanent presence within the empire. Domnica, the widow of Valens, is referred to in the most poignant episode of the imperial exempla, when Chrysostom describes Valens' violent death following Adrianople. Having related how Valens was burnt alive after his retreat from the battle, Chrysostom completes the description with how only the news of his death could be brought back to Domnica, in place of a body.[38]

The impact of Adrianople shaped imperial policy in both East and West in the decades which followed as the emperors and their administrations negotiated how to deal with the permanent presence within the

ἀναπεύσασα συμφορῶν ἀναμεμιγμένην ἔχει πολλὴν τῇ ἡδονῇ τὴν ὀδύνην διὰ τὸ σφόδρα ἔτι νέον εἶναι καὶ ἄπειρον τὸν κρατοῦντα καὶ πολλοὺς πολλαχόθεν ἔχειν τοὺς ἐπιβουλεύοντας. ἡ δὲ ἀποτέθηκε τῷ δέει καὶ τῶν καταδίκων ἀθλιώτερον ζῇ διὰ τὸ τὸν ἄνδρα αὐτῆς, ἐξ οὗ τὸ διάδημα ἀνεδήσατο μέχρι τῆς σήμερον, ἐν πολέμοις διατρίβειν καὶ μάχαις καὶ τῶν συμφορῶν πλέον ὑπὸ τῆς αἰσχύνης ἀναλίσκεσθαι καὶ τοῖς παρὰ πάντων ὀνείδεσιν. Ὁ γὰρ μηδέποτε γέγονε, συνέβη νῦν, καὶ τὴν αὐτῶν ἀφέντες οἱ βάρβαροι χώραν μυρίους σταδίους τῆς ἡμετέρας καὶ πολλάκις τοσούτους ἐπέδραμον.

[35] Amm. Marc. 29.6.7–8 describes the attempted abduction by the Quadi, which is discussed by Vihervalli and Leonard 2023, 211. I look at her appearance in Procopius' usurpation in the next section.

[36] Omissi 2018, 250–90, argues that Valentinian II and Theodosius usurped. See also G. Kelly 2013, who examines the accession of Valentinian II and Gratian's response.

[37] The only surviving mention of Laeta is provided by Zos. 5.39.4, who describes her living in Rome with her mother during the Visigothic sack of the city in 410.

[38] 5.332–340. The specific details about how Valens died at Adrianople differ: Amm. Marc. 31.12.10 and 31.14.1. *Cons. Const.* s.a. 378. Zos. 4.24.2. Socrates, *Hist. eccl.* 4.38.7. Sozom. *Hist. eccl.* 6.40.3–5. Theod. *Hist. eccl.* 4.36.2. Domnica is described in some primary sources as helping to defend Constantinople in the aftermath of Adrianople: Socrates, *Hist. eccl.* 5.1.3. Sozom. *Hist. eccl.* 7.1.2. Theoph. Conf. AM 5870. Woods 1996 and Lenski 2002, 52, discuss her involvement.

empire of the Goths. The same period also saw the development of the emperor and his court from being itinerant to becoming permanently based in a capital and the emperor no longer directly participating in military campaigns. This development, which started with Valentinian II's accession to Augustus, changed how an emperor could promote the stability of their rule, and the way in which imperial women themselves could play a role.[39] I will look at these trends, along with other themes that emerge from the *Letter*, in the next section.

The Broader Historical Context: Women's Reported Involvement with Regime Changes

Within a short passage of a brief letter, Chrysostom presents for dramatic effect extreme examples of imperial women who suffered more distress than the grief felt by Chrysostom's addressee. In doing so, Chrysostom's summary describes uniquely in our extant literature the events at which lesser-known fourth-century imperial women appeared, i.e. points of regime change and usurpation.

Within the period in which Chrysostom sets his references for the *Letter*, imperial women appear frequently in the surviving narrative for usurpations. In this section I will look at a series of fourth-century usurpations which would have been in the living memory of Chrysostom's audience and involved some of the women identified in the previous section. I also consider these appearances within the context of the wider imperial period. The three points of crisis I will look at here are the usurpations of: Magnentius (350–353); Nepotianus (350) and Vetranio (also 350); and Procopius (365–356). Below are a list of the imperial women and the key relationships by which they appear in the narratives for these usurpations:

- Justina (wife of first Magnentius then Valentinian I, and mother of Valentinian II);
- Eutropia (daughter of Constantius I, half-sister of Constantine I, aunt of Constantius II, and mother of Nepotianus);
- Constantina (daughter of Constantine I, sister of Constantius II, wife of Hannibalianus and then Gallus Caesar);
- Constantia (posthumous daughter of Constantius II and first wife of Gratian); and
- Faustina (last wife of Constantius II and mother of Constantia).

---

[39] Lee 2013, 81–82, notes the change of role expected for an emperor following Theodosius I's death and a "shift away from a peripatetic lifestyle". See also Icks 2017 for analysis of the literary reception for this change.

The 350–353 Usurpations

The uprisings in this period took place after the death of the western Augustus, Constans, who was killed by the forces of Magnentius in 350.[40] In quick succession, following Magnentius' acclamation in Gaul, Vetranio was acclaimed Augustus in Illyricum and Nepotianus in Rome. Both Vetranio and Nepotianus' usurpations ended in 350, but Magnentius went on to control most of the western empire until he was finally defeated by Constantius II's forces at Mursa in 353.[41] After Magnentius' death, Constantius became sole Augustus of the empire and restored Constantinian rule in the West.

The usurpations of Vetranio and Nepotianus have been convincingly argued as being directed not against Constantius II in the East, but rather as a response to Magnentius' proclamation in the West.[42] It is not coincidental to this line of argument that imperial women feature in the narrative for both events because their actions served to ensure the survival of the Constantinian dynasty. In the case of Vetranio, his acclamation as Augustus was supported by the physical presence of Constantina (sister of Constantius).[43] Nepotianus' rebellion was ended within a month by Magnentius' forces.[44] Nepotianus died along with his mother, Eutropia, and other Constantinian relatives in Rome. Although Magnentius' usurpation happened first, I will look initially at the two shorter usurpations of Nepotianus and Vetranio.

Nepotianus

Although there is little extant information for Nepotianus' brief uprising, he would likely have drawn support from his Constantinian descent through his mother, Eutropia, who was the daughter of Constantius I from his

---

[40] Omissi 2018, 164–92, provides a summary of this period, although he does not discuss Nepotianus.

[41] Drinkwater 2022, 49–51, offers a recent detailed reconstruction of the battle.

[42] Omissi 2018, 164–65 and 181–92, argues convincingly (based on the evidence from panegyrics) that Vetranio rebelled out of loyalty to Constantius – see also Holm, this volume, 62. Drinkwater 2022, 39–42, offers a different assessment of Vetranio's motivations.

[43] Bleckmann 1994, 42–49, looks at Constantina's role in the most detail. Omissi 2018, 164–65 and 181–92, suggests that Constantina's subsequent marriage to Constantius' Caesar, Gallus, shows her loyalty to the regime. Vetranio was proclaimed by the Illyrian army. Constantina's presence shows that she had left Rome where she had been resident for most of the 340s. See *PLRE* 1 (Vetranio 1), for a list of the primary sources detailing Vetranio's proclamation.

[44] It took place in June – see *PLRE* 1 (Nepotianus 5).

second marriage to Theodora.[45] Eutropia was therefore the half-sister of Constantine I, aunt of Constantius II, and also the granddaughter (on her mother's side) of the Augustus Maximian. One detail from the piecemeal information we have about the usurpation, provided by the contemporary Athanasius of Alexandria in his *Apologia ad Constantium*, is that both Eutropia and Nepotianus were killed in Rome. The death of Nepotianus would be expected, but associated women often survived regime change – as is the case for Justina once Constantius II defeated her husband Magnentius in 353.

It is possible that Eutropia helped to fund her son's rebellion given it was likely, as Hillner has recently set out, that Eutropia, like her Constantinian and Maximian relatives, had property in Rome.[46] Fausta (Eutropia's aunt) had owned at least one house in the city, which had been within the territory of her father, Maximian, then her brother, Maxentius, and eventually her husband Constantine I.[47] As well as Fausta, Constantina (Eutropia's niece), who also lived in Rome in the 340s, dedicated a church which is commemorated with an acrostic poem celebrating her Christian piety.[48] In comparison to fourth-century emperors, imperial women visited Rome regularly and had local prominence thanks to their wealth and imperial connections.[49] As we will see with Eudoxia in the next section, this prominence took on a greater political aspect when the woman was resident at the imperial court.

---

[45] Nepotianus was the son of Flavius Nepotianus and Eutropia (and therefore grandson of Constantius I and Maximian). Burgess 2008, 10 n. 34, makes the interesting point that Nepotianus was not mentioned by any source as having survived the family massacre of the descendants of Constantius I and Theodora in 337 which was orchestrated (as Burgess shows) by Constantius II. Burgess argues that, since Nepotianus is not mentioned by Julian, a fellow survivor, then Eutropia was likely still pregnant with him at the time. This would mean Nepotianus was about 13 when he led the revolt in Rome. Burgess and more recently Omissi 2018, 154–62, offer reconstructions of the events in 337. There is little information about Nepotianus generally: Amm. Marc. 28.1.1. Aur. Vict. *Epit.* 42.3 and *Caes.* 42.6–8. Zos. 2.43.2–4. Eutrop. 10.11. Oros. 7.29.11. Socrates, *Hist. eccl.* 2.25.10. Sozom. *Hist. eccl.* 4.1.2. *Chron. Pasch.* s.a. 349 and Jer. *Chron.* 350.

[46] Hillner 2018 analyses the local importance of the descent from Maximian of the Constantinian women who resided in Rome (via their mother Theodora, wife of Constantius I). See in particular 85–88 for Eutropia's local network and Christian patronage in Rome.

[47] The *Domus Faustae* is mentioned by Optatus 1.23 and discussed by Hillner 2018, 81–83.

[48] The acrostic is CONSTANTINA DEO: *ICUR* 8.20752. *ILCV* 1768. *CLE* 201. A statue was also set up to her in Rome by Flavius Gavianus: *CIL* 6.40790. Hillner 2018, 89, describes Constantina "as the central imperial woman in the city in the 340s".

[49] Drinkwater 2022, 33, argues that the members of the Roman senate who opposed Magnentius may have been influenced by local Constantinian residents.

Eutropia's death is mentioned by Athanasius of Alexandria in his *Apologia ad Constantium* in which he defends himself to Constantius against accusations that he colluded with Magnentius' regime:

> What sort of opening could I affix to my letter if I had written to him [Magnentius]? 'Congratulations on murdering the one [Constans] who honoured me, whose favours I can never forget'? 'I welcome your killing of my friends who were very firm and devoted Christians'? We admire your slaughter of those who received us nobly in Rome, the emperor's aunt of blessed memory, the aptly named Eutropia, Abuerius that noble man, the faithful Sperantius, and many other good men'?[50]

Athanasius' sympathetic description shows that Eutropia, like her relatives in Rome (and later women in Constantinople), was also involved in ecclesiastical patronage.

Eutropia's violent death is unusual for imperial women in the fourth century and suggests she was closely involved in Nepotianus' revolt. The last firmly attested violent deaths of imperial women had been those of Galerius' widow Valeria, her mother Prisca (the widow of Diocletian), and the widow of Maximinus Daza (whose name is unknown). After Galerius' death Valeria and Prisca had fled to the territory of Maximinus Daza, but were killed after he was defeated by Licinius in 313, which established the latter's dyarchy with Constantine I.[51] The elimination of Maximinus and these women removed for the dyarchy of Constantine I and Licinius any focus for residual support for the families of Galerius and Diocletian.

---

[50] Athan. *apol.* 6.5: ποῖον προοίμιον τῆς ἐπιστολῆς ἔτασσον γράφων αὐτῷ; ὅτι ‹τὸν τιμῶντά με, οὗ τῶν εὐεργεσιῶν οὐκ ἄν ποτε ἐπιλαθοίμην, τοῦτον φονεύσας καλῶς ἐποίησας, καὶ ἀποδέχομαί σε τοὺς γνωρίμους ἡμῶν Χριστιανοὺς καὶ πιστοτάτους ἄνδρας ἀνελόντα, καὶ θαυμάζομέν σε σφάξαντα τοὺς ἐν Ῥώμῃ γνησίως ἡμᾶς ὑποδεξαμένους›, τὴν μακαρίαν σου θείαν τὴν ἀληθῶς εὔτροπον καὶ Ἀβουρήιον τὸν γνήσιον ἐκεῖνον καὶ Σπειράντιον τὸν πιστότατον καὶ ἄλλους πολλοὺς καλούς. The translation is from Barnes 1993, 53, who connects Eutropia's death with that of her son based on this passage. This work was written within a decade of the usurpation.

[51] These deaths are attested by a contemporary source, Lactantius (*De mort. pers.* 49.1–7, 50.6–7 and 51.1–2), in an amount of detail unusual for the imperial women of this period. According to Lactanius (39.1–42.3), Valeria and Prisca sought protection from Maximinus after Galerius' death but ended up banished (*relegata*) to a remote desert part of Syria. Maximinus' unnamed widow was killed and her body thrown into the Orontes after his defeat in 313: 50.6. Valeria and her mother were beheaded on the orders of Licinius and their bodies thrown into the sea in 314 (51.1–2). For the dates of their deaths see Creed 1984, xxxiii. For a good overview of Lactantius' account see James 2013, 103–106. Vihervalli and Leonard, 2023, 215–17, look at Valeria's violent treatment after the death of her husband (along with similar later treatments of imperial women) – see also Holm, this volume, 63–64.

Chrysostom's dramatically vague reference to fourth-century imperial widows dying of either despondency or poison in his *Letter* seems to be an exaggeration. However, it is likely that Constantine I's wife, Fausta, suffered a violent death, which many modern scholars suggest was a forced suicide and somehow connected to the execution of Constantine I's eldest son Crispus.[52] Fausta's death is exceptional though as it occurred during Constantine's reign and, it seems, was sanctioned by him.[53]

The usual trend was for imperial women to survive regime change, such as the widows who Chrysostom mentioned were still alive when he wrote his *Letter*, including wives of usurpers. Other examples include Constantina (sister of Constantius) who survived the violent death of her first husband Hannibalianus in 337 and Justina, second wife of Valentinian I, who survived the death Magnentius, her first husband.[54] Both Constantina and Justina are mentioned in the narratives for the usurpations of Magnentius and Vetranio whose usurpations are described below.[55] After the death of Eutropia, the next violent death of an imperial woman at a point of regime change was that of Serena, wife of the western *magister militum* Stilicho, in 408, although this heralded an internal regime change as to who controlled the court of her nephew and son-in-law Honorius.[56]

---

[52] Primary sources for Fausta's death include Julian. *Caes.* 336A–B, *Epit. de Caes.* 41.11–12, and Sid. Apoll. *Epist.* 5.8.2–3. James 2013, 107–12, provides an analysis of the different accounts. There has been a lot of debate in modern scholarship as to whether her death was accidental. Barnes 1982, 219–22, Drijvers 1992b, 500–506, and Pohlsander 1984, 79–106, argue it was as a punishment and connected to the death of Crispus. Woods 1998, 70–86, argues she died from an attempted abortion. Desnier 1987, 297–309, suggests it was accidental and James 2013, 107–12, argues Fausta died a natural death. Potter 2013, 245, has put forward an interesting argument that she died while in a sort of internal exile – discussed further by Hillner 2020, 15–27.

[53] Earlier precedents for Fausta's (possible) violent death were those of Messalina (Tac. *Ann.* 11.29.3–34.3) and Julias Soaemias and Mammaea (Hdn. 5.8.8–10 and 6.9.6–8) who were all killed without the intermediary step of exile.

[54] Amm. Marc. 14.1.2 and Philostorg. *Hist. eccl.* 3.22, refer to Constantina's first marriage. Justina's first marriage is mentioned by Zos. 4.19.1 and 43.1 (for more sources see *PLRE* 1).

[55] Survival after regime change seems to have been the norm for imperial women in the fourth century – see Washington 2016, 209–44. For an alternative assessment see Harries 2014, 200, who compares the deaths during the tetrarchy with the high mortality rate during the Julio-Claudian dynasty. Vihervalli and Leonard 2023, 201–18, examine the violent treatment of imperial women at moments of regime change (not all necessarily resulting in violent deaths).

[56] Serena was killed by the senate in Rome after the death of her husband Stilicho: Olymp. *fr.* 7.3 and Zos. 5.38.1–2. Hillner 2020, 20, examines this particularly demeaning method of execution.

82 *Empresses-in-Waiting*

Eutropia's death suggests she was closely associated with her son's actions. The mother of the emperor was often portrayed as an influential figure throughout the imperial period and is possibly the relationship whereby an imperial woman held most clout at court.[57] Prominent imperial mothers in the Late Antique period (who survived into their sons' reigns) were Helena, Justina, and Galla Placidia (Gratian's mother may also have had influence over her son following her return to court).[58] The best comparisons for Eutropia's death are those of Julia Soaemias and Julia Mamaea at the end of the Severan dynasty in the third century. All three women met violent ends when their sons were overthrown. The deaths of both Julias were especially violent. Julia Soaemias (mother of Elagabalus) was decapitated and her body, along with that of her son, was thrown into the Tiber.[59] Julia Mamaea was reportedly killed while shielding her son from his own troops, while on campaign.[60] The brutality of both deaths shows the negative consequence of the close identification of dowager empresses with (especially) young sons.[61] Such maternal anxiety is sympathetically depicted in Chrysostom's *Letter* when referring to one of the widows whose son is now in power.

---

[57] For the importance of this relationship see Leonard 2019, 343. However, see Roggo this volume, who cautions against ascribing too much influence to such a relationship in the later case of the empress Sophia. An early imperial example is Livia's influence at her son Tiberius' court which was indicated by the decree *Senatus Consultum Pisone Patre*. The decree describes events also referred to in Tac. *Ann.* 3.15.1–17.2. For Julia Domna's prominence as mother of Caracalla see Langford 2013, 21–22. Boatwright 2021, 99–105, argues that the mother of an emperor was the most lauded role a women could hold in the early Principate.

[58] Amm. Marc. 28.1.57 refers to her influence at Gratian's court (after her return) which is discussed by Al. Cameron 2012, 345, and McLynn 1994, 85. Helena, mother of Constantine I, would be the most prominent Late Antique example of lauded imperial mothers. She appeared on coinage struck throughout the empire (alongside her daughter-in-law Fausta): Longo 2009, 97–118, discusses their coin types. Near the end of her life, Helena toured the Holy Land and engaged in building patronage. Lenski 2004, 121–22, and Drijvers 1992a, 55–72, discuss her dedications there. Whiting 2022, 117–18, looks at her journey. Barnes 1982, 221–22, argues Helena carried out dedications to promote Constantine and his court after the scandal surrounding the deaths of Crispus and Fausta. McLynn 1994, 85.

[59] Herodian, 5.8.8–10. Cass. Dio 80[79].20.2. SHA. *Heliogab.* 18.2–3. The degradation of Soaemias' corpse was exceptional for an imperial woman and indicates that she was considered a *hostis* – my thanks to Matilda Brown and Alex Imrie for this observation. There are similarities with the treatment of the bodies of Maximinus Daza's widow, and Valeria and Prisca – see n. 51 above.

[60] Other examples of imperial women on campaign with the emperor are uncommon. One exception is Agrippina the Elder – see Tac. *Ann.* 1.34.1–45.2.

[61] See n. 45 above for Nepotianus' young age when he revolted in Rome (supported by his mother Eutropia).

Vetranio

Vetranio's revolt in Illyricum is better documented than the brief uprising by Nepotianus. However, the narrative is still unclear and the purpose of his usurpation has been disputed in modern scholarship as to whether it was spontaneous or calculated to protect Constantius' regime from Magnentius. Vetranio was an elderly general who allegedly gained legitimacy for his usurpation from the participation of Constantina (the sister of Constantius II) in his election.[62] Unlike other usurpers, Vetranio was allowed to retire by Constantius. Such clemency strongly suggests that Vetranio was a reluctant usurper whose revolt was designed to stall Magnentius and allow Constantius time to secure his position in the East before gathering forces to head West.[63] Constantina's support of Vetranio's election served to protect her brother's regime against the aggression of Magnentius. Just as Vetranio was allowed to retire afterwards, Constantina was soon married to Constantius' Caesar Gallus showing her continued value to Constantius.[64]

Constantina is not an attractive character in Ammianus' history, the main historiographical source for the fourth century.[65] However, her actions in this episode exhibit her familial loyalty to her brother Constantius' regime and the value her physical presence had for Vetranio as a representative of the Constantinian family. Such familial *pietas* can often be inferred as the underlying motive of imperial women's actions when they appear in literary accounts of imperial crises, especially the dowager empresses mentioned in the previous section. That their actions could also be so easily divorced from the wishes of the emperor, as so often conveyed by the literary sources, was part of the benefit of their actions for the emperor as well, serving to protect his own authority should such attempts be unsuccessful.[66] Moving beyond the fourth-century example of Constantina, one might infer such

---

[62] Philostorg. *Hist. eccl.* 2.2.4. Constantina's involvement is discussed by Bleckmann 1994, 42–49, and more recently by Drinkwater 2022, 40–41, who argues that Constantina became involved after Constantius recognized Vetranio as Caesar. Building on Bleckmann's analysis, Hillner 2018, 88, draws attention to Constantina's kinship with the Roman aristocrat Vulcacius Rufinus (the maternal uncle of her future husband Gallus Caesar) who was sent as an envoy by Magnentius to Constantius II.

[63] Omissi 2018, 164–65 and 181–92; however, see Drinkwater 2022, 39–42, for a different assessment.

[64] Drinkwater 2022, 41, makes the point that the chief Constantian negotiator was more likely Vulcacius Rufinus.

[65] Amm. Marc. 14.1.2 describes her as "fury in mortal form" (*Megaera quaedam mortalis*) during her marriage to Gallus.

[66] Eutropia's patronage of Athanasius (see preceding section) indicates that she observed Nicene Christianity, unlike Constantius II. For comparison see Holm's discussion of Eusebia's patronage in this volume.

a motivation in the fifth-century patronages of different Christian sects in Constantinople by Theodosius II's wife, Eudocia, and his sister, Pulcheria, and later with the Christian patronages by Justinian and Theodora. Their support of different causes, and their position of influence, which was reliant on Theodosius' continued reign, allowed him to draw on different avenues of support, but at the same time distance himself (to some extent) from antipathy between the different factions. This was especially important for the emperors who became Augusti at a young age and found themselves permanently based in one city; a phenomenon which was at a nascent stage when Chrysostom wrote his *Letter*.[67] Arcadius was the first emperor in the East not to serve a military role and therefore he and his court sought other ways to establish and secure his position, which included the local prominence of his wife through public displays of Christian piety.[68] When Chrysostom became bishop of Constantinople his freedom of speech and popularity at times challenged this authority, especially when his speeches were interpreted as criticisms of the emperor's wife.[69]

Magnentius

To reinforce his position after the death of Constans, Magnentius married Justina, one of the widows referred to in Chrysostom's *Letter* in relation to her second marriage to Valentinian I. As with many imperial women, the early biographical details for Justina are mostly unreported, but both her marriages suggest that she shared kinship with the Constantinian dynasty, which her two husbands sought to capitalize on.[70]

Constantina also appears in accounts of this usurpation. She was reportedly part of Magnentius' final petition to Constantius to recognize his position as western Augustus. Although Magnentius had already married the young Justina, future wife of Valentinian I, he proposed a reciprocal marriage alliance between himself and Constantius. Constantina's

---

[67] McEvoy 2013, 48–70, examines the precedent set by the appointment as Augustus of Gratian and Valentinian II. Omissi 2018, 289–99, summarizes the change in imperial promotion which this development brought about and the implication this had for the role of women like Eudoxia. Icks 2017 and Maier 2019 look at the change in the emperor's role. G. Kelly 2013 and Meier 2007a discuss the importance of imperial displays of Christian piety.

[68] The coinage struck for Theodosian women celebrated their Christian piety: see Longo 2009, 56–57, for a full list of different coin types.

[69] Holum 1982, 69–78, discusses Eudoxia's *basileia* in direct relation to her altercations with Chrysostom. Liebeschuetz 1990, 198–202, cautions against overstating Eudoxia's active political role.

[70] Chausson 2007, 179–84, argues for Justina's Constantinian descent based on an onomastic study. See also Barnes 1975, 181, and Woods 2004, 326–27.

position as an immediate member of Constantius' family made her a more appealing bride than Justina, while Magnentius proposed in exchange that Constantius marry his daughter.[71] Instead, after the defeat of Magnentius, Constantius married his sister to his new Caesar Gallus. Constantina's marriage to Gallus served as the context for Ammianus' more animated references to her, portraying her in a manner similar to the Julio-Claudian imperial woman Agrippina the Younger, who encroached into imperial administration, overstepping her expected role as dutiful wife.[72]

Justina's survival following Constantius II's eventual defeat of Magnentius touches on another trend, in counterbalance to that described in the previous section, of imperial women's survival after regime change. The underlying reason for this can be examined in relation to the later fourth-century usurpation of Procopius.

Procopius

Procopius claimed power in Constantinople and other eastern territories in 365, soon after Valentinian I had made his brother, Valens, Augustus for the eastern half of the empire.[73] Like the usurpations of 350–3, Procopius also made use of Constantinian kinship via imperial women during his usurpation.[74] Procopius did not pursue marriage to secure his position, but instead used the physical presence in Constantinople of Constantius II's widow, Faustina, and infant daughter, Constantia, to confer legitimacy on his actions, as Vetranio had done with Constantina. Ammianus describes Procopius carrying Constantia before the troops to engender loyalty and Faustina's presence adding legitimacy to his acclamation.[75] Conversely,

---

[71] Petrus Patricius, *fr.* 16, refers to the proposition. Drinkwater 2022, 41, discusses Magnentius' offer. Vihervalli and Leonard 2023, 204–208, discuss Justina's age for her first marriage and compare it to the young age of Maria, Honorius' first wife. The episode has echoes of the description by Lactant. *De mort. pers.* 39.1–5, of Maximinus Daza's marriage proposal to Valeria (Galerius' widow), despite him being already married.

[72] Amm. Marc. 14.1.2–8 describes Constantina acting in concert with Gallus in his administration. Tac. *Ann.* 1.5.3–4 and 12.68.1–69.2 describes Livia and Agrippina's roles in their sons' accessions. Santoro L'Hoir 1994, 5 and 12–13, discusses the *dux femina* archetype for early imperial women. Cass. Dio 78.18.2–3 refers to Julia Domna managing imperial correspondence during the reign of her son Caracalla.

[73] Amm. Marc. 16.7.3–16.10.15 provides a narrative for the usurpation and its aftermath. Omissi 2018, 223–54, offers a recent analysis.

[74] *PLRE* 1 (Procopius 4), suggests he was related to Julian via his maternal line based on Amm. Marc. 23.3.2, 26.6.1, 18.7.10 and 17.5.1.

[75] Amm. Marc. 16.7.10; Amm. Marc. 16.9.3 mentions Procopius then took them with him on campaign.

some emperors married daughters of deceased generals perhaps also to draw on residual loyalty to their family among the military. One such example was Eudoxia who was the daughter of the general Bauto.[76] Although Valens was able to defeat Procopius, the usurper's use of Constantinian women may well have prompted actions later described by Chrysostom in his *Letter*.

As set out in the previous section, Chrysostom likely referred in the *Letter* to the marriages of Valentinian I to Justina and his son Gratian to Constantia. These nuptials seem to have been a calculated response by Valentinian I, in response to Procopius' actions. The two marriages entwined Valentinian's own dynasty with that of Constantine. If this was the motivation for his marriage to Justina (whose Constantinian descent can only be inferred), then it also prompted the exile of his first wife, Marina Severa, both of whom were likely referred to in Chrysostom's *Letter*.[77]

The exile described in Chrysostom's *Letter* was not a common fate for fourth-century imperial women. As mentioned above, Valeria and her mother, Prisca, fled to Maximinus Daza's territory after the death of Galerius, but this may be the only fourth-century example other than the case of Marina Severa.[78] Exiles had been common in the Julio-Claudian dynasty and, as in the case of male relatives, were usually to an island. Augustus exiled his daughter Julia and granddaughter Julia to Pandateria, as did Tiberius for Agrippina the Elder and Nero for Octavia. Agrippina the Younger and Livilla were also island exiles and were banished by both Gaius and Claudius. Later, Commodus sent Lucilla and Crispina to islands, as did Caracalla for his wife Plautilla.[79] In contrast to these examples of

---

[76] Lee 2013, 90, notes the political advantages Arcadius' marriage to Eudoxia presented. Zos. 5.3 mentions that Rufinus had wanted Arcadius to marry one of his daughters. This would have reinforced Rufinus' power at court, as Stilicho managed in the West through the consecutive marriages of his daughters to Honorius. Vihervalli and Leonard 2023, 204–208, look at the marriages of Maria and then Thermantia to Honorius.

[77] Marina's exile is otherwise mentioned by three late sources: Joh. Malal. 13.31–33, *Chron. Pasch.* s.a. 369, and John of Nikiu 82.10–15.

[78] Lactantius describes them being banished by Maximinus after Valeria's rejection of him, but it seems they remained in (a remote part of) his territory: *De mort. pers.* 39.1–41.3. Justina may be a further example when Valentinian II was at Gratian's court. Paulinus *Vit. Ambr.* 11–12 refers to her presence in Sirmium. For the debate as to her location see McLynn 1994, 85, and Errington 1996, 442 n. 24.

[79] An exception was the exile by Alexander Severus of his wife Orbiana who was sent to Africa. Corbier 1995, 186–90, Flower 2006, 160–96, and more recently Boatwright 2021, 47–82, discuss the punishments given to imperial women in the early Principate, which were usually dealt with privately; Hillner 2020, looks at similar Late Antique examples (including Fausta). Suet. *Aug.* 65.4 lists the exiles carried out by Augustus; Suet. *Tib.* 53.2 describes the exile of Agrippina the Elder; Tac. *Ann.* 14.63.1–64.3 relates

women removed to isolated locations, Marina's absence from court seemed less punitive.[80] Marina also did not pose the same threat and had not been removed due to a transgression, but merely to allow her husband to remarry.

Later absences from court followed a similar pattern to that of Marina, rather than the punitive early imperial examples, and similarly are poorly documented. Theodosius I's widow, Galla, and Theodosius II's sister, Pulcheria, both removed themselves from the eastern court, but only so far as their own properties in the suburbs of the capital.[81] The underlying cause of their break in relations is unclear, but was not related to the charge of adultery which was the most common reason given for the early imperial examples.[82] Theodosius II's wife, Eudocia, eventually lived permanently in Jerusalem where she became a prominent local benefactor.[83] Like Marina, Galla Placidia also left the western court (along with her young son Valentinian III) for the eastern empire, following the deterioration of her relationship with her half-brother Honorius after the death of her husband, Constantius III.[84] Such departures seem to have been underplayed at the time with motives only suggested by much later sources.

Marriage to women of a former dynasty was perhaps the most straightforward way to promote one's own legitimacy and, to some extent, this protected imperial women when a relative lost power – although, as we have seen, this was not always assured. Procopius and Vetranio's use of imperial women of a former dynasty, outside of a marriage alliance, to bolster their own claims to legitimacy showed that there were other ways

---

the exiles of Livilla and Agrippina the Younger (and the violent death of Octavia); Cass. Dio 67.14.2 describes the exile of Domitilla and Lucilla. Kienast, Eck, and Heil [6]2017, 173, discuss Orbiana's exile.

[80] The first two exiles of imperial women, Julia the Elder and Younger, were enforced by armed guard: Suet. *Aug.* 150.4; Tac. *Ann.* 1.53.1 and 4.71.4.

[81] *Chron. min.* 390.2 refers to Galla's expulsion. Holum 1982, 191–92, and Burgess 1993–1994, 65, discuss Pulcheria's withdrawal from court. Serena and Galla Placidia were in Rome, rather than the court in Ravenna, when the city was besieged by Alaric's Visigoths in 410: Zos. 5.38.1 and Marc. Comes s.a. 410.

[82] Fagan 2002, 79, discusses the close association between the charge of adultery and *maiestas* in relation to the early imperial period.

[83] Lenski 2004, 117–18, describes Eudocia's tours of Jerusalem (including her final residency in the city). Whiting 2022, 117–18, discusses Eudocia's earlier journey to Jerusalem. Eudocia reportedly removed herself from Constantinople following allegations of an affair; the later source Joh. Malal. 14.8 provides one of the more detailed accounts. Burgess 1993–1994, 50, discusses the different accounts. Av. Cameron 1981, 254–70, argues against an adultery charge being the cause of Eudocia's departure from Constantinople. Scott 2010, 120–21, discusses Eudocia's extensive patronage in Jerusalem.

[84] See Olymp. *fr.* 40 and Philostorg. *Hist. eccl.* 12.13.

to use an imperial woman's connections. Another example of this was Constantine I's brief promotion of his sister Constantia on coinage struck at the Constantinople mint soon after he took control of the East following his defeat of her husband, Licinius.[85] This brief coin series shows how an imperial woman could be used to draw on local popularity of a displaced regime, outside of a marriage pact.[86] It seems that the violent death of Eutropia was an exception to this trend and that even the exiles of imperial women later in the fourth century were less punitive.[87]

John Chrysostom in Constantinople

After Chrysostom wrote his letter to Therasios' widow, he became bishop of Constantinople in 397 when Arcadius was senior Augustus.[88] Unlike his father, Theodosius I, Arcadius never served a military role and his court resided in Constantinople throughout his reign. In the preceding section, we saw a number of Constantinian women who wielded influence outside of the imperial court. Arcadius' reign saw a reappreciation of the role imperial women could have local to the court. This was a development advanced by his wife Eudoxia and taken further during the reign of their son Theodosius II by both their daughter, Pulcheria, and daughter-in-law Eudocia.[89] Eudoxia's local prominence eventually led her into conflict with Chrysostom, but was similar to the roles of Christian patronage carried out by Eutropia and Constantina in Rome (away from the emperor and the court), and Justina in Milan (at the western court of her son Valentinian II) in the preceding generations.[90]

Chrysostom's time as bishop of Constantinople (397–404) was tumultuous, resulting in two exiles, with the second ending at his death.

---

[85] E.g., see *RIC* VII,15. The coinage was only struck at the Constantinople mint.

[86] The emperors Galba, Otho, and Titus featured Augustus' wife Livia on their coinage: *RIC* II, 13 and II, 218.

[87] Boatwright 2021, 47–82, traces the punishments of imperial women in the early Principate. She notes (69–78) the interesting transition from imperial women's transgressions being dealt with initially in court to becoming a private matter.

[88] Barnes and Bevan 2013, xii–xiii, give a chronology of Chrysostom's career.

[89] Holum 1982 and more recently Busch 2015 provide important surveys of the women of the Theodosian dynasty.

[90] Constantina's poetic inscription with the acrostic, CONSTANTINA DEO, for the church she funded for St. Agnes in Rome is a prominent advertisement of her personal Christian piety and patronage (and makes no mention of the rest of her family) – see n. 48 above. Hillner 2018 provides a good overview of the patronage in Rome by women of the Constantinian dynasty. Valentinian II was a non-Nicene Christian like his mother Justina (and unlike his father Valentinian I and brother Gratian). For Justina's religious patronage in Milan see Washington 2016, 173–88.

The later ecclesiastical sources who describe Chrysostom's relationship with the court provide a far less sympathetic literary treatment of Eudoxia than Chrysostom had afforded the imperial exempla in the *Letter*.[91] The (reported) causes of the deterioration of Chrysostom's relationship with the imperial court touch on some of the themes which emerge from the *Letter*. The main themes are the legacy of the Battle of Adrianople for the court and the value of imperial women in promoting the position of emperors whose own role had undergone significant changes since the time the *Letter* had been written. A key change was the transition from military leader to figurehead of a court removed from the frontier and therefore reliant on other means by which to promote the emperor's authority.[92] Such a change had already taken place in the West with the accession of Valentinian II as senior Augustus and which had notably also resulted in criticism of an imperial woman (in Valentinian II's case his mother Justina) 'meddling' in church affairs local to the imperial court (specifically with Ambrose, the bishop of Milan).[93]

Adrianople provides the backdrop of Chrysostom's most detailed account of an imperial death in the *Letter*, that of Valens. The aftermath of Adrianople also informs the description of one of the current consort's anxieties as her husband deals with the barbarian incursions since the battle. The political legacy of Adrianople has been thoroughly examined from many angles in modern scholarship.[94] The Gothic War, of which the Battle of Adrianople forms a part, ended with the Gothic Treaty in 382.[95] One of the conditions of the treaty was further recruitment of Goths into the Roman armies, which were severely depleted following Adrianople. Some

---

[91] Barnes and Bevan 2013, 24–32, provide an overview of Eudoxia's relationship with Chrysostom. The most vicious surviving account of Eudoxia's death, as the result of a stillbirth, is also the one written closest to the events, by Pseudo-Martyrius in his funerary speech for Chrysostom: 121. The passage resonates with the description by Lactantius of the death by cancer of the emperor Galerius, a persecutor of the Church: *De mort. pers.* 33.1–11. Later descriptions of Eudoxia's death by the ecclesiastical historians Socrates (*Hist. eccl.* 6.19) and Sozomen (*Hist. eccl.* 8.27) are less graphic and shorter.

[92] Icks 2017 and Lee 2013, 81–82, describe the change in the role of the eastern emperor.

[93] For further discussion of Justina's opposition to Ambrose see McLynn 1994, 185–86, Humphries 2000, 122, and Liebeschuetz 2005, 126–28. See also n. 28, above.

[94] Kulikowski, 2006, 123–43, provides an overview of the battle. Lenski 1997, 129–168, explores the evolving contemporary literary responses to Adrianople and refers to Chrysostom's mentions of it in the *Letter*.

[95] Kulikowski 2006, 144–53, and Lee 2013, 35–38, discuss Theodosius' actions during this period.

90 *Empresses-in-Waiting*

of these new recruits observed non-Nicene 'Arian' Christianity, and their need for spaces of worship caused divisions among the local population.[96]

Arcadius was the first eastern emperor to be permanently based in Constantinople throughout his reign.[97] The development of young emperors who were never involved in military campaigns meant they had to rely on other displays of imperial authority such as their religious piety, while their young age at the time of accession also made them reliant on, and vulnerable to a number of powerful men.[98] In the West, the power behind the throne was a succession of generals, starting with the relatively stable hegemony established by Stilicho, who confirmed his position by marrying Honorius to his daughters, first Maria and then Thermantia. In the East, however, there were a number of internal regime changes which determined who had control of Arcadius' court, in which Eudoxia was implicated.[99] Unlike the West, the dominant figures at Arcadius' administration tended to hold civilian, rather than military, high office.[100]

Arcadius' administration was first controlled by Rufinus and then by Eutropius, who saw to Chrysostom's election as bishop. During this period there was also a power grab made by the military general (and non-Nicene Goth) Gainas who, it seems, used the billeting of some of his troops in Constantinople to gain office and influence with Arcadius in early 400.[101]

---

[96] Lenski 1997, 133–144, summarizes the treaty. Liebeschuetz 1990, 104–25, cautions against overstating anti-Germanic sentiment at both court and the local population of Constantinople.

[97] Theodosius I had spent an increasing amount of time in Constantinople after the conclusion of the Gothic War, but died in Italy. Heather and Moncur 2001, 199–218, offer a succinct overview of how Theodosius courted the Constantinople senate (via the prism of Themistius's panegyrics). See also Croke 2010.

[98] McEvoy 2013 traces this development in the West – there has not yet been a similar detailed analysis of the change in the East. Icks 2017, 472–82, looks at the literary perceptions of military inactive rulers in both the East and West and the emphasis on their Christian piety to covey authority. Kuefler 2001 provides further discussion of the shifting displays of power, away from military prowess in the Late Antique period.

[99] Lee 2013, 90, discusses Eutropius' involvement in the marriage of Eudoxia to Arcadius which, if true, was to the detriment of Rufinus who hoped to marry his own daughter to the emperor. Cameron, Long, and Sherry 1993, 309, offer an assessment of the political situation in East and West in this period.

[100] Lee 2013, 89–94, notes the resilience of Arcadius' court to the events early in his reign compared to the West. Liebeschuetz 1990, 126–31, demonstrates that the eastern court was less reliant on powerful generals and armies than that of the West. For the dominance of military figures in the West see O'Flynn 1983.

[101] Zos. 5.18.8–9 provides a narrative for Gainas' occupation of Constantinople. Gainas' revolt (399–400) was not a straightforward usurpation, in contrast to those described in the previous section. Cameron, Long, and Sherry 1993, 323–33, provide a good summary of the rebellion based on Synesis' *De regno*; see also Heather 2006,

However, Gainas' ambitions were thwarted on 12 July when some of his troops were killed within Constantinople by the local population. Gainas and the remainder of his forces were pushed beyond the empire's frontier by Arcadius' general Fravitta, and Gainas and his forces were eventually defeated by Uldin, a Hunnic leader.[102]

At the time Gainas sought influence at Constantinople, he tried to obtain a church within Constantinople for the Arian contingent of his forces, which was successfully resisted by Chrysostom with the support of Eudoxia who joined the bishop in night-time processions through Constantinople.[103] This episode shows that the bishop and empress at least at this point in time had good relations and acted in concert with those of the city's Nicene population who had resisted Gainas. The actions of Gainas also resonate with the earlier Basilica Conflict in the West, between the court of Valentinian II and Ambrose (bishop of Milan). A key difference however, was that Valentinian II (influenced by his mother Justina) was a non-Nicene Christian, like the troops for whom he was seeking a space for worship in the city.[104] The need to create spaces of worship for an important component of the imperial army, local antipathy to this contingent, and the need for a court-based emperor to show authority through religious piety, in the absence of military prowess, were factors in both episodes.[105]

A large proportion of Gainas' soldiers were eventually massacred in Constantinople by a proportion of the local population on 12 July 400.[106]

---

215. Holum 1982, 61–69. Kulikowski 2006, 169. Lee 2013, 81–109. Liebeschuetz 1990, 111–31.

[102] This is a very truncated summary of a period for which the surviving evidence is especially difficult to navigate. Liebeschuetz 1990, 111–31, gives a good summary of the sources with a particular focus on Chrysostom's role. See also Lee 2013, 89–93.

[103] Pseudo-Martyrius 49 describes the united front of Chrysostom and Eudoxia in opposition to Gainas' request. Other accounts are provided by Sozom. *Hist. eccl.* 8.4.6–10, Socrates, *Hist. eccl.* 6.5.8, Theod. *Hist. eccl.* 5.32.2–8, and Photius 96. Liebeschuetz 1990, 111–25, provides a reconstruction of events in 400 and describes Eudoxia's early support of Chrysostom (166–68). There were also Nicene Christian Goths in Constantinople and elsewhere, on whose behalf Chrysostom often acted – see Allen and Mayer 1999, 9 and 45. Cameron, Long, and Sherry 1993, 405–408, refer to Chrysostom's important intermediary role in negotiating with Gainas.

[104] *CTh* 16.1.4 was issued by Valentinian to allow freedom of religious assembly. See n. 28 and 29 above for further discussion of the Basilica Conflict.

[105] Parallels can also be drawn with the promotion of the young emperor Elagabalus in the Severan dynasty: see Kemezis 2016, 376.

[106] Zos 5.19.1–5; Sozom. *Hist. eccl.* 8.4.14–17; Marc. Comes s.a. 399. Cameron, Long, and Sherry 1993, 333, make the important point that the massacre in Constantinople was a response to local animosity towards Gainas, rather than the Gothic or the non-Nicene Christian community as a whole, since many were unharmed in the event. See also Liebeschuetz 1990, 111–25.

This event was evocative of the local response following Adrianople when, reportedly facilitated by Valens' widow Domnica, a local militia was recruited to defend the city.[107] In early 400, while Gainas sought to strengthen his position with Arcadius and his court, Eudoxia is surprisingly prominent. She supported Eutropius, who was killed as a result of Gainas' influence, and was involved in the night-time processions which Chrysostom led in Constantinople for his Nicene congregation. As well as this she received the title of Augusta on 9 January 400 from Arcadius.[108] Theodosius I had reintroduced the practice of the emperor giving his wife the title of Augusta in the previous generation, a practice which had stopped after Constantine I's award of the title to his mother Helena and wife Fausta. Theodosius did not have the authority to make Aelia Flaccilla Augusta since he was the junior Augustus to the childless Gratian and Valentinian II, but notably, he did give the title to his first wife, Aelia Flaccilla, although not to his second wife, Galla, even though she was the sister of the by-then senior Augustus, Valentinian II. The use of the title Augusta for Flaccilla served to celebrate the dynastic security she provided with her sons, Arcadius and Honorius, which was the typical motive for the title.[109] Eudoxia, however, received the title before the birth of her son Theodosius II. An alternative motive has to be sought and it seems likely to relate to Gainas who was trying to leverage influence with the court at this time.[110] Such a move by Arcadius suggests that he was using his wife's local popularity in Constantinople, maybe in part due to her coordinated actions with Chrysostom, which in turn supported his own position.

The uprising of Gainas was serious and Arcadius' promotion of his wife Eudoxia to Augusta and her local prominence during the crisis, early in his reign, set a precedent for a more prominent local role for eastern Augustae

---

[107] See Socrates, *Hist. eccl.* 5.1.3 and Sozom. *Hist. eccl.* 7.1.2. Woods 1996 discusses the episode further. Lee 2013, 36, suggests this hints at the local influence of Domnica, for whom general information is lacking. Lenski 1997, 132, describes eastern cities' makeshift defences in the immediate aftermath of Adrianople.

[108] Eudoxia's receipt of the title Augusta is attested by the *Chron. Pasch.* s.a. 400. See also Holum 1982, 64–65 and 69. The coin types produced for Eudoxia around this time have a military tone with the legends VIRTUS EXERCITI (e.g., *RIC* X, 74) and GLORIA ROMANORUM (*RIC* X, 77). For further discussion see Longo 2009, 179–80.

[109] Theodosius I's second wife, Galla, was the mother of Galla Placidia, who was made Augusta once her son, Valentinian III, became western Augustus.

[110] *Chron. Pasch.* s.a. 400 (4 January 400). Holum 1982, 64–69, and Cameron, Long, and Sherry 1993, 170–73, also connect Eudoxia's receipt of the title and Gainas' revolt. Liebeschuetz 1990, 199, suggests conversely that Eudoxia received the title because of Gainas' influence.

in the promotion of the emperor's rule.[111] In a letter Chrysostom wrote while in his second exile, he noted that a woman could have equality with men in ecclesiastical affairs: "In contests on God's behalf and in labours for the Church… it is quite possible for a woman to join in these fine contests and labours with greater strength than a man."[112] Eudoxia's actions in opposition to Gainas would have been a positive example of this for the bishop. In his earlier *Letter*, Chrysostom concluded with a petition to Therasios' widow not to remarry and instead to devote her time (and probably wealth) to the Church. For each, Chrysostom implies the deference of Christian devotion by women to the authority of the Church, which was represented, in both cases, by Chrysostom. Later events showed Eudoxia, from the perspective of the bishop's supporters, subverting this important hierarchy. Eudoxia's receipt of the title Augusta and the local prominence this gave her was criticized by John Chrysostom.[113] Although such criticism was not one of the charges listed against Chrysostom at the Synod of the Oak (which precipitated his first exile), Chrysostom's disapproval of the empress tarnished imperial authority, by association.[114]

The bishop's exile and Eudoxia's title of Augusta were even objected to by the western Augustus Honorius in a letter written to his older brother Arcadius. Honorius opens his letter with a passage describing the promotion of Eudoxia's image throughout the eastern provinces, presumably as part of the pageantry associated with her receipt of the title Augusta (as was the erection of the statue in Constantinople).

> Although, I reproached you in an earlier letter about the image of a woman being unprecedentedly [*nouo exemplo*] carried about throughout the provinces and the whispers of critics being spread abroad through the whole world, so that by repentance from such a deed and by cessation from this scheme envious rumour may grow stale and the public discourse may have nothing to complain about in the character of the times.[115]

---

[111] Holum 1982, 48–78, describes Eudoxia's influence at court. Holm, in this volume, considers the power networks empresses could build via their relationship with the emperor.

[112] *Ep.* 29 'To Italica' (170M) Spring 406: *At in divinis certaminibus, iisque laboribus, qui Ecclesiae causa subeuntur, hoc locum non habet: verum fieri potest ut femina in praeclaris his certaminibus laboribusque capessendis virum quoque fortitudine superet.* The translation is by Barnes and Bevan, 2013.

[113] The base of a statue erected for Eudoxia in Constantinople still survives: *CIL* 8614=*ILS* 822=*LSA* 27. The later accounts by Socrates and Sozomen interpret a derogatory speech by Chrysostom as a reaction to such a statue near his church: Socrates, *Hist. eccl.* 6.18 and Sozom. *Hist. eccl.* 8.20.

[114] Barnes and Bevan 2013, 153–59, provide a translation and analysis of the charges.

[115] *Coll. Avell.* 38: '*De persona sancti Iohannis*': *Quamuis super imagine muliebri nouo exemplo*

94 *Empresses-in-Waiting*

The letter then goes on to refer to the bloody riots which followed Chrysostom's second exile.[116] While Chrysostom's objection may not have been intended as political, Honorius' objection was and he did not give either of his wives, or his cousin (and mother-in-law) Serena, a title.

Arcadius was not subverting the imperial hierarchy by making his wife Augusta, since he was the senior Augustus (unlike Theodosius I), but the practice had not been standard in recent memory.[117] Eudoxia predeceased Arcadius, while Chrysostom's memory was later rehabilitated under her son's rule.[118] Honorius, who had given neither of his wives a title, eventually died a widower isolated at court. The installation of Valentinian III in the West, by eastern forces, saw the reintroduction of the title of Augusta in the West for Valentinian's mother, Galla Placidia, who had not been made Augusta while her husband (Constantius III) had reigned with Honorius.[119]

Conclusion

The imperial exempla Chrysostom presents in his letter provide a means by which he could console his subject by referring her to the greater troubles that concerned women of higher status. In doing so, Chrysostom incidentally offers a rare collective analysis of a group of fourth-century women who are otherwise poorly documented in extant sources. Chrysostom may well have employed artistic licence in his portrayals to maximize the effect on his addressee. Nevertheless, the biographical information, which often relates contemporary rumours about both the women and their husbands, offers a sympathetic viewpoint of imperial women's position in the late fourth century at moments of regime change.

There was no universal pattern in the fourth century when imperial women found themselves involved in usurpations, although fewer suffered violent deaths than in the earlier imperial period. After the revolt of

---

per prouincias circumlata et diffusa per uniuersum orbem obtrectantium fama litteris aliis commonuerim, ut talis facti paenitenia et intermission propositi rumor aemulus consenescat et, quod in moribus temporum carpat, publica lingua non habeat. The translation is my own, with the assistance of Matt Hoskin and Gavin Kelly.

[116] The two events are not connected in the letter. The riots took place four years after Eudoxia was made Augusta.

[117] See Washington 2016, 87–90, for further discussion.

[118] Theod. *Hist. eccl.* 5.36, describes the internment of Chrysostom's remains in Constantinople during Theodosius II's reign. Holum and Vikan 1979, 123, discuss this later event.

[119] Galla Placidia first appeared on coinage in the East with the title Aelia Placidia (e.g., *RIC* X, 231). Her western coinage was produced after she returned to the western empire with her son Valentinian III: Longo 2009, 183. Aelia Flaccilla's cognomen was adopted by her successors as part of their nomenclature on eastern coinage.

Gainas, Arcadius and his court enjoyed a relatively stable regime, in which Eudoxia was publicly honoured, probably in acknowledgement by the court of her local popularity. The disapproval of her public presentation by Chrysostom (and his many local supporters) in Constantinople and the objection from Honorius in the West showed that such a role for an imperial woman was still at an early stage of development and not accepted by everyone. Eudoxia's death in childbirth was described in graphic detail by later hostile ecclesiastical sources as a form of retribution for her actions against Chrysostom. Such depictions present the negative inverse of the representations of her predecessors in Chrysostom's *Letter* where they also served a literary purpose. Even when such literary descriptions served a clear agenda, the information which Chrysostom provides in the *Letter*, especially for the Valentinianic women, is illuminating. The *Letter* offers a snapshot of imperial women's position at a time when the role of emperor was beginning to change and both parts of the empire were adapting to the political and military situation created by Adrianople. The later promotion of Eudoxia as part of imperial presentation led to even more prominent, and possibly influential, women such as Galla Placidia in the West and Eudoxia's daughter, Pulcheria, in the East.

4

The Empress Sophia Reconsidered

Silvio Roggo

On 4 October 578, Emperor Justin II (565–578) died after a protracted illness, which had severely impaired his ability to rule and necessitated the installation of Tiberios as Caesar in late 574.[1] On Justin's death, his widow, the Augusta Sophia, soon turned her thoughts towards remarriage. This is at least what John of Ephesos wanted us to believe. John, a contemporary of Justin and Sophia and author of an *Ecclesiastical History* covering parts of the reigns of Justin II and his successors Tiberios (578–582) and Maurice (582–602),[2] reported that there were rumours in Constantinople that Sophia hoped to keep her exalted position at court by either marrying the new emperor Tiberios herself or by arranging a marriage between him and her own daughter, the princess Arabia, who was also a widow.[3] John records that Sophia proposed her plan to Tiberios through intermediaries, among them the patriarch, the head of the Church of Constantinople. However, there was a significant obstacle to this plan: Tiberios was already married to Ino, a woman of humble origin, and had children with her.[4] It is therefore hardly astonishing that Tiberios was enraged by the patriarch's suggestion that he divorce Ino. John has Tiberios exclaim: "Will it please God, as well as you, for me to leave my wife, by whom I have had three children, and who took me to share all she had when I had nothing? And now that God has raised me to power, am I to leave her and take another?"[5]

---

[1] Pfeilschifter 2013, 142–47. Mi. Whitby 2001, 94–95. Av. Cameron 1976a. I am very grateful to the Hardt Foundation in Geneva, Switzerland, for their generous support and for providing a quiet research environment that enabled me to work on this chapter in March 2022.
[2] The best available discussion of John of Ephesos and his oeuvre is van Ginkel 1995.
[3] Joh. Eph. *Hist. eccl.* 3.7; cf. *PLRE* 3a (Arabia), 102.
[4] See Joh. Eph. *Hist. eccl.* 3.8 for how Tiberios, originally engaged to Ino's daughter, ended up marrying Ino after both her daughter and her husband had died.
[5] Joh. Eph. *Hist. eccl.* 3.7: ܪܒܐ ܐܠܗܐ ܡܢ ܠܝ ܐܝܬ ܐܢܬܬܐ ܕܐܫܒܘܩ ܐܢܐ ܠܟܘܢ ܕܐܝܟ (trans. Payne Smith 1860, 179).

Is this story anything more than malevolent gossip? Could there actually be a kernel of truth in it? In her seminal article, 'The Empress Sophia', published in 1975, Averil Cameron argued that the portrayal of Sophia in the sources available to us is highly credible.[6] Cameron concluded that Sophia frequently managed to impose her will in an empire dominated by powerful men. She showed that Sophia's influence during the reign of her husband Justin in the 560s and 570s was exceptional and surpassed that of other late Roman empresses.[7] Consequently, she was inclined to believe John of Ephesos' account of Sophia's marriage scheme.[8] Endorsing Cameron's arguments, most modern scholarship on Late Antique empresses has tended to accept John's testimony at face value,[9] while only a few scholars have been more cautious.[10] However, no one has subjected his bold claims, which are not attested in any other source, to a more thorough examination. Yet such an analysis is much needed: this is one of very few episodes in which an empress is depicted acting independently in order to preserve her political influence in the male-centred world of Late Antiquity. Moreover, it would be nothing short of sensational if the patriarch, arguably the empire's most important bishop, had actively promoted a divorce for the emperor at a time when imperial legislation increasingly enshrined the indissolubility of marriage.[11] In what follows, I do not seek to dispute the notion that Sophia was a central figure at court, but I aim to demonstrate that we should be wary of uncritically accepting accounts that credit her with considerable independent agency.

Sophia as Co-Ruler of the Empire

Sophia was the niece of a previous empress: Justinian's wife Theodora (d. 548). This connection may have provided her husband Justin, himself a nephew of Justinian (527–565), with additional legitimacy and thus helped to secure his accession to the throne in 565.[12] John of Ephesos records that Sophia actively supported the imperial ambitions of her husband

---

[6] Av. Cameron 1975c.
[7] Already Stein 1919, 47 and 56–57, had described Sophia's unique position. See also Dagnall, this volume.
[8] Av. Cameron 1975b. 1975c.
[9] See, e.g., McClanan 2002, 150–58. Evans 2002, 117. Garland 1999, 40–57. Van Ginkel 1995, 153.
[10] Notably James 2001b, 64 and 68.
[11] For the development of divorce legislation in Late Antiquity, see the overview in Hillner 2015, 323–26. Stolte 1999, 77–86. Arjava 1996, 177–92. Clark 1993, 17–27. Puliatti 1991, 53–87. Beaucamp 1990, 174–77 and 223–29.
[12] McClanan 2002, 150. James 2001b, 64 and 109–10. Garland 1999, 40. Av. Cameron 1975c, 6f.

and attempted to convince the ageing Justinian to nominate Justin as his successor.[13] Despite her efforts, Justinian never officially designated the next emperor, and Justin relied on the help of his own network at court when securing his succession.[14] After Justin had acceded to the throne, Sophia was portrayed on the same level as her husband in the contemporary panegyrical poems by Corippus and Venantius Fortunatus, who both celebrated the new imperial couple.[15] Moreover, according to the ninth-century chronicler Theophanes, Sophia helped her husband to avert a looming conflict with the Constantinopolitan moneylenders by repaying the debts the empire had incurred under Justinian.[16] Finally, she is also found in the numismatic record: bronze *folles* depicted her together with her husband – the first appearance of an empress on coinage since the issue of the *solidi* commemorating the marriage of Anastasios (491–518) and Ariadne.[17]

Given these testimonies to Sophia's importance in the 560s, it comes as no surprise that Cameron identified her as the real ruler of the empire after the onset of Justin's illness.[18] The emperor famously reacted badly to the news of the loss of the stronghold of Dara on the eastern frontier to the Persians in November 573. There is evidence that bouts of illness had already affected his ability to govern prior to this, but his condition deteriorated decisively after the devastating defeat of the Roman army.[19] The *communis opinio* holds that Sophia assumed the regency of the empire and, together with Tiberios, negotiated a ceasefire with the Persians.[20] When Justin's health improved temporarily, he was able, on Sophia's instigation,

[13] Joh. Eph. *Hist. eccl.* 2.10.
[14] The most recent treatments of Justin's succession are Lin 2021, 136–41. Roggo 2019, 442–45.
[15] Corippus, *Iust.* 2.169–73. 3.71–84. 4.272–80. Venantius Fortunatus, *Ad Iustinum et Sophiam Augustos.*
[16] Theoph. Conf. AM 6060. See Corippus, *Iust.* 2.399–406 and *Nov.* 148 for Justin's repayment of debts. For all these sources on Sophia, see also James 2001b, 12. Garland 1999, 41–46. Av. Cameron 1975c, 9–14.
[17] McClanan 2002, 158–63. James 2001b, 102 and 109–10. Av. Cameron 1975c, 10–11. However, Brubaker and Tobler 2000, 583–85, argue against a particular importance for Sophia since she is never depicted alone, and only on low-value bronze coins. For Sophia's numismatic record, see Gkantzios Drápelová, this volume.
[18] Av. Cameron 1975c, 15.
[19] Evagr. *Hist. eccl.* 5.11. Joh. Eph. *Hist. eccl.* 3.1–4. Theophylact, *Hist.* 3.11.2–3. Theoph. Conf. AM 6066. Cf. Bleckmann 2021, 52–53. Greatrex and Lieu 2002, 147–49. Mi. Whitby 2001, 92–94.
[20] Schreiner 2010, 405–406. McClanan 2002, 154–55. James 2001b, 97. Mi. Whitby 2001, 94. Garland 1999, 50–52. Av. Cameron 1975c, 15–16. For the ceasefire, see Evagr. *Hist. eccl.* 5.12. Theophylact, *Hist.* 3.11.3 and 12.2–3. Men. Prot. *fr.* 18.1–2. Sophia's role in foreign policy is covered by Dagnall, this volume.

to designate Tiberios as his successor. On 7 December 574, Justin elevated Tiberios to the rank of Caesar and made him the effective ruler of the empire.[21]

Despite this shift in power, Sophia preserved her exalted status as Augusta. Before his accession as Caesar, Tiberios had sworn an oath that he would always honour Sophia.[22] She is thought to have issued orders to the new Caesar: according to John of Ephesos, she forbade him to bring his wife Ino to the imperial palace, declaring that she would never accept the presence of another empress. For this reason, Ino was forced to live in another palace in Constantinople, and Tiberios commuted daily from there to the imperial palace. John informs us that Sophia prohibited the women of the court from visiting Ino. In the end, Ino was allegedly so lonely that she moved back to the place where she had grown up, located on the coast outside of Constantinople, thereby forcing Tiberios to travel even further if he wanted to see his wife.[23] Furthermore, John of Ephesos asserts that Sophia remained in control of the imperial finances, criticizing Tiberios for his expenditure and financial liberality and therefore restricting his access to the imperial treasury.[24]

Sophia's Influence Re-Examined

If Sophia had indeed been able to dominate the imperial court to such an extent even after Tiberios was made Caesar, John's account of her marriage plan in 578 would seem quite credible. However, a comparative reading of other sources with attention to the historical background casts doubt on Sophia's agency in the period of Justin's illness. In fact, only Gregory of Tours, writing at the end of the sixth century far away from Constantinople in Gaul, explicitly states that Sophia ruled the empire between Justin's lapse into insanity in 573 and Tiberios' accession as Caesar in late 574.[25] In his *Historiae*, Gregory provides some unique information on Constantinopolitan affairs and in particular on the influential position of Sophia.[26] For instance, Gregory is the sole source for a plot that was supposedly orchestrated by Sophia soon after Justin's death in 578 with the aim of removing Tiberios from the throne. While Averil Cameron has argued that

---

[21] Joh. Eph. *Hist. eccl.* 3.5. Evagr. *Hist. eccl.* 5.13. Theophylact, *Hist.* 3.11.4–13. Theoph. Conf. AM 6070. See the discussion in Bleckmann 2021, 47–63, and Av. Cameron 1976a.
[22] Joh. Eph. *Hist. eccl.* 3.7; cf. Theophylact, *Hist.* 3.11.8.
[23] Joh. Eph. *Hist. eccl.* 3.7f.
[24] Joh. Eph. *Hist. eccl.* 3.11 and 14; cf. Av. Cameron 1977, 12–13. For Tiberios' financial liberality, see also Evagr. *Hist. eccl.* 5.13 and *Nov.* 163.
[25] Gregory of Tours, *Hist.* 5.19.
[26] Gregory of Tours, *Hist.* 4.40. 5.19. 5.30. 6.30.

these elements are generally trustworthy, her view has been increasingly challenged in recent years, as scholars have highlighted Gregory's inaccuracies and mistakes.[27] It is indeed conspicuous that the eastern sources are far less clear on the question of Sophia's regency. Neither John of Ephesos nor the historian Menander, writing in the 580s, state that Sophia had actually taken over the government in 573.[28] The latter author highlights that Tiberios was powerful already prior to his official designation as Caesar, and Sophia does not appear in any decisive role in the writings of the historians Evagrios and Theophylact, who both recorded these events a few decades later. They attribute all agency to Justin and Tiberios and imply that Sophia performed only a subordinate function.[29] Evidently, we cannot exclude the possibility that these authors intentionally minimized the role of Sophia, but the dubious testimony of Gregory alone should not lead us to assume that Sophia occupied the role of regent.

Nor is it clear that she really had much say in the selection of Tiberios. Certainly, we have no reason to doubt that Sophia encouraged the ailing Justin to proclaim Tiberios Caesar. John of Ephesos and Evagrios agree in this regard.[30] Yet to assume that she wielded enough authority to freely choose her husband's successor is likely a step too far. As *comes excubitorum*, the commander of the imperial bodyguard, Tiberios held a uniquely powerful office at court. This was a key position whenever there was a disputed imperial succession in the sixth century. Previously, Justin I (518–527) had come to the throne in 518 as commander of the bodyguard, and Tiberios had already been *comes excubitorum* in 565, when his support was a decisive factor in the accession of Justin II.[31] Tiberios' prestige may have further grown in the wake of his triumph over the Avars around 570 and he was no doubt ideally placed to exert pressure on the imperial couple in 574.[32] Crucially, as Rene Pfeilschifter has shown, the status of the late Roman emperor was never fully institutionalized, and the authority of any emperor depended upon his personal ability to find continuous acceptance

---

[27] The view of Av. Cameron 1975b was shared by Schreiner 2010, 405–13; McClanan 2002, 157–58; Evans 2002, 117; Garland 1999, 54–57. But see the counterarguments of Loseby 2015, 482–84; Pfeilschifter 2013, 174 n. 96 and 278 n. 48; Mi. Whitby 2001, 94f; Heinzelmann 1994, 126–27 and 157.
[28] Joh. Eph. *Hist. eccl.* 3.4. Men. Prot. *fr.* 18,1f.
[29] Evagr. *Hist. eccl.* 5.12; Theophylact, *Hist.* 3.11.3 and 12.2–3; cf. Pfeilschifter 2013, 143–45.
[30] Joh. Eph. *Hist. eccl.* 3.5. Evagr. *Hist. eccl.* 5.13.
[31] See Pfeilschifter 2013, 165–172, for the accession of Justin I. For Tiberios' role in 565, see Corippus, *Iust.* 1.202–25; Av. Cameron 1976b, 138.
[32] John of Biclar, *Chron.* 13. However, Tiberios also suffered a defeat when campaigning against the Avars in the early 570s; cf. Men. Prot. *fr.* 15.3–5; Evagr. *Hist. eccl.* 5.11; Theoph. Conf. AM 6066.

among important powerbrokers such as the senate, the people of Constantinople, and the leadership of the Church.[33] The sources, first and foremost John of Ephesos, leave no doubt that Justin, due to his mental illness, was no longer able to meaningfully interact with the dignitaries whose cooperation was necessary for the stability of his rule.[34] Pfeilschifter has argued convincingly that in such circumstances, Justin's imperial authority had all but disappeared and could be seized by anyone who gained the backing of the decisive groups.[35] In his interpretation of the events, Sophia was thus far more vulnerable than has hitherto been thought.

It is indeed likely that Tiberios used his influential position at court to secure power before anyone else could do so. After all, Justin had a son-in-law (Baduarios), a brother (Markellos), and two cousins (Markianos and Justinian) who all held important offices and were valid candidates for the throne.[36] The repeated tensions between Tiberios and Sophia, as recorded by John of Ephesos, strongly hint at the possibility that the transition of power was not entirely amicable.[37] Despite this, the safest option for Sophia was probably to support the ambitions of Tiberios, as he had been one of Justin's allies already in 565. By making Tiberios Caesar, the imperial couple were able to prevent the loss of their status as soon as it had become clear that a complete recovery of Justin was very unlikely. Tiberios offered security to the Augusta.[38] With an incapacitated husband who was in constant danger of being overthrown, this was probably the best she could hope for, but it may well have left her embittered.

Tiberios was made Augustus on 26 September 578 – only a few days before Justin's death on 4 October – but, as has been argued, he alone had ultimately been responsible for all decisions following his proclamation as Caesar by Justin four years earlier. Theophylact and Theophanes state that Justin had adopted Tiberios on that occasion in December 574, which may suggest that the strategy had been to legitimize the new emperor with no need for Sophia's involvement.[39] In all likelihood, it was even beneficial

---

[33] Pfeilschifter 2013. His understanding of the Late Antique Empire as a 'Akzeptanzsystem' has been influenced by Flaig 1992 and Diefenbach 1996; see also Greatrex 2020 for the most recent treatment of Pfeilschifter's approach in Anglophone scholarship.

[34] Joh. Eph. *Hist. eccl.* 3.2–5. Evagr. *Hist. eccl.* 5.11. Theophylact, *Hist.* 3.11.3–4. Theoph. Conf. AM 6066.

[35] Pfeilschifter 2013, 142–47.

[36] Cf. *PLRE* 3a (Baduarius 2), 164–65; (Iustinianus 3), 744–47; (Marcellus 5), 816–17; (Marcianus 7), 821–23. However, there were tensions between Justin and Baduarios in the early 570s (Theoph. Conf. AM 6065), and at the same time, Markianos had lost Justin's favour as commander against the Persians (Joh. Eph. *Hist. eccl.* 6.2).

[37] Joh. Eph. *Hist. eccl.*3.7–11; 3.14–15; 3.23–24.

[38] Joh. Eph. *Hist. eccl.* 3.7 and 3.10; cf. Theophylact, *Hist.* 3.11.8.

[39] Theophylact, *Hist.* 3.11.4. Theoph. Conf. AM 6067.

for Tiberios to appear only as the junior emperor alongside Justin, who was still the nominal sovereign. As Caesar, Tiberios could present himself as Justin's son and underline his filial piety by respecting the prerogatives of his adoptive father. Similarly, John of Ephesos, Theophylact, and Theophanes agree with each other that the Caesar Tiberios regarded Sophia as his mother – undoubtedly to her frustration, if she indeed intended to eventually marry him.[40] The respect Tiberios paid to her in this role may explain why he did not insist on Ino's moving into the imperial palace before he had become sole Augustus in 578. It is, however, telling that Sophia was unable to prevent Ino's arrival after Justin's death when Tiberios asked for her permission to live together with his wife.[41] This again indicates that we should not overestimate Sophia's power at court. In Pfeilschifter's view, John also exaggerated Sophia's influence when he asserted that she restricted Tiberios' liberal spending behaviour and even denied him access to the treasury.[42]

John also claims that Tiberios had to extend the imperial palace after Justin's death in order to create sufficient space for his own family and Sophia. He suggests that Sophia refused to leave her apartments – where she had lived ever since 565 – thereby creating a major difficulty for Tiberios who was too mild to have her forcibly removed.[43] Yet this story appears quite distorted and we should not attribute much importance to it. First, Sophia's continued presence at the imperial court might not (solely) have been based on her own preference: we can safely assume that it was also in Tiberios' interest that Sophia remained somewhere in the palace and did not leave it altogether, since this would have allowed him to control her actions more easily. Indeed, in another passage by John, Tiberios insists that Sophia should be content with staying in the palace, and, according to the heading of a now-lost chapter of John's *Ecclesiastical History*, Sophia still lived in a part of the palace complex at the start of the reign of Maurice in 582.[44] However, it is possible that Sophia's quarters were moved within the palace: Theophanes records that Tiberios had Sophia relocated to the so-called Sophiae, a south-western part of the imperial palace on the seashore.[45] Finally, John's assertion that Sophia forced Tiberios to build new imperial quarters for himself and his family may refer to the ample

---

[40] Joh. Eph. *Hist. eccl.* 3.10. Theophylact, *Hist.* 3.11.8. Theoph. Conf. AM 6072.
[41] Joh. Eph. *Hist. eccl.* 3.9; cf. Pfeilschifter 2013, 495.
[42] Pfeilschifter 2013, 146 n. 52; cf. Joh. Eph. *Hist. eccl.* 3.11 and 14.
[43] Joh. Eph. *Hist. eccl.* 3.23; see van Ginkel 1995, 153.
[44] Joh. Eph. *Hist. eccl.* 3.10; the heading of the lost chapter 3.50 (see Brooks' 1923 edition, 119) is "about the three queens who lived together in the palace after the death of Tiberios" (ܥܠ ܬܠܬ ܡܠܟܬܐ ܕܥܡܚܕܐ ܗܘܝ ܒܒܝܬ ܡܠܟܐ ܡܢ ܒܬܪ ܡܘܬܗ ܕܛܒܪܝܘܣ; my own translation).
[45] Theoph. Conf. AM 6072. For the Sophiae, see Av. Cameron 1967.

building activity that was ongoing in the palace complex under both Justin II and Tiberios.[46] John might have presented the temporal coincidence of these construction works and Sophia's continued stay in the palace as causally related in order to highlight the power she allegedly exercised over Tiberios, as this would have suited his own narrative.

The Image of Sophia in John of Ephesos' *Ecclesiastical History*

The arguments above suggest that the sources, and especially John's *Ecclesiastical History*, attribute to Sophia more influence over Tiberios than she, in fact, had. John's portrayal of Sophia as a scheming and power-hungry empress was probably influenced by religious issues: he introduced Justin and Sophia as the instigators of the persecution of the Miaphysites which started in 571.[47] John himself was a Miaphysite bishop, one of the leaders of a significant Christian group that did not accept the doctrinal decisions of the Council of Chalcedon (451) which were embraced as orthodox by the imperial Church.[48] For his rejection of Chalcedon, he was repeatedly imprisoned in the first half of the 570s when the imperial couple, together with the patriarch of Constantinople, John Scholastikos (565–577), attempted to force the Miaphysite bishops to enter into a union with the imperial Church.[49]

Given the hardship John had to endure, it is not surprising that he viewed the imperial couple very negatively in his *Ecclesiastical History*. In particular, John did not connect Justin's illness to the Roman defeat at Dara, but instead presented this as divine punishment for his merciless persecution of the Miaphysites.[50] For the same reason, John creates the impression that Sophia responded without compassion when her husband had become severely ill. Apparently, "the empress Sophia was not only not chastened or alarmed by his affliction and calamity and punishment, but rather elated".[51] But John is eager to show that such unchristian behaviour did not go unpunished: Sophia eventually lost all her influence, her schemes failed, and the empire was given to the truly Christian and

---

[46] For the building activity in the imperial palace under Tiberios, see Westbrook 2020, 95 n. 212; 106; 131; 169; 207; 222–23; see also Av. Cameron 1980b.

[47] Joh. Eph. *Hist. eccl.* 1.5 and 11.

[48] For Miaphysitism and the dispute over Chalcedon, see Price 2009, 1–23. Menze 2008. Gray 2005.

[49] Joh. Eph. *Hist. eccl.* 1.5–30 and 2.4–7.

[50] Joh. Eph. *Hist. eccl.* 3.2–4.

[51] Joh. Eph. *Hist. eccl.* 3.4: ܣܘܦܝܐ ܡܠܟܬܐ ܕܠܘ ܒܠܚܘܕ ܠܐ ܪܓܫܬ ܒܗ ܕܚܠܬܐ ܘܙܘܥܐ ܕܟܘܪܗܢܗ ܐܠܐ ܐܦ ܡܬܚܕܝܐ (trans. Payne Smith 1860, 171).

merciful Tiberios, who also put a stop to the persecution.[52] In the end, John of Ephesos was able to report that the imperial couple had received a just punishment for their deeds, for Sophia lived "bitter, and vexed, and out of temper, and full of grief and lamentation at her present state, to think that she was humiliated, and reduced in rank, and deserted by all people, and in her lifetime had become like one dead".[53]

These observations indicate that John had personal reasons and a clear motive for introducing Sophia as a scheming empress who tried to preserve her power at all costs. John cast her as the very opposite of her imperial predecessor Theodora, whom he frequently praised as a supporter of the Miaphysite cause.[54] Importantly, the contrast with Sophia also allowed him to construct Tiberios as the perfect example of a good and righteous emperor who was full of reverence even for those who attempted to harm him. John's description of the interactions between Sophia and Tiberios is thus ultimately governed by his desire to prove that God is on the side of the Miaphysites and brings the plans of their enemies to naught. Moreover, John expressed his enmity towards Sophia by depicting her in a particularly 'unfeminine' way: when claiming that she did not grant Tiberios unlimited access to the treasury, that she contrived plots, and that she behaved as if she were the sole ruler, John portrayed her as a woman who had forgotten her place in society. His *Ecclesiastical History* almost exclusively focusses on men, and it is very probably no coincidence that no other woman features as prominently in it as Sophia.[55] She is presented as subverting the traditional gender roles of Late Antiquity because of the considerable agency that John attributed to her. By highlighting her independence and her attempts to dominate Tiberios, John was once again able to show his male readership how depraved the persecuting empress Sophia was.

Having recognized John's main motivations in his chapters dealing with Sophia, we should be wary of taking his information at face value and, evidently, we need to be even more wary of the mere rumours he reported about Sophia's supposed marriage plan. This story fits excellently into his carefully constructed narrative of an empress who was deeply unwilling to share her power with another imperial wife and desperately wanted to prevent the loss of her former importance. Averil Cameron and

---

[52] For the positive depiction of Tiberios, see Joh. Eph. *Hist. eccl.* 3.11–14. Cf. Pfeilschifter 2013, 495 n. 101. Mi. Whitby 1998, 327–29. Van Ginkel 1995, 108. Av. Cameron 1977, 9–13.
[53] Joh. Eph. *Hist. eccl.* 3.10: ܒܠܚܕܪܗ̇ ܚܡܝܪܐ ܘܠܐ ܘܟܪܝܐ ܘܚܒܝܨܐ ܘܥܩܝܪܐ ܚܝܬܐ ܒܕ ܗܘܬ ܒܕܘܟܬܐ ܕܗܝ ܐܦ ܐܝܟ ܗܘܝܐ ܐܝܟ ܡܝܬܐ ܒܝܬ ܦܘܠܗ̇ ܡܢ ܚܕܘܬܐ ܘܬܚܬܝܘܬܐ (trans. Payne Smith 1860, 185).
[54] E.g., in *Hist. eccl.* 1.10 and 4.6.
[55] See van Ginkel 1995, 151–55, for John's depiction of imperial women.

the other scholars who have looked into Sophia in the last decades have not considered this dimension of John's *Ecclesiastical History* when analysing the relationship between Sophia and Tiberios. In John's version of events, Sophia's plans failed without exception, the traditional gender roles were restored, and consequently, she all but disappeared once Tiberios had managed to secure his position against her. However, another source, the chronicle of Theophanes, attests that Sophia still enjoyed all the privileges befitting an empress and was on a par with Maurice's wife Constantina more than twenty years later, in 601, when "on holy Easter day, [the two empresses] made a precious crown which they offered to the emperor [Maurice]".[56] The supposed setbacks she had suffered according to John seem therefore to not have diminished her status in a lasting manner.

It remains probable that Sophia was discontent with the fact that she was obliged to share the title of Augusta with someone else after Justin's death and Ino's move into the imperial palace in 578. Yet this does not mean that she really hoped that Tiberios would divorce his wife and marry her or her daughter Arabia instead. This episode is doubtful not only because of John's intrinsic motivations in his portrayal of Sophia, but also because it conflicts with other developments of the same period. In what follows, I shall examine these points.

The Adoption of Tiberios

One fact which casts doubt on the rumours as reported by John is that Tiberios had been adopted by Justin before his proclamation as Caesar in December 574.[57] Legally, Justin had become Tiberios' father, and there were thus good reasons why Tiberios should regard his relation to Sophia as that between mother and son. We have already seen that Tiberios treated Sophia like his mother.[58] However, strictly sticking to the letter of the law, Sophia had not received a mother-like status because of the adoption. Roman law as codified in Justinian's *Digest* holds that adoption creates a parent-child relationship only between the one who adopts and the one who is adopted.[59] The wife of an adopting man remains unrelated to the adopted person and, consequently, there would be no legal obstacles to their marriage. Yet we can be sure that such a union, especially when involving the emperor, would have been considered highly irregular, if not incestuous,

---

[56] Theoph. Conf. AM 6093: τῇ ἡμέρᾳ τοῦ ἁγίου πάσχα Σοφία ἡ αὐγούστα, ἡ γυνὴ Ἰουστίνου, ἅμα Κωνσταντίνῃ, τῇ γυναικὶ Μαυρικίου, στέμμα κατασκευάσασαι ὑπέρτιμον τῷ βασιλεῖ προσήγαγον (trans. Mango and Scott 1997, 406).

[57] Theophylact, *Hist.* 3.11.4. Theoph. Conf. AM 6067. Cf. Bleckmann 2021, 56–57.

[58] Joh. Eph. *Hist. eccl.* 3.10. Theophylact, *Hist.* 3.11.8. Theoph. Conf. AM 6072.

[59] *Dig.* 1.7.23; cf. *Inst.* 1.10.1.

by large parts of the population that were unaware of the subtleties of the law. Tiberios' esteem for Sophia as his mother indicates that also in his view, the adoption had made him the son of the couple Justin and Sophia, and not of Justin alone.

In John's *Ecclesiastical History*, Tiberios addresses Sophia as his mother when she wishes to leave the imperial palace with a large amount of gold after her failure to prevent Ino's installation as Augusta in late 578. Tiberios thwarts this plan (and remains in control of the gold) by insisting that she should "dwell here [in the palace], and be content, as our mother (ܐܡܐ ܕܝܠܢ), and whatever you command, we will do".[60] But John never spells out the real reason why Tiberios could call Sophia his mother. This is hardly a coincidence, since any mention of Tiberios' adoption would have weakened his sensational story about the supposed plot of Sophia and the patriarch for her to secure a marriage with Tiberios. It would have made the rumours of Sophia's marriage scheme seem less credible, and John would have been deprived of another opportunity to denigrate Sophia as a desperate and power-hungry empress. Unsurprisingly therefore, Theophylact, our main source for Tiberios' adoption, does not say anything about such a marriage project.

Apart from John of Ephesos, only the ninth-century chronicler Theophanes recorded Sophia's hope for marrying Tiberios. Theophanes clearly had access to more than one source, since he is the sole author to mention both that Justin adopted Tiberios and that Sophia "wanted to marry Tiberios and remain Augusta, but she did not know that he had a wife".[61] Theophanes' account is different from John's: he omits Sophia's demand that Tiberios should divorce his wife. As it stands, Theophanes' version is evidently wrong since it is impossible that Sophia only learned after Justin's death that Tiberios was already married. After all, Tiberios had been commander of the imperial bodyguard at least since 565 and already had daughters old enough for marriage. The source of Theophanes' information remains mysterious, but it might be that it was based on John of Ephesos himself. Theophanes used some Syriac sources that had been translated into Greek, and especially in his treatment of the reigns of Justin II and Tiberios, "there are several items which are curiously similar to, but not identical with, the Syriac *Ecclesiastical History* by John of Ephesos".[62] It is conceivable that Theophanes used a fragmentary epitome of the

---

[60] Joh. Eph. *Hist. eccl.* 3.10: ܕܗܕܐ ܐܬܕܟܪܝ ܐܦ ܐܢܬܝ ܕܗܠ ܠܟܐ ܗܘܝ ܕܝܪܬܐ ܕܝܠܢ ܐܟ ܐܡܐ ܕܝܠܢ (trans. Payne Smith 1860, 185).

[61] Theoph. Conf. AM 6067 (for the adoption) and 6071 (for the marriage project: ἐβούλετο γὰρ λαβεῖν Τιβέριον καὶ μεῖναι αὐγούστα. Οὐ γὰρ ᾔδει ὅτι εἶχε γυναῖκα; trans. Mango and Scott 1997, 370).

[62] Mango and Scott 1997, lxxxii–lxxxvii, with the quotation on page lxxxvii.

108 *Empresses-in-Waiting*

Ecclesiastical History. Perhaps its author shared neither John's Miaphysite convictions nor his resulting hatred of the persecutor Sophia. Therefore, he did not include those elements which presented Sophia in a bad light – hence his omission of her suggestion that Tiberios should divorce Ino and inclusion of the awkward alternative explanation that she did not know that Tiberios was already married. Evidently, it is not possible to offer conclusive proof for this hypothesis, but be that as it may, Theophanes' version remains implausible and cannot be used to corroborate John's account.

The Patriarchal Involvement in Sophia's Plans

So far, we have seen that Tiberios, adopted by Justin, desired a relationship between Sophia and himself similar to that between mother and son and that for these reasons, marrying Sophia – or her daughter Arabia – was not a realistic option for him. But this is not yet sufficient to reject Sophia's marriage project as mere fiction. After all, she might, despite Tiberios' views, still have had such hopes since there was no law explicitly preventing a widow from marrying someone her late husband had adopted as his son. The rumours as reported by John claim that Sophia was in alliance with the patriarch of Constantinople to achieve her goal, and we should now turn our attention to this connection.

According to these rumours, the patriarch was willing to assist Sophia and proposed to Tiberios that he should divorce his wife Ino. There is no clear indication when this took place, and John's account is contradictory: it refers to Tiberios still as Caesar (ܩܣܪ), but it implicitly describes Sophia as a widow when it says that her daughter Arabia "was *also* (ܐܦ) a widow".[63] Tiberios was made Augustus on 26 September 578, shortly before Justin's death on 4 October. Hence, there was never a moment when Tiberios was Caesar and Sophia a widow, and this mistake does not strengthen the episode's claim to authenticity. If it is historical at all, the story can only be placed quite soon after Justin's death, since John himself insists that Tiberios brought his wife Ino to the palace and made her Augusta when he had become sole emperor.[64] Consequently, the patriarch in question – John does not name him – was Eutychios (552–565; 577–582), who had returned to Constantinople in October 577 after having spent more than twelve years in exile.[65]

An analysis of Eutychios' relationship with Justin and Sophia on the one hand and with Tiberios on the other renders his alleged backing for Sophia

---

[63] Joh. Eph. *Hist. eccl.* 3.7: ܐܪܡܠܬܐ ܗܝ ܐܦ ܗܘܬ ܕܒܪܬܗ ܡܛܠ ܐܘ ܠܡܦܩܗ (trans. Payne Smith 1860, 179).
[64] Joh. Eph. *Hist. eccl.* 3.9.
[65] For the career of Eutychios, see Av. Cameron 1988. 1990.

quite doubtful. In all likelihood, Eutychios was not on good terms with Justin and Sophia. As I have argued elsewhere, there is strong evidence that Eutychios was deposed in January 565 and sent into exile because he had become victim of a plot orchestrated by a circle of influential dignitaries who wished to install another patriarch who supported Justin's imperial ambitions.[66] Given Justinian's unsettled succession, it was vital for any contender for the imperial throne to have as many high-ranking officials as possible on his side. The leader of the Constantinopolitan Church was evidently a particularly valuable ally because he also played a role in the investiture of a new emperor.[67] Eutychios' successor as patriarch, John Scholastikos, was close to Justin already in the early 560s and therefore an ideal choice for those favouring Justin.[68] As recorded in Corippus' panegyrical poem, Scholastikos readily assisted at Justin's investiture only hours after Justinian's death on 14 November 565, before any rival could have reached Constantinople.[69] During his exile, Eutychios always perceived Scholastikos as an illegitimate usurper and never acknowledged him as patriarch. When he returned to Constantinople in 577 after Scholastikos' death, he embarked on a campaign of a proper *damnatio memoriae* and ordered the destruction of all images of Scholastikos.[70] Considering both Eutychios' hatred of Scholastikos and the close connection between Justin and Scholastikos, Eutychios is hardly likely to have been very supportive of Sophia after his reinstatement as patriarch, all the more so since Sophia had also been active in securing Justin's claim for the throne in the early 560s.[71]

At the same time, Eutychios had known Tiberios already for a long time. He had, in the late 550s or early 560s, even introduced Tiberios to service in the imperial palace.[72] Eutychios was thus ultimately responsible for Tiberios' rise to the post of commander of the imperial bodyguard and, eventually, to the throne. During his exile, Eutychios had also remained in touch with Tiberios through letters.[73] We may assume that it was their friendly relationship which prompted Tiberios to call Eutychios back

---

[66] I have collected the arguments for this view in Roggo 2019.

[67] For the imperial investiture in Late Antiquity, see Rollinger 2024 (ch. 14–16). Pfeilschifter 2013, 138–74 and 378–83. Szidat 2013. Trampedach 2005. Dagron 1996, 74–99.

[68] *Vit. Sym.* 202–206; cf. van den Ven 1965, 320–23.

[69] Corippus, *Iust.* 2.159–64.

[70] Joh. Eph. *Hist. eccl.* 2.27 and 31–34; 3.17–18. Cf. Av. Cameron 1988, 239–42.

[71] Joh. Eph. *Hist. eccl.* 2.10. *Vit. Eut.* 1850–51 claims that Justin and Sophia favoured Eutychios, but this conflicts with the fact that he remained exiled until John Scholastikos died; cf. Av. Cameron 1988, 240–41.

[72] *Vit. Eut.* 1883–84; see also Joh. Eph. *Hist. eccl.* 3.5. Lin 2021, 138. Stein 1919, 53–54.

[73] *Vit. Eut.* 1884–99.

from exile as soon as there was a vacancy on the patriarchal throne.[74] Eutychios was thus indebted to Tiberios, and this is hard to reconcile with his supposed attempt to convince the emperor to repudiate his wife. It is true that there were occasional tensions between emperor and patriarch since Tiberios took issue with some of Eutychios' doctrinal ideas and his eagerness to persecute the Miaphysites.[75] But John of Ephesos writes that Eutychios did not fail to support Tiberios on a crucial occasion: when Ino arrived at the palace soon after Justin's death, Eutychios was immediately ready to assist Tiberios in her elevation to the rank of Augusta. The day of Ino's investiture ended with a procession to Hagia Sophia, where Eutychios celebrated a liturgy for the new imperial couple.[76]

There is a curious tension between this episode of John's *Ecclesiastical History* and the alleged patriarchal involvement in the marriage scheme, for only very little time can have elapsed between the two events. If we treat them both as historical, we have to accept that after Justin's death, Eutychios first attempted to convince Tiberios to divorce Ino on behalf of the widowed Sophia, but then participated in Ino's investiture as soon as she had arrived in the city. The two episodes appear mutually exclusive, and the one that has Eutychios siding with Tiberios is more credible than the rumours which present him forming an alliance with Sophia, who had been closer to his hated rival John Scholastikos.

Furthermore, if John of Ephesos' account of Sophia's plot to remarry were considered credible, we would have to believe that Eutychios encouraged a divorce. We cannot exclude this, but it is highly improbable given the view of the indissolubility of marriage that was espoused by the Church.[77] It is striking that despite this allegedly unorthodox behaviour by the patriarch, John did not grasp the opportunity to criticize him for it. Throughout the *Ecclesiastical History*, John is generally very negative towards Eutychios because he was an eager persecutor of the Miaphysites; accordingly, John depicts him as a heretic and dangerous innovator of the faith.[78] The fact that John stated the rumours about the supposed scandalous involvement of Eutychios in an imperial divorce in a relatively neutral manner suggests that he himself doubted whether these rumours were actually true. The story simply allowed him to denigrate Sophia, and this seems to have been his main aim in this passage. John's *Ecclesiastical History* was later used as a source by other Miaphysite authors, first and foremost by Michael the Syrian, the compiler of a monumental

---

[74] *Vit. Eut.* 1826–44.
[75] Joh. Eph. *Hist. eccl.* 2.35–37; 40 and 51–52. 3.15–21. *Vit. Eut.* 2449–502.
[76] Joh. Eph. *Hist. eccl.* 3.9.
[77] Cf. Hillner 2015, 323–26. Stolte 1999, 77–81. Clark 1993, 26f.
[78] Joh. Eph. *Hist. eccl.* 2.31–41 and 51–52; 3.15–22; cf. van Ginkel 1995, 145–47.

twelfth-century world chronicle. Michael repeated John's account of Sophia's marriage scheme and Eutychios' involvement in it, yet unlike John, he did not describe the episode as a rumour. He was certain that Eutychios, the head of the Church, had indeed supported a divorce, and consequently, he criticized him heavily for his immorality.[79] It appears thus that Michael made the same mistake as some modern scholars who took the rumours of Sophia's marriage plan at face value.

Finally, the ever-growing importance of Christianity increasingly influenced divorce legislation in Late Antiquity. In a series of laws, Justinian had rendered divorce more difficult so that only few valid reasons remained.[80] These included adultery, attempted murder of the spouse, impotence, and the choice of a monastic lifestyle, none of which applied to the situation of Tiberios and Ino. It is true that Justin had, in 566, reintroduced the possibility of getting a divorce by mutual consent between the partners, but he had also stressed in the same constitution that the rest of the Justinianic legislation on divorce remain in force.[81] We do not have the slightest indication that there was consent for a divorce between Tiberios and Ino. On the contrary, Tiberios was adamantly opposed to the idea, and according to John's description of Ino's arrival at the imperial palace, her desire to be reunited with her husband was such that she even hurried ahead of the dignitaries who had come to escort her from her residence in the suburbs of Constantinople to the palace.[82] Her behaviour on that occasion may not only have been motivated by her longing for Tiberios: she may also have feared that those dignitaries might act on orders of Sophia and attempt to prevent her investiture or even harm her.[83] Be that as it may, it must remain a mystery as to how Sophia could have hoped to convince this couple to agree to a divorce neither of them wanted. Moreover, Justinian had also decreed that whenever a wife lost her husband, be it through death or divorce, she was not allowed to remarry before one year had passed.[84] Consequently, Sophia would not have been able to marry Tiberios anytime soon after Justin's death, unless she thought it possible that Tiberios would break the law for her.

---

[79] Michael the Syrian, *Chron.* 10.17 (342–43).
[80] Notably in *Nov.* 22, 117, and 134; see note 11 above for divorce legislation in Late Antiquity.
[81] *Nov.* 140; cf. Puliatti 1991, 81–87.
[82] Joh. Eph. *Hist. eccl.* 3.9.
[83] This is the plausible explanation of van Ginkel 1995, 153.
[84] *Nov.* 22.22.

Conclusion

All the arguments presented above suggest that it is improbable that Sophia could ever realistically have hoped to benefit from a marriage with Tiberios. The available evidence leads us to the conclusion that we should regard Sophia's marriage scheme as nothing more than a wild rumour. John of Ephesos himself never claimed that it was true but reported it as mere hearsay. However, a large part of the modern scholarship on Sophia has taken John's account at face value, thereby overlooking the author's intention to simply present yet another scandal in which the persecuting empress, his antithesis to the tolerant Tiberios, was involved. There is no serious support for the view that Sophia wanted to marry her husband's imperial successor and secure her power in this way. Such a plan would not only have been unrealistic, but also unnecessary: Tiberios honoured her as his mother despite occasional tensions, and we have seen that she preserved her position at court until the end of Maurice's reign.

To sum up, the image of Sophia that has dominated scholarship ever since Averil Cameron's article from 1975 needs to be corrected in some regards. Careful and critical examination of her influence at court has revealed that she has often been credited with too great a degree of independent agency, especially after Tiberios' accession as Caesar in 574. Particularly important is the hitherto rather neglected observation that Sophia's depiction in our main source for the 570s, John's *Ecclesiastical History*, is strongly influenced by John's antipathy towards her. This prompted him to portray Sophia very negatively, and one strategy to achieve this was to show that she had repeatedly transgressed traditional gender boundaries and even imposed her will on the ruling emperor, the Caesar Tiberios. However, this chapter demonstrates that strong arguments can be advanced against John's episodes where Sophia features as a dominant empress who, for instance, allegedly created problems for Tiberios by refusing to vacate her apartments, prevented Ino from entering the palace, and, as a widow, even hoped to marry Tiberios himself. Yet we have seen that, in all likelihood, Tiberios wanted her to stay in the palace, that she was not able to prevent Ino from moving into the palace after Justin's death, and that a marriage with Tiberios never was a realistic possibility. John's shrewdly constructed and misleading image of Sophia is founded on the fact that Tiberios was engaged in enlarging and embellishing the imperial palace, that Ino lived outside the palace when Tiberios was Caesar, and that rumours spread among the population, who knew of Sophia's bitterness at having her power curtailed.

Sophia may indeed have played a central role at court from Justin's accession in 565 to the time after the onset of her husband's illness, when emissaries acting in her name succeeded in concluding a truce with the Persians. But her importance waned after Tiberios' accession as Caesar in 574, and there is no conclusive evidence that she controlled him. On the contrary, it is probable that she had no choice but to accept Tiberios' rise to the imperial throne and the secure, but largely powerless status of empress-mother that he offered her. Sophia did not allow herself to be easily dominated by the men around her in the male-centred world of Late Antiquity, but she was no longer able to act independently to any significant degree after Justin's demise, contrary to what some modern scholars have thought.

5

The Empress Sophia and East Roman Foreign Policy

Lewis Dagnall

> Barbarian wars shall increase the triumphs of Rome and the strongest kingdoms shall come beneath your feet. See, the leaders of the state are treading the threshold of your doorway, asking Justin and Sophia to succeed to their father.[1]

The emperor Justin II (565–578) made bold threats to his enemies upon coming to power.[2] Within days of his accession, he began demolishing the intricate diplomatic edifice bequeathed by his uncle, the emperor Justinian (527–565).[3] In decrying the payment of φόρος, 'tribute', to barbarian kings, Justin adopted the rhetoric of Justinian's bitterest critics against what was, in fairness, merely the latest instance of a long-standing instrument of Roman foreign policy.[4] Justin's uncompromising approach led to war: the Avars attacked across the Danube in 568 and 573/74, the Lombards invaded Italy in 568, and the Sāsānian Persians invaded Syria in 572. Fighting on three fronts, the Romans suffered dramatic defeats. In the winter of 573/74 Justin is said to have suffered a sharp decline in his health, allegedly experiencing

---

[1] Corippus, *Iust.* 1.62–65: *barbara Romanos augebunt bella triumphos regnaque sub vestris venient fortissima plantis. ecce tuae proceres pulsantes limina portae Iustinum Sophiamque rogant succedere patri* (trans. Av. Cameron 1970, 88). For discussion of this passage, see McEvoy 2018, 107–15. On Corippus, see Av. Cameron 1980a.
[2] On Justin II: *PLRE* 3b (Iustinus 5), 754–56. Bury 1889, II 67–82. Mi. Whitby 2001. Main 2019. For discussion of primary sources, see below.
[3] On Justinian's foreign policy: Bury 1889, I 333–482. Rubin 1986, 48–49. Halsall 2007, 499–506. Sarris 2011, 145–68. Heather 2020, 303–311. Mi. Whitby 2021, 115–280.
[4] For an overview of Roman/East Roman use of subsidies in Late Antiquity: Gordon 1949, 65–69. Hendy 1985, 260–64. Blockley 1985b, 62–63. Blockley 1992, 108. Heather 2001, 25–27. Lee 2007, 105–22. For Justinian's use of subsidies: Gordon 1959, 24–26. Blockley 1985b, 69–71. Sarantis 2016, 325–74.

catastrophic mental illness after hearing of the loss of the fortress of Dara to the Persians.[5] For the next four years Justin lived on, while apparently unable to govern the empire. The resultant power vacuum gives us a unique insight into the performance of power by a Late Antique empress, with the highest political stakes for herself and her empire.

Several, but not all, of our primary sources evidence that the empress Sophia rose to play a central role, or perhaps indeed *the* central role, in determining foreign policy in this period. One-by-one, the subsidy arrangements that Justin had cancelled were restored. Sophia's supposed influence coincides, therefore, with a crucial change of course: the abandonment of Justin's radical foreign policy and the reinstatement of key elements of the Justinianic system. When Justin died and was succeeded as emperor Augustus by Tiberius II (578–582),[6] and then by Maurice (582–602),[7] Sophia retained her title of Augusta but was by all accounts marginalised from day-to-day decisions. As will be shown, though, even when sharing Justin's rhetorical denunciations of tribute, these emperors continued the Justinianic approach that had been restored under Sophia.

Much of the historiography has done a disservice to Sophia, portraying her in the sexist image of the 'domineering wife'.[8] She has often been compared unfavourably with her aunt, the empress Theodora,[9] and received relatively modest interest in comparison.[10] However, following a groundbreaking study by Averil Cameron, several more sympathetic studies have sought to correct the record and instead emphasize Sophia's influence and agency.[11] In Cameron's judgement:

> For forty years she had been a dominant influence in politics. During the reign of Justin she exercised a power no less than the emperor's and almost

---

[5] The report of Justin's 'insanity' has been taken at face value in much of the scholarship: see Av. Cameron 1970, 11. Blockley 1985b, 73. Mi. Whitby 1988, 6. Isaac 1995, 126–27. Greatrex and Lieu 2002, 151. For a somewhat problematic attempt to understand Justin's illness using modern psychiatry, see Kroll and Bachrach 1993, 40–67. For defences of this methodology, see Kroll and Bachrach 2005, 5–6. Kroll and Pouncey 2016, 226–35.
[6] *PLRE* 3b (Tiberius Constantinus 1), 1323–26.
[7] *PLRE* 3b (Fl. Mauricius Tiberius 4), 855–60.
[8] Mi. Whitby 1988, 6–7, describes the "domineering wife Sophia".
[9] *PLRE* 3b (Theodora 1), 1240–41.
[10] For example, Bury 1889, II 71: "Sophia had the ambition, without the genius, of her aunt Theodora".
[11] Av. Cameron 1975c, 5–21. Garland 1999, 40–58. McClanan 2002, 149–78.

succeeded in making the Imperial power into a collegiality. Once Justin's illness had set in she came into her own...[12]

While it is now recognized that this perhaps overstates the case,[13] it remains clear that Sophia had an unusual level of involvement in the governance of the empire.

In this chapter I want to look beyond the usual debate about Sophia's constitutional role, instead considering both the ways in which she was involved in foreign policy and the scale of the resultant changes. We shall see how Sophia could not have been the co-author of Justin's dogmatic rejection of subsidies, as Cameron's interpretation would imply, because of the sheer contrast in the substance of their policies. We shall also see how the machinations of the imperial court shaped the way the empire looked outwards and interacted with its neighbours. In this way, this chapter suggests that the serious study of empresses, often treated as a discrete field within the historiography of the later Roman Empire, can also be of vital importance to 'mainstream' political topics, in this case, the dynamics of foreign policy.

The chapter proceeds by first establishing the complex legacies of Justinian and Theodora, which formed the political context for the accession of Justin and Sophia. The second part then presents an analysis of foreign policy under Justin's leadership in the period 565 to 573/74, demonstrating the radicalism of his deliberate and dogmatic rejection of 'tribute payments'. I also show that, contrary to images of Sophia as the 'power behind the throne', the sources for this period provide no direct evidence for the empress' close involvement in foreign policy decisions before her husband's decline. Once Justin was incapacitated, however, that changed: in the third part, discussing the period of Justin's illness (573/74–78), we find that the empire dramatically overturned Justin's foreign policy and reinstated the system inherited from Justinian. The decision making in these years is explicitly associated with the empress, even if she worked closely with Tiberius as *comes excubitorum* and later Caesar. After the death of Justin, upon whom Sophia's position depended, she was marginalized, but the continuities between her foreign policy and that of Tiberius and then Maurice show that she had a greater influence in the long-term than her husband's brief and garish reign.

---

[12] Av. Cameron 1975c, 21.
[13] Pfeilschifter 2013, 142–47. See also Roggo, this volume.

The Inheritance from Justinian and Theodora

Justin acceded to the throne in a febrile political atmosphere, with the circumstances of the succession itself contested.[14] The new emperor then had to confront a whole range of issues – including religious[15] and fiscal[16] policy – where Justinian's long-standing policies had become increasingly questioned. The outstanding area of anxiety for many, however, was foreign policy, and in particular Justinian's increasing reliance on paying subsidies. In this first section we shall consider Justinian, and how he and the empress Theodora bequeathed complex legacies to Justin and Sophia.

In his early reign Justinian had paid Persia for peace, enabling a military pivot to the western Mediterranean and the reconquest of North Africa and much of Italy.[17] Following these successes, he donned the image of the 'imperial victor' through iconography, games and triumphs.[18] Yet as the wars of the 540s and 550s dragged on, Justinian was seen to increasingly favour diplomatic intrigue to open hostility, offering further money to the Persians, Laz, Moors, Huns, and Avars.[19] Regardless of whether this constituted "measured Realpolitik", in the words of one modern study,[20] the contemporary perception was that Justinian had abandoned his earlier military daring for a submissive and reactive stance.

Criticism was of course subdued for most of Justinian's rule. Even if Procopius was exaggerating that he composed the *Secret History* from fear of "hordes of spies" and "the most horrible of deaths",[21] the publication of overt criticism was not without risk. Yet by the twilight of Justinian's reign, intellectual opinion was bristling at his perceived reliance on the empire's fiscal power rather than military might. As John of Ephesus later recalled, "the murmuring against him grew general on the part of the senate and the people, for they said, 'He is stripping the whole kingdom and giving it to the barbarians.'"[22]

---

[14] Lin 2021, 136–42. Also Roggo 2019, 444–45.
[15] Av. Cameron 1976c. Bell 2013, 160–212.
[16] Mi. Whitby 2001, 87–90.
[17] Greatrex 1998. Rubin 1986.
[18] McCormick 1986, 64–68.
[19] Dagnall (forthcoming). Blockley 1985b, 70–72. Sarantis 2016, 325–74.
[20] Sarantis 2016, 326.
[21] Procop. *Anecd.* 1.2: αἴτιον δὲ, ὅτι δὴ οὐχ οἷόν τε ἦν περιόντων ἔτι τῶν αὐτὰ εἰργασμένων ὅτῳ δεῖ ἀναγράφεσθαι τρόπῳ. οὔτε γὰρ διαλαθεῖν πλήθη κατασκόπων οἷόν τε ἦν οὔτε φωραθέντα μὴ ἀπολωλέναι θανάτῳ οἰκτίστῳ: οὐδὲ γὰρ ἐπὶ τῶν συγγενῶν τοῖς γε οἰκειοτάτοις τὸ θαρρεῖν εἶχον (trans. Williamson and Sarris 2007, 66). See Av. Cameron 1985, 50. For Procopius as a 'dissident', see Kaldellis 2004b, 2–4.
[22] Joh. Eph. *Hist. eccl.* 3.6.24: ܐܬܘܟܠܡ ܗܠܟ ܢܡܕ ܢܝܪܡܐܘ ܐܡܥܘ ܐܛܠܩܢܘܣ ܗܠܟ ܢܡ

The death of Justinian allowed an intellectual thaw in which critical discussion of the late emperor's policies became permissible. This is evident in how two continuators of Procopius' history, Agathias[23] and Menander,[24] included far stronger criticism than the original author had dared. Agathias gave a stark portrait of the late emperor relying on subsidies due to old age:

> At an earlier date the emperor had reduced Africa and the whole of Italy, becoming as a result of those epoch-making campaigns almost the first of the rulers of Byzantium to be Emperor of the Romans in fact as well as in name. He had accomplished these and similar feats when he was still in the full vigour of his youth, but now in his declining years when old age was upon him, he seemed to have wearied of vigorous policies and to prefer to play off his enemies against one another and, if necessary, to coax them away with gifts rather than rely on his own powers and expose himself to the hazards of a sustained struggle.[25]

Menander offered a similar picture:

> Justinian's body was weak and his strength, of course, had diminished from the time when, as a young man, he had made captive both Gelimer the Vandal and Vittigis the Goth. Now he was an old man, and his bold and warlike spirit had become feeble, and he sought ways other than war to ward off the power of the barbarians. He would have crushed and utterly destroyed them, if not by war than by wisdom, if he had not met his destined end first.[26]

܀ܟܬܒܐ ܗܘ ܡܘܡܐ ܕܚܘܠܡܢܐ ܗܘ ܠܗ ܡܢܗ ܡܢܝ ܀ܚܘܝܬܐ (trans. Payne Smith 1860, 429). Cf. Joh. Ant. *fr.* 312.

[23] *PLRE* 3a (Agathias), 23–25. For dating of Agathias' *Histories*, see Av. Cameron 1970, 11; 124.

[24] *PLRE* 3b (Menander 1 [Menander Protector]), 873. See Blockley 1985a, 1–30.

[25] Agath. 5.14.1: ὁ γὰρ βασιλεὺς ἐπειδὴ πρότερον Ἰταλίαν ξύμπασαν ἐχειρώσατο καὶ Λιβύην, καὶ τοὺς μεγίστους ἐχείνους πολέμους διήνυσε, καὶ πρῶτος ὡς εἰπεῖν ἐν τοῖς κατὰ τὸ Βυζάντιον βεβασιλευκόσι Ῥωμαίων αὐτοκράτωρ ὀνόματί τε καὶ πράγματι ἀπεδέδεικτο· ἐπειδὴ οὖν αὐτῷ ταὐτά τε καὶ ἄλλα ὅμοια τούτοις νεάζοντι ἔτι καὶ ἐρρωμένῳ ἐξείργαστο, τότε δὴ ἀμφὶ τὴν ἐσχάτην τοῦ βίου πορείαν, (ἤδη γὰρ καὶ ἐγεγηράκει,) ἀπειρηκέναι τοῖς νόμοις ἐδόκει, καὶ μᾶλλόν τι αὐτὸν ἤρεσκε ξυγκρούειν ἐν σφίσι τοὺς πολεμίους, δώροις τε αὐτούς, εἴπῃ δεήσοι, καταθωπεύειν, καὶ ταύτῃ ἀμωσγέπως ἀποκρούεσθαι, ἢ ἐφ' ἑαυτῷ πεποιθέναι καὶ μέχρι παντὸς διακινδυνεύειν (trans. Frendo 1975, 149). See Av. Cameron 1970, 126. Treadgold 2007, 290.

[26] Men. Prot. *fr.* 5.1.17–26: οὐ γὰρ ἐσφρίγα οἱ τὸ σῶμα οὐδὲ ἤκμαζεν ἡ ἀλκή, ὥσπερ ἀμέλει ἡνίκα Γελίμερά τε τὸν Βάνδηλον καὶ Οὐίττιγιν τὸν Γότθον ἄμφω ἔτι νεάζων ἔθετο δοριαλώτω, ἀλλ' ἤδη γηραλέος τε ἦν καὶ τὸ ἀνδρεῖον ἐκεῖνο φρόνημα καὶ φιλοπόλεμον μετεβέβλητο ἐς τὸ ῥᾳθυμότερον, ταῦτα ἔγνω ἑτέρῳ τρόπῳ καὶ οὐχὶ πολέμῳ τὴν βαρβαρικὴν ἀποκρούσασθαι δύναμιν. καὶ κατηγωνίσατο ἂν καὶ ἄρδην ἠφάνισεν, εἰ καὶ μὴ πολέμῳ, ἀλλ' οὖν εὐβουλίᾳ, εἴ γε μὴ τῷ ὀφειλομένῳ τέλει πρότερον ἠφανίσθη αὐτός (trans. Blockley

This criticism was not limited to intellectuals. In making such arguments, both writers exactly echoed the rhetoric attributed to Justin himself by Corippus:

> Let the world rejoice that whatever was not done or put into practice because of our father's old age has been corrected in the time of Justin.[27]

As Sarris has highlighted, the public deprecation of Justinian's policies in such a "highly critical" manner can only be understood as Justin deliberately courting those disillusioned with the late emperor.[28]

It must, however, be said that others have found these writers to have been not wholly unsympathetic to Justinian.[29] By labouring the emperor's old age and presenting a parallel with the passivity of the elderly Khosrow, Menander may have been seeking to excuse policies that looked unwise in retrospect.[30] Indeed, in the different context of subsidies to Arab kings, Menander comfortably employed the rhetoric of a "generous and noble Emperor", suggesting he might not have been opposed to subsidies in all circumstances.[31] That Corippus, Agathias, and Menander hedged their critique of Justinian's foreign policy perhaps reveals that the tide of opinion had not gone quite as far as Justin believed: educated Romans still despised tribute, but when it worked they understood the logic of Justinian's actions. We are safe to conclude, though, that contemporary and later sources all point to a growing disquiet about Justinian's policies among the intellectual elite that Justin sought to respond to.[32]

Before we proceed though, there is one further legacy from the reign of Justinian of relevance to our present inquiry: the role of Sophia's aunt, the empress Augusta Theodora.[33] While it is infamous that amidst the wide-ranging invective of the *Secret History*, Procopius particularly deplored Theodora,[34] we must not downplay his evidence. Justinian himself was

---

1985a, 49). Note that Menander still regards it as a victory of sorts to defeat an enemy "if not by war by wisdom": he was not amongst the most rabid opponents of 'tribute'.
[27] Corippus, *Iust.* 2.263–4: *quod minus ob senium factumve actumve parentis, tempore Iustini correctum gaudeat orbis* (trans. Av. Cameron 1976b, 99).
[28] Sarris 2011, 162. See also Sarris 2006, 226.
[29] Corippus: Av. Cameron 1976b, 170. Agathias: Av. Cameron 1970, 126. Menander: Baldwin 1978, 112–13. Blockley 1985a, 22. Treadgold 2007, 29.
[30] Men. Prot. *fr.* 16.1.12–16. As noted by Blockley 1985a, 22 n. 98. On the discourses surrounding Justinian's policy of subsidies, see also Rollinger (forthcoming a).
[31] Men. Prot. *fr.* 9.1.34–35: μεγαλόφρων ἀνήρ καὶ βασιλικώτατος (trans. Blockley 1985a, 99).
[32] Börm 2008, 327–46.
[33] On their relationship, see Potter 2015, 201–202.
[34] Procop. *Anecd.* 10.14.

candid about the influence of the empress, explaining in one law that he reached his conclusions after "taking our God-given and most pious consort into consultation".[35] Theodora played a notable role in several episodes of foreign relations.[36] Taking one example, the empress made a personal appeal to Khosrow for peace in the 540s. She met personally with the Sāsānian ambassador, Zabergan,[37] and sent him with a letter urging Khosrow to come to terms. In this instance, Theodora was actively trying to further Justinian's own objective of peace.[38] She did not, however, limit herself to shoring up her husband's position. John of Ephesus relates how Theodora sent a rival Miaphysite mission to the Sudan, competing against the official orthodox missionaries dispatched by her husband.[39] When we come to consider Sophia's role, Theodora's involvement in foreign policy provides instructive context.

Justin's Foreign Policy (565–573)

Given the rising disquiet, there was a weight of expectation that the new emperor would signal an immediate break with Justinian's most unpopular policies. One first example is Agathias' short panegyric to Justin,[40] which offered a warlike depiction of the new emperor:

> Let no barbarian, freeing himself from the yoke-strap that passes under his neck, dare to fix his gaze on our king, the mighty warrior.[41]

The barbarians threatened by Agathias were enumerated in another source, an anonymous epigram:

> Another statue loaded with spoils shall the bold Persian erect within Susa to the Emperor for his victory, and yet another the host of the long-haired Avars beyond the Danube shearing the locks from their squalid heads…

---

[35] *Nov.* 8.1: *hic quoque participem consilii sumentes eam quae a deo data nobis est reverentissimam coniugem* (trans. Miller and Sarris 2018, I 130).
[36] Evans 2002, 59–66.
[37] *PLRE* 3b (Zabergan 2), 1410.
[38] Evans 2002, 60–61.
[39] Joh. Eph. *Hist. eccl.* 3.4.6–7. However, it has been argued that John over-emphasized the mission to flatter his Miaphysite Church; for a critical evaluation of this passage, see Zacharopoulou 2016, 75–76. For Theodora and Justinian's divergent theological views, see also Procop. *Anecd.* 10.13–5 and Evagr. *Hist. eccl.* 4.10.
[40] The subject of the panegyric was established as Justin II by Cameron and Cameron 1966 and McCail 1969, notwithstanding the scepticism of Baldwin 1977 and 1980.
[41] *Anth. Gr.* 4.3 (Agathias *Cycle*, 47–48): μή τις ὑπαυχενίοιο λιπὼν ζωστῆρα λεπάδνου βάρβαρος ἐς βασιλῆα βιημάχον ὄμμα τανύσσῃ (trans. Paton 1916, 119).

But mayst thou stand firm, O fortunate Byzantine Rome, who hast rewarded the god-given might of Justin.[42]

Of course, these sources, written early in the new emperor's reign and in the panegyric form, cannot be taken literally. It has been said of Agathias' panegyric that "not much could yet be said about Justin himself, so the poet has recourse to the set themes of Byzantine imperial ideology".[43] That is precisely its value. These sources give us a sense of the general expectations among the senatorial elite for the new emperor – and in the case of foreign policy, they were hungry for "victory and triumph".[44]

If commentators had found martial vigour wanting in the ageing Justinian, they also resented his attempts to stabilize imperial finances by raising taxes and demanding compulsory loans. Justin quickly acted to relieve the pressure on taxpayers by remitting taxes and repaying public debt.[45] There was a role too for Sophia in this effort: according to the later chronicler Theophanes, the empress met with bankers to instruct them to absolve their debtors, in what Cameron described as "an extraordinary intervention by an empress in financial affairs".[46] Besides being perceived as burdensome, Justinian's fiscal policies were also regarded as failing in their stated aim: a concern Justin recognized in law by declaring his horror "on finding the public treasury burdened with numerous debts and heading towards utter destruction".[47] So although easing the burden on taxpayers was welcomed, the new emperor was still expected to balance the books, and the combination of reducing income and expenditure necessitated finding economies elsewhere.

Conveniently, there was an obvious way that Justin could both demonstrate austerity and prove how he favoured 'martial virtue' over diplomacy.[48] The belief that the extra money raised to the treasury simply drained to the barbarians, as exemplified by the John of Ephesus quote

---

[42] *Anth. Plan.* 72: Ἄλλον ὑπὲρ νικας ἐναρηφόρον ἔνδοθι Σούσων ὁ θρασὺς ἀνστήσει Μῆδος ἄνακτι τύπον· ἄλλον ἀκειρεκόμας Ἀβάρων στρατὸς ἔκτοθεν Ἴστρου, κείρας ἐκ κεφαλῆς βόστρυχον αὐσταλέης... ἔμπεδος ἀλλὰ μένοις, Βυζαντιὰς ἔμμορε Ῥώμα, θεῖον Ἰουστίνου κάρτος ἀμειφαμένα (trans. Paton 1927, 197 and 199).

[43] Av. Cameron 1977, 4.

[44] Av. Cameron 1977, 4.

[45] Corippus, *Iust.* 2.361. See Sarris 2011, 227–32, on Justin's placation of his senatorial supporters.

[46] Theoph. Conf. AM 6060. Av. Cameron 1975c, 9–10.

[47] *Nov.* 148.pr: *fiscum enim cum multis debitis oneratum et ad extremam inopiam adactum inveniremus...* (trans. Miller and Sarris 2018, II 957).

[48] For the discussion of 'martial virtue' in the Late Roman Empire see Stewart 2016, 1–11 and *passim*.

earlier,[49] shows how the failures of foreign and fiscal policy were understood to be closely bound together. Cutting foreign subsidies would therefore demonstrate Justin's commitments to austerity and to martial prowess over diplomacy. The first opportunity for this came in the days following his accession.

Justin received a delegation of Avars, nomads who had reached the Danube frontier in the previous decade and secured accommodation with Justinian in return for subsidies.[50] This famous embassy was recorded in multiple sources of different genres, thereby widely advertising Justin's actions. The first and most prominent of these was Corippus' panegyric, *In Praise of Justin the Younger*. Bound by convention to offer a supportive presentation of imperial authority, its date (566/67)[51] means it was also written without full knowledge of how Justin's foreign policy would eventually unwind. The source therefore provides good insight into how Justin wished his policy to be presented at the opening of his reign. One important element was the presentation of the imperial couple together as joint bearers of a holy duty to restore the might of the empire, as exemplified in the quote from Corippus taken as this chapter's epigram. Despite this, however, Corippus gives no direct account of Sophia's involvement in foreign policy, as do our sources for the 570s.

Corippus has the Avars enter the imperial audience and after a long speech, request that Justin "send our king the gifts that are his due".[52] Corippus insists that the emperor was "tranquil" and "not moved in anger",[53] yet he responded forcefully:

'Do you think my father did it through fear, because he gave gifts to the needy and exiled out of pity?'[54]

Justin made an explicit threat to wage war on the Avars:

'Against those we find ungrateful, we go to war. Are we to stand in the way of kings, yet open our doors to exiled slaves?... I tell you the truth. We are

---

[49] Joh. Eph. *Hist. eccl.* 3.6.24: ܐܝܟ ܡܢ ܘܐܦ ܣܝܥܬܐ ܐܝܟ ܡܢ ܕܢܦܝܩ, ܡܠܐ ܒܗ ܕܐܪܥܐ ܕܪܗܘܡ ܠܐ ܐܝܬܘܗܝ. ܬܚܘܡܐ (trans. Payne Smith 1860, 429). Cf. Joh. Ant. *fr.* 312.
[50] Sarantis 2016, 325–74.
[51] Av. Cameron 1967, 12–13.
[52] Corippus, *Iust.* 3.305: *debita quaerenti transmittes munera regi* (trans. Av. Cameron 1976b, 108).
[53] Corippus, *Iust.* 3.308–10: *nulla commotus in ira, tranquillus princeps oculis pietate serenis aspexit iuvenem* (trans. Av. Cameron 1976b, 108).
[54] Corippus, *Iust.* 3.347–49: *terrore putatis id nostrum fecisse patrem, miseratus egenis et profugis quod dona dedit?* (trans. Av. Cameron 1976b, 109).

offering aid to the unworthy. Does the Cagan think that he is feared and dare to assail my standards in war? Very well, go. Prepare your battles, dispositions and encampments, and wait with certainty for the generals of my army.'[55]

As would be expected in a panegyric, Corippus wrote that the Avar ambassador "trembled in horror and stiffened in great fear".[56] Yet it was not only panegyrists, bound by convention to laud imperial policy and diminish barbarians, who celebrated Justin's new approach.

In Menander's record of the embassy, he bemoaned Justinian's policy and celebrated Justin's treatment of the Avars:

> During the reign of the younger Justin the envoys of the Avars came to Byzantium to receive the usual gifts which the previous emperor, Justinian, had given to their tribe... On this occasion the envoys of the Avars wished to come to try the Emperor and see if they would in the same way be able to obtain gifts, make mock of the Romans' inertia and turn their negligence to their own profit.[57]

He reported how Justin dismissed this entreaty in the strongest terms:

> 'Depart, therefore, having purchased from us a gift of the greatest value – your lives – and having received, instead of Roman gold, a terror of us which will ensure your survival. I shall never need an alliance with you, nor shall you receive from us anything other than we wish to give, and that as a free gift for your service, not, as you expect, a tax upon us.'[58]

---

[55] Corippus, *Iust.* 3.393–98: *quos contra ingratos offendimus, arma paramus. obstamus dominis, profugis damus ostia servis? legibus hoc nostris non convenit. arguo factum. Indignis praebemus opem. Caganque timeri se putat, et bello mea signa lacessere temptat? ite, licet. campos acies et castra parate, signorumque duces certo sperate meorum* (trans. Av. Cameron 1976b, 110).

[56] Corippus, *Iust.* 3.399–400: *contremuit stupefactus Avar, magnoque timore diriguit* (trans. Av. Cameron 1976b, 110).

[57] Men. Prot. *fr.* 8.1–3 and 5–10: Ὅτι ἐπὶ Ἰουστίνου τοῦ νέου οἱ τῶν Ἀβάρων πρέσβεις παρεγένοντο ἐν Βυζαντίῳ τὰ συνήθη δῶρα ληφόμενοι, ἅπερ τῷ κατ' αὐτοὺς ἔθνει Ἰουστινιανὸς ὁ πρὸ τοῦ βασιλεὺς ἐδίδου ... τότε δὴ οὖν οἱ πρέσβεις τῶν Ἀβάρων ἐς πεῖραν ἰέναι τοῦ βασιλέως ἐβούλοντο, εἴ γε οὐκ ἄλλως <ἐνεῖν> δῶρα λαμβάνειν αὐτοῖς καὶ τῇ Ῥωμαίων ῥαθυμίᾳ ἐπεντρυφᾶν καὶ τὸ ἀμελὲς αὐτῶν οἰκεῖον τίθεσθαι κέρδος καὶ δὴ παρὰ βασιλέα φοιτᾶν ἠξίιουν (trans. Blockley 1985a, 93).

[58] Men. Prot. *fr.* 8.53–55: ἄπιτε τοιγαροῦν πλείστου πριάμενοι παρ' ἡμῶν κἂν γοῦν ἐν ζῶσι τελεῖν καὶ ἀντὶ τῶν Ῥωμαϊκῶν χρημάτων τὸν καθ' ἡμᾶς φόβον εἰς σωτηρίαν εἰληφότες. οὔτε γὰρ δεηθείην ποτὲ τῆς καθ' ὑμᾶς συμμαχίας, οὔτε τι λήψεσθε παρ' ἡμῶν ἢ καθ' ὅσον ἡμῖν δοκεῖ, ὥσπερ δουλείας ἔπανον, καὶ οὐχ, ὡς οἴεσθε, φορολογίαν τινά (trans. Blockley 1985a, 95).

5 The Empress Sophia and East Roman Foreign Policy 125

The embassy is also described in John of Ephesus' *Ecclesiastical History*. He names Justin as "one of those who were vexed and grumbled at the amount which these barbarians received".[59] In an echo of the epigram discussed above, John wrote that Justin threatened to "shave off those locks of yours"[60] – an instance of Romans' recurrent fascination with the Avar hairstyle and a bait for chauvinistic attitudes to ethnicity and gender. All in all, the ambassadors who had expected a resumption of the payments they had received from Justinian had a rude awakening.

This diplomatic rebuke soon had consequences. First, the Avar *khagan* Bayan[61] joined with the Lombards to invade and destroy the kingdom of the Gepids in the north-west of the Danube frontier. The Gepids were imperial clients, albeit unreliable ones, and Menander says Justin's cancellation of subsidies motivated the Avars to attack.[62] The Gepid king Cunimund[63] sent a plea for aid to Justin which was refused.[64] Instead, the Romans took the opportunity of the crumbling Gepid kingdom to reoccupy the city of Sirmium, a former imperial capital that had been under their control. After destroying the Gepids, however, in spring 568, the Avars turned their attention south of the Danube and laid siege to Sirmium.[65] Early in the siege Bayan sought to negotiate with the city's commander, the *magister militum* Bonus,[66] and offered to withdraw upon the receipt of gifts. This lends weight to the idea that the Avar rampage was self-inflicted by Justin's refusal to pay subsidies. To Bayan's fury, however, Bonus insisted that he could only make such gifts with the express approval of Justin, knowing full well the stance the emperor had taken.[67]

Following this, Bayan sent Targitius,[68] the ambassador who had been rebuked in 565, on two embassies to Justin (likely in 567/8)[69] to make a direct request for Sirmium and annual subsidies. In the meantime, he convinced another Roman authority, the prefect of Illyricum, to give him 800 *nomismata* in return for the Avars not pillaging his territory.[70] When Targitius met Justin, he made his case legalistically: since the Avars had subjugated the Utigur, Cutrigur, and Gepid groups, who had been

---

[59] Joh. Eph. *Hist. eccl.* 3.6.24 (trans. Payne Smith 1860, 429).
[60] Joh. Eph. *Hist. eccl.* 3.6.24 (trans. Payne Smith 1860, 429).
[61] *PLRE* 3a (Baianus), 167–69.
[62] Men. Prot. *fr.* 12.2.1–12.
[63] *PLRE* 3a (Cunimundus), 364–65.
[64] Men. Prot. *fr.* 12.2.12–31.
[65] See Mi. Whitby 1988, 86–88.
[66] *PLRE* 3a (Bonus 4), 241–42.
[67] Men. Prot. *fr.* 12.5.64–83. Pohl ²2018, 222.
[68] *PLRE* 3b (Targitius), 1217.
[69] Pohl 2018, 76.
[70] Men. Prot. *fr.* 12.6.1–5.

subsidized by Justinian, the Avar *khagan* could lay claim to those subsidies.[71] Regardless of the irony that those groups had received subsidies to defend the Danube from the Avars themselves, Justin would have had no intention of paying even a legitimate request and dismissed the question of subsidies. Justin did, however, agree to send the future emperor Tiberius to negotiate directly with Bayan.[72]

The Avars' destruction of the Gepids had knock-on effects. Rather than stay within striking distance of his erstwhile allies, the Lombard king Alboin[73] decided to make his own move west. In 568 the Lombards invaded Roman Italy and quickly seized territory across the north of the peninsula. Whereas previous invaders had largely maintained Roman administrative structures, the Lombards instead began carving out duchies.[74] Italy, which Justinian's armies had fought long and hard to reclaim, once again became the scene of war.

While these events unfolded in the west of the empire, Justin's hard-line policy against subsidies caused upset in the east, too. We understand the Arab tribes bordering Rome and Persia as having increasingly cohered into rival federations: successive sixth-century Roman emperors promoting the Jafnid dynasty to rule over Ghassanid tribes, while the Sāsānians had long favoured the Nasrid rulers of the Lakhmid federation.[75] Justinian's subsidies cut across such spheres of influence, however: he made gifts of gold to al-Mundhir III,[76] the pro-Sāsānian Nasrid king, just as he did to the Jafnid king al-Harith,[77] a Roman ally.[78]

In keeping with his policy against subsidies, Justin spurned Arab requests for money. In response, 'Amr,[79] the Nasrid successor to al-Mundhir, persuaded his Sāsānian benefactors to intervene. In July 567 Khosrow raised the matter with Justin's ambassador, John,[80] only to be rebuffed.[81] John lamented Justinian's "excess of generosity" and explained that rather than hand out donatives, "the present emperor wishes to be an object of

---

[71] Men. Prot. *fr.* 12.6.14–86. Curta 2006, 63–65. Sarantis 2016, 333–52.
[72] Men. Prot. *fr.* 12.7.15–19.
[73] *PLRE* 3a (Alboin), 38–40.
[74] Christie 1995, 73–90. Sarris 2011, 179–80.
[75] Fisher 2011, 49–70.
[76] *PLRE* 2 (Alamundarus 2), 40–43.
[77] *PLRE* 3a (Arethas), 111–13.
[78] Men. Prot. *fr.* 6.1.288–91 and *fr.* 9.1.34–36. See Fisher 2011, 122–23.
[79] *PLRE* 3a (Ambros ['Amr] 2), 54–55. Note that while Justinian had subsidized al-Mundhir III, he apparently declined to send money to 'Amr. See Men. Prot. *fr.* 6.1.288–91 and Blockley 1985a, 255 n. 46, *contra* Stein 1949, 521.
[80] *PLRE* 3a (Ioannes 81), 672–74.
[81] Dated by Greatrex and Lieu 2002, 135.

the greatest fear to all".[82] This explanation did not satisfy the Persians, who allowed a Nasrid delegation to accompany a subsequent Sāsānian embassy to Constantinople later that year.[83] Justin refused to receive the Arab envoys, declaring:

> 'He says that he wishes to receive the usual payment from us, instead of which, I think, the accursed criminal will receive misfortune. It would be laughable if we, the Romans, became tributary to the Saracen race, nomads at that.'[84]

This response was both significant and revealing. Not only did Justin demolish his uncle's policy, but he adopted exactly the line of attack that critics had used against his uncle – that making diplomatic payments reduced the empire to tributary status.

If this was the response to the Persian-aligned Nasrids, there was an even worse reception to the request for money by the Romans' own clients, the Jafnid dynasty. After being rebuffed by Justin, the Nasrids had recommenced raids against Jafnid lands. The Jafnid king al-Mundhir sent to Justin in 572 to request gold to fund his defences.[85] Justin responded furiously, ordering an assassination attempt on the Jafnid king. This plot was bungled and consequently, during what was to be a crucial period for the defence of the Roman East, al-Mundhir withdrew his cooperation with Roman security for three years.[86]

Alongside the Arab alliance system, other sources of tension between Rome and Persia began flaring up in the borderlands of Armenia, Yemen, and the Eurasian steppe. In one case Yazan, the Himyarite king of Yemen, had his request for Justin's support dismissed, so instead submitted as a vassal of the Sāsānian *Šâhanšâh*.[87] In and of themselves, these conflicts were not certain to precipitate direct conflict between the great powers: under Justinian, Roman and Persian forces had fought directly and through proxies in peripheral regions, while maintaining peace in Mesopotamia.[88]

---

[82] Men. Prot. *fr.* 9.1.86–87: ὁ δὲ νῦν Ῥωμαίων αὐτοκράτωρ πρὸς πάντας εἶναι βούλεται φοβερώτατος (trans. Blockley 1985a, 101).

[83] Men. Prot. *fr.* 9.3.30.

[84] Men. Prot. *fr.* 9.3.105–10: φησί γὰρ ὡς ἐθέλοι τὰ συνήθη χρήματα κομίσασθαι πρὸς ἡμῶν, ἀνθ' ὧν, οἶμαι κομιεῖται ξυμφορὰς ὁ κατάρατός τε καὶ ἀπολουμενος. γελοιῶδες γάρ, εἰ Σαρακηνῶν ἔθνει, καὶ ταῦτα νομάδων, Ῥωμαῖοι γε ὄντες τεταξόμεθα ἐς φόρων ἀπαγωγήν (trans. Blockley 1985a, 110).

[85] Joh. Eph. *Hist. eccl.* 3.6.3. See Edwell et al. 2015, 255–57. *PLRE* 3a (Alamundarus), 34–37.

[86] Joh. Eph. *Hist. eccl.* 3.6.4. See Greatrex and Lieu 2002, 136, and Fisher 2011, 72.

[87] Al-Tabari *History*, 949–50.

[88] For example, Lazica was excluded from Justinian's truces of 545 and 551: see Greatrex and Lieu 2002, 113 and 124.

Crucial to that peace, however, was the Roman willingness to underwrite treaties with payments.

Given this, Justin's refusal to send money to Persia was tantamount to a declaration of war. After several bouts of warfare in the early and middle decades of the century, Justinian and the Persian *Šâhanšâh* had reached a position of grudging stability.[89] In Persia, the receipt of money from the Roman emperor had ideological significance. Regular payments were used by the *Šâhanšâh* as evidence that the Roman emperor was but another subject king.[90] For this reason, Roman negotiators tried to avoid formally agreeing to annual payments. Even when payment terms were written in secret annexes to treaties or paid as a lump sum to avoid the appearance of an annual obligation, they were derided by Romans, as we have seen.

It was such an arrangement that shielded Justin in the early years of his reign. Justinian's treaty of 562 had committed to annual payments of 30,000 *solidi*, with a lump sum for the first seven years paid immediately in advance.[91] A further payment of 90,000 *solidi* should have been due in 568/69, but whether payments were ever started by Justin is not made clear in our sources.[92] What we do know is that in 572 a Persian embassy to Justin requested the commencement of annual payments of 30,000 *solidi* agreed by the treaty. Justin refused to honour the agreement. He lectured the Sāsānian ambassador Sebokht[93] that "a friendship secured by money was not good (for such a thing when bought was shameful and servile)".[94]

The toughening of the stance between 569 and 572 may well have been encouraged by geopolitical shifts. Menander wrote that the prospect of an alliance with Turks in Central Asia, which could enable the envelopment of the Sāsānian empire, was the consideration that "most encouraged" Justin to challenge Persia directly, a view shared by other writers.[95] Building on his refusal, Justin boasted that he was "confident that were he to make war, he would destroy Khosrow and himself give a king to the Persians" – a threat that would soon be shown to be empty.[96]

---

[89] Mi. Whitby 2021, 115–172.
[90] Payne 2013, 3–33. Also Canepa 2009, 22.
[91] Men. Prot. *fr.* 6.1.134–54. Turtledove 1983. Also Turtledove 1977.
[92] Mi. Whitby 1988, 251, and 2001, 88, argues that this must have been paid if war did not break out that year, but there is no positive evidence. Indeed, John of Epiphania, *Chron.* 3 = *FHG* IV.274 states that this embassy was sent at the conclusion of the advance payment; see Greatrex and Lieu 2002, 142 and 282.
[93] *PLRE* 3b (Sebochthes), 1119–20.
[94] Men. Prot. *fr.* 16.1.28–30: ἔφη τοιγαροῦν ὡς αὐτὸν ὡς ἡ φιλότης χρήμασι βεβαιουμένη οὐκ ἀγαθή (αἰσχρὰ γὰρ καὶ ἀνδραποδώδης ὠνητή τε ἡ τοιάδε) (trans. Blockley 1985a, 153).
[95] Men. Prot. *fr.* 13.5.2 μᾶλλον ἀναπτερῶσαν. See also John of Epiphania, *Chron.* 2 = *FHG* IV.273–4 in Greatrex and Lieu 2002, 141. Joh. Eph. *Hist. eccl.* 3.6.22.
[96] Men. Prot. *fr.* 16.1.53–55: θαρρεῖν τε ὡς, εἰ πρὸς πόλεμον ὁρμήσοι, καθελεῖ τε Χοσρόην

In these ways, Justin inherited a stable empire from Justinian and plunged it into war on multiple frontiers at once. By adopting the scathing criticism of Justinian's diplomatic manoeuvres and ruling out making diplomatic payments, whether to tribal kings or the Sāsānian *Šâhanšâh*, Justin dramatically destabilized East Roman foreign policy for short-term political gain at home. This was, it seems, very much Justin's own policy. While sources emphasized the partnership between Justin and Sophia, none attribute a direct role in these decisions to Sophia or give any reason to think she fully subscribed to her husband's views.

Sophia's Foreign Policy? (574–578)

As we have seen, Justin's hard-line refusal to honour treaties and pay subsidies brought an end to the stable system of foreign relations he had inherited from Justinian. By provoking direct confrontation with the Persians, Justin courted disaster. Any expectation that the Persian armies would be locked down on multiple fronts proved vain. For six decades the fortress of Dara had been the keystone of Roman defences in Mesopotamia and, after a major reconstruction under Justinian, it was believed to be impregnable.[97] Yet when Persian forces massed to besiege Dara in the autumn of 573, the Arab allies whom Justin had scorned did not arrive to the city's defence.[98] In November 573 the Persians overwhelmed the fort, allowing their forces to directly threaten the prosperous Roman Levant and thereby achieving an enormous strategic victory.

This military setback triggered a political crisis. The story given by several sources is that Justin experienced acute mental illness. In the view of Evagrius, this was directly triggered by the news from Dara:

> When Justin heard of these events, after such delusion and pretension he had no healthy or sane thoughts, nor did he endure what had happened like a mortal, but fell into mental disorder and madness, and thereafter had no understanding of events.[99]

For a critic like John of Ephesus, this was a fitting and divine punishment for Justin. John includes a lengthy account of how the emperor was reduced

καὶ αὐτὸς βασιλέα χειροτονήσοι Πέρσαις (trans. Blockley 1985a, 155).

[97] Procop. *Aed.* 2.1.14–21. Croke and Crow 1983. Croke 1984. Nicholson 1985. Keser-Kayaalp and Erdoğan 2017.

[98] Mi. Whitby 1988, 210–11.

[99] Evagr. *Hist. eccl.* 5.11: ἄπερ ἐπειδὴ ἠκηκόει ὁ Ἰουστῖνος, ἐκ τοσούτου τύφου καὶ ὄγκου οὐδὲν ὑγιὲς ἢ φρενῆρες ἐννοήσας οὐδὲ ἀνθρωπίνως τὸ συνενεχθὲν ἀνατλὰς ἐς φρενίτιδα νόσον καὶ μανίαν ἐμπίπτει, οὐδὲν λοιπὸν τῶν γιγνομένων συνείς (trans. Mi. Whitby 2001, 270). On Evagrius, see Allen 1981. This claim is backed by Men. Prot. *fr.* 18.1.1.

to being towed around the palace in a wagon, only soothed by constant organ music.[100] While Justin could have lucid moments – presiding over the appointment of Tiberius to Caesar in 574 and Augustus in 578 – our sources concur that he was unable to maintain a day-to-day role in the governance of the empire.

Had Justin died, a new emperor Augustus would have immediately arisen. With the emperor alive but incapacitated, the empress Augusta was left in an unusual position to act on the authority of her husband. Some sources, such as John of Epiphania, omit Sophia and imply Tiberius was immediately elevated to Caesar after Justin's collapse.[101] This was not the case: there was almost a full year between Justin's incapacitation in the winter of 573/74 and the appointment of Tiberius as Caesar in November 574.

At the other extreme, however, Gregory of Tours describes Sophia as having "assumed sole power".[102] While this was once accepted by Cameron and others working on Sophia, the value of Gregory's testimony about events in Constantinople has since been downgraded.[103] Most important, as Pfeilschifter has observed, is that there was no conception of an "empress regent" in the Late Roman Empire except for mothers of underage children.[104] There could not be "sole power", as Gregory suggested. Indeed, as per Justinian's *Digest*, it was "emperors [who] give the empress the same privileges as they have themselves";[105] that is to say, empresses held no authority independent of their emperor.[106] This makes the question of regency somewhat of a red herring: rather than focusing on the legal role, we should instead seek to evaluate the role that Sophia is attested to have played.

In our most reliable sources it is made clear that Sophia did step up to manage the empire's affairs, with the assistance of Tiberius, acting from his

---

[100] Joh. Eph. *Hist. eccl.* 3.3.2–5. For John's biases regarding Justin II, see van Ginkel 2020, 35–36.

[101] John of Epiphania, *Chron.* 5 = *FHG* IV.275–6 (trans. Greatrex and Lieu 2002, 151).

[102] Gregory of Tours, *Hist.* 5.19: *Cum autem Iustinus imperator, amisso sensu, amens effectus esset et per solam Sophiam augustam eius imperium regiretur, populi, ut in superiore libro iam diximus* (trans. Thorpe 1974, 283).

[103] Av. Cameron 1975c, 18–19. Garland 1999, 54–57. McClanan 2002, 157. See Pfeilschifter 2013, 142 n. 46 and Roggo, this volume, for further discussion.

[104] Pfeilschifter 2013, 495: "So etwas wie eine Regentschaft konnten Frauen nicht als Witwen oder Gattinnen erlangen. Sie vermochten es nur als Mütter unmündiger Kinder."

[105] *Dig.* 1.3.31: *Princeps legibus solutus est: Augusta autem licet legibus soluta non est, principes tamen eadem illi privilegia tribuunt, quae ipsi habent* (trans. Watson 1998, I 13).

[106] McCormick 1991, 694.

powerful position of *comes excubitorum*.[107] Even Menander describes how, at the outset of Justin's illness, "Tiberius and the empress Sophia were at a loss how to manage the war", acknowledging Sophia's role.[108] The relationship became increasingly fractious, but while Sophia is supposed to have criticized Tiberius's lavish donatives or where he housed his wife,[109] she is never reported as criticizing his foreign policy. Given, as we shall see, how dramatically the empire changed its position on the key question of foreign subsidies in the period from 574 to 578 and beyond, might she not have had good reason to? Had she indeed been the joint author of Justin's hard-line policy or, at the very least, felt any loyalty to it, such criticism would have been natural. Instead, Sophia is best understood to have taken an active role in undoing Justin's doctrine and restoring a pragmatic approach that owed much more to Justinian.

The first challenge faced following Justin's incapacitation was how to respond to the Sāsānian capture of Dara. This was eased by Khosrow's decision to send an embassy following the fall of the fortress; he sought to consolidate Persian gains and end the war on favourable terms. Sophia alone gave a formal audience to this embassy, not accompanied by Justin or Tiberius.[110] Moreover, she responded by sending a personal ambassador in her name back to the Sāsānian *Šâhanšâh*, who would be competent "to discuss all the points at dispute" towards reaching a ceasefire.[111]

The choice of ambassador was "one of the palace physicians", Zacharias.[112] Menander explicitly states that Zachariah was chosen and dispatched by Sophia.[113] The choice of a doctor was not as unusual as it might first seem. Of course, the palace doctor would have intimate contact and a direct relationship with the imperial couple.[114] The palace physicians were also senior administrative officers who ranked as senators.[115] It was an approach that had been well received on previous occasions: Khosrow's father Kavādh had formally requested the ministration of a Roman doctor in one episode of negotiations,[116] and Khosrow met doctor-ambassadors on

---

[107] Lin 2021, 128. Discussed further below.
[108] Men. Prot. *fr.* 18.1.2–4: ἐν ἀπόρῳ ἦσαν αὐτός τε Τιβέριος καὶ ἡ βασιλὶς Σοφία ὅπως διάθοιντο τὰ τῶν πολέμων (trans. Blockley 1985a, 157).
[109] See Roggo, this volume.
[110] Men. Prot. *fr.* 18.1.26–31.
[111] Men. Prot. *fr.* 18.1.29–30: καί ἀμφὶ τῶν ὁπωσοῦν κεκινημένων διαλεχθησόμενον (trans. Blockley 1985a, 159). See Nechaeva 2014, 107.
[112] Men. Prot. *fr.* 18.1.30–31: ἐν τοῖς βασιλείοις καταταττόμενος ἰατροῖς (trans. Blockley 1985a, 159). Also Men. Prot. *fr.* 18.2.1–2. *PLRE* 3b (Zacharias 2), 1411–12.
[113] Men. Prot. *fr.* 18.2.1–3.
[114] Blockley 1980, 94.
[115] Blockley 1980, 89–90, on palace physicians and 91–92 on Zacharias in particular.
[116] Procop. *Bell.* 2.31. Discussed in Blockley 1980, 89–90.

two occasions under Justinian.[117] However, it is clear that Zacharias was an important figure to Justin and Sophia, and indeed later to Tiberius.

Zacharias's task was to totally reverse the policy of Justin that had led to the war. While Sophia's husband had insisted that no Roman emperor would pay tribute to barbarians, her envoy carried 45,000 gold coins to buy a one-year truce, from 574 to 575.[118] The Sāsānians agreed, giving Sophia time to prepare a further embassy. The decision to pay for a truce has been criticized: Whitby calls it an act of "desperation".[119] Taken in the wider context of restoring a Justinianic approach to foreign policy, however, it seems far from desperate, but deliberate and considered.

This deferment also allowed the imperial court to stabilize. Had Justin have suffered a further decline in health without a clear successor, a political crisis would have consumed the court at a perilous moment. This risk was resolved with the appointment of a Caesar, whom by sixth-century convention would serve as the presumptive successor. The appointment of a favourable Caesar ought to have served Sophia's advantage, by offering a guarantee of longevity for her position beyond her ailing husband. The emperor alighted on Tiberius, apparently – according to John of Ephesus – on the "counsel of the queen".[120] Tiberius had long been an ally of the imperial couple.[121] Having served as *comes excubitorum*, commander of the imperial guard, in Justinian's last years,[122] Tiberius would have worked closely alongside, and perhaps under the direction of, Justin as *curopalates*.[123] The weight of the imperial guard was crucial to a smooth succession. Following Justin's accession, Tiberius continued as *comes excubitorum* alongside serving as a *magister militum*, in which role he campaigned on the Danube frontier and conducted negotiations with the Avars.[124] All in all, upon his appointment by Justin in December 574 he was well placed to assist with foreign policy.

In the winter of 574/75, the Romans moved to settle relations on the Danube and in Italy. The Romans and Avars agreed a treaty predicated on the payment of 80,000 *nomismata* (*solidi*) per annum,[125] reversing Justin's dramatic rejection of the Avar embassy in the first days of his reign. This decision acknowledged Avar hegemony over the north bank of the Danube, accepting it was better to return to diplomatic relations if the war could not

---

[117] Blockley 1980, 90–91.
[118] Men. Prot. *fr.* 18.2.1–5.
[119] Mi. Whitby 2001, 94.
[120] Joh. Eph. *Hist. eccl.* 3.3.5.
[121] Lin 2021, 128.
[122] Corippus, *Iust.* 1.212–25.
[123] Lin 2021, 128.
[124] Men. Prot. *fr.* 12.7.15–19.
[125] Men. Prot. *fr.* 15.5.1–6 and 27.3.27–29. See Pohl ²2018, 77–78.

be won. The political situation in Italy was different: in 574 the Lombard kingdom had split into multiple, competing duchies following the death of King Cleph,[126] who had succeeded Alboin upon the latter's assassination in 572.[127] After a dismal military expedition led by Baduarius,[128] Justin and Sophia's son-in-law, Tiberius tried two alternative approaches. Firstly, he sent the patrician Pamphronius[129] with "a large amount of gold, about thirty *centenaria*" (3,000 lbs of gold) to buy peace from Lombard dukes.[130] In a further passage, Menander attests to another embassy conveying gifts in 579, as a result of which "very many of the chiefs did accept the Emperor's generosity and came over to the Romans".[131] The second approach revived Justinian's frequent stratagem in the Gothic Wars: drawing the Franks into Italy to fight the Lombards.[132] The Frankish kingdom of Burgundy had emerged in 561 from the division of Merovingian territories.[133] They were persuaded to mount a campaign in 575 that imposed tribute on Lombard duchies in northern Italy.[134]

With Persia, the approach taken under Sophia was deepened. Tiberius recommissioned Zacharias as ambassador in late 574, this time accompanied by a senior senator, Trajan.[135] Menander specifically states that Tiberius and Zachariah reported back to Tiberius for instruction.[136] The Roman ambassadors offered a three-year truce, underwritten by 30,000 *nomismata* per year. While the Persians had sought a minimum term of five years, they ultimately agreed to the Roman proposal. The truce excluded Armenia, so fighting continued in the North.

This truce bought time to negotiate a full peace treaty. In early 575 Khosrow received an embassy led by the *silentarius* Theodore[137] seeking to progress talks. After accompanying Khosrow on an ill-fated attack on

---

[126] *PLRE* 3a (Cleph), 318–19.
[127] Wickham 1981, 28–32.
[128] *PLRE* 3a (Baduarius 2), 164–65. See Goffart 1957, 80–81.
[129] *PLRE* 3b (Pamphronius), 962–63.
[130] Men. Prot. *fr.* 22, 1–2: χρυσίον συχνὸν ἄχρι κεντηναρίων τριάκοντα (trans. Blockley 1985a, 197, amended by Dagnall).
[131] Men. Prot. *fr.* 24.10–15: τῶν ἡγουμένων τοῦ Λογγιβάρδων ἔθνους δεξιώσηται δώροις ὑποπείθων καὶ μεγίστας ἐπαγγελλόμενος χάριτας, ἤδη τε πλεῖστοι τῶν δυνατῶν μετετίθεντο ὡς Ῥωμαίους τὴν ἐκ τοῦ αὐτοκράτορος ὠφέλειαν προσδεχόμενοι (trans. Blockley 1985, 217).
[132] Goffart 1957, 75–77. Sarantis 2018, 7–8. Reimitz 2019.
[133] Wood 1994, 55–57.
[134] Fredegar, *Chron.* 45. Discussed by Goffart 1957, 82. See Fisher 2019.
[135] *PLRE* 3b (Traianus 3), 1334. Evagr. *Hist. eccl.* 5.12. Men. Prot. *fr.* 18.3 and 18.4. Blockley 1980, 92. For dates, see Greatrex and Lieu 2002, 285.
[136] Men. Prot. *fr.* 18.4.1–2.
[137] *PLRE* 3b (Theodorus 33), 1254–55.

Roman-aligned Armenia, which had been excluded from the previous truce, Theodore returned to Constantinople to convey that the Persians wished to enter full peace talks. A further embassy was dispatched for this purpose in 576 led by Justin's former *magister officiorum*, the patrician Theodore,[138] and accompanied by the doctor Zacharias and the senators John[139] and Peter.[140] The Persian negotiator Mebodes[141] sought a return to annual payments of 30,000 *solidi* amongst other measures, but during negotiations he withdrew that demand and conceded "that peace must come on equal terms".[142] Instead the Romans recognized Persian suzerainty over Eastern Armenia and Iberia, while their ambition to buy back Dara was never concluded.[143] The ultimate conclusion of a peace treaty without payments was the fruit of the pragmatism of Sophia and Tiberius, in contrast to Justin's bellicose dogmatism.

Indeed, as we have seen, such an approach bore fruit across the empire. Money bought ceasefires in the East, while an annual subsidy was also agreed with the very Avars whom Justin had humiliated in court. An embassy was sent with money to Italy, to seek allies amongst Lombard dukes or Frankish kings. Roman ambassadors maintained a preference to make deals without subsidies, even at the expense of territorial concessions, as in the case of negotiations with Persia in 576/77. However, the willingness to concede subsidies or one-off payments as necessary demonstrates that foreign policy in the period 574–578 reflected far more the legacy of Justinian than it did the agenda set by Justin.

Although Sophia was to maintain her title of empress Augusta until her last recorded mention in 601,[144] she became politically marginalized after her husband's death in 578. Her claim to pre-eminence was compromised when Tiberius's wife Ino,[145] taking the regal name Aelia Anastasia, took the title empress Augusta as well.[146] In policy terms, however, both Tiberius and his successor Maurice showed continuity with the course charted under Sophia, rather than the dogmatic approach of Justin. It is true they still regarded the idea of 'tribute' as poisonous. Even during the talks with the Persians in 576, Tiberius insisted that "this could not be called a peace if the Persians hoped to receive payment from the Romans and to have

---

[138] *PLRE* 3b (Theodorus 34), 1254–56.
[139] *PLRE* 3a (Ioannes 90), 676–77. John was the empress Theodora's grandson.
[140] *PLRE* 3b (Petrus 17), 1003.
[141] *PLRE* 3b (Mebodes 2), 868–70.
[142] Men. Prot. *fr.* 20.2.79–80: περὶ μὲν οὖν τοῦ χρῆναι ἐξ ἰσοτιμίας τὴν εἰρήνην προελθεῖν (trans. Blockley 1985a, 187).
[143] Men. Prot. *fr.* 20.2.68–78. Mi. Whitby 1988, 219.
[144] Theoph. Conf. AM. 6093.
[145] *PLRE* 3a (Ino), 622, and (Aelia Anastasia 2), 60–61.
[146] For Sophia and Ino's relationship, see Roggo, this volume.

them as tributaries, as it were".[147] This position was reprised when Tiberius negotiated with the Persians in 578.[148] Yet despite expressing this view, both men eschewed the dogmatic position of Justin for the pragmatic approach that Sophia had reinstituted. The emperors made payments to the Avars for peace,[149] and to the Franks in a failed attempt to lure them to Italy.[150] This is significant: it shows Justin's attempt to mark a clear break with Justinian's system of subsidies had been undone by Sophia's diplomacy.

Given this change of policy, it seems impossible to conclude that Sophia had co-authored Justin's hard-line policy of non-payment of subsidies from 565 to 573. Her readiness to abandon this principle makes it seem likely that Sophia harboured doubts about her husband's approach. Why would this be? Perhaps an empress was less beguiled by the sabre-rattling of intellectuals safely ensconced in Constantinople. However, we should not read too much into a gender distinction and follow the chauvinistic primary sources which disparage Sophia (just like they had disparaged Theodora). The use of religious missions or subsidy payments was not to resort to 'softer' options than military might, but to pursue alternative stratagems of imperial expansion. The empresses were just as committed imperialists: they sought to achieve Roman aims by exploiting the religious and fiscal hegemony of the empire instead of raw force. Moreover, while Justin's uncompromising approach was a radical break, it was Sophia who oversaw a return to more traditional imperial foreign policy.

Conclusion

Previous studies have, either sympathetically or chauvinistically, implied that Sophia was the mastermind behind Justin's disastrous policies. The corollary of this interpretation is that she must have shared the dogmatic rejection of 'tribute' attributed to her husband. In contrast, I have argued that the rapid retreat from Justin's approach during Sophia's regency and the return to paying for peace must be taken as evidence that, at the very least, she did not share such hard-line views. In the crucial year of 574, between the onset of Justin's illness and the appointment of Tiberius as Caesar, Sophia personally engaged in diplomatic relations to restore

---

[147] Men. Prot. *fr.* 20.2.15: αὐτίκε οἵγε τοῦτο αὐτὸ οὐδὲ τοὔνομα προσίεσθαι ἔφασαω τῆς εἰρήνης, εἴπερ ἐπὶ συντελείᾳ τινὶ καὶ ἅτε ἐς φόρου ἀπαγωγὴν Πέρσαι ἐλπίζοιεν Ῥωμαίους ἕξειν τοῦ λοιποῦ (trans. Blockley 1985a, 183).
[148] Men. Prot. *fr.* 26.1.25–34.
[149] For the years 582–84 see Men. Prot. *fr.* 27.3; for 575–97 see Theophylact, *Hist.* 1.3.7 and 1.5.4–6; for 598–603 see Theophylact, *Hist.* 7.15. Discussed by Pohl ²2018, 163–98.
[150] To Childebert II, king of Austrasia in 584, 585, and 590. See *PLRE* 3a (Childebertus 2), 287–91, and Wood 1994, 167–68.

subsidies and bring about a truce with Persia. The Sāsānian ambassador was received in her audience, and she sent a senior palace official to negotiate and carry correspondence in her name. These actions were not unprecedented: her own aunt, the empress Theodora, had also engaged in diplomacy to supplement, and sometimes undermine, Justinian's strategy. In the period after Justin's death, Sophia was marginalized by Tiberius and Maurice, but the approach she had re-established was nonetheless preferred to that of Justin.

These arguments underline the value and opportunities of studying Late Antique empresses. Sophia has been shown to have had agency, not necessarily sharing the views of her husband, and to be worthy of study in her own right. Re-evaluating Sophia in this way thus changes the narrative of foreign policy in the 570s. Therefore, the study of empresses can be shown to be of interest not only for its own sake, but also to help answer the broad questions of foreign policy in Late Antiquity that we continue to debate.

Acknowledgements

My thanks to Silvio Roggo for his assistance with the Syriac quotations and to the editors for their helpful advice. The research for this chapter was supported by UKRI via the White Rose College of the Arts and Humanities, under grant AH/L503848/1.

An Open Access version of this chapter will be available on the Liverpool University Press website.

6

Dynasty, Endogamy, and Civil Strife: Martina Augusta and the Role of Imperial Women in the Early Seventh Century

Nadine Viermann

After this [i.e., the burial of the emperor Herakleios] the Augusta Martina summoned the archpriest Pyrrhos and the dignitaries of the court, and having gathered the people of Byzantium in an assembly, showed the testament of Herakleios and the provisions he had made concerning herself and her children. All the people who were present clamored for Emperors Constantine and Herakleios; so she brought them out while expressing her claim that she, as empress, would have the first place in the empire. But some of the people present cried to her: 'You have the honor due to the mother of the emperors, but they that of our emperors and lords!' They paid particular respect to Constantine because, by reason of his seniority, he was first to have been appointed emperor when he was still a child. 'Nor can you, O Lady,' they said, 'receive barbarian or ⟨other⟩ foreign ⟨emissaries⟩ who come to the palace or hold converse with them. May God forbid that the Roman State should come to such a pass.' And they came down ⟨from their seats⟩ acclaiming the emperors. When ⟨Martina⟩ had heard these things, she withdrew to her palace.[1]

---

[1] Nik. *Brev.* 28: Μετὰ τοῦτο Μαρτῖνα ἡ Αὐγούστα προσκαλεῖται Πύρρον τὸν ἀρχιερέα καὶ τοὺς βασιλικοὺς ἄρχοντας, ἐκκλησιάσασα καὶ τὸν περὶ τὸ Βυζάντιον λαόν, τάς τε διαθήκας Ἡρακλείου ὑπεδείκνυ, ὡς περὶ αὐτῆς καὶ τῶν τέκνων διέθετο. ὁ δὲ παρὼν ἅπας δῆμος Κωνσταντῖνον καὶ Ἡράκλειον τοὺς βασιλεῖς ἐπεζήτει· ἡ δὲ ἦγεν αὐτούς, καὶ ἅμα διελέγετο νομίζουσα ἅτε βασίλισσα τὰ πρῶτα εἰς τὴν βασιλείαν φέρεσθαι. τινὲς δὲ τοῦ συνεστῶτος λαοῦ ἀνεφώνουν πρὸς αὐτὴν ὅτι "σὺ μὲν τιμὴν ἔχεις ὡς μήτηρ βασιλέων, οὗτοι δὲ ὡς βασιλεῖς καὶ δεσπόται". ἐξαίρετον δὲ ἐδίδουν γέρας Κωνσταντίνῳ ὡς πρώτῳ εἰς τὴν βασιλείαν κατὰ τὴν ἡλικίαν ἐκ παιδὸς προχειρισθέντι. "οὐδὲ γὰρ βαρβάρων ἢ ἀλλοφύλων πρὸς τὰ βασίλεια εἰσερχομένων, ὦ δέσποινα," ἔφασκον, "δύνασαι ὑποδέχεσθαι ἢ λόγοις ἀμείβεσθαι· μηδὲ δοίη θεὸς ἐν τούτῳ τάξεως τὴν Ῥωμαϊκὴν ἐλθεῖν πολιτείαν". καὶ κατήρχοντο ἀνευφημοῦντες τοὺς βασιλεῖς. ταῦτα ἀκούσασα πρὸς τὸ ἑαυτῆς ὑπεχώρει παλάτιον (trans. Mango 1990b).

This passage from Nicephorus' *Short History* relates a crucial moment in the political history of the East Roman Empire. In early 641, the emperor Heraclius died after having ruled for more than thirty years, leaving behind his second wife, the Augusta Martina, and children from his first and second marriage, two of whom, the above-mentioned half-brothers Constantine (i.e., Heraclius Constantine) and Heraclius (i.e., Heraclonas), held the rank of Augustus. What becomes evident from Nicephorus' account is that after Heraclius' death, imperial succession was all but clear. Not only were there several contenders for precedence in the imperial college, but also a number of political and religious actors and interest groups involved in the negotiations. The year 641 saw the coronation of two further Augusti and ended with the overthrow of Martina and her sons, leaving Heraclius' grandson from his first marriage, Constans II, as sole emperor in Constantinople.[2]

This chapter assesses Martina's role at a time when Constantinople was facing internal and external insecurities. While the Muslim Arabs, who had started expanding into territories formerly held by the Romans in the 630s, were at the brink of taking over Egypt, the situation in the capital was further destabilized due to recurrent unrest and civil strife. Nicephorus' account, as well as other primary evidence, suggests that Martina was actively involved in the negotiations that followed her husband's death, trying to secure her own and her children's position in opposition to the other family line, the offspring of Heraclius' first marriage. Her involvement, however, needs to be read against the backdrop of male-dominated political structures in which imperial women usually played subordinate and passive roles as wives and mothers. Based on an analysis of the strategies that shaped the Heraclian dynasty, including the role of imperial women and the rationale behind marriage politics, I explore how Martina sought to navigate the contest for political power, her network within and beyond Constantinople, and her relation to the relevant interest groups. This analysis will not only shed light on the political dynamics that shaped the early seventh century, but also flesh out the set of norms and expectations that female members of the imperial family were subjected to, and the extent to which they could (or could not) impact the struggle around imperial rule in a patriarchal society.

---

[2] For the succession crisis of 641, see Stratos 1972, 175–205. Kaegi 1981, 154–57. Treadgold 1990 (with a reconstruction of the timeline). Cosentino 2021. For Heraclius' reign in general see Viermann 2021. Kaegi 2003. Cf. Raum 2021, whose analysis only goes up to 630.

Niece and Wife: Martina in the Heraclian Dynasty

After the premature death of his first wife Eudocia in 612, Heraclius married Martina, the daughter of his sister, who would become a contested figure, triggering controversy in both (near-)contemporary sources and modern historiography.[3] By marrying his niece, Heraclius acted against Roman law which explicitly banned this kind of incestuous connection.[4] The extent to which there was opposition against the marriage from the start is difficult to determine;[5] what seems clear, at least, is that when Heraclius' position was weakened due to military losses against the Arabs and a failing religious policy in the later years of his reign, criticism of his connection to Martina became a means to challenge his position.[6] The stigma of being an illegitimate consort tainted Martina's public image during the above-mentioned succession crisis and had a negative impact on her legacy.

Before exploring the dynamics of events in 641, the question of why Heraclius decided to break Roman law and risk public opposition by marrying his niece needs to be addressed. The approach taken in this chapter does not focus on potential personal reasons but suggests that Heraclius acted out of a political rationale which becomes evident when considering his dynastic policies in general.

The Roman monarchy had no institutionalized order of succession; amidst a range of factors that impacted the question of who would become emperor, dynastic connections played an important role but could be trumped by a contender who managed to galvanize the necessary support based on, for example, military achievement.[7] As the eastern Roman emperors settled in Constantinople from ca. 400 onwards, the city's populace and elites became a crucial political factor in negotiating imperial succession.[8] This was still the case in the early seventh century. When Heraclius came to power in 610 by overthrowing Phocas, who had

---

[3] On Martina, see Garland 1999, 63–72.

[4] For the legal aspects, see Boudignon 2011.

[5] Nik. *Brev.* 11 relates that Heraclius married Martina despite the patriarch Sergius and the circus factions condemning the wedding, but the question remains to what extent Nicephorus, or his sources, projected later criticism back onto the time of the wedding. A contemporary source is an appendix to Antiochos Strategos' account of the siege of Jerusalem by the Persians (Conybeare 1910, 516); however, the transmission history of this source is highly problematic.

[6] For more criticism of Heraclius' marriage, see Nik. *Brev.* 20. Mich. Syr. 11.3a (Chabot 1901, 410). *Chron. 1234*, 98 (Chabot 1916, 182–83).

[7] For monarchic succession in the Roman Empire, see Humphries 2019a. Börm 2015a.

[8] For the sedentary monarchy in Constantinople, see Pfeilschifter 2013. Diefenbach 1996.

lost the backing of the metropolitan interest groups, his main challenge was to build a more stable rule; in a highly charged political climate, shaped by outbursts of civil strife and exacerbated by foreign threats, Heraclius had to find ways to root his position within the capital as well as the military sphere in order to curb potential contenders.[9]

One means to this end was for Heraclius to explicitly promote his family from very early on in his reign.[10] The Augusta Eudocia gave birth to two children, a girl and a boy, both of whom were invested with the highest imperial honours at a remarkably young age. The daughter, Epiphania, was made Augusta in October 612, aged 1,[11] and the son, Heraclius Constantine, Augustus in January 613, not even 1 year old.[12] That a Roman emperor should elevate his son at a young age was not uncommon; this way of strengthening the ruling dynasty and designating an heir had been a well-established practice for centuries.[13] In Late Antique Constantinople, however, this practice had decreased in relevance, as so few emperors produced sons. After the death of Theodosius II in 450, the only instance of a male heir being made Augustus throughout the fifth century was the coronation of Leo II, aged 6, by his grandfather Leo I in 473.[14] It was not until the late sixth century that the practice of making an infant son Augustus was reassumed: Maurice, who was the first emperor in more than a century to have not just one but several sons who survived childhood, elevated his firstborn, Theodosius, in 590.[15]

While the elevation of Heraclius' children is not entirely surprising in this context, the remarkably young age, the specific circumstances, as well as the clarity with which Heraclius communicated his actions, are noteworthy. Starting with the year of Heraclius Constantine's coronation, the obverse of all newly minted coins bore the portraits of the two Augusti, father and son, emphasizing dynastic unity and promoting the designated successor.[16] The date of Heraclius Constantine's elevation, right before Heraclius left Constantinople to lead the Roman army against the Persians,

---

[9] For Heraclius' usurpation, see Stratos 1968, 80–91. Olster 1993, 117–38. Kaegi 2003, 37–52. Roberto 2010. Pfeilschifter 2013, 584–605. Viermann 2021, 93–104.
[10] Humphries 2019b. Cosentino 2021, 274.
[11] *Chron. Pasch.* s.a. 612. Theoph. Conf. AM 6104 (De Boor 1883, 300).
[12] *Chron. Pasch.* s.a. 613; Theoph. Conf. AM 6104 (De Boor 1883, 300) with a different date.
[13] Humphries 2019a, 17–22; on the imperial college created by Heraclius throughout his reign, see Humphries 2019b, 31–33.
[14] *PLRE* 2 (Leo 7).
[15] *Chron. Pasch.* s.a. 590. Theoph. Conf. AM 6082 (De Boor 1883, 267). *PLRE* 3b (Theodosius 13).
[16] For Heraclius' coins see DOC II/1, 216–21, pl. 8–22 and *MIB* III, 83–122, pl. 1–19; cf. Olster 1982, Viermann 2021, 165–70, and Gkantzios Drápelová, this volume.

was deliberately chosen.[17] By taking up personal command, Heraclius broke with imperial precedent (for more than two centuries, emperors had remained in the capital instead of leading the armies) and risked alienating the metropolitan environment that was crucial for the stability of his rule.[18] With Heraclius Constantine, co-Augustus to his father, an emperor was left in Constantinople to represent the Heraclian family and, despite his young age, take on the emperor's ceremonial function.[19]

In a similar vein, Heraclius' decision to marry his niece Martina should be seen as an attempt to strengthen the emperor's position. Throughout the centuries of Roman monarchy, marriage politics had been a crucial instrument of forming alliances between families, asserting political influence, and displaying power structures. The same applies to Constantinople in Late Antiquity: when it was not possible to pass on imperial rule from father to son, or within the family, marriage was a means of legitimizing a candidate after an emperor's death. This was the case for Marcian, who married Theodosius' sister Pulcheria, or for Anastasius, who married Zeno's widow Ariadne.[20] Marrying into the imperial family, however, also became a means for powerful political stakeholders to position themselves for imperial succession during an emperor's lifetime.[21] It was mainly military men who had the means to pressure the emperor into including them, or their offspring, into their family; in some cases, this coincided with being bestowed with the rank of Caesar or even Augustus, equivalent to being designated successor. This was the case, for example, for Patricius, son of the Alan general Aspar, who married Leo's daughter Leontia and was made Caesar in 470.[22] The only way Leo could emancipate himself from Alan influence, and break free from Aspar and Patricius, was to promote Isaurian contingents in Constantinople and marry his other daughter Ariadne to their leader Zeno, who eventually succeeded him on the throne.[23] In 582, the successful general Maurice married Tiberius' daughter Constantina, was crowned Caesar and later Augustus, succeeding his father-in-law after his death.[24] Phocas honoured

---

Maurice's son Tiberius only appeared on the reverse of coins from Chersonesos, see Olster 1982, 400–401; *MIB* II, 74–75, pl. 28.

[17] This connection is made explicit by Sebeos 34 (Thomson and Howard-Johnston 1999, I 57–58).

[18] See n. 8 and 9 above; for Heraclius' break with established patterns, see Viermann 2021, 138–75.

[19] For Heraclius Constantine cf. Hächler 2022.

[20] Herrin 2013, 174. Croke 2015b. Humphries 2019a, 22.

[21] Croke 2015b describes this phenomenon as "ties of blood and office" (110); Viermann 2021, 60–61.

[22] *PLRE* 2 (Iulius Patricius 15).

[23] Croke 2005. 2015b, 106–10.

[24] *PLRE* 3b (Fl. Mauricius Tiberius 4).

one of his leading generals, Priscus, by marrying him to his daughter Domentzia in 607 – a gesture that the people of Constantinople understood as designation for imperial succession.[25]

Having overthrown Phocas, Heraclius not only promoted family members to the highest military offices to create a loyal surrounding,[26] but also pursued an endogamous marriage strategy that was meant, I argue, to prevent ambitious men from marrying their offspring into the imperial family and thus potentially impacting succession.[27] In fact, Heraclius' marriage to Martina was not the only endogamous connection within the family. In 613, Heraclius engaged his infant son Heraclius Constantine to the daughter of his cousin Nicetas, Gregoria; the couple was married in 630.[28] Although in this case the degree of kinship was not close enough to trigger controversies, it indicates Heraclius' attempts to weave a tightly knit family network. In this context, it is also relevant that Heraclius' firstborn daughter Epiphania was not married to a Roman nobleman but promised as wife to the Turkish *khagan* with whom Heraclius intended to form an alliance against the Sāsānians.[29] The agreement fell through only due to the *khagan*'s untimely death. Some years later, Heraclius betrothed children of his to the offspring of the Sāsānian general Shahrbaraz, whom he supported in an attempt to overthrow the weak Sāsānian heir to the Persian throne.[30] Apart from forming strong diplomatic bonds which were needed at a time of substantial geopolitical shifts, this practice had the further advantage that the (potential) spouses or their families did not have the same stakes in, or influence on, Roman imperial succession as high-achieving Roman officials.

Heraclius' decision to marry Martina is thus in line with the marriage policies he implemented on a broader scale, aiming to stabilizing his dynasty. What remains unclear is when exactly the wedding took place.[31] Theophanes Confessor's *Chronographia* is the only source to give a concrete year, mentioning

---

[25] *PLRE* 3b (Priscus 6).
[26] Most explicitly his cousin Niketas: *PLRE* 3b (Niketas 7). For further family members, see Viermann 2021, 160–62.
[27] Viermann 2021, 171–75. Cf. Cosentino 2021, 284–85.
[28] Nik. *Brev.* 5 (engagement); 17 (wedding). These were not the first instances of endogamous weddings in Roman imperial families: Claudius had married his niece Agrippina, which was condemned by Suet. *Caes.* 5.39. In 437, Theodosius II had married his daughter Licinia Eudoxia to his cousin Valentinian III; see Herrin 2013, 305.
[29] Nik. *Brev.* 12. Zuckerman 1995, esp. 117. Herrin 2013, 302; 308. For diplomacy between Romans and non-Romans through marriage connections, see Croke 2015b; on Heraclius' alliance with the Turks, see Howard-Johnston 2021, 295–304.
[30] Nik. *Brev.* 17. Mango 1985, 105–106. Cf. Howard-Johnston 2021, 336–46.
[31] For a detailed discussion, see Cosentino 2021, 274–80.

the wedding and Martina's coronation in his entry that corresponds to 613/14 CE.[32] However, the dating is complicated by Nicephorus, who does not give an exact date but relates an account of the wedding in the wake of Heraclius' counteroffensive against Persia in 624, nearly a decade later.[33] In both Theophanes and Nicephorus, there are at times serious problems with chronology so that one cannot generally prioritize one over the other. As further evidence, we can draw on a set of bronze coins, issued between 615/16 and 628/29: next to two male figures, the Augusti Heraclius and Heraclius Constantine, these coins' obverses show a crowned female figure whose identity is disputed.[34] Scholars are divided between identifying her as either Heraclius' daughter Epiphania, Augusta since 612, or his second wife Martina, the latter of which would imply Theophanes' early date for the wedding.[35] From a numismatic perspective, identifying the female figure as Martina seems more likely, as depicting the emperor's spouse on copper coins next to her husband had become common in the late sixth century, ever since Justin II included his wife, Sophia.[36] While including the emperor's daughter would have been unconventional, depicting his wife on bronze coins was in line with established practice.[37] Based on this evidence, an early date for the wedding becomes more plausible. Aiming to build a strong dynasty and to wall off his family against external influence, Heraclius seems to not have waited long before re-marrying.

In the sources for Heraclius' reign, Martina does not make much of an appearance apart from the above-mentioned hints about the controversies surrounding the marriage, her accompanying Heraclius on some of his travels to the East, and her bearing several children, some of which were disabled.[38] In 626, Martina gave birth to a healthy son, who went by the name Heraclius, dubbed Heraclonas by our authors, and was made Caesar in 632.[39] In 638, after Heraclius had returned from the disastrous campaign

---

[32] Theoph. Conf. AM 6105 (De Boor 1883, 300).
[33] Nik. *Brev.* 11; cf. *Chron. 1234*, 98–99 (Chabot 1916, 182–83). Mich. Syr. 11.3a (Chabot 1901, 410).
[34] *MIB* III, pl. 11, n. 161–62; DOC II/1, 226–27 with pl. 12, n. 90a.1–96; see Gkantzios Drápelová, this volume.
[35] For Martina and an early date, see Grierson in *DOC* II/1, 227. Olster 1982, 401. Whitby and Whitby 1989, 167 n. 452. Garland 1999, 62. Viermann 2021, 174. Cosentino 2021, 280. For Epiphania and a later date, see Mango 1990b, 79–80. Zuckerman 1995. Speck 1997. Kaegi 2003, 106.
[36] See Gkantzios Drápelová, this volume.
[37] Olster 1982. Viermann 2021, 165–70.
[38] On Martina, see Garland 1999, 63–72; on their children, see Cosentino 2021, 278–79.
[39] For the elevation, see Theoph. Conf. AM 6108 (De Boor 1883, 301), who dates it to the wrong indiction cycle; cf. Mango and Scott 1997, 433 n. 2, and Nik. *Brev.* 19.

against the expanding Muslim Arabs in Palestine and Syria, he elevated Heraclonas to the rank of Augustus.[40] As the lustre of Heraclius' success against the Sāsānians faded,[41] he seems to have felt the need to revert to the time-proven strategy of strengthening his family in times of crisis, this time positioning the offspring from his second marriage for imperial succession as well. This setting (several sons being crowned Augustus), however, would be the trigger for the 641-succession crisis.

According to Nicephorus, Heraclius decreed in his testament "that his sons Constantine and Herakleios were to be emperors of equal rank and his wife Martina was to be honored by them as mother and empress".[42] Several sons succeeding their father as emperors – as expressed here – was an established practice in Late Antiquity; it had been the mode of succession, for example, for Constantine I and Theodosius I, whose sons took responsibility over distinct parts of the empire.[43] According to Theophylact Simocattes, the emperor Maurice stated in his testament that he wanted his firstborn Theodosius to reign in Constantinople, his second son Tiberius as emperor in Old Rome, and his younger sons to govern the rest of the Roman realm, which would have meant a return to a tetrarchic form of government modelled on fourth-century patterns.[44] However, how this would have played out in practice remains an open question, as the entire imperial family was murdered during the coup of 602.[45] In contrast to Maurice's plan, we find no hint of a geographical assignment of the Augusti in Heraclius' will. Constantinople was indeed used to hosting several Augusti, usually a senior who was the *auctor imperii* of his junior partner; however, with the two half-brothers Heraclius Constantine and Heraclonas the hierarchy was not as clear-cut. After Heraclius' death, it quickly materialized that having two Augusti "of equal rank" in Constantinople was not a sustainable solution.

---

[40] Nik. *Brev.* 25. *De cer.* 2.27. Heraclius also made his younger sons David and Martinus Caesar, and his daughters Augustina and Martina Augusta: Nik. *Brev.* 27 and *De cer.* 2.29.

[41] For the Arab expansion and the consequences on the Roman Empire, see Kaegi 2003, 229–99.

[42] Nik. *Brev.* 27: ὥστε Κωνσταντῖνον καὶ Ἡράκλειον τοὺς υἱοὺς αὐτοῦ βασιλεῖς ἰσοτίμους εἶναι, καὶ Μαρτῖναν τὴν αὐτοῦ γυναῖκα τιμᾶσθαι παρ' αὐτῶν ὡς μητέρα καὶ βασίλισσαν (trans. Mango 1990b).

[43] Humphries 2019a, 17–22.

[44] Theophylact, *Hist.* 8.11.7–10.

[45] For the coup, see Mi. Whitby 1988, 24–27; 165–69. Olster 1993, 53–57. Pfeilschifter 2013, 261–69. Viermann 2021, 80–93.

Martina in the Succession Crisis of 641

Judging from Nicephorus' account quoted at the beginning of this chapter, which seems to be based on a seventh-century source,[46] Martina entered the political spotlight after her husband's death by convening Constantinople's relevant stakeholders and interest groups: the patriarch Pyrrhus, "the dignitaries of the court", i.e., the highest officeholders, and "the people of Byzantium". Nicephorus does not specify where exactly the assembly took place, but the fact that the account closes with Martina withdrawing "to her palace" indicates that it happened in a more public space. In early seventh-century Constantinople, the prime assembly venue in which the imperial family would meet the broader strata of the city's populace was still the hippodrome where Heraclius himself, in 610, had closed off his accession festivities with horse races.[47] More than thirty years later, when Martina sought to assert her own authority – she not just supported her underage son Heraclonas, but insisted on "the first place in the empire" for herself – she most likely claimed the space that was crucially linked to imperial power, the imperial box of the hippodrome.[48]

This gesture, however, did not have the desired effect as the response by the assembly to Martina's foray was negative. The fact that she was left with no option but to concede to popular will and accept the primacy of her stepson Heraclius Constantine, whose authority was based on having been co-emperor for almost two decades, serves as evidence for how impactful the urban interest groups were in processes of political decision making; without their consent, Martina could not rule. Furthermore, Nicephorus' account is clear about what kind of power empresses were allowed to strive for and what was considered out of their reach: they were relevant to sustain a dynasty but were not granted any kind of 'official' political role, like receiving emissaries.[49]

---

[46] For Nicephorus' sources, see Mango 1990b, 12–14. Howard-Johnston 2010, 244–50. Zuckerman 2013a, 206–209, followed by Booth 2016 and Boudignon 2021, suggests attributing the source to the patriarch Pyrrhus or his circle. This is based on the idea that Pyrrhus, when preparing his return to Constantinople after having been exiled, felt the need to cover up his close connection to Martina and Heraclonas to appeal to their successor Constans II; see Booth 2016, 518–19.

[47] *Chron. Pasch.* s.a. 610; the same goes for Phocas, see *Chron. Pasch.* s.a. 602. For the hippodrome as political space, see Av. Cameron 1976b, 157–92. Viermann 2021, 122–23.

[48] The Augusta Ariadne had appeared in the hippodrome after her husband Zeno's death, see *De cer.* 1.92.

[49] Although it is believed that Nicephorus took this passage from a mid-seventh-century source (n. 46), the explicit disapproval of an empress' involvement in foreign policy might be read as a reference to the author's contemporary, the empress Irene, who

Despite the strong resistance Martina faced within Constantinople, she could draw on a network of supporters who were determined to implement the late Heraclius' will in honouring Martina and her offspring. One of Martina's allies was Pyrrhus, patriarch of Constantinople since 638. Just like his predecessor Sergius, Pyrrhus sustained a strong bond with the imperial family, Heraclius in particular, who, according to Nicephorus, considered the clergyman his brother.[50] After the emperor's death, his alliance with the patriarch seems to have passed on to Martina. Nicephorus informs us that Heraclius, anticipating the potentially difficult situation Martina would find herself in after his death, entrusted Pyrrhus with funds that were meant to support the empress.[51] The patriarch's influence, however, was limited. Against his will, Pyrrhus had to surrender the money to the treasurer Philagrius,[52] who used the funds to strengthen Heraclius Constantine's position against his stepmother. Because of his ill health, Heraclius Constantine arranged generous payments to the Roman field army in Asia Minor to guarantee support for his infant son Constans, born in 630, in case of his own demise.[53] Papyrological evidence adds further detail to our understanding of this situation as its dating formula suggests that Heraclius Constantine elevated his son to the rank of Caesar.[54]

Heraclius Constantine indeed died in May 641,[55] leaving Heraclonas, aged 15, as sole emperor. Judith Herrin has pointed out that empresses could "enhance their powers through guardianship over their sons after they suffer widowhood".[56] And indeed, Nicephorus states that Heraclonas "shared the administration of the empire with his mother",[57] supporting the idea that the dowager empress indeed possessed political agency. With

---

acted as regent for, and finally co-ruler with her son, Constantine VI, from 780 to 797 (with a brief interruption), and as sole ruler from 797 to 802; see Mango 1990b, 8, with further references. This, however, is based on the question of when to date the composition and redaction of the *Short History*; cf. Mango 1990b, 8–12, and Howard-Johnston 2010, 238–44. For empresses and foreign policy, see James 2001b, 69–70, as well as Dagnall, this volume.

[50] Nik. *Brev.* 26: Heraclius' sister was Pyrrhus' godmother. For Pyrrhus, see Van Dieten 1972, 57–75. *PMBZ* #6386. For the importance of a strong bond between emperor and patriarch, see Viermann 2021, 184–85.
[51] Nik. *Brev.* 29.
[52] *PLRE* 3b (Philagrius 3).
[53] Nik. *Brev.* 29.
[54] Zuckerman 2010, 869–74. If we follow Zuckerman's reconstruction, the dating formula grants precedence to Constans over his step-uncles David and Martinus who already held the rank of Caesar (see n. 40 above).
[55] Theoph. Conf. AM 6132 (De Boor 1883, 341); cf. Mango 1990b, 192.
[56] Herrin 2013, 181.
[57] Nik. *Brev.* 30: ᾧ συνελάμβανεν εἰς τὰ τῆς βασιλείας πράγματα καὶ ἡ μήτηρ Μαρτῖνα (trans. Mango 1990b).

Heraclius Constantine out of the way, the new regime sought to strengthen alliances and restructure political hierarchies in the capital, exiling the late emperor's henchmen such as the aforementioned treasurer Philagrius,[58] and – as the dating formula of another papyri suggests – demoting Constans from the rank of Caesar.[59] After Heraclius Constantine had allied himself with the army stationed in Asia Minor, Martina likewise sought military support to bolster her position; according to John of Nikiu, she brought Thracian contingents into the capital.[60]

In Late Antique Constantinople, it was not unheard of for emperors to rally support from military units. This had been particularly common in the fifth century, when emperors formed alliances with Gothic, Alan, and Isaurian troops to strengthen their position – sometimes to the extent that military units were stationed within the capital, as had been the case with the commander Gainas during Arcadius' reign.[61] In the 640s – at a time when the army had regained much of its importance in negotiating the imperial position[62] – opposing factions in the capital drew on different contingents. As dowager empress, Martina actively furthered the trend of garrisoning Constantinople; John of Nikiu has one of the protagonists of the 641-struggle uttering that "Martina's strength lies in the fighting men which are with her and her sons."[63]

This *Chronicle* of John of Nikiu also gives further information on Martina's network. Written in Coptic in seventh-century Egypt, the text comes down to us only in an Ethiopic translation from a lost Arabic intermediary.[64] Phil Booth has argued convincingly that parts of the text were interpolated at a later point from a Constantinopolitan source and that, despite the difficult transmission history, they bear genuine information on the events of 641.[65] This evidence connects Martina to Cyrus, patriarch of Alexandria, who had been appointed in 630/31 but, after initial successes in solving doctrinal rifts amongst Egypt's Christian communities, had fallen from the Heraclius' grace over the question of how to deal with the Arab threat – Cyrus' approach of paying tribute was not received well in the capital – and was sent into exile.[66] The *Chronicle*, in conjunction with

---

[58] Nik. *Brev.* 30. Joh. Nik. 120.23.
[59] Zuckerman 2010, 875–77.
[60] Joh. Nik. 120.23; cf. Kaegi 1981, 155–56.
[61] Liebeschuetz 1990. Cameron, Long, and Sherry 1993. Croke 2005.
[62] For the remilitarisation of the imperial office, see Viermann 2021, 150–60; 176–85. Raum 2021.
[63] Joh. Nik. 210.40.
[64] For the textual history and subsequent problems, see Booth 2011, 555–60; cf. Howard-Johnston 2010, 181–89. The English translation used here is by Charles 1916.
[65] Booth 2016, 527–36.
[66] Booth 2016, 511–17.

a brief note in Nicephorus, suggests that after Heraclius Constantine had continued his father's foreign policy, it was Martina and Heraclonas who opposed the faction that rooted for a more confrontational strategy against the Arabs and sent Cyrus back to Egypt to negotiate peace.[67]

Martina was, it seems, not only involved in foreign policy but also intervened with regards to religious issues, like other empresses before her.[68] This is evidenced by a letter by Maximus Confessor, a staunch Chalcedonian and one of the prime opponents against Heraclius' attempt to implement a doctrinal compromise that would reunite the different Christian communities. As Maximus reports, Georg, the prefect of Africa, received a letter by Martina in which she took a stand for Miaphysite nuns who, after having fled Egypt in face of the Arab expansion, resisted the authorities' attempts to incorporate them into the Chalcedonian Church.[69] Martina thus returned to the unionist policy of reconciling different Christological positions that her late husband had promoted in the early 630s.[70] This is coherent not only with her support of the unionist figurehead Cyrus, but also with her connection to Arcadius, bishop of Cyprus and another prominent supporter of said policy.[71]

In Constantinople, meanwhile, it did not take long for opposition to arise against Martina and Heraclonas from various sides; Heraclius Constantine's precautionary measure of bribing the army paid off. Under the lead of a certain Valentinus, who had been appointed commander of the army in the East,[72] the troops marched on Chalcedon with the declared aim of securing Heraclius Constantine's legacy against the rival family line.[73] For the time being, Martina and Heraclonas, supported by the patriarch Pyrrhus, managed to deescalate the situation by asserting that Heraclius Constantine's son was not to be harmed;[74] but as Valentinus increased the pressure by destroying the harvest around Chalcedon and preventing people from crossing over, demands were raised amongst the citizens to meet Valentinus' claim and make Heraclius Constantine's son Augustus as

---

[67] Joh. Nik. 119.18–22 (whereas Charles 1916, 191, translates the Ethiopic *kirs* as Pyrrhus, and Booth 2016, 525–26, argues convincingly that it refers to Cyrus) and 119.66–67. Nik. *Brev.* 30. See Booth 2016, 520–27 and 536–39.
[68] Cf. Theodora's involvement with Miaphysites, see Garland 1999, 23–29.
[69] Max. Conf. *Ep.* 12 (*PG* 91, col. 460A–509B).
[70] Booth 2016, 539–50. Cf. Van Dieten 1972, 67–69. Boudignon 2011, 231–35.
[71] Joh. Nik. 120.64. Cf. Booth 2016, 548–49.
[72] Sebeos 44 (Thomson and Howard-Johnston 1999, I 104). Valentinus had been Philagrius' shield-bearer: see Nik. *Brev.* 30, with *PLRE* 3b (Valentinus 5) and *PMBZ* #8545.
[73] Nik. *Brev.* 30. Joh. Nik. 120.40.
[74] Nik. *Brev.* 30; cf. Joh. Nik. 120.41–43.

6 Dynasty, Endogamy, and Civil Strife 149

well. Probably sometime around September 641,[75] the patriarch Pyrrhus, acting as Martina and Heraclonas' representative, had no choice but to concede.[76] The boy, known to history as Constans II, was brought into Hagia Sophia and crowned Augustus by his uncle, Heraclonas, in accordance with the prevailing practice of imperial coronations.[77] After a brief period of nominal sole rule by Heraclonas, there were again two Augusti in Constantinople – neither of which was mature enough to effectively take charge of political affairs.

For Valentinus, still encamped in Chalcedon with his troops, however, the elevation of Constans was not enough. To alleviate the military pressure, Martina and Heraclonas' faction made further concessions to the general, appointing him *comes excubitorum*, commander of the palace guards.[78] The office of *comes excubitorum* was one of the most powerful and influential positions within Constantinople due to the officeholder's proximity to the emperor and his control over the imperial palace. With the rise in importance of the excubitors throughout the sixth century, the commander's position had become a stepstone towards imperial office. Several emperors such as Justin I, Tiberios, and Maurice had been *comites excubitorum* before their elevation; Priscus, *comes excubitorum* and son-in-law of Phocas, was seen as a promising candidate for imperial succession.[79] With Valentinus, we have an example of an ambitious military man using his resources and influence amongst the troops to catapult himself into highest office. As *comes excubitorum*, he crossed over from the military camp in Chalcedon into the city; he gained access not only to Constantinople but also, crucially, the imperial palace. In these negotiations, Martina seems to have had at least some leverage, as another son of hers, David, was promoted from Caesar to Augustus.[80] Overall, however, Valentinus'

---

[75] See Mango 1990b, 192.
[76] Nik. *Brev.* 31.
[77] For coronation rituals in Constantinople, see Trampedach 2005 and Rollinger 2024, ch. 14–16; for the seventh century specifically, see Viermann 2021, 104–28 and Rollinger (forthcoming b). According to Nik. *Brev.* 31, the crowd in Hagia Sophia pressed on Heraclonas to perform the coronation instead of Pyrrhus; according to custom the patriarch only performed the coronation if no senior Augustus was present. In Joh. Nik. 120.44, it is Valentinus who "placed the imperial crown on the younger Constantine"; cf. Sebeos 44 (Thomson and Howard-Johnston 1999, I 104). The latter version of events is not credible as it goes directly against contemporary conventions of imperial coronations; what John of Nikiu reflects are the actual power relations in the capital, with Valentinus having the means to induce the elevation.
[78] Nik. *Brev.* 32.
[79] When Heraclius came to power, he removed Priscus from office as soon as possible and replaced him with his own loyal ally, his cousin Nicetas: see *Chron. Pasch.* s.a. 612.
[80] Nik. *Brev.* 32.

150 *Empresses-in-Waiting*

intrusion into Constantinople's political affairs severely limited the empress' manoeuvring space. Martina's situation was exacerbated as one of her closest allies, the patriarch Pyrrhus, was pushed out of his position and had to leave the capital due to rising public pressure.[81]

The *Chronicle* of John of Nikiu offers further insight into how Martina tried to prevail against Valentinus. Having already brought Thracian contingents into Constantinople earlier that year, she now approached military units stationed in Anatolia. According to the *Chronicle*, a letter emerged amongst the Cappadocian troops, sent by Martina and Pyrrhus to a certain David "the Translator".[82] David's identity remains unclear, but he seems to have been a military man with authority over troops, as the empress and patriarch urged him to "make a vigorous war" and "to put down the sons of [Heraclius] Constantine". As an incentive, they offered "Martina to be his wife".[83] To further complicate the picture, the stakeholders in Constantinople suspected that Martina and Pyrrhus' initiative was connected to "Kubratos, chief of the Huns, the nephew of Organa, who was baptised in the city of Constantinople, and received into the Christian community in his childhood and had grown up in the imperial palace."[84] This Kubrat, who is in fact known from other sources as the ruler of the Onogur-Bulgars, apparently supported Martina and her sons based on his personal bond with the late Heraclius.[85]

In discussions of the events of 641, this set of evidence is often overlooked or discredited as untrustworthy.[86] However, when considering it from the broader perspective of late Roman history, it appears in line with established political practice. In Late Antiquity, it was common for Romans to form military alliances with non-Roman confederations in the empire's peripheries; this often went hand in hand with mutual

---

[81] Nik. *Brev.* 31 and Joh. Nik. 210.53 present two slightly different accounts of this; Pyrrhus must have left the city before Paul was consecrated patriarch on 1 October 641; cf. Theoph. Conf. AM 6133 (De Boor 1883, 341). For the circumstances of Pyrrhus' exile, see Zuckerman 2010, 207. Based on the translation of Joh. Nik. 116.5 and 119.19–20, it is sometimes assumed that Pyrrhus had been exiled from Constantinople already earlier that year but returned after Heraclius Constantine's death (see Mango 1990b, 193). Booth 2016, 522–27, however, has argued that this is based on a translation error, with the Ethiopic *kirs* referring not to Pyrrhus but to Cyrus.
[82] *PMBZ* #1242. Booth 2016, 528 with n. 109.
[83] Joh. Nik. 120.46.
[84] Joh. Nik. 120.47.
[85] *PLRE* 3b (Koubratos). For the baptism of a Hun chieftain, see Nik. *Brev.* 9; for the alliance between Kubratos and Heraclius, see Nik. *Brev.* 22; cf. the comments in Mango 1990b, 177–78; 188.
[86] See, for example, Stratos 1972, 201; 219–20. Cosentino 2021 does not take it into account.

exchange of hostages (as in the case of the above mentioned Kubrat) and attempts at Christianization. Barbarian chieftains in turn, based on their command over fighting units, had the means to impact Roman policies more or less directly.[87] Female members of the imperial house also sought to exploit the power dynamics between Romans and non-Roman tribes, or between opposing sections of the military, to their own advantage. When the western Roman Emperor Valentinian III tried to neutralize his sister, Honoria, she approached Attila, ruler of the Huns, for support; her sending her signet ring to Attila was understood as an offer of marriage.[88] Licinia Eudoxia, wife to Valentinian III, acted along similar lines. Finding herself in a precarious position after her husband's assassination and having been forced into a new marriage by the emperor Petronius Maximus, she allegedly asked the Vandal king Gaiseric for help, which contributed to the Vandal's subsequent invasion of Italy.[89]

In Martina's case, it remains unclear how David and Kubrat the Bulgar were connected. What is evident, however, is that Martina approached military men, holding out the prospect of marriage – the ultimate ticket into the imperial palace – in order to impact political dynamics in her favour. The only way for her to emancipate herself from Valentinus and to counter the resources he had with his troops was for Martina to invite another commander into the city as her husband. The marriage, however, never came to pass and Martina's efforts proved in vain.

Not even a year after Heraclius' death, at some point in the winter of 641/42,[90] Martina and her sons Heraclonas, David, and Martinus were overthrown, mutilated, and exiled to Rhodes, leaving Constans II as sole emperor.[91] Valentinus was confirmed as *comes excubitorum* and supreme commander of the army. The evidence is ambiguous with regards to the exact details of the coup. Theophanes Confessor describes the senate of Constantinople as main actor;[92] but according to the Armenian chronicle of Ps.-Sebeos, Valentinus attacked Constantinople with his army, deposed Martina and her sons, and confirmed Constans as emperor.[93] John of Nikiu outlines how, after Martina's attempt to cooperate with David "the Translator" had become public, "all the soldiers in Constantinople and

---

[87] Halsall 2007. Meier 2019a.
[88] James 2013, 305. Croke 2015b, 112–16.
[89] Joh. Malal. 14.26; cf. James 2013, 306. Croke 2015b, 104–105. Börm 2018, 109–10. After the looting of Rome by Vandal troops, the empress was brought to Carthage and one of her daughters, Eudocia, married to Gaiseric's son Huneric.
[90] The exact date is debated; see Treadgold 1990, 433, who argues for November 641; cf. Cosentino 2021, 288.
[91] Stratos 1972, 200–203.
[92] Theoph. Conf. AM 6133 (De Boor 1883, 341).
[93] Sebeos 44 (Thomson and Howard-Johnston 1999, I 104).

the people rose up", led by a "Jûtâlîjûs, the son of Constantine, named Theodore".[94] This enigmatic commander fought and killed Martina's champion David, then took Constantinople by military force and deposed the empress and her sons (the latter part in accordance with Sebeos' account).[95]

Compared to the fifth and sixth centuries, seventh-century Constantinople saw a particularly high frequency of civil strife in which the ruling emperor(s) were deposed: Maurice and his sons in 602, Phocas in 610, and Heraclonas and his brothers in 641.[96] The first two coups, for which there is more detailed evidence, came about through an interplay of several factors: an approaching army or fleet put external military pressure on the capital but could only effect a regime change when the populace of Constantinople rose up against the respective emperor.[97] Neither the army as such, nor the senate as an institution or its individual members had the means to overthrow an emperor; instead, it needed a concerted popular effort from inside the city.[98] For the coup of 641, a similar dynamic is most likely.[99] As external military pressure rose, it became unmistakably clear that Martina and Heraclonas had lost the support of the Constantinopolitan populace, which gave Valentinus the opportunity to remove them. The emphasis on the senate, present in the account of Theophanes, appears to be a retrospective attempt to strengthen the role of this institution in times of political turmoil (when an underage emperor, effectively, stood under the control of the military man Valentinus).[100]

The notion of the political impact of Constantinople's populace is supported by Valentinus's own fate. Having overthrown Martina and her sons, Valentinus tightened his grip on Constans II by betrothing his daughter to him,[101] and seems to have made several attempts to become Caesar or

---

[94] Joh. Nik. 120.50. For Jûtâlîjûs' identity, see *PMBZ* #3568/corr. Stratos 1972, 201; 220. Booth 2016, 529 with n. 111, suggests 'Euthalius' as the most likely reading; a person of this name, however, is otherwise unknown.

[95] Joh. Nik. 120.51–52.

[96] This continued in the second half of the century, see Haldon 1990, 41–91.

[97] For the coups, see n. 45 above.

[98] See Pfeilschifter 2013 for a detailed analysis of the political impact these groups had in Late Antique Constantinople, and Kaldellis 2015 for the power of the people. Scholarship often assumes that at a time of weak (male) political leadership of underage emperors, the senate as political body gained in importance. For the 640s, see Haldon 1990, 53. 2016, 32.

[99] Against Stratos 1972, 203; cf. Cosentino 2021, 29.

[100] Theophanes' account is characterized by a strong emphasis on the role of the senate in general, suggesting his use of a senate-friendly source for the period in question; AM 6134 (De Boor 1883, 342) relates a (fictitious) speech by Constans to the senate.

[101] Joh. Nik. 120.61–63; the daughter was made Augusta.

even Augustus himself.[102] This, in conjunction with the heightened military presence in the city, must have overstretched the people's tolerance. Years of concerted public campaigns to promote Heraclius' family seemed to pay off:[103] with a strong attachment to the Heraclian dynasty, the people would not allow a military man to take over. In 644/45, riots broke out during which Valentinus' contingents were outnumbered and Valentinus himself executed.[104] Again, it was not the senate, but the population of Constantinople that had the necessary leverage to effect a regime change.

Conclusion

In the Roman political system, structured by patriarchal norms and conceived, in Late Antiquity, in a framework of Christian values, female members of the imperial family had a very limited set of roles or public personae at their disposal.[105] Most famously, there was the option of the pious empress, modelled on Helena, mother of Constantine, and Pulcheria, virgin sister of Theodosius II, the latter of which made a considerable impact on Constantinople's political climate through public displays of Christian piety.[106] Any deviation from this could be met with slander, as in the case of Theodora, who had sought to play a more active role in her husband Justinian's politics.[107] Procopius, in his *Secret History*, assails her with misogynistic stereotypes and aims to discredit her by referring to her humble background and alleged promiscuity.[108] In that respect, the early seventh century did not see any substantial changes. What was considered the emperor's core responsibilities and public function could not be fulfilled by a female member of the imperial house, not even an Augusta. It does not come as a surprise, then, that in order to discredit Martina's attempt to maintain her ground, the male-authored sources portray her as illegitimate,

---

[102] Sebeos 44 (Thomson and Howard-Johnston 1999, I 106). Joh. Nik. 120.61. The *Commemoratio*, a document in connection with the trial against Pope Martin (*PL* 129, 594C), relates that Valentinus "was clad in purple at the emperor's behest and sat next to him" (trans. Viermann); cf. Booth 2016, 538–39.
[103] This becomes particularly evident in coin images: see Viermann 2021, 160–70; cf. n. 16 above.
[104] Sebeos 44 (Thomson and Howard-Johnston 1999, I 106–107). Theoph. Conf. AM 6136 (De Boor 1883, 343). Cf. Kaegi 1981, 157–58. Stratos 1975, 10–13; 266. Haldon 1990, 305–306.
[105] James 2001b, 11–25.
[106] Holum 1982, 79–111. Busch 2015, 110–35.
[107] Garland 1999, 11–39.
[108] Grau and Febrer 2020.

cunning, and intriguing; she is even accused of having caused Heraclius Constantine's death.[109]

However, when trying to leave aside the misogynistic stereotypes that the sources confront us with, what remains is the image of a woman who tried to break out of her ascribed role as wife and mother and assert her position in Constantinople's political landscape. For the greater part of the year 641, the sources are patchy at best, but – based on a firm contextualization within Roman political structures and patterns of political behaviour – Martina's involvement can be assessed, nevertheless. The evidence collected here suggests that she was active not only in the guardianship of her son Heraclonas but also in directing imperial strategy with regards to the confrontation with the Arabs in Egypt and the question of how to deal with inner-Christian doctrinal conflicts. When facing strong resistance within Constantinople, she held on to her connection with the patriarch Pyrrhus, who could at least temporarily impact public opinion in the dowager empress' favour. But as Valentinus gathered his troops in Chalcedon, it quickly transpired that ecclesiastical backing would not suffice for Martina to compete for her son's and her own position. In this precarious situation, she tried to beat Valentinus at his own game by rallying support from the military. Having first brought Thracian contingents into the city, she eventually resorted to the most impactful means at her disposal: offering herself in marriage to a military commander, which was synonymous with bringing in another contender for imperial succession. But what seems to have been Martina's last resort did not play out as planned. Her trying to escalate the civil strife triggered an adverse reaction from the populace of Constantinople. When Martina's popularity reached rock bottom, Valentinus took the opportunity to remove the empress and her sons from palace and capital.

---

[109] Sebeos 44 (Thomson and Howard-Johnston 1999, I 104). Theoph. Conf. AM 6132 (De Boor 1883, 341); AM 6133 (De Boor 1883, 342). Cf. Stratos 1972, 183.

Section 2

Performance and Representation

7

Constructing Power through Rituals: The Case of Theodora

Mads Ortving Lindholmer

In the increasing scholarship of recent decades on Roman and Byzantine imperial women, scholars have moved away from viewing empresses as mere appendages to the emperor, and towards seeing them as important actors and objects of study in their own right.[1] The same is true for Theodora: due to the unparalleled *Secret History* by Procopius, scholars have long been interested in this figure, but publications have become more plentiful in the last twenty years or so.[2]

Theodora's influence and power have naturally received attention: for example, research has underlined her wealth and her patronage (for example of building projects) as sources or signs of power.[3] More broadly, Theodora's power is often conceptualized as centred on her personality and her ability to influence or dominate Justinian on a personal level through her marriage and proximity to him.[4] In this chapter, I intend to explore a facet of Theodora's power that has so far received limited attention, namely her inclusion in imperial rituals. The lack of attention paid to Theodora's involvement in rituals contrasts markedly with the long-standing focus on imperial rituals and partly also with the less intense focus on the

---

[1] See, e.g., Garland 1999. James 2001b. Busch 2015.
[2] See, e.g., Pazdernik 1994. Garland 1999, 11–39. Leppin 2000a. Foss 2002. McClanan 2002, 93–148. Meier 2004. Croke 2006. Harvey 2010. Unterweger 2014. Ravegnani 2016. Becker 2017. See also Herrin 2001, 185–239. Evans 2002. Leppin 2002. Evans 2011 and Potter 2015 aim partly at a wider audience and are more lightly footnoted.
[3] Wealth: Garland 1999, 6; 21. Foss 2002, 151–52. Patronage: McClanan 2002, 93–106. Unterweger 2014.
[4] E.g., Garland 1999, 11, asserts that Theodora "possessed great sway in matters of state through her influence over her husband". See also Garland 1999, 29–37. Likewise, Av. Cameron 1985, 74: Theodora "worked behind the scenes and through processes of intrigue". See also James 2001b, 5.

involvement of empresses in these.[5] That rituals are in fact intrinsic to the construction of power and legitimacy has been highlighted by a mass of scholarship by both anthropologists and historians of various periods.[6]

In the following, I will mainly focus on Theodora's involvement in "the admission": this ritual is often called the *salutatio* during the Principate and the *adoratio* during Late Antiquity, and was a regular ritual during which the elite, by virtue of their status or offices, greeted the emperor, first through a kiss (during the Principate) and later through kneeling (in Late Antiquity).[7] These collective, institutionalized, and regular ritualized greetings should be distinguished from the *ad hoc* reception and greeting of individuals due to specific circumstances, such as embassies or petitions. Procopius provides a lengthy description of ritualized greetings of the imperial couple, which I will argue is a continuation of the admission of earlier times. Importantly, he asserts that Theodora was the first empress ever to be greeted in this way with the emperor. This is highly significant but has received little attention. I will trace the history of the admission from Augustus to Justinian and hereby show that Procopius is likely right in his assertion that the inclusion of Theodora broke with precedent. Hereafter, I will contextualize Theodora's involvement in the admission by exploring other rituals and argue that she played a limited or non-existent role in these. Lastly, I will explore how the admission constructed power for Theodora and presented a new and distinctive picture of imperial rule.

Theodora's Involvement in the Admission

Procopius' *Secret History*, an unpublished work written in the 550s, was meant as a correction to the more positive portrayal of Justinian in Procopius' earlier work on this emperor's wars.[8] The *Secret History* avows "to disclose all the base deeds committed by Justinian and Theodora".[9]

---

[5] MacCormack 1981 and McCormick 1986, but see also, e.g., Goldbeck and Wienand 2017. Imperial women in rituals: see, e.g., James 2001b, 50–59.
[6] The bibliography on this field is enormous, but see, e.g., Geertz 1973. Bell 1992. Beihammer, Constantinou, and Parani 2013.
[7] On the imperial admission, see, e.g., Avery 1940. Alföldi 1970, 3–79. Winterling 1999, 117–44. See also Lindholmer 2021 for a new perspective on this ritual. I am currently turning this doctoral thesis into a monograph.
[8] 550 or 551 are often favoured: e.g., Av. Cameron 1985, 8. Kaldellis 2004a, 3. Pfeilschifter 2022, 131. Recently, however, Battistella 2019 opted for a slightly later date.
[9] Procop. *Anecd.* 1.10: ὅσα Ἰουστινιανῷ καὶ Θεοδώρᾳ μοχθηρὰ εἴργασται ἐγὼ δηλώσω. See n. 10 below on translations used here. On this work, see, e.g., Av. Cameron 1985, 47–66. Kaldellis 2004, vii–lix. Pfeilschifter 2022. On Procopius more generally, see also the various chapters in Greatrex and Janniard 2018. Lillington-Martin and Turquois 2018. Meier and Montinaro 2022.

7 Constructing Power through Rituals 159

It consistently demonizes Theodora in particular and, towards the end of the work, Procopius includes a lengthy description of how Theodora and Justinian were greeted by the senators and patricians, which is supposed to support this demonization:

> And among the innovations of Justinian and Theodora in the administration of the government there is also the following. In ancient times, the Senate, as it came into the emperor's presence, was accustomed to performing *proskynesis* in the following manner. Any man of patrician rank performed *proskynesis* to the emperor on the right breast. And the Emperor would kiss him on the head from above and then dismiss him; but all the rest first bent the right knee to the emperor and then withdrew. However, it was not at all customary to offer *proskynesis* to the empress. But in the case of Justinian and Theodora, all the other members of the Senate and those as well who held the rank of patricians, whenever they entered into their presence, would throw themselves to the floor, flat on their faces, and holding their hands and feet stretched far out they would touch with their lips one foot of each before rising. For even Theodora was not disposed to forego this testimony to her dignity.[10]

Procopius here describes the mode of greeting when the senators and patricians were received by Justinian but the context is not immediately clear. However, the admission is not an unlikely candidate: in continuation of the *salutatio* of the Principate, a Late Antique admission had been common in the fourth century, as evidenced for example by Eusebius who describes how numerous large groups at Constantine's funeral came to greet the emperor, exactly as they had been accustomed to do during his lifetime.[11] Likewise, Ammianus indicates that Julian conducted a regular admission

---

[10] Procop. *Anecd.* 30.21–26: Τῶν δὲ πρός τε Ἰουστινιανοῦ καὶ Θεοδώρας ἐπὶ τῇ πολιτείᾳ νεοχμωθέντων καὶ ταῦτά ἐστι. πάλαι μὲν ἡ σύγκλητος βουλὴ παρὰ βασιλέα ἰοῦσα τρόπῳ τοιῷδε προσκυνεῖν εἴθιστο. πατρίκιος μέν τις ἀνὴρ παρὰ μαζὸν αὐτοῦ προσεκύνει τὸν δεξιόν. βασιλεὺς δὲ αὐτοῦ καταφιλήσας τῆς κεφαλῆς ἐξίει· οἱ δὲ λοιποὶ ἅπαντες γόνυ κλίναντες βασιλεῖ τὸ δεξιὸν ἀπηλλάσσοντο· βασιλίδα μέντοι προσκυνεῖν οὐδαμῇ εἴθιστο. παρὰ δὲ Ἰουστινιανόν τε καὶ Θεοδώραν τὰς εἰσόδους ποιούμενοι οἵ τε ἄλλοι ἅπαντες καὶ ὅσοι τὸ πατρικίων ἀξίωμα εἶχον ἔπιπτον μὲν ἐς τὸ ἔδαφος εὐθὺς ἐπὶ στόμα, χειρῶν δὲ καὶ ποδῶν ἐς ἄγαν σφίσι τετανυσμένων τῷ χείλει ποδὸς ἑκατέρου ἁψάμενοι ἐξανίσταντο. οὐδὲ γὰρ ἡ Θεοδώρα τὴν ἀξίωσιν ἀνεδύετο ταύτην. I have used the Loeb translation of Dewing 1935 with some modifications. Elsewhere, I have likewise used the Loeb translations when available, with occasional adjustments. When these were not available, I have either provided my own translation or noted in the footnote which translation was used.
[11] Euseb. *Vit. Const.* 4.67. Given the large groups regularly greeting the emperor irrespective of personal circumstances but merely on account of their official positions, it seems probable that the funerary rites described by Eusebius are purposefully mirroring an admission ritual that was conducted when Constantine was alive.

ritual as a certain Gallus was "prohibited from adoring the emperor and being present at the ceremony among the other dignitaries".[12] Some form of admission ritual, in which the emperor was adored, seemingly continued in the fifth century: for example, Honorius and Theodosius in a rescript from 415 declared that the palace decurions could decide to attain the rank of *illustris* upon the completion of their service, and that this was "extended to them in adoring Our Serenity, and in connection with the salutation of officials, and with respect to the other privileges of the aforesaid honor, as well as in Our Council".[13] Adoring the emperor is quite clearly presented as a self-contained, regularly recurring event, apparently comparable to the certainly regular ritual of the *salutatio* of officials.[14]

Lastly, it is worth noting, as indicated by the just quoted *constitutio*, that adoration of the emperor became part of imperial patronage in the fourth and fifth centuries, and numerous middling officials were granted this privilege, both as a one-off honour and as a general right.[15] The latter especially necessitated a somewhat regular admission ritual, since these middling officials would generally not have had the chance to adore in contexts such as consistory meetings. Importantly, fifth-century evidence for this dates as late as the emperor Zeno, who reigned until 491, and we in fact also have a *constitutio* from Justinian's reign showing that middling officials continued to adore the emperor.[16]

Against this background, it seems likely that what Procopius is testifying to and describing is the continuation of a regular admission ritual under Justinian during which the imperial aristocracy present in the capital greeted the imperial couple. The fact that Procopius envisions the senators greeting as a collective group shows that he is not here referring to *ad hoc* visits by individuals. Furthermore, Procopius seems to be contextualizing this supposedly new form of greeting within the tradition of admissions in the fourth century: Procopius contrasts the abominable present with a past where "the Senate" merely knelt before the emperor and this, importantly, parallels Eusebius' description of Constantine's admission.[17] It is also noteworthy that Procopius elsewhere seems to describes how Theodora, like

---

Avery 1940, 72, thinks likewise. On this passage, see, e.g., Avery 1940, 72–73, and MacCormack 1981, 117–21.

[12] Amm. Marc. 22.9.16: *adorare adesseque officio inter honoratos prohibito*. For Julian's admission, see also Greg. Naz. 4.80; *Pan. Lat.* 3(11).28.1–4.

[13] *CJ* 12.16.1: *in adoranda nostra serenitate quam in salutandis administratoribus et reliquis praedicti honoris privilegiis nec non in nostro consistorio his honor omnifariam observetur* (trans. Frier 2016).

[14] *Salutatationes* of officials: e.g., *CIL* 8.17896; *CTh* 1.15.16. 6.18.1. 6.28.8.

[15] See, e.g., *CJ* 12.16.1; *CTh* 6.13.1. 8.7.4.

[16] *CJ* 12.4.pr. 12.29.2. 12.33.7.1.

[17] Euseb. *Vit. Const.* 4.67.

other imperial women and elite individuals had done in the past, conducted her own personal admission ritual, and this included the same key elements, the prostration and kiss on the feet, as the apparent admission of Justinian.[18] Overall, then, it seems likely that a somewhat regular admission ceremony continued under Justinian and that Procopius is describing it above.

The key in Procopius' description is that the admission had changed drastically through the introduction of prostration and kisses on the feet and the inclusion of the empress, Theodora. The *Secret History*, however, has a clear aim of slandering Justinian and Theodora, and therefore cannot be accepted uncritically. Scholarship has long argued that Procopius' depiction of Theodora is structured around negative female stereotypes, and some therefore see it as mostly invented.[19] Against this background, it is possible that Procopius simply invented the supposed change to the admission and Theodora's role in it in order to demonize the imperial couple. Indeed, Liz James asserts that Procopius' description "represents an attack on Theodora rather than anything necessarily 'real' about ceremony".[20] However, this seems unlikely: firstly, it is clear from the contemporary Peter the Patrician that kisses on the emperor's feet were in fact common in other Justinianic ceremonies.[21] More importantly, whereas Procopius could present unverifiable gossip about the empress' private life, it would have been glaringly obvious to his elite audience if his claim that Constantinople's imperial aristocracy regularly had to kiss the feet of Justinian and Theodora during the admission was invented.[22] Thus, it seems highly likely that Theodora was in fact included in Justinian's admission.

---

[18] Procop. *Anecd.* 15.13–16. This occurred regularly, included the elite, and the greeters normally left without uttering a word. These factors make it clear that Procopius is describing the ritual of the admission, rather than *ad hoc* visits by individuals to the empress. Elite admissions in general: Amm. Marc. 14.6.12–13. *CTh* 6.24.4. Sen. *Ben.* 6.33–34 with Goldbeck 2010 and Badel 2007. That the admission as a ritual continued under Justinian is likewise indicated by Procop. *Anecd.* 4.20.21, to which I will return below.

[19] See, e.g., Fisher 1978. Av. Cameron 1985, 47–82. McClanan 2002, 107–20. Grau and Febrer 2020. Foss 2002, 163, and Kaldellis 2004a, 130, disagree.

[20] James 2001b, 51 n. 6. Likewise, Alföldi 1970, 24–25. McClanan 2002, 127, also questions the reliability of Procopius' account, but accepts that "some degree of transformation" of ceremonial is possible. By contrast, Garland 1999, 20, accepts Procopius' depiction. See also Herrmann-Otto 1998, 355–59. Pazdernik 2009, 66–68. Ravegnani 2016, 60.

[21] See, e.g., *De cer.* 1.84. 1.86–87.

[22] As pointed out by Kaldellis 2004a, 135–36. Procopius envisions his audience as future emperors and the elite in general: *Aed.* 1.1. *Anecd.* 1.1–10. *Bell.* 1.1–2. His classicizing historiographical approach and use of Attic Greek likewise suggest an audience among the cultural and intellectual elite. Likewise, Whately 2016, 222–24. See also Pfeilschifter 2022, 132–33.

Procopius' assertion that Theodora's central role in the admission was a break with the past may of course still be invented or stem from ignorance of past practice. If the empress traditionally had been included in the imperial admission, Theodora's inclusion would simply be an unremarkable continuation of tradition. Consequently, we must verify Procopius' depiction by tracing, where we can, the role of women in the imperial admission from the start of the empire: during the Principate, three women are mentioned in connection with the admission, namely Livia, Agrippina the Younger, and Julia Domna.[23] Livia's admission is mentioned in Cassius Dio: "She occupied a very exalted station, far above all women of former days, so that she could at any time receive the Senate and such of the people as wished to greet her in her house; and this fact was entered in the public records."[24] Dio's mention that Livia was repeatedly greeted in her house and received "the Senate" is likely a reference to the admission, and Dio does indeed use his preferred word for the admission, ἀσπάζομαι.[25]

Patrizia Arena places great emphasis on this and argues that it shows that Livia became part of the emperor's admission and attained a central position in this ritual.[26] However, Cassius Dio's wording does not give any impetus to suppose that Livia was involved in the emperor's admission, since the emperor is never mentioned. Rather, Livia seems to have organized her own admissions, which is arguably not surprising: the admission had been a key ritual during the Republic, where it functioned as a tool to establish links of patronage and *amicitia* and advertise one's popularity by the number of one's *salutatores*.[27] As the empire came into being, both emperor and elite continued conducting admissions, and these were key to the networks of patronage that continued to suffuse imperial society.[28] In a situation where Livia and other imperial women, by virtue of their proximity to the emperor, had considerable influence and possibilities to informally petition the emperor, it is not surprising that Livia would start holding admissions, just like all other powerful individuals in Rome.[29]

---

[23] On the admission of these and other women, see Goldbeck 2010, 67–73, and Lindholmer 2021, 66–69.

[24] Cass. Dio 57.12.2–3: πάνυ γὰρ μέγα καὶ ὑπὲρ πάσας τὰς πρόσθεν γυναῖκας ὄγκωτο, ὥστε καὶ τὴν βουλὴν καὶ τοῦ δήμου τοὺς ἐθέλοντας οἴκαδε ἀσπασομένους ἀεί ποτε ἐσδέχεσθαι, καὶ τοῦτο καὶ ἐς τὰ δημόσια ὑπομνήματα ἐσγράφεσθαι. On Livia in Dio, see Sion-Jenkis 2016.

[25] He consistently uses this word when writing about the admission: see, e.g., 56.26.2. 57.11.1. 80[79].14.4.

[26] Arena and Goldbeck 2010, 437.

[27] As argued by Goldbeck 2010, 252–62.

[28] Admission: Winterling 1999, 117–44. Badel 2007. Goldbeck 2010, 263–81. Patronage: Saller 1982 remains foundational.

[29] Ovid, e.g., uses Livia to petition Augustus: *Pont.* 3.1.131–38.

Agrippina's admission is mentioned in both Tacitus and Cassius Dio. The latter writes that she "used to greet in public all who desired it, a fact that was entered in the records".[30] Dio again uses ἀσπάζομαι here to describe a repeated greeting, which is likely the admission. Indeed, the description closely parallels Dio's depiction of Livia's admission.[31] Tacitus also testifies to Agrippina's involvement in admissions:

> And, to prevent her being greeted by a throng of well-wishers, he [Nero] made his own establishment separate, installed his mother in the house once belonging to Antonia, and, at his visits to her new quarters, came surrounded by a throng of centurions and left after a perfunctory kiss.[32]

It has been argued that this passage shows that Agrippina was involved in the emperor's admission.[33] Yet nothing in the passage directly suggests so. Indeed, if Agrippina were greeted by many due to her involvement in Nero's admission, the emperor could have just excluded her from the ritual. Rather, he moves her to another *domus*. This suggests that Agrippina, like Livia, held her own admissions and that more people naturally frequented these when they were held in the same place as the emperor's. In Dio's description, likewise, we get the clear impression that Agrippina conducted her own admissions, as the emperor is not mentioned.

Lastly, Julia Domna, wife of Septimius Severus, is also described by Dio as conducting admissions during the reign of Caracalla.[34] Dio mentions the many governmental responsibilities of Julia Domna and then writes: "Need I add that she publicly greeted all the most prominent men, precisely as did the emperor?"[35] The mention of Julia Domna's repeated greetings of the foremost men is almost certainly a reference to the admission. It has been argued that the passage shows Julia Domna conducting the imperial admission instead of Caracalla.[36] However, Dio quite clearly indicates that both Julia and Caracalla greeted these men. There is no indication that they did so together in the same admission, and it is most likely that Julia

---

[30] Cass. Dio 61[60].31.1: καὶ ἐν κοινῷ τοὺς βουλομένους ἠσπάζετο· καὶ τοῦτο καὶ ἐς τὰ ὑπομνήματα ἐσεγράφετο.

[31] E.g., Dio writes that the admissions of Livia and Agrippina were both mentioned in the public records.

[32] Tac. *Ann.* 13.38: *Ac ne coetu salutantium frequentaretur, separat domum matremque transfert in eam, quae Antoniae fuerat, quotiens ipse illuc ventitaret, saeptus turba centurionum et post breve osculum digrediens.*

[33] Arena and Goldbeck 2010, 437–39. Likewise, Goldbeck 2010, 71.

[34] On Julia Domna, see Langford 2013.

[35] Cass. Dio 78[77].18.3: τί γὰρ δεῖ λέγειν ὅτι καὶ ἠσπάζετο δημοσίᾳ πάντας τοὺς πρώτους καθάπερ καὶ ἐκεῖνος.

[36] Goldbeck 2010, 71 n. 2.

Domna, like Livia and Agrippina, conducted her own separate admission. This admission would be a natural result of her significant influence and important governmental responsibilities, which Dio emphasizes.

These are all the surviving descriptions of imperial women being involved in the admission during the Principate.[37] They suggest that imperial women were not included in the imperial admission but instead conducted their own admissions, very much like other powerful individuals of imperial society. The suggestion that imperial women were not involved in the imperial admission during the Principate receives further support from the fact that no imperial woman is mentioned in any of the surviving descriptions of imperial admissions.[38] This is perhaps not surprising: the admission of the Principate presented the emperor as *primus inter pares*, through the kiss exchanged with the elite and the use of the toga by all, for example, and was essentially a continuation of a republican elite ritual where women had not been involved.[39] Conducting the imperial admission with the empress would have smacked of monarchic rule in a way that would not have fit the imperial self-presentation of the Principate.

In Late Antiquity, imperial self-presentation changed dramatically and the ideal of *primus inter pares* was largely rejected. Yet there is nothing to suggest that this caused imperial women to be involved in the emperor's admission. Firstly, it is worth noting that no imperial woman is portrayed as conducting her own admission in the fourth century, in contrast to the Principate. Regarding the imperial admission, it is unfortunate for our purposes that the most detailed fourth-century descriptions of this ritual, contained in Eusebius' biography of Constantine and Mamertinus' panegyric of Julian, were written at times when the emperor had no spouse.[40] However, it is still noteworthy that in both examples the emperor remains the sole focus of the ritual with no family members, such as children or female relatives, involved. Fortunately, we do have some other useful depictions of the imperial admission, namely the numerous mentions of *adoratio* in the codices of Theodosius and Justinian. Importantly, here the emperor is likewise always portrayed as the sole object of greeting. For example, a *constitutio* from 413 by Honorius and Theodosius starts thus: "We have directed that the commandants and tribunes of the imperial guard, who are summoned to imperial banquets and have long received

---

[37] Goldbeck 2010, 69–70, suggests that Tac. *Ann.* 4.68 shows that Agrippina the Elder also held admissions, but this is not clear from the passage.
[38] See, e.g., Cass. Dio 56.26.2–3. 57.11.1. 62[63].13.3. Plut. *Mor.* 508b with Lindholmer 2021, 17–80.
[39] Suet. *Aug.* 60; *Otho* 6.2; *Tib.* 34.2 with Winterling 1999, 117–44, Goldbeck 2010, 67–69, and Lindholmer 2021, 17–34.
[40] Euseb. *Vit. Const.* 4.66–67. *Pan. Lat.* 3(11).20.4–21.4.

the right of adoring the Emperor (*adorandi principis*)...".[41] This picture, of the emperor being the sole object of the *adoratio*, recurs numerous times in *constitutiones* from the fourth and fifth centuries.[42]

The same picture is evident in other Late Antique references to the admission: for example, Ambrose, in his funeral speech for Theodosius, tells the story of how Helena, the mother of Constantine, found the True Cross and used one of the holy nails to fashion a diadem for her son. He then comments: "Wisely did Helena act when she placed a cross on the head of kings so that the cross of Christ might be adored among rulers. [...] By the generosity of Christ our princes are to have the privilege that what has been said of the Lord can be said of the Roman emperor: 'You have placed on his head a crown of precious stones.'"[43] This is a fascinating passage on multiple counts: it constitutes the first time in surviving literature that Helena is credited with using one of the holy nails for the imperial diadem, and it is part of the increasing mythologizing of Constantine as the founder of a Christian empire. Ambrose mentions the *adoratio* of the emperor, which is at least partially a reference to the admission, the most frequent context in which the emperor was adored. Importantly, Ambrose gives the clear impression that only the emperor is adored.

To this can be added another passage from Ambrose: in his *Hexameron*, Ambrose mentions "the purple of kings which adorn their banquet halls and give colour to their garments", and immediately hereafter asserts that "from water comes that which is adored in kings; of water, too, is the brilliance of their array".[44] Ambrose is quite clearly here referring to the *adoratio purpurae* and, again, it is only the emperor who receives this honour in Ambrose's depiction. In other words, just like in the funeral speech for Theodosius quoted above, no empresses or other imperial family members are mentioned. More broadly, the fourth-century use of the word *adorare* and its cognates shows a noteworthy narrowing: whereas during the early Roman Empire, potential allies, the audience of a speech, and even the tongue of a patron, for example, can be presented as *adorati*, in the fourth century it is consistently the emperor and God who are presented as adored.[45] Only three exceptions can be found among the more than

---

[41] *CJ* 12.11.1 (trans. Frier 2016).
[42] *CJ* 12.4.pr. 12.29.2. *CTh* 6.24.3. 8.7.9. 10.22.3.
[43] *Sapienter Helena, quae crucem in capite regnum locavit; ut crux Christi in regibus adoretur. [...] Habeant hoc etiam principes Christi sibi liberalitate concessum, ut ad imitationem Domini dicatur de imperatore Romano: Posuisti in capite ejus coronam de lapide pretioso.* Ambr. *De Ob. Theod.* 47–48 (trans. Liebeschutz 2005).
[44] *Aquarum est igitur quod in regibus adoratur, aquarum est species illa quae fulget.* Ambr. *Hexam.* 5.2.6–7.
[45] Ov. *Ex Pont.* 2.2.53; *Fast.* 4.880. Tac. *Hist.* 1.36.

1,000 instances of *adorare* in the fourth century, and none of them refers to imperial women.[46] Likewise, in the more than 2,000 instances of *adorare* in fifth-century literature, no imperial woman is adored and it is again almost exclusively the emperor and especially God who are presented as the objects of adoration.[47] This suggests that the emperor increasingly monopolized the *adoratio*, as part of the admission and in general, as a privilege only fitting for himself and God. Indeed, Ambrosiaster mentions that officials could be severely punished for receiving *adoratio*.[48] All this indicates that empresses were not adored in the fourth century and probably the fifth as well.

Overall, then, empresses had likely not had a prominent role in the imperial admission before Theodora. Procopius' assertion that Theodora's involvement was a break with tradition also deserves attention, since Procopius evinces some knowledge about the praxis of the admission in the past: as previously mentioned, Procopius' claim that kneeling was the common greeting at the admission in earlier times is confirmed by Eusebius.[49] Consequently, it is at least unlikely that Procopius' portrayal of Theodora's inclusion in the admission as untraditional stems from ignorance about past practice. Lastly, although Justinian was a remarkably long-lived emperor, some sort of general knowledge among the educated elite, first- or second-hand, about the admission of his predecessors is likely, which militates against the possibility that Procopius would claim that Theodora's inclusion in the admission was untraditional if this was not the case.

Contextualizing the Admission

Overall, then, it appears that Theodora's prominent inclusion in the imperial admission contrasted with past practice. However, in order to gauge the significance of this innovation, it is necessary to contextualize it by exploring whether Theodora was involved in other imperial rituals. Firstly, it is worth noting that, while empresses could occasionally be crowned, no fixed coronation ceremony was seemingly dedicated specifically to the Augusta in the sixth century; the first example of a fixed ceremony devoted to the Augusta in the *Book of Ceremonies* is from the crowning of Eirene in 768.[50] Whether Theodora was crowned in some ceremony is difficult to

---

[46] Ambr. *De Virginate* 3.20. Jer. *Adv. Iovinian* 2.14. *Vit. Malch.* 5.
[47] These numbers come from the Latin Library database.
[48] Ambrosiast. *Q.* 114.2. See also Ambrosiast. *Comm. Rom.* 1:22.
[49] Euseb. *Vit. Const.* 4.67. The kiss "on the right breast" may sound strange and invented. However, this type of greeting is in fact mentioned twice in Lucian (*Menip.* 12; *Nigr.* 21), probably in the context of aristocratic admissions.
[50] *De cer.* 1.41 with James 2001b, 52. The *Book of Ceremonies* is a tenth-century handbook detailing the procedure of imperial rituals but preserves substantial material from

say with certainty. Theophanes claims that she was "crowned (ἔστεψεν)",[51] but the contemporary Malalas, narrating the reign of Justin, writes that "the most sacred Justinian became co-emperor with him, together with the *Augusta*, Theodora, and was crowned by his most sacred uncle".[52] The key here is that only Justinian is crowned, as στεφθεὶς is singular masculine. The somewhat vague phrase μετὰ τῆς Αὐγούστας Θεοδώρας may have meant that Theodora, as Justinian's wife, was presented with him as Augusta. More importantly, Theodora seems to have played no prominent role in Justinian's coronation: Peter the Patrician, as preserved in the *Book of Ceremonies*, describes the ritual of Justinian's accession to the throne, and there is no mention of Theodora.[53] The same is the case in Zonaras.[54] This is a continuation of a tradition in which empresses did not have prominent roles as part of accessions, at least as far as can be judged from Peter the Patrician.[55]

On the other hand, it is sometimes asserted that Theodora played an important role in the triumph of 534.[56] The basis for this is Zonaras who writes that when Belisarius and Gelimer, as part of the triumph, "had arrived in front of the ruler, Belisarius persuaded Gelimer to throw himself on the ground and thus offer *proskynesis* to the emperor".[57] Belisarius did the same to show that "it was customary to perform *proskynesis* to the Roman emperor, as if thereby lightening his [Gelimer's] misfortunes. And after Gelimer had also offered the same *proskynesis* to the empress, he was received with splendid, royal hospitality which had been prepared for him

---

Peter the Patrician. On this work, see Av. Cameron 1987. Dagron and Flusin 2020. Occasional crowning of empresses: Theoph. Conf. AM 6094. 6102.

[51] Theoph. Conf. AM 6016.
[52] Joh. Malal. 17.18: συνεβασίλευσεν αὐτῷ ὁ θειότατος Ἰουστινιανὸς μετὰ τῆς Αὐγούστας Θεοδώρας, στεφθεὶς ὑπὸ τοῦ θειοτάτου αὐτοῦ θείου. *Chron. Pasch.* s.a. 527 parallels Malalas: Justinian "was proclaimed with his wife, Theodora (μετὰ τῆς γαμετῆς αὐτοῦ Θεοδώρας ἀναγορευθείς)", but only he is crowned. Likewise, Zonar. 14.5. The contemporary John of Ephesus, if the translation of the Syriac by Brooks 1923, 189, is accurate, likewise mentions nothing of a crowning of Theodora. Her description as "God-crowned" in a dedicatory inscription (Croke 2006, 47–48) may have been figurative and does not necessitate an actual crowning ritual.
[53] *De cer.* 1.95.
[54] Zonar. 14.5.
[55] *De cer.* 1.91–95. Ariadne is an exception: see n. 65 below. It may also be noted that in the coronation of Justinian's successor, Justin II, the latter's wife, Sophia, played a somewhat prominent role: Corippus, Iust. 2.167–73.
[56] See, e.g., Evans 2002, 26. Foss 2002, 151. On this triumph more broadly, see, e.g., Börm 2013. Meier 2019b.
[57] Zonar. 7.41: ἐφθακὼς ἔναντι τοῦ κρατοῦντος ὁ Βελισάριος πείθει τὸν Γελίμερα εἰς τοὔδαφος καταβαλεῖν ἑαυτὸν καὶ οὕτως ἀπονεῖμαι τῷ βασιλεῖ τὴν προσκύνησιν.

before."⁵⁸ This could appear to attribute a central position to Theodora in the triumph, receiving *proskynesis* next to Justinian.

If read closely, however, this is not clear from Zonaras: rather, Belisarius and Gelimer stand in front of one ruler (τοῦ κρατοῦντος), and they both then perform *proskynesis* to "the emperor (τῷ βασιλεῖ)" since this was common to do in front of Roman emperors (τῶν Ῥωμαίων τοὺς βασιλεῖς). Thus, Zonaras consistently paints a picture of Belisarius and Gelimer prostrating themselves in front of Justinian alone. Hereafter, only Gelimer offers *proskynesis* to the empress, and the same sentence then describes the royal reception offered to the former Vandal king. In other words, the *proskynesis* offered to Theodora is not explicitly set in the context of the triumph, and the fact that only Gelimer, and not Belisarius, offered it suggests that this prostration in front of Theodora took place at a later time, just like the reception mentioned in the same sentence.

This picture is confirmed by Procopius, who may have been an eyewitness, as he writes that Gelimer, when he reached the hippodrome, "saw the emperor sitting upon a lofty seat and the people standing on either side [...] And when he came before the emperor's seat, they stripped off the purple garment, and compelled him to fall prone on the ground and perform *proskynesis* to the Emperor Justinian. This also Belisarius did, as being a suppliant of the emperor along with him."⁵⁹ The account is very close to Zonaras', and it is again only Justinian who is explicitly mentioned in the context of the triumph. If any doubt remained about the recipient of *proskynesis*, Procopius makes it abundantly clear that it was Justinian alone: προσκυνεῖν Ἰουστινιανὸν βασιλέα.

Lastly, some scholars assume that Theodora received foreign ambassadors, which is based on the following passage from Procopius: Theodora "was by no means averse to receiving even the ambassadors of the Persians and of the other barbarians and to bestowing upon them presents of money, a thing which had never happened since the beginning of time".⁶⁰ This is from the *Secret History*, and Procopius is obviously highly critical here, so we should be cautious. A century after Theodora, the people

---

⁵⁸ Zonar. 7.41: νενόμισται προσκυνεῖσθαι τῶν Ῥωμαίων τοὺς βασιλεῖς, καὶ οἱονεὶ κουφίζων αὐτῷ τὸ δυστύχημα. καὶ τὴν ἴσην δὲ τῇ βασιλίσσῃ προσκύνησιν ἀπονείμαντα τὸν Γελίμερα καταγωγὴ δέχεται λαμπρὰ καὶ θεραπεία βασιλικὴ προετοιμασθεῖσα αὐτῷ.
⁵⁹ Procop. *Bell.* 4.9.12: βασιλέα ἐπὶ βήματος ὑψηλοῦ καθήμενον τόν τε δῆμον ἐφ' ἑκάτερα ἑστῶτα εἶδε [...] ἀφικόμενον δὲ αὐτὸν κατὰ τὸ βασιλέως βῆμα τὴν πορφυρίδα περιελόντες, πρηνῆ πεσόντα προσκυνεῖν Ἰουστινιανὸν βασιλέα κατηνάγκασαν. τοῦτο δὲ καὶ Βελισάριος ἐποίει ἅτε ἱκέτης βασιλέως σὺν αὐτῷ γεγονώς.
⁶⁰ Procop. *Anecd.* 30.24: τοὺς πρέσβεις προσίεσθαι Περσῶν τε καὶ τῶν ἄλλων βαρβάρων, χρήμασί τε αὐτοὺς δωρεῖσθαι, ὥσπερ ὑπ' αὐτῇ κειμένης τῆς Ῥωμαίων ἀρχῆς, οὐδαμῇ ἀπηξίου, πρᾶγμα πώποτε οὐ γεγονὸς ἐκ τοῦ παντὸς χρόνου. This is accepted by Pazdernik 1994, 268 n. 53. Evans 2002, 26.

of Constantinople, in response to Heraclius' widow Martina's attempted intervention in politics, clamoured that "nor can you, O Lady, receive barbarian or ⟨other⟩ foreign ⟨emissaries⟩ who come to the palace or hold converse with them. May God forbid that the Roman State should come to such a pass."[61] This cautions against accepting Procopius too readily and, as Liz James has observed, "the presence of a woman before foreigners could not have enhanced the prestige of the empire. Above all […] foreign policy was the emperor's concern".[62]

Most importantly, we possess Peter the Patrician's detailed descriptions of the reception of ambassadors under Justinian: in the sixth century, such receptions had evolved a highly complex choreography and were a key part of foreign policy. It is significant that Theodora is never mentioned by Peter and, given his minutely detailed descriptions (which, for example, pinpoint the three exact places where ambassadors should perform *proskynesis*), it is difficult to imagine that the empress held a key role but was ignored by Peter.[63] Peter's detailed descriptions are certainly more reliable than Procopius' brief, biased passage. However, it is important to note that Procopius does not say that Theodora received the ambassadors with Justinian in an official capacity. It was not unusual for empresses to receive individuals in private audiences, for example people in need of assistance, and Procopius above may be criticizing Theodora for receiving ambassadors in this context, outside of the official ceremonial framework described by Peter.[64] Overall, then, the absence of Theodora from Peter's descriptions of the official reception of ambassadors strongly suggests that she was not involved or at most played a very minor role in these proceedings.

Constructing Power through the Admission

Strikingly, it seems that Theodora did not have a central role in key rituals such as the accession of Justinian, imperial triumphs, or the continuous reception of ambassadors. In fact, judging from the *Book of Ceremonies*, this pattern seems to have been common in the centuries after Theodora, as the earliest surviving records of formalized ritual involvement of imperial women is the above-mentioned coronation ritual of the empress Eirene

---

[61] Nik. *Brev.* 28 (trans. Mango 1990b).
[62] James 2001b, 69. In the exceptional case of the long-term illness of Justin II, however, his wife, Sophia, seems to have received foreign ambassadors alone: see Dagnall, this volume.
[63] Details: *De cer.* 1.89 [R406]. The empress was also not part of ambassadorial receptions under Justinian's successor: Corippus, *Iust.* 3.151–407.
[64] See Marc. Diac. *Vit. Porph.* 39. Procop. *Anecd.* 15.25–27.

170 *Empresses-in-Waiting*

in 768.[65] This contextualizes Theodora's unprecedented inclusion in the admission and makes it all the more striking. However, this also raises the question of why she was only involved in the admission. Fundamentally, as suggested above, it may have been problematic to include an empress in the reception of ambassadors, and the same applies to the triumph which was likewise connected to war and foreign policy. Furthermore, since empresses had seemingly not played a central role in imperial rituals before Justinian, it may have been judged too radical to include Theodora in spectacular, large-scale rituals such as the triumph or the accession.

The admission, by contrast, took place inside the palace with no participation from foreign powers, and the audience was instead the participants of the ritual, whom Procopius describes as "senators" and "patricians". The latter was the highest honorary court dignity while the former status under Justinian was tied to the rank of *illustris*, which was obtained either through a range of important offices or the favour of the emperor.[66] Procopius is not here focused on providing a detailed and exhaustive list of participants, but he gives the clear impression that it was not a small, closed group of imperial favourites but rather the imperial aristocracy more broadly that was included in this ritual.

However, arguably the most important advantage of the admission was its regularity: admittedly, the exact frequency of the admission, both under Justinian and in Late Antiquity in general, is unclear. However, we know that the Senate participated in meetings of the *consistorium* from 537 onwards, and these meetings must have been preceded by the admission ritual described by Procopius, if he is correct in underlining that the senators had to perform prostration "whenever they entered into their [Justinian and Theodora's] presence".[67] Another passage from Procopius may be of interest here: he writes that "once Belisarius came early in the morning to the Palace, exactly as he was wont to do, accompanied by a small and pitiful escort",[68] and he then mentions the presence of other people at the

---

[65] As pointed out by James 2001b, 52, who suggests that Ariadne's untraditional involvement in Anastasius' accession "perhaps formalizes the empress's role in the choice of successor". However, there is no evidence to support this, and the *Book of Ceremonies*, our main source for Ariadne's role in the accession, mentions no involvement by subsequent imperial women in this ceremony. Furthermore, Ariadne's involvement seems to be tied to the specific historical situation: she married Anastasius and thereby secured him the throne, despite the fact that Zeno's brother, Longinus, was expecting to become emperor: *De cer.* 1.92. Theoph. Conf. AM 5983.

[66] Jones 1964, 528–29.

[67] *Nov.* 62.1.2. Theodora seemingly participated in consistory meetings: see, e.g., *Nov.* 8.1. Procop. *Anecd.* 14.7–8 with Garland 1999, 30.

[68] Procop. *Anecd.* 4.20.21: ἦλθε μέν ποτε Βελισάριος πρωῒ ἐς Παλάτιον, ᾗπερ εἰώθει, ξὺν ἀνθρώποις οἰκτροῖς τε καὶ ὀλίγοις τισίν. Cf. Dewing 1935. Williamson and Sarris

palace at this time as well. This may be a reference to the admission given that Belisarius, as well as others, regularly came to the palace at a specified time for no specified reason. It should also be noted that the morning in fact was the traditional time for the admission, and the *Historia Augusta* could still in the late fourth or early fifth century criticize Elagabalus for not following this tradition.[69] The passage is admittedly vague but, if it refers to the admission, ᾗπερ εἰώθει ("exactly as he was wont to do") suggests that Belisarius attended this ritual on most if not all mornings.

However, the exact frequency is not decisive here. Scholarship on imperial rituals has traditionally focused firmly on grand events such as triumphs, accessions, or funerals but these were infrequent affairs which most of the emperor's subjects witnessed only a few times in their entire lives.[70] The key here is that under Justinian, as well as under his predecessors, the admission was a far more prominent feature of the daily ritual landscape of the imperial aristocracy than such grand rituals. The admission in fact probably constitutes the most frequently occurring context of interaction between the emperor and the imperial aristocracy more widely. There were other relatively frequent rituals, such as the ceremonial surrounding circus games, but these events, like triumphs and funerals, for example, communicated not only with the elite but also with the population of the capital more broadly. On the other hand, the admission constituted an arena in which only the emperor and the imperial aristocracy interacted.

Theodora's prominent position in such a ritual was naturally a significant source of power for her: on a basic level, it made her visible in the eyes of the imperial aristocracy and underlined her closeness to the emperor, which made her attractive as a patron, and the resulting extension of her patronage networks translated into tangible influence and power.[71] The admission was also connected to power in more subtle ways: in the words of Constantine VII, who commissioned the *Book of Ceremonies*, imperial rituals made the imperial power (τοῦ βασιλείου κράτος) "appear more awesome (σεμνοπρεπέστερον) to those subject to it and through this more agreeable and more marvellous (ἡδύτερον τε καὶ θαυμαστότερον)".[72] An important part

---

2007 see εἰώθει as referring to the escort. However, it seems unlikely that the great general Belisarius had traditionally been accompanied by ἀνθρώποις οἰκτροῖς τε καὶ ὀλίγοις τισίν. More importantly, the position of ᾗπερ εἰώθει makes it quite clear that it is Belisarius' morning visit to the palace which was customary. Signes Codoñer 2000, Veh 2005, and Kaldellis 2010 agree in their translations.

[69] Fronto, *Ep. M. Caes.* 1.3.4. SHA *Heliogab.* 28.6. Suet. *Aug.* 60 with Winterling 1999, 125.
[70] See, e.g., MacCormack 1981. Goldbeck and Wienand 2017.
[71] E.g., Procopius mentions an unnamed patrician who asked Theodora for assistance, rather than Justinian: *Anecd.* 15.27.
[72] *De cer.* Pref. (R5).

of this more subtle power of the admission stemmed from its long history: during both the Republic and Empire, the elite had conducted admissions, and the size of one's admission was a significant status symbol. This praxis was still common in Late Antiquity.[73] Moreover, the emperor's admission had already in the first century become a symbol of rulership, as the senatorial elite was obligated to attend this ritual, and the introduction of kneeling in Late Antiquity further emphasized this symbolic role.[74] Thus, by the time of Justinian, the admission was a traditional symbol of power which had been used by the emperors, and throughout Roman elite society more broadly, for centuries. Theodora's inclusion in the imperial admission thus presented her as powerful and prominent in a language of power that was familiar to and accepted by the elite.

The admission also allowed Theodora and Justinian to articulate a distinctive vision of imperial government. As mentioned above, the admission of the Principate presented the emperor as a *primus inter pares*, whereas the fourth-century admission supported the wider Late Antique re-conceptualisation of the emperor as a divine (or at least divinely supported) monarch, for example through the demand of kneeling and the use of bejewelled clothes in this ritual.[75] In other words, the admission presented a narrative to the imperial aristocracy about who the Roman emperor was, his place in the empire, and his relationship with the elite. Consequently, the unprecedented inclusion of Theodora in the admission arguably presented a distinctive vision of the Roman Empire: its government was no longer constituted only by the emperor, as implied by earlier admissions, but rather by the imperial couple as a whole. This imbued Theodora with part of the power and authority of the emperor, which would have increased her power significantly and widened her scope of independent action and spheres of influence.[76] It is worth noting that the elite already encountered this new presentation of imperial government in the entrance to the palace where the imperial couple was depicted together in a mosaic as receiving the spoils of Belisarius' victories – in sharp contrast to the actual triumph where Justinian was the sole protagonist.[77]

Another important aspect of the admission under Justinian is its emphasis on the distance between subject and ruler. This had already

---

[73] See n. 18 above.
[74] Obligation: Plin. *Pan.* 48.2. Suet. *Otho* 6.2 with Winterling 1999, 123–24. See also Avery 1940. Lindholmer 2021.
[75] See, e.g., Avery 1940. Alföldi 1970, 3–79. Winterling 1999, 117–44. Lindholmer 2021.
[76] This ties into Busch 2015 who argued that the use of imperial symbols of power, such as the title Augusta and the imperial insignia, by the Theodosian empresses increased their power significantly.
[77] Procop. *Aed.* 1.11.16–18.

been underlined in the fourth-century admission, for example through the emperor's purple, bejewelled clothes, and many such fourth-century elements likely continued in Justinian's admission despite not being mentioned by Procopius. For example, the San Vitale mosaic, among others, shows Justinian dressed in purple, bejewelled clothes, which strongly suggests that he, like his predecessors, wore such attire at the admission as well. Furthermore, it is clear that the *proskynesis* demanded by both fourth-century rulers and Justinian as part of their admissions retained the strong religious connotations that it had traditionally had: Procopius writes that, after Theodora became empress, "the senators were all to perform *proskynesis* to the woman as though she were a god".[78]

However, Justinian and Theodora also strengthened this emphasis on subjection in novel fashion: previously, senators had merely knelt in front of the emperor, and patricians had been accorded the special honour of kissing the emperor's chest and of receiving a kiss on the head by the ruler, an almost paternal gesture. Under Justinian, on the other hand, the manner of greeting was more submissive, as all prostrated themselves and kissed the feet of the imperial couple.[79] This also removed the differentiation between ordinary senators and the patricians, which obliterated the internal hierarchy of the imperial aristocracy in this ritual. Hereby, Justinian and Theodora were further elevated over their subjects who were now all equal in their subjection to the imperial couple. The more marked emphasis on the distance between ruler and ruled inherent in Justinian's admission is connected to an increased use of slavery imagery by this

---

[78] Procop. *Anecd.* 10.6: αὐτὴν ἅπαντες ἴσα θεῷ προσκυνήσοντες. The same conception of *proskynesis* is likewise repeatedly evident in Joh. Malal. 12.7–9 and has a long tradition: Alföldi 1970, 49–79. Lindholmer 2021, 82–94.

[79] Whether this was an innovation introduced by Justinian, as claimed by Procopius, is difficult to say with certainty: however, under Constantine, people clearly knelt at the admission (Euseb. *Vit. Const.* 4.67), and nothing is mentioned of prostration and kisses on the feet in the numerous fourth- and fifth-century *constitutiones* that mention the *adoratio*. It should also be noted that during the traditional coronation ceremony before Justinian only the relatively lowly "*kometes* of the *scholai* who guard the City and the Palace" kiss the feet of the emperor, whereas the archons perform obeisance (presumably without kisses on the feet), while "the leading senator, with the eparch of the City" are even offered a kiss by the emperor: *De cer.* 1.91. On the other hand, kisses on the feet are often mentioned in ceremonial, such as the appointment of officials, from Justinian's time: *De cer.* 1.84. 1.86–87. In fact, Peter the Patrician says that, previously, *protectores* only performed *proskynesis* but now (i.e. under Justinian) kissed the feet of the emperor as well: *De cer.* 1.86. Thus, it seems likely that Procopius is correct in claiming that it was an innovation that even senators and patricians were forced to prostrate themselves and kiss the emperor's feet. Indeed, it seems unlikely that Procopius could claim this if senatorial prostration and kisses on the imperial feet were a well-entrenched tradition before Justinian.

emperor: Procopius, immediately after the description of the admission, asserts that Theodora and Justinian, in contrast to their predecessors, insisted on being called only δεσπότης and δέσποινα and their subjects being called slaves (δουλοῖ). Procopius' claim is supported by the fact that this presentation of imperial government only became common in official documents under Justinian.[80] This tied into and supported the reconceptualization of imperial government inherent in the new form of greeting at Justinian's admission.

This ritual self-presentation likely affected the elite's perception of the imperial government: a key insight of anthropological scholarship in recent decades is that rituals affect the worldviews of participants. In the words of Nancy Jay, "ritual practices and traditions have been critical to the establishment and naturalization of cultural hierarchies based on age and gender".[81] Likewise, Barbara Myerhoff succinctly asserted that: "Doing is believing."[82] Of course, the participants were not docile *tabulae rasae* who could passively be inculcated with narratives. However, what this strand of scholarship shows is that participation in the admission would have caused the worldviews and hierarchies expressed in this ritual to be naturalized and internalized by the participants to some degree, especially given the frequency of the admission. Essentially, then, the inclusion of Theodora in the admission and the presentation of her as an integral part of a divinely supported imperial government would have fundamentally affected the imperial aristocracy's perception of her, and thus functioned as a significant source of power and authority for this empress.

Conclusion

In this chapter, I have argued, firstly, that Procopius' depiction of Theodora as participating in the imperial admission and his claim that this participation was a break with the past are likely correct. Strikingly, this ritual inclusion of Theodora appears to be unparalleled as she was seemingly not involved in Justinian's accession, the triumph of 534, or the continuous reception of ambassadors. Thus, Theodora's inclusion in the admission appears a specific and targeted choice. It was also a wise choice: the admission communicated with the imperial aristocracy present in Constantinople, not foreign powers, and it was a traditional ritual of rulership and power. Furthermore, it presented a new narrative of Roman government that accorded Theodora a central place alongside Justinian, and which

---

[80] Kaldellis 2004a, 137. Pazdernik 2009, 70–72. See also Lydus, *Mag.* 1.6. On earlier uses of δεσπότης and *dominus*, see Dickey 2001, 1–5. 2002, 77–109.
[81] Jay 1992, 89.
[82] Myerhoff 1977, 223.

further elevated the imperial couple over their subjects. Through the aristocracy's continuous participation, these narratives of the power and authority of Theodora and Justinian were internalized to some degree.

More broadly, the admission is likely to have coloured the imperial aristocracy's understanding of other presentations of Theodora, such as the above-mentioned mosaic in the palatial entrance depicting Theodora with Justinian receiving conquered enemies; the law in which Justinian presents himself as discussing governmental matters with Theodora; or the oath imposed on all magistrates in which they swore to be faithful to "our most sacred masters, Justinian and his wife Theodora".[83] In other words, the admission's regular presentation of Theodora as a co-ruler, or at least as central to imperial government, invited the imperial aristocracy to understand other presentations of Theodora, such as the ones just mentioned, in a similar light.[84] Thus, the admission adds a new layer to and ties into the broader imperial presentation of Theodora.

Overall, then, the admission was not merely a reflection of broader social, economic, and political structures, but rather played an intrinsic role in the construction of this reality and of imperial power and authority more specifically. In other words, Theodora's inclusion in the admission was a significant source of power for her. It invested her further with imperial authority, which widened her scope for action and patronage. Thus, this chapter allows Theodora to emerge as a strikingly innovative empress who exploited the imperial admission for self-presentation for the first time. However, this is also part of a long-term continuity: Anja Busch argued that publicly displayed imperial symbols were key to the power of the Theodosian empresses, and James has explored how Theodora's Byzantine successors employed ceremonial to construct power.[85] When factoring in Theodora's innovative use of the admission, it thus appears that the powerbase of Roman and Byzantine imperial women, throughout a significant part of the first millennium AD, was to a large degree characterized by 'soft power' obtained through public self-presentation. This public aspect of female imperial power in Late Antique Rome and Byzantium qualifies the common scholarly depictions of Theodora and

---

[83] Appended after the epilogue of *Nov.* 8: *sacratissimis nostris dominis, Iustiniano et Theodorae coniugi eius. Nov.* 8.1. Procop. *Aed.* 1.11.16–18.

[84] Against this background, it is curious that Theodora is not included on any coins, which contrasts with her predecessors and successors: McClanan 2002, 121. Foss 2002, 151. Pavla Gkantzios Drápelová, in this volume, points out that numismatic representations of empresses were often the consequence of them producing a male heir, and Theodora's inability to do so may partly explain why no coins seemingly included her image. See also Gkantzios Drápelová, this volume, for the depiction of empresses on coins more generally.

[85] Busch 2015. James 2001b, 50–59.

other empresses as mainly being powerful through their private, conjugal influence on the emperor, through covert female "intrigue".[86] Thus, the exploration of Theodora's inclusion in the admission not only illuminates the power of this empress but sheds light on the alternative sources of power available to empresses in the absence of the 'hard power' of political offices or military resources, and thus illuminates the *longue durée* nature of female imperial power in Rome and Byzantium.

---

[86] See n. 4 above.

8

Empresses on Early Byzantine Coins (Sixth to Seventh Centuries): Evidence of Power?

Pavla Gkantzios Drápelová

The representations of Roman empresses on coins struck in the sixth and seventh centuries display substantial changes from how imperial women figured in coinage of previous centuries. In this late period, fifteen emperors ascended the imperial throne, but only five of them included imperial women on coins. By contrast, imperial women had appeared on coins under the reign of almost all of the fifth-century emperors; in total nine Augustae were represented on these issues.

The practice of including representations of actual women on Roman coins ultimately dates back to the late Republic, while Roman imperial coins featuring women had been a feature since the Julio-Claudian era.[1] It may be argued that this was a comparatively prevalent practice, even though depictions varied in frequency across time. Some Roman empresses never appeared on coins; others did so frequently. It is clear that there were specific political motivations behind the representation of women on coins, such as the need to highlight ties between particular families, commemorate dynastic marriages, or highlight the importance of women's positions of authority within the imperial system. For instance, it is readily apparent that women were important to the political strategy of Constantine and to the idea and communication of dynastic legitimization.[2] Notably, it was during the Constantinian dynasty that several imperial women appeared on coins. In the second half of the fourth century, by contrast, only one Augusta – Aelia Flaccilla – was represented on coins following the end of the Constantinian dynasty, before Augustae again became a regular part of numismatic iconography in the fifth century.[3] The situation changed again in later decades and during the sixth and seventh centuries, the

---

[1] For an overview, see, e.g., Wainwright 2018, 26–30. Kahrstedt 1910.
[2] Frakes 2006, 96–98.
[3] On Aelia Flaccilla and the other Theodosian empresses and their representation in coinage, see Holum 1982, 32 and *passim*.

practice of depicting Augustae on coins existed exclusively in the period between 565 and 629.

All Augustae whose effigies appeared on coins in this period were portrayed together with the emperor and/or a male heir; they were never presented alone, as had been usual on coins struck up to the fifth century.[4] Another characteristic feature of sixth and seventh century coins is that empresses almost exclusively featured on bronze denominations, which is again a significant difference to previous centuries, when Augustae were portrayed on coins struck in various metals including gold coins of the highest value. Remarkably, none of the imperial women of the sixth and seventh centuries appeared on the most precious gold coins or multiples, i.e., issues that were addressed to the highest strata of contemporary society and very often also to the representatives of non-Roman peoples.[5] Finally, aside from minor regional exceptions in the case of the empress Sophia, it is striking that the empresses' names do not feature in the legends of the coins on which they do appear.

These features suggest a significant shift in the representation of imperial women on coins, compared to previous centuries when empresses were frequently depicted alone, their representations were not limited to a particular metal, and their full names and the abbreviation of their title Augusta (AVG) were usually stated in the legends.[6] It is the aim of this chapter to present the evidence for empresses on coins in the sixth and seventh centuries and explore the underlying causes for and symbolism of these portraits.

✱✱✱

The empress Sophia, consort of Justin II (565–578), was the first Byzantine empress to be depicted on coins struck in the sixth century. Her effigy appeared more than seven decades after the empress Ariadne had been depicted on a gold multiple celebrating her wedding to Anastasius in 491.[7]

---

[4] For the purposes of this article, all the coins minted before the end of the fifth century are referred to as Roman, thus following the traditional convention, according to which most modern catalogues use the term 'Byzantine' for coins minted after 498, when Emperor Anastasius introduced a major coin reform; see DOC, *MIBE*, BNP I and others.

[5] On the significance of multiples, see Bastien 1988, 28–41. Morrisson 2012, 25–28.

[6] It remains debated why women stopped appearing on coins from the end of the fifth century. Philip Grierson and Melinda Mays offer an explanation that the break could have been related to the fact that after the death of empresses that could have been labelled as scandalous or unpopular there followed a break in the representation of Augustae on regular issues (e.g., after Fausta, Verina, or Martina); see LRC, 8.

[7] The issue was acquired by Dumbarton Oaks Collection, see DOC I, 4–5. For details

Sophia was represented on issues struck in Constantinople,[8] Thessalonica,[9] Cyzicus,[10] Nicomedia,[11] Antioch,[12] Carthage,[13] and probably also Cherson.[14] In the vast majority of cases, the coins are exclusively bronze; only the Carthage mint also struck silver coins with the portrait of the empress (see Table 1). In Constantinople, coins with Sophia's effigy were minted from the beginning of Justin II's reign in 565 (fig. 8).[15] The Constantinopolitan issues depict the imperial couple enthroned, wearing chlamyses, with the emperor holding a *globus cruciger*. The empress is holding a traverse sceptre surmounted by a cross. Both are nimbate and crowned, with the emperor on the left, i.e. the more 'honourable' side. One of the features that enables the precise identification of the other figure as an empress is the crown with *pendilia* and pinnacles as a traditional feature of Byzantine empresses' representations which appears on coins depicting Augustae throughout Byzantine history.[16]

In some regions the representation of the enthroned couple gradually spread over the following years, but in other provincial mints the empress'

---

about this issue, see Zacos and Veglery 1959, 154–55. Ernst H. Kantorowicz studied the issue among older similar issues whose reverse iconography was the same: Christ blessing the newly married couple with a legend FELICITER NVBTIIS. Such issues were also struck on the occasion of the wedding of Licinia Eudoxia and Valentinian III or Marcian with Pulcheria; see Kantorowicz 1960, 7–8, figures nos. 21–23. Some specimens can be consulted in the Dumbarton Oaks online catalogue: http://museum.doaks.org/objects-1/info/36666.

[8] *MIBEc*, 92–95. DOC I, 204–17. BNP I, 124–25; 129–32.
[9] *MIBEc*, 104–106. DOC I, 221–25. BNP I, 134.
[10] *MIBEc*, 98–99. DOC I, 234–39. BNP I, 137–39.
[11] *MIBEc*, 96–97. DOC I, 226–33. BNP I, 135–37.
[12] *MIBEc*, 101–103. DOC I, 243–45; 248–49. BNP I, 142–45.
[13] *MIBEc*, 89–90; 107–108. DOC I, 254–56. BNP I, 148; 150–52.
[14] *MIBEc*, 112–13.
[15] See *MIBEc*, 92. DOC I, 204/205 (no. 22). BNP I, 130 (nos. 1–3).
[16] Such a crown is, for example, part of the depiction of Empress Theodora on a mosaic in San Vitale (fig. 20). Triangular pinnacles were characteristic for empresses' crowns; see Rousseau 2004, 10. Examples can also be seen in sixth-century sculpture, e.g., ivory of Ariadne displayed in the Kunsthistorisches Museum in Vienna (fig. 7) or the marble head of Euphemia from Niš (see James D. Breckenridge in Weitzmann 1979, 31–32). The motif also appeared on coins representing empresses in previous centuries but is recognizable mainly in those issues that depict the bust frontally (a relatively unusual practice prior to the sixth century), see, e.g., commemorative issues of Licinia Eudoxia from the first half of the fifth century (*RIC* X, no. 2023). On the diadems and *pendilia* and its representation on coins in the sixth and seventh centuries, see the table by Ph. Grierson in DOC II/1, 82. The imperial crown with *pendilia* can be seen not only on issues struck in our period of interest, but also on coins of, e.g., the empresses Irene of Athens (DOC III/1, 349 [no. 1]), Zoe Karbonopsina (DOC III/2, 541 [no. 1]), Theodora Porphyrogenita (DOC III/2, 750–53 [nos. 1–2]), and others.

180 *Empresses-in-Waiting*

effigy did not appear at all (e.g., Alexandria, Rome, and Ravenna). One year after the introduction of this new iconographic type on Constantinopolitan bronze coins, i.e. in 566/67, the same representation also appeared in the mints of Nicomedia and Cyzicus.[17] In Justin's fourth regnal year (568/69), the mint of Thessalonica started to strike coins with the same reverse type.[18] One year later, the mint of Antioch initiated production of these coins, but in this case the iconography differed on a minor point: on Antiochene coins, both the emperor and empress hold individual sceptres and a large *globus cruciger* between them.

The coins of Carthage, minted from 572, possess various rather extraordinary features. Firstly, the Carthage mint was the only one to portray the empress not only on bronze but also on silver half-*siliquae*.[19] The iconography of the enthroned imperial couple on Carthaginian silver coins diverges from that employed on the Constantinopolitan coins in that each of the figures holds a scroll. The other details correspond more or less to those features known from other mints: both imperial figures are crowned, sometimes also nimbate; occasionally, a cross is depicted between their heads. The Carthaginian mint also struck bronze coins depicting the imperial couple and the representation again diverges from the usual iconography known from other mints. The *folles* and half-*folles* struck in Justin's eighth regnal year (572/73) show two frontal busts on their obverse, with the emperor helmeted and the empress crowned (fig. 9). Two frontal busts of the imperial couple on some Carthaginian coins represent an iconographic type that had appeared earlier, on bronze coins struck exclusively in Antioch in 527 during the joint reign of Justin I and Justinian.[20] This iconography was not widespread in previous centuries, however examples of two frontal busts can be found, e.g., on late Roman *exagia solidi* (coin weights for weighing gold *solidi*).[21] The Carthaginian *folles* and half-*folles* that were struck some years

---

[17] In Cyzicus, the earliest *folles* are dated to the third year of Justin II's reign (567), but there exists evidence of half-*folles* with such a representation already from the second regnal year (566); see *MIBEc*, 98 (type 50b) and 99 (type 51b).
[18] Fourth regnal year, *MIBEc*, 105.
[19] *MIBEc*, 26–27; 89–90 (types 33a–c). BNP I, 148 (no. 5). These coins were erroneously assigned to the mint of Constantinople at the beginning of the twentieth century; cf. BMC I, 77–78 (nos. 26 and 27) or DOC I, 204 (nos. 19–21). In some modern publications, therefore, the erroneous information that Sophia was depicted on Justin II's Constantinopolitan silver coins can still be found.
[20] DOC I, 60–61 (14–16). BNP I, 52. *MIBE*, 41 (types 10–13).
[21] *MIBEc*, 41. Two frontal busts also appear on *solidi* struck during the short joint reign with Tiberius II at the very end of Justin II's life (see *MIBEc*, 35). Furthermore, frontal busts of Justin II and Sophia were employed also on the contemporary lead seals of the imperial *xenon* (*DO Seals* 5, no. 36.1); however, in this case the half-length figure of the Virgin Mary was included in the centre.

later[22] bear the representation of the enthroned imperial couple like coins struck in other mints, but again with a noticeable difference: the figures on these coins do not hold any insignia.

The obverse legend of all Carthaginian bronze coins representing the empress includes the full names of the imperial couple: DN IVSTINO ET SOFIAE.[23] In the exergue of the bronze *folles* and some half-*folles*, the exclamation VITA completes the legend in the sense of "Long life to Justin and Sophia".[24] This is the only instance of an empress' name being fully stated on coins struck in the period under study.

However, it has been argued that Sophia's name was also included in the imperial monogram that was widespread on *pentanummia*, a bronze coin worth five *nummi* struck by various mints (fig. 10).[25] John B. Bury was the first to interpret the monogram as IOVCTINOV KAI COΦIAE.[26] In Antioch, bronze *pentanummia* with this monogram appeared at the same time as the iconography of the imperial couple was introduced.[27] Other mints, however, did not use the monogram at all, either because they used different types of monograms or a completely different iconography on *pentanummia* (e.g., Carthage, Sicily, Rome), or because they did not strike *coins* of such a denomination (e.g., Alexandria, Cherson). The attribution of the *pentanummia* with this monogram to individual mints was long uncertain and it is due to Bury's argument that they are identified as connected to Justin II, an attribution now widely accepted.[28]

This evidence of Sophia's name being explicitly stated on coinage alongside the name of her consort has no parallel among other early Byzantine empresses from the sixth and seventh centuries. Just as her representation was limited to scenes that included the emperor, her name was combined with that of her male counterpart who was stated first.

Although Theodora, the famous consort of Justinian, had enjoyed a prominent position at court, she never appeared on coins.[29] Possible explanations for Sophia appearing on coins have centred on the fact that she, unlike Theodora, gave birth to a male heir.[30] Striking coins with the portrait of the empress after the birth of an heir was common during the

---

[22] The *folles* were struck exclusively in the tenth regnal year (574/75) and the half-*folles* did not bear a reference to a particular year; *MIBEc*, 107–108.
[23] BMC I, xix. BNP I, 150 (nos. 15 and 16). DOC I, 254–55 (no. 198).
[24] Grierson 1982, 48.
[25] In Constantinople (*MIBEc* type 45), Nicomedia (*MIBEc* type 49), Cyzicus (*MIBEc* type 53), Antioch (*MIBEc* type 65a–b), Thessalonica (*MIBEc* type 72).
[26] Bury 1924, 302.
[27] *MIBEc*, 29.
[28] BNP I, 125. DOC I, 218. *MIBEc*, 28. Grierson 1982, 49.
[29] For her position at court, see Lindholmer, this volume.
[30] E.g., C. Morrisson in BNP I, 25. Grierson 1982, 45.

fourth and fifth centuries with only minor exceptions.[31] In addition, the birth of a son was sometimes associated with awarding the title of Augusta to an empress.[32] Some scholars, however, have expressed their doubts with regards to the direct connection between empresses' representations and the birth of an heir in general.[33] Strikingly, the only son of Justin II and Sophia died just before Justin ascended the throne and Sophia's assumption of the title Augusta, [34] i.e. well before coins with her effigy were designed, which makes a direct connection less likely.

Another aspect of Sophia's reign that is often emphasized and adduced as a possible explanation for her figure appearing on coins, is her influence on her husband and later direct role in government.[35] The shared nature of Justin II's and Sophia's reign is noted already in Corippus.[36] I consider it significant that the iconography of the enthroned imperial couple presented on their coins resembles the iconography of two enthroned co-emperors from previous centuries, including during the short period of co-rule by Justin I and Justinian in 527.[37] Interestingly, this type of iconography was more or less limited to gold coins in the past. This means that in the case of Sophia, a type of iconography was introduced that was not previously used for empresses but was common in the case of two male co-rulers, which in essence underlines Sophia's significant position.

Furthermore, the representation of the imperial couple is sometimes interpreted as aiming at complementing the image of the emperor as a

---

[31] Grierson 1982, 44–45.
[32] Herrin 2000, 23.
[33] E.g., McClanan 2002, 162–63. James 2001b, 110–22. Kenneth G. Holum, in his review of James' book (Holum 2003, 1326), indirectly opposed James' opinion that the practice of depicting empresses was unrelated to providing a male heir and noted that the practice of portraying the empress after giving birth to a male heir could vary.
[34] *PLRE* 3a, 759. *PLRE* 3b, 1179.
[35] See Brubaker and Tobler 2000, 583. Nikolaou 1999, 123. Garland 1999, 56–57. Louth 2008, 125. Av. Cameron 1975c, 9–16. That direct power was also emphasized by contemporary sources, e.g., Gregory of Tours, *Hist.* 5.19: *Cum autem Iustinus imperator, amisso sensu, amens effectus esset et per solam Sophiam augustam eius imperium regiretur.* For an analysis of Sophia's direct rule during the time of her husband's incapacitation, see Dagnall and Roggo, both this volume.
[36] Corippus, *Iust.* 1.205 and 290; 2.170; and *passim*.
[37] See the following examples: two enthroned emperors were depicted on *solidi* struck between the 360s and 380s (*RIC* IX, 2, no. 2. *RIC* IX, 16–17, nos. 16–18. *RIC* IX, 21, no. 39. *RIC* IX, 24, no. 49. *RIC* IX, 28, no. 75. *RIC* IX, 76, nos. 3, 5. *RIC* IX, 76, nos. 8–9 and others); on *solidi* of Honorius and Arcadius struck at the end of the fourth century (*RIC* X, 3 and 127); and on *solidi* of Basiliscus and Marcus struck in Constantinople in 475/76 (*RIC* X, 1022). For Justin I and Justinian, see *MIBEc*, 108–10 (*solidi* from the Constantinople mint) and *MIBEc*, 111 (bronze coinage from Antioch). Cf. Olster 1982, 399 and McClanan 2002, 159.

Christian ruler. Leslie Brubaker and Helen Tobler offered an explanation that the introduction of Sophia's portrait on Justin II's coins could have been intended to evoke memories of Constantine and Helena.[38] This hypothesis is consistent with the fact that the Latin poet Venantius Fortunatus, a contemporary of Justin II and Sophia, referred to the emperor as Constantine and the empress as Helena.[39] Such a connotation is also documented in the case of the following emperor, Tiberius, and his wife Ino Anastasia.[40] Arguably, a certain connection also existed between the rank of Augusta and Helena, who was the first Christian to hold this imperial title.[41] However, the connection with Helena is simultaneously associated with the perception of an empress as a symbol of family and dynastic stability within the Christian empire.[42] There is no evidence that coins of the fourth and fifth centuries reflected the connection between the imperial couple and the couple Constantine and Helena, who, in fact, had never been depicted together on coins.

The introduction of this new iconographic type – a seated imperial couple or two busts – can be viewed from yet another perspective. In general, the period of Justin II brought several significant changes in coin iconography with some older models returning; e.g., a personification of Constantinople re-appeared on the reverse of his *solidi*.[43] The *globus cruciger* in the emperor's hand was replaced by a globe with Victory on the obverse of *solidi* and the reverse legend stated CONCORDIA AVCC instead of VICTORIA AVCC as had been common on Justinian's gold issues.[44] Cécile Morrisson noted that the style of Justin II's *solidi* was rather close to the *solidi* struck by Arcadius and Theodosius II.[45] Evidently, there

---

[38] Brubaker and Tobler 2000, 583–84; 587.

[39] Fortunatus Venantius, *MGH* 4 (1), 277, ed. F. Leo, Berlin 1881, 277. Garland 1999, 48. Jones 2016a, 111–12.

[40] On the evidence see Mi. Whitby 1994, 83–84. Angelova 2015, 311. Joh. Eph. *Hist. eccl.* 3.5 and 3.10.

[41] Brubaker 1997, 60. Spieser 2002, 601.

[42] See, e.g., Brubaker 1997, 63. Jean-Michel Spieser speaks about "a new model of Christian femininity" that was closely linked to the image of Empress Helena; see Spieser 2002, 602–604.

[43] See DOC I, 198–201 (nos. 1–11). *MIBE*, 79–88. As Joh. Eph. *Hist. eccl.* 3.14 shows, traditional ancient personification was not universally comprehensible anymore.

[44] In the cases of Antioch and Thessalonica, this iconography appeared also on some bronze coins, see *MIBEc*, 100 (types 54–55); 102 (type 58); 103 (type 62); 104 (type 68a).

[45] See BNP I, 124. Coins from the Carthage mint also display a line reminiscent of older motifs: On the reverse of silver coins depicting the enthroned imperial couple, a half-figure of Constantinople appears with the inscription VICTORI in the exergue (*MIBEc*, 89–90, types 33a/c). Personifications of cities were noticeably declining in coin iconography during the sixth century, with just a few examples found on Byzantine coins from Antioch (Tyche of Antioch), Carthage (the personification of Carthage), and

is a certain tendency to adopt older iconographic motifs on coins, perhaps in the hopes of emphasizing continuity with the imperial past. Similar reminiscences and allusions are also visible in the art production of this period, as Averil Cameron has shown, which combined old traditions with new models.[46] The use of two enthroned figures on Justin's coins, which had been commonly used to represent male co-emperors, could be interpreted as part of this broader phenomenon.

The practice of depicting the imperial couple continued under Justin II's successors, Tiberius II (578–582) and Maurice (582–602), but the production occurred on a substantially smaller scale and was limited to several regional mints and, in some cases, to a short time period (Table 2). The Empress Ino Anastasia, wife of Tiberius II, has been identified on coins struck in Thessalonica (fig. 11), where the enthroned couple continued to be depicted on local half-*folles* just as they had been during the reign of Justin II.[47] The figure of Constantina, consort of Emperor Maurice, appeared exclusively on coins struck in Thessalonica,[48] Cherson,[49] and Carthage.[50] Thessalonica struck bronze half-*folles* with representations of the enthroned imperial couple only during the first two regnal years of Maurice (582/83–583/84).[51] The iconography continued the model established under Justin II. One type, however, shows a variation with a long cross between the imperial heads, which had previously been exclusive to Antioch under Justin II.[52] Wolfgang Hahn supposes that either an Antiochene coin served as a model or that the die engraver in Thessalonica was just experimenting.[53] The fact that the production in Thessalonica was relatively short-lived suggests the continuation of the previous type used under Tiberius and Justin II, rather than the intention to express a particular message.[54]

---

on Justin II's *solidi* (Constantinople). Moreover, on one type of Carthaginian half-*follis* depicting the imperial couple enthroned on the obverse, two Victories holding a shield with a star are depicted on the reverse. Such a composition involving the personification of Victory was quite unusual in this period and it is a certain reminiscence of older compositions common, e.g., in the fourth century.

[46] See Av. Cameron 1975a, 130–32.
[47] *MIBEc*,127 (type 65). BNP I, 166 (nos. 1–3). DOC I, 277 (nos. 23–25).
[48] *MIBEc*, 164–65. DOC I, 320 (nos. 70–90). BNP I, 166 (no. 6).
[49] BMC, xxii. *MIBEc*, 173 (types 157 and 160). DOC I, 373–75 (nos. 297–303: including also types which are attributed to Justin II or Tiberius in other catalogues). BNP I, 214–15 (nos. 1–8).
[50] *MIBEc*, 144 (types 59a–b). BNP I, 179 and 204 (type 3).
[51] See *MIBEc*, 55.
[52] See *MIBEc*, 164 (type 111).
[53] *MIBEc*, 55.
[54] Grierson 1982, 45.

Under Maurice, the Cherson and Carthage mints provide evidence of rather specific issues with an emphasis on dynastic promotion, striking the so-called family coinage that bore a representation of the imperial couple and the male heir. The introduction of the representation of the imperial couple on Cherson bronze coins remains a subject of debate, and some anonymous coins have been attributed to the period of the emperors Justin II and Tiberius.[55] The Cherson mint struck *folles* and half-*folles* with a representation of a standing imperial couple on the obverse (fig. 12), the figures holding the same insignia as on the coins from Constantinople representing the imperial couple struck under Justin II: the *globus cruciger* in the hands of the emperor and a cross-topped sceptre in the hands of the empress.[56] The reverse depicts a standing male figure next to the denomination mark that is commonly interpreted as Theodosius, the male heir of Maurice, crowned Augustus in 590. These coins led to various hypotheses as to why it was important to mint coins promoting dynasties in Cherson, with conflicting interpretations as to their exact dating. Philip Grierson suggested these issues to be insurrectionary coinage from the late phase of the sixth century or 602, when local rebel units might have wanted to depose the emperor and to appoint Theodosius as a new ruler.[57] Warwick Wroth suggested that both family coinages of Maurice – that of Cherson and Carthage – might be dated to 596/97, when the emperor Maurice bequeathed the empire to his sons in his will.[58] An earlier date of 589/90 has been proposed in connection to Maurice re-establishing the administrative and military organization in the Black Sea region.[59] The possibility of connecting the coinage with the appointment of Theodosius Augustus in 589/90 also exists.[60] In essence,

---

[55] Wolfgang Hahn dated the anonymous series to an earlier period based on their weight standard, see *MIBEc*, 34, 112–13 (types 158c; 159; 161b; 162). The earlier date was also proposed by V.A. Anokhin (Anokhin 1977, 99–100, types 315–319).

[56] The third series of these Cherson coins bears a legend that includes the name of Emperor Maurice; see *MIBEc*, 58. As this series did not bear the name of the city in contrast to the previous series attributed to Justin II and Tiberius, they have sometimes been attributed to Thessalonica, but this is not widely held; cf. Anokhin 1977, 101–102.

[57] Grierson 1982, 73.

[58] BMC I, xxii. Furthermore, he considered it unlikely that these coins could be from the period around 601/602, because relations between Theodosius and Maurice were already strained by this point; however, this hypothesis is doubtful as no direct evidence on problematic relations between Theodosius and his father exists.

[59] Sidorenko 2007, 81.

[60] Such a context is considered by some scholars in the case of the minting of the so-called family coinage during the reign of Maurice in Carthage. However, the exact dating and attribution of particular types remains a problem. For example, Wolfgang Hahn hypothesized that these coins could have been minted early in Maurice's reign, i.e., before Theodosius was appointed co-regent, and this fact casts doubt on the

all hypotheses associate these coins with the need to present dynastic legitimacy to the army and consolidate Roman power in the region. However, Wolfgang Hahn proposed dating the issues to the early phase of Maurice's reign, i.e., 583/84–584/85, which would cast doubt on the identification of the figure with Theodosius.[61]

The representation of busts of the imperial couple also re-appeared in Carthage (fig. 13) on the reverse of some silver half-*siliquae*,[62] depicting two imperial busts, a long cross between them and in exergue AGTI (for AVGVSTI).[63] The obverse of these coins bears the frontal bust of Theodosius. Maurice's son also appeared on other Carthaginian silver issues without the inclusion of his parents on the reverse.[64] As in the case of the Cherson family coinage, various hypotheses have been expressed on the reasons why and when precisely these coins appeared in North Africa.[65] Some scholars proposed that the coinage could be related to the occasion of the young Theodosius' proclamation as Augustus in 589/90.[66] Others have hypothesized that rumours spread in Africa of Theodosius' survival of Phocas' massacre of Maurice and his family in 602.[67]

On a larger scale, the empress again began to appear on coins minted by Phocas (602–610) in various mints, including Constantinople (Table 3). It is noteworthy that the iconography of these coins was very similar to that on the obverses of the family coinage from Cherson: the imperial couple is depicted standing, not enthroned (fig. 14). The figures are crowned and nimbate, the emperor holding the usual *globus cruciger* and the empress a cross-sceptre. It has been suggested that Phocas was familiar with this type from his service on the northern frontiers.[68]

Leontia, Phocas' consort, was the first empress after Sophia to be depicted in the capital mint. She was represented on Constantinopolitan,[69]

---

identification of the figure on the reverse as a successor (*MIBEc*, 34 and 59). Hahn also noted that a practice of depicting the emperor on the reverse was common in Chersonese issues.

[61] *MIBEc*, 59; the earlier date is discussed on the basis of a version of the imperial name common in the early phase in the capital included on Cherson issues.

[62] *MIBEc*, 144 (types 59a–b). BNP I, 179.

[63] See *MIBEc*, 144 (type 59). BNP I, 204 (type 3).

[64] *MIBEc*, 144 (types 60 and 62). BNP I, 203 (nos. 6–8).

[65] An overview is provided by C. Morrisson in BNP I, 179.

[66] BNP I, 179. Grierson 1982, 45. *MIBEc*, 52.

[67] A.R. Bellinger in DOC I, 376, n. 305.1. Grierson 1982, 45.

[68] Hahn 1978, 521.

[69] *MIBEc*, 188 (types 60a–b); 190 (types 64a–b). DOC II/1, 162–63 (nos. 24–25). BNP I, 226 (nos. 1–2).

Nicomedian,[70] Cyzicene,[71] and Antiochene [72] bronze *folles* and half-*folles* struck immediately after the ascension of Phocas. On coins minted in Thessalonica, the standing couple appeared exclusively on one type of undated half-*folles* considered to have been struck in the fourth and fifth regnal years (604/605 and 605/606).[73] The activity of the Cherson mint under Phocas is controversial, with attributions hypothetical at best.[74] In Constantinople, Nicomedia, and Cyzicus the production of these coins ceased during the first two regnal years (602/603–603/604). Only the mint of Antioch continued to strike these issues until 608 when it introduced the imperial consular bust on the obverse, thus adapting a type that had been common in other mints since 603/604. The question remains whether the Antioch mint followed a special policy in this case, or whether the adoption of types from the capital was simply delayed – a phenomenon common in Antioch also in the sixth century. [75]

An Augusta again reappears after a few years on coins struck during the reign of Heraclius (610–641) (fig. 15), which represents a rather complicated topic. In some cases, the precise identification of effigies depicted on Heraclius' coins is uncertain – due to them being executed rather carelessly and details are often hardly recognizable – and so the figure, which is interpreted as Augusta in some catalogues, is identified elsewhere as Heraclius' son.[76] Sometimes numismatists preferred to leave the represented

---

[70] *MIBEc*, 191 (type 68); 191 (type 171). DOC II/1, 176 (nos. 53–54). BNP I, 230–31 (nos. 1–8).

[71] *MIBEc*, 194 (types 75 and 78). DOC II/1, 180–81 (no. 69). BNP I, 232 (nos. 1–2).

[72] *MIBEc*, 195–97 (types 83a–b; 85; 87). DOC II/1, 186–88 (nos. 83–89). BNP I, 234–35 (nos. 1–23).

[73] *MIBEc*, 98 (type 94).

[74] Anokhin 1977, 102. *MIBEc*, 68.

[75] See Gkantzios Drápelová 2019. Wolfgang Hahn proposed that Antioch possibly ceased to strike coins with the imperial couple after the empress' death, the precise date of which is unknown; however, the hypothesis does not explain why the empress' representation continued to be employed in Antioch longer than elsewhere; see *MIBEc*, 66.

[76] This is the case for several types of coins struck under Heraclius. Philip Grierson identified the empress Martina on bronze coins struck in Rome between 621/22 and 624/25 depicting three busts, see DOC II/1, 363–64 (nos. 263–67), interpreting the left figure as Martina, while in BNP I and BMC the same figure has been interpreted as Heraclonas; see BNP I, 307 (nos. 9–13) and BMC, 243 (nos. 20–23). Wolfgang Hahn noted that these coins correspond to the issues struck in Constantinople and Ravenna that depicted the empress but emphasized that in the case of the coins struck in Rome no distinguishing element is present in the Augusta representation; see *MIB* III, 120. For Ravenna, Philip Grierson recognized the empress' figure on a silver ceremonial hexagram held in the Bibliothèque nationale that depicts three standing figures. The left figure, supposedly the Augusta, is almost invisible. Cécile Morrisson and Wolfgang

188 Empresses-in-Waiting

figures without any further identification.[77] In addition, some issues are rare with little evidence existing on particular specimens.[78] Finally, the question of which Augusta was depicted on Heraclius' coins is heavily debated.[79]

The earliest examples of female figures on Heraclius' coins appeared in his sixth regnal year, 615 (see Table 4). Commonly, the nineteenth regnal year (628/29) is considered to be the end of coins with female portraits under Heraclius;[80] however it seems that in some mints the production continued even after that date.[81] In any case, the intensity and regularity of production differed between the mints. The Constantinopolitan mint is the only mint that produced a complete series of coins depicting women in the period from 615/16 to 628/29. Other mints usually provide examples from a limited number of years (see Table 4) and some did not include the effigy of the Augusta in their repertoire at all.[82]

Altogether, a female effigy appeared on Heraclius' coins from nine mints (Constantinople, Thessalonica, Nicomedia, Cyzicus, Carthage, Ravenna, Cyprus, Rome, and Cherson). This is the highest number of mints striking coins with a representation of a woman in the period under study. In the vast majority of these mints, representations including the empress

---

Hahn preferred to identify the figure as Heraclonas– see BNP I, 310, no. 4 and *MIB* III, 101 (type 154) – and their identification is followed in this article. Similar controversies exist concerning the coins struck in Cherson, see below.

[77] E.g., in the case of Thessalonica's *folles* and half-*folles*, Philip Grierson just noted that three standing figures are depicted on the obverse, see DOC II/1, 312–13 (nos. 146–150) and 314 (no. 151). Similarly, Wolfgang Hahn (*MIB* III, 116) leaves the description without specifying the identification. On the contrary, Cécile Morrisson and Warwick Wroth identified the figure on the Thessalonica issues as the empress, because the iconography corresponds to the type in Constantinople, which depicts three standing figures, of which the one on the left is an Augusta; see BNP I, 282 (type 3) and BMC, 213 (no. 219).

[78] E.g., this is the case for half-*folles* from Cyzicus with the representation of three standing figures; see *MIB* III (type 189). In other catalogues (e.g., DOC II/1. BNP I) only Cyzicene *folles* have been included. In some other cases, no complete series is known and only specimens from specific years have been documented – for example, in the case of Cyzicus, *folles* with references to the years 625/26, 627/28, and 628/29 are well documented, but specimens from 626/27 are lacking in most catalogues.

[79] Zuckerman 1995. 1997. Speck 1997. Pottier 1997. Morrisson 1997.

[80] E.g., DOC II/1, 216; 227–28. Grierson 1982, 106.

[81] The mint of Thessalonica evidently continued to strike these coins also in the twentieth regnal year (629/30); see DOC II/1, 313 (no. 150). *MIB* III, 232. Rodolfo Ratto mentioned the existence of a Thessalonican *follis* struck in the twenty-first year (630/31), but the information remains unverified: Ratto 1930/1959, no. 1475. Another mint that possibly struck these coins even after 629 is Carthage; cf. p. 199 (this chapter).

[82] E.g., the mint of Cyzicus provides bronze coins with a representation of an Augusta exclusively in the years 625/26–628/29 and the mint of Cyprus struck the Augusta representation only between 626/27 and 628/29.

appeared exclusively on bronze coins (see Table 4). Only the Carthage mint also struck silver coins with the empress' representation on the reverse.

In most mints the Augusta appeared in a composition of three standing figures. The female figure was usually depicted to the left, which, in the case of representations of three figures, was the least honoured position.[83] The emperor Heraclius was represented in the centre and his son from the first marriage, Heraclius Constantine, who had been elevated to the rank of Augustus in 613, was depicted to the right. However, examples of transposition exist, with the Augusta depicted on the right.[84] Each figure wears a chlamys. The male figures also bear a crown with a cross. In cases where the details are recognizable, and the empress' crown is visible, there are two pinnacles on each side and *pendilia* hanging from the shoulders. For these coins, two phases can be distinguished which differ mainly by the presence of Heraclius' monogram on the reverse. The issues without a monogram were struck during the first phase that is dated between the sixth and fourteenth regnal years (615/16–623/24).[85] The second phase, when the Heracleian monogram was included on the reverse, covers the period from the fifteenth until the nineteenth regnal years (624/25–628/29).[86] The iconography of the obverse remained unchanged; however, some scholars have pointed out that in the later years, the style is rougher and the details even less recognizable.[87] In 628/29 the female figure disappeared from coins; instead, a new iconographic type was introduced, which emphasized Heraclius' military character.[88] It can be argued that the figure of the woman was no longer relevant on the coins depicting the emperor in a military style.

A distinctive iconography was employed in Rome, Ravenna, Cherson, and Carthage. In Ravenna and Rome (fig. 16), three frontal busts were depicted on the obverse instead of the standing figures and the iconography appears exclusively on bronze coins dated to specific years (see Table 4).[89] The mint of Cherson struck bronze *folles* with an iconography similar to that employed on local coins struck under Heraclius' predecessors: two standing figures were depicted on the obverse, and a third next to the

---

[83] If two figures were depicted, the more important figure was to the left and the less important to the right. If three figures were represented, the most important was depicted in the centre, the second most important to right and the least important to the left, see DOC II/1, 69.

[84] See, e.g., DOC II/1, 289 (no. 92a, Constantinople, date: 619/20); 320 (no. 164, Nicomedia, date: 617/18).

[85] See *MIB* III, 224 (type 161). Philip Grierson ends this phase in 622/23; see DOC II/1, 217.

[86] See *MIB* III, 224–25 (type 162).

[87] DOC II/1, 227.

[88] E.g., C. Morrisson in BNP I, 257, and Morrisson 1997, 454.

[89] See *MIB* III, 234 (types 244; 251; 252; 259; 260; and 264).

denomination mark was on the reverse.[90] However, the identification of the portraits remains debated.[91]

As with the reigns of Justin II and Maurice, during Heraclius' reign the mint of Carthage was the only one that included the representation of a female figure on silver coins. The fraction of *siliqua* depicted the emperor's frontal bust on the obverse and two frontal busts on its reverse (fig. 17). The two reverse busts are usually interpreted as Martina, Heraclius' second wife, and Heraclius Constantine. The iconography was thus similar to some issues from Maurice's reign. Judging from the diadem, the Augusta is depicted on the right side, with the more honourable place again given to the male successor.

Neither the bronze coins from Cherson nor the silver coins from Carthage bear any references to regnal years. Generally, the opinion prevails that both mints started to strike these issues in 615/16, when an Augusta appeared for the first time on the coins in Constantinople.[92] In Cherson, the production of these coins probably ended in 624;[93] while the mint of Carthage presumably struck these coins throughout Heraclius' reign.[94]

Heraclius' coins with the representation of an Augusta have provoked an intense scholarly debate concerning the identity of the depicted woman. Traditionally, the figure has been identified as Martina, Heraclius' second wife.[95] In contrast to that, some scholars have argued that the effigy represents Heraclius' daughter from his first marriage, Epiphania-Eudocia who was elevated to the rank of Augusta in 612.[96] The main reason for the conflicting interpretation is the debate around when exactly Heraclius married Martina. Based on the chronicle of Theophanes Confessor, the wedding has been dated to 613/14, shortly after the death of Heraclius'

---

[90] *MIB* III, 121 (type 265).
[91] Numerous scholars identified the obverse figures as Emperor Heraclius and his consort Martina and the reverse figure as Heraclius Constantine (see *MIB* III, 121. Sokolova 1983, 27). Philip Grierson interpreted the two figures as Heraclius and Heraclius Constantine and the reverse figure as Martina (see Grierson 1982, 120. DOC II/1, 381, no. 311). Cécile Morrisson saw the obverse figures as Heraclius and Heraclius Constantine and suggested identifying the reverse figure as Heraclius' other son, Heraclonas (see BNP I, 316).
[92] DOC II/1, 235. *MIB* III, 125. Wolfgang Hahn dates the introduction of the particular coinage in Carthage to ca. 617; see *MIB* III, 100 (immobilized coinage). Philip Grierson suggested that the striking started about the same period as in the capital in 615; see Grierson 1982, 126.
[93] Wolfgang Hahn concludes this based on the coins' weight standard; see *MIB* III, 121.
[94] *MIB* III, 100–101.
[95] BMC I. DOC II/1. BNP I. *MIB* III and many other catalogues.
[96] Zuckerman 1995. 1997. Speck 1997.

first wife Eudocia in 612.[97] This early date for the wedding and Martina's elevation to the rank of Augusta suggests identifying the female effigy on Heraclius' coins as her. However, the situation is complicated by the fact that there is a time gap between the wedding, if Theophanes' dating is accepted, and the Augusta's first appearance on coins in 615/16, several years later. Philip Grierson explained this by noting that the award of the Augusta title itself did not automatically imply a right to appear on coins and suggested that Martina's appearance on coins was connected to her giving birth to a son, Constantine, which is usually dated between 614 and 616.[98] The disappearance of the female figure in 628/29 has been explained by Martina's unpopularity among the population, together with the fear that she might plot against the male successor, Heraclius Constantine, who was the son of Heraclius' first wife.[99]

However, various scholars have challenged the early date of the wedding due to Theophanes' inaccuracy in dating numerous events of Heraclius' reign and instead suggested a later date, around 622.[100] The later date by default rules out the identification of the female figure as Martina on coins minted before 622. In consequence, the female figure is either identified as Epiphania-Eudocia throughout,[101] or it is suggested that earlier coins depict

---

[97] Theoph. Conf. AM 6105 (De Boor 300); *PLRE* 3b, 837. The date 6105 corresponds to 612/13 in accordance to the edition of *The Chronicle of Theophanes Confessor* by C. Mango and Roger Scott, 430. Cf. Viermann, this volume.

[98] Grierson 1982, 44; 106 (616), and DOC II/1, 227. Theophanes dates the birth to AM 6106; see Theoph. Conf. AM 6016 (De Boor 301) which corresponds to 613/14. For alternative dates (615 or 616), see *PLRE* 3a, 348 (615).

[99] Grierson 1982, 88 and 106. Philip Grierson in his catalogue cited in the footnotes a note by A. Bellinger, who, in the case of one specimen in DO collections. remarked that "the figure of Martina seems to have been obliterated by subsequent hammering"; see DOC II/1, 292 (note 99a.1). Lynda Garland understood this as an act of the coins' user who "disapproved of her morals or political involvement" and acknowledged this to be an indication that the figure should be identified as Martina; see Garland 1999, 62. Nevertheless, we can only agree with Lauren Ann Wainwright, who emphasized that on the basis of just one specimen, it is not possible to draw such conclusions; see Wainwright 2018, 174. For an analysis of the causes of Martina's unpopularity, see Viermann, this volume.

[100] Apart from Speck 1988 and Zuckerman 1995, see also Bolotov 1907 and commentaries by C. Mango on Nikephoros in Mango 1990b, 179–80. Paul Speck pointed out several inconsistencies in the sequence of events in Theophanes' *Chronicle* and concluded that the only possible explanation for certain events was the postponement of Martina and Heraclius' wedding to a later period; see Speck 1988, 34–36. Henri Pottier preferred to date the marriage to 620; see Pottier 1997, 469–72.

[101] The identification of the Augusta on Heraclius' coins as Martina was critically questioned by Constantin Zuckerman who accepted the later dating suggested by Paul Speck; see Zuckerman 1995. 1997.

Epiphania while later issues represent Martina.[102] If we accept the identification of the female figure on Heraclius' coins as Epiphania-Eudocia, it means a significant development in the Byzantine numismatic iconography as it would be the first time after the fifth century for a Byzantine princess to appear on coins.[103] All Augustae that appeared on the sixth-century coins were emperor's consorts. In previous centuries, we do see the inclusion of women on imperial issues who were not emperor's spouses, but played a specific role in the dynastic policy, with some political influence and potentially even a role in deciding who would be depicted on coins (e.g., Galla Placidia; Pulcheria).[104] The representations of imperial daughters was definitely not a common practice in Byzantium; some rare examples exist from several centuries later.[105]

After Heraclian coinage ceased to include female figures in 628/29, more than 150 years passed before another imperial woman appeared on coins. The female figures on Heraclius' coins thus conclude a series of depictions of Augustae on early Byzantine coins.

***

The Augustae who were depicted on the coins during the sixth and seventh centuries (Tables 1–4) present a very disparate group of imperial women. Each case requires an individual approach and presents a set of different problems. Some of the empresses appeared on coins only over short periods of time; others were displayed on coins throughout the reign of their consorts. Some were represented on coins struck in the capital and mints in its vicinity (e.g., Cyzicus and Nicomedia), whose output was significant for the whole empire and whose coins circulated on a large scale.[106] Other Augustae (e.g., Ino Anastasia and Constantina) appeared exclusively on coins struck in particular regions and/or just in particular years. Moreover, the issues from regional mints sometimes showed specific iconographic features

---

[102] Speck 1988, 36. 1997. Henri Pottier supported this identification by the study of the figures' sizes and concluded that the effigy of the Augusta was enlarged after 624, which would suggest the female figure represented was no longer the Epiphania, but Martina; Pottier 1997, 470.

[103] Zuckerman 1995, 120.

[104] LRC, 229–32; 152–54.

[105] In the ninth century, Theophilos' daughters Thecla, Anna, and Anastasia appeared on rare gold *solidi* (DOC III/1, 407. BNP I, 524, no. 11) and later, after Theophilos' death, *solidi* were struck representing the regent Theodora on the obverse and Michael III the Drunkard and his sister Thecla on the reverse (DOC III/1, 457. BNP II, 533, nos. 1–3).

[106] For the significance of various early Byzantine mints, see mainly *MIBE* and *MIBEc*.

that had no parallels elsewhere and sometimes struck coins with empresses' representations in years when other mints preferred different images.

From the perspective of this study, the empress Sophia has a privileged position. Although it is difficult to pinpoint the specific motive behind Sophia's inclusion on coins and the choice of the specific iconographic type, which was previously used exclusively for two male co-rulers, it is important to point out that Sophia was the first empress to appear on coins after a hiatus of several decades. The question remains to what extent the empress could have played a direct role in deciding that her effigy would be included in coin imageries. In general, no details are known as to how the images that appeared on the coins were selected. Various regional differences indicate that sometimes local authorities may have played a certain role. Still, it is supposed that the emperor himself, or people within his close circle, played the main role in deciding how he would be depicted and what sort of symbolism would be employed.[107] Only in her case, and only hypothetically, can one consider the possibility that her personality played some role in the decision to include her image on coins, and only in her case is a direct influence on the government considered.[108] Even so, it is not certain whether the placement of the imperial couple on the obverse of bronze coins in most large mints could be related to Sophia's significant position, or rather to Justin II's need to emphasize dynastic legitimacy.

For the period under study, it is likely that only the empress Sophia was in the position to impact the decision to be included in coin imagery; the following empresses might not have appeared on coins at all if this practice had not been reintroduced under Justin II and Sophia.

A number of elements may have affected the reintroduction of empresses' effigies on coins, with Sophia's significant position and active role in the political affairs as one potential factor. Furthermore, a heightened need to emphasise dynastic continuity and legitimacy might have influenced the decision to reinclude imperial women on coins.[109] Empresses represented an important factor in dynastic legitimacy, both in terms of giving birth to a male heir and in terms of their ties to an established dynasty; Sophia was Theodora's niece, after all, and Constantina, the consort of Maurice, was a daughter of Tiberius II. Dynastic continuity and legitimacy were particularly precarious in the period under study, as the majority of emperors ruling between the first half of the fifth century and the early

---

[107] Morrisson 2013, 68–78.
[108] On Sophia's role in imperial government, see Roggo and Dagnall, both this volume.
[109] On the symbolism of female effigies on coins and the idea of the empire's security and legitimacy, see also, e.g., Olster 1982, 399–408. Odahl 1986, 5–6. Brubaker and Tobler 2000, 590.

seventh century had no male offspring to whom they would have been able to hand over their rule.[110] The Heraclian succession in 641 was, after all, the first instance of power passing from father to biological son(s) since the brief rule of Leo II, i.e. roughly 150 years earlier.[111] In the time of Heraclius, the emphasis shifted to presenting the male heir, who remained part of the coin imaginary after the Augusta's portrayal disappeared from coins in 629.[112] In the case of Leontia, who appeared in various mints in the early days of her husband Phocas' reign, it was not possible to evoke ties to the previous ruler Maurice, who had been violently overthrown. Leontia never provided a male heir,[113] but still could have served to evoke the image of a new dynasty.

The Augusta's role on coin issues struck in the sixth and seventh centuries seems to be mainly that of an abstract symbol, which is supported, for example, by the fact that in the vast majority of cases, they remain unnamed.[114] In some cases, it remains unclear whether the coins depicting Augustae were struck based on a specific policy, or whether they were simply the continuation of a previously introduced type (e.g., in Thessalonica under Tiberius and Maurice, and under Heraclius after 628 when most mints ceased to include the Augusta; or in Antioch under Phocas). Various examples have demonstrated that the mints in the provinces often functioned differently from the capital mint. In some places the empress' representation never appeared on coins (e.g., in Alexandria). At the same time, some depictions of Augustae in the provinces seem to have had a specific meaning or arisen out of specific circumstances. Two areas in particular stand out: Cherson and Carthage. Both mints not only often resorted to a different type of iconography, but more than once included the figure of a potential successor in their repertoire at a time when this was not common in other mints (in Carthage under Maurice; in Cherson possibly also under Justin II, Tiberius, and Phocas). The mint in Carthage also stands out in that it was the only one to include the full name of the empress Sophia. The fact that these mints departed from models common elsewhere, had a certain tendency to mint 'family coins', and included unusual elements (e.g., paying homage to the imperial couple with the exclamation VITA that included Sophia's full name or the unusual representation of a male heir under Maurice in Carthage) indicate that

---

[110] On the role of empresses as transmitters of dynastic legitimacy in the case of the male heir's absence, see, e.g., Croke 2015a, 291. Herrin 2013, 174–76. Olster 1982, 399–400.

[111] Cf. Viermann, this volume, 140.

[112] Cf. Viermann, this volume, 140.

[113] E.g., Philip Grierson emphasized the fact that Leontia did not provide a male heir, but just a daughter, thus he considers her presence on coins to be inspired by the coins of Cherson; see Grierson 1982, 45.

[114] See, e.g., Brubaker and Tobler 2000, 587.

they emphasized the role of empresses in projecting dynastic prosperity and legitimacy to a larger extent than did other contemporary mints. In addition, the Augustae appeared in Carthage on silver issues, which makes it the only mint where women were depicted on coins from precious metal. These observations suggest that the issues discussed above were not random aberrations, but pursued certain objectives, though it is difficult to say more. It has been attested that both Carthage and Cherson made efforts to introduce better civil and military administration in the sixth and early seventh centuries.[115] With imperial coin production mainly covering state expenditures, a large part of which served to pay the army, soldiers are considered prime recipients of messages conveyed via coins.[116] In the case of Maurice's series of Chersonese 'family coinage', the iconography might have been intended to present the imperial successor to the army.[117]

For the period under consideration, coins representing Augustae are not so much evidence of their own power, it seems, but rather an indication of imperial power as a whole. Overall, the Augustae's role in imperial propaganda seems to have been limited as they did not feature on gold coins or multiples, which addressed the highest strata of Roman society or were used for diplomatic purposes. The messages delivered by bronze coins depicting Augustae aimed primarily at emphasizing legitimacy and dynastic stability to the general public (and, in some cases, to soldiers in particular). The representations of women on coins in this period of Roman history mainly testify to specific political situations and challenges that the emperors had to face.

---

[115] Carthage was a centre of the newly created African Exarchate in 590, see *MIBEc*, 52. For the first mention of the Exarch of Africa in 591, see BMC I, xxi. For military challenges by the Moors, see Barker 1966, 266. The Cherson region also witnessed a Byzantine effort to consolidate the situation as it was regularly challenged by the Turks. Some scholars suggest that the military administration established there under Maurice could have been a precursor for the future Byzantine *thema*, see, e.g., Ajbabin 2011, 83, 120–28, or the commentary to IOSPE V 330 by Andrey Vinogradov and Irene Polinskaya: https://iospe.kcl.ac.uk/5.330.html (last accessed 4 November 2023).
[116] For earlier centuries see, e.g., Hekster 2007. Manders 2012, 29–30.
[117] Grierson 1982, 45 and 73. Gkantzios Drápelová 2016, 82–83.

196 Empresses-in-Waiting

Table 1: The empress Sophia on Justin II's coins

Mint	Period	Metal	Denomination	Obverse legend	Iconography	Type
Constantinople	565–77/78	Cu	M (=*follis*), K (=half-*follis*)	DN IVSTINVS (PPAVC)	Enthroned couple	*MIBEc* 43a–f (M); *MIBEc* 44a–d (K)
		Cu	E		Monogram	*MIBEc* 45
Nicomedia	566–77/78	Cu	M, K	DN IVSTINVS PPAVC	Enthroned couple	*MIBEc* 46a–b (M); *MIBEc* 47a–b (K)
		Cu	E		Monogram	*MIBEc* 49
Cyzicus	566–77/78	Cu	K	IVSTI(A)NVS PPAVC	Enthroned couple	*MIBEc* 51a–c
	567–77/78	Cu	M	DN IVSTINVS PPAVC	Enthroned couple	*MIBEc* 50a–d
		Cu	E		Monogram	*MIBEc* 53
Antioch	569/70–77/78	Cu	M, K, I	Blundered legend	Enthroned couple	*MIBEc* 56a–b and 57a–b (M); *MIBEc* 59, 60a–b (K); *MIBEc* 63a–b (I)
		Cu	E		Monogram	*MIBEc* 65a–b
Thessalonica	568/69–77/78	Cu	K	DN IVSTINVS PPAVC	Enthroned couple	*MIBEc* 70a–f
		Cu	E		Monogram	*MIBEc* 72
Carthage	After 572/73–77/78 (?)	Ag	Half-*siliqua*	DN IVSTINVS	Obverse: enthroned couple	*MIBEc* 33a–c

Mint	Period	Metal	Denomination	Obverse legend	Iconography	Type
	572/73	Cu	M, K, I	DN IVSTINO ET SOPHIAE	Frontal busts	*MIBEc* 73 (M); *MIBEc* 76 (K)
	574/75	Cu	M, K	DN IVSTINO ET SOPHIAE	Enthroned couple	*MIBEc* 74 (M); *MIBEc* 77 (K)
	572/73–77/78	Cu	I	DN IVSTINO ET SOPHIAE	Frontal busts	*MIBEc* 80a–b
Cherson	?	Cu	H (=M), Δ (=K)	Cherson	Standing couple	*MIBEc* 159–62; Δ u Anokhina

Table 2: Empresses Anastasia and Constantina

Empress	Mint	Period	Metal	Denomination	Iconography	Type
Anastasia	Thessalonica	578–81/82	Cu	K	Enthroned couple	*MIBEc* 65
	Cherson (?)	578–81/82	Cu	H (=M)	Standing couple	*MIBEc* 185b
Constantina	Thessalonica	582/83–83/84	Cu	K	Enthroned couple	*MIBEc* 110B–111B
	Cherson	582/23–602	Cu	H (=M), Δ (=K)	Standing couple	*MIBEc* 157a–c; 160a–b
	Carthage	590–92	Ag	Half-*siliqua*	Reverse: frontal busts	*MIBEc* 59a–b

Table 3: Empress Leontia

Mint	Period	Metal	Denomination	Iconography	Type
Constantinople	602–603/604	Bronze	M, K	Standing couple	*MIBEc* 60a–b and 64a–b
Nicomedia	602–603/604	Bronze	M, K	Standing couple	*MIBEc* 68 and 71
Cyzicus	602/603	Bronze	M, K	Standing couple	*MIBEc* 75 and 78
Antioch	602/603–608	Bronze	M, K, I	Standing couple	*MIBEc* 83a–b, 85, and 87
Thessalonica	604/605–605/606	Bronze	K	Standing couple	*MIBEc* 94

Table 4: Augusta on Heraclius' coins

Mint	Period	Metal	Denomination	Iconography	Type
Constantinople	615/16–628/29[118]	Bronze	M	Obverse: three standing figures	
Thessalonica	621/22–629/30[119]	Bronze	M	Obverse: three standing figures	*MIB* III 221
	622/23 and 627/28	Bronze	K	Obverse: three standing figures	*MIB* III 229
Nicomedia	615/16–17/18 and 625/26–27/28	Bronze	M	Obverse: three standing figures	*MIB* III 176 and 177

[118] Without evidence on folles struck in 617/18 and 621/22.
[119] Without evidence on folles struck in 625/26 and 626/27.

8 Empresses on Early Byzantine Coins 199

Mint	Period	Metal	Denomination	Iconography	Type
Cyzicus	625/26–28/29[120]	Bronze	M	Obverse: three standing figures	*MIB* III 186
	627/28	Bronze	K	Obverse: three standing figures	*MIB* III 189
Carthage	615/16–41 (?)	Ag	third *siliqua*	Reverse: two facing busts (male heir and Augusta)	*MIB* III 149
Ravenna	616/17–18/19, 622/23, and 625/26	Bronze	M	Obverse: three facing busts	*MIB* III 251 and 252
	616/17–18/19 and 625/26	Bronze	K	Obverse: three facing busts	*MIB* III 259 and 260
		Bronze	X	Obverse: three facing busts	*MIB* III 264
Cyprus	626/27–28/29	Bronze	M	Obverse: three standing figures	*MIB* III 198
Rome[121]	622/23–24/25	Bronze	K	Obverse: three facing busts	*MIB* III 244
Cherson	615/16–24 (?)	Bronze	H (=M)	Obverse: two standing figures (emperor and Augusta)	*MIB* III 265

[120] Without evidence on folles struck in 626/27.
[121] There are no iconographic elements (e.g., pinnacles or pendilia on crown) that would enable the identification of one of the busts as an Augusta without any doubt. In some catalogues the figure is identified as Heraclonas.

Catalogues

DO Seals 5
E. McGeer, J. Nesbitt, and N.Oikonomides, *Catalogue of Byzantine Seals at Dumbarton Oaks and in the Fogg Museum of Art, Volume 5: The East (continued), Constantinople and Environs, Unknown Locations, Addenda, Uncertain Readings,* Washington 2005.

DOC I
Alfred R. Bellinger, *Catalogue of the Byzantine Coins in the Dumbarton Oaks Collection and in the Whittemore Collection, Volume 1: Anastasius I to Maurice, 491–602,* Washington 1965.

DOC II/1
Philip Grierson, *Catalogue of the Byzantine Coins in the Dumbarton Oaks Collection and in the Whittemore Collection, Volume 2: Phocas to Theodosius III, 602–717,* Washington 1968.

DOC III/1
Philip Grierson, *Catalogue of the Byzantine Coins in the Dumbarton Oaks Collection and in the Whittemore Collection, Volume 3, part 1: Leo III to Michael III, 717–867,* Washington 1973 (2nd impression 1993).

DOC III/2
Philip Grierson, *Catalogue of the Byzantine Coins in the Dumbarton Oaks Collection and in the Whittemore Collection, Volume 3, part 2: Basil I to Nicephorus III, 867–1081,* Washington 1973 (2nd impression 1993).

BNP I
C. Morrisson, *Catalogue des monnaies byzantines de la Bibliothèque nationale I, D'Anastase Ier à Justinien II (491–711),* Paris 1970.

BNP II
C. Morrisson, *Catalogue des monnaies byzantines de la Bibliothèque nationale II, De Philippicus à Alexis III (711–1204),* Paris 1970.

LRC
P. Grierson and M. Mays, *Catalogue of Late Roman Coins in the Dumbarton Oaks Collection and the Whittemore Collection,* Washington 1992.

MIB III
W. Hahn, *Moneta Imperii Byzantini, Volume 3: Von Heraclius bis Leo III/Alleinregierung (610–720)*, Vienna 1981.

MIBE
W. Hahn and M.A. Metlic, *Money of the Insipient Byzantine Empire (Anastasius I – Justinian I, 491–565)*, Vienna 2000.

MIBEc
W. Hahn and M.A. Metlich, *Money of the Incipient Byzantine Empire Continued (Justin II – Revolt of the Heraclii, 565–610)*, Vienna 2009.
Ratto 1930/1959
R. Ratto, *Monnaies byzantines et d'autres pays contemporaines a l'époque Byzantine*, Reprint, Amsterdam, 1959.

RIC IX
J. Pearce, *The Roman Imperial Coinage, Volume 9: Valentinian I – Theodosius I*, London 1933.

RIC X
J. Kent, *The Roman Imperial Coinage, Volume 10: The Divided Empire and the Fall of the Western Parts, AD 395–491*, London 1994.

Section 3

Non- and Near-Imperial Women at the Imperial Court

9

Augusta Unrealized: Anicia Juliana and the Logistics of Place

Geoffrey Nathan

Omnium consensu capax imperii nisi imperasset.
"By the agreement of all, he would have been thought capable of ruling had he never ruled."

Tacitus on the emperor Galba, Histories 1.49.

In a review of Anne Kolb's edited volume *Augustae*, Jörg Fündling remarked that the term "imperial woman" is "as comprehensive as it is vacuous".[1] His comment underlies a basic problem consistent with examining such women in the pre-modern world: that it is difficult to create a taxonomy of behaviours, expectations, or ideology that is readily applicable to females of the ruler's household, empresses or otherwise. Nor is this necessarily a gender-specific concern. It might be true of Roman rulers as well: Andrew Wallace-Hadrill, for example, described the homogenous conglomeration of virtues that made up an unreal, 'ideal' emperor.[2]

This is equally applicable to the Byzantine era, in part due to the prominent roles imperial women often played, starting with Constantine's family itself.[3] Perhaps because of this challenge, they are often characterized as possessing considerable 'unofficial' power. This is a tacit acknowledgement of an association between their ability to wield authority and the challenges of broader cultural (masculine) constructions of the feminine. Three regnant imperial women underscore this problem: the sisters Zoe and Theodora co-ruled with the feminine title *porphyrogenite* in the eleventh century, while Irene insisted upon the masculine *basileus* in the ninth. The tensions created between sex and gendered activities greatly contributed to such ambiguity.

---

[1] Fündling 2011.
[2] Wallace-Hadrill 1981.
[3] James 2013. Brubaker 1997.

As a means of establishing a clearer typology of the imperial woman (or women), we can examine, for the lack of a better term, a 'near-imperial'. Considering someone who was proximate to, but never *of* the ruling household offers several advantages. First, such an individual can serve as a model of privileged womanhood and could more openly display behaviours and expectations than those whose position within the palace might circumscribe their agency. Second, the life and actions of such a woman can, if at variance with those behaviours and expectations, better define the normative limits of imperial womanhood. Third, such a comparison can indicate the parameters under which women might exercise and express authority as well as less formal means of influence.

To these ends, the aristocrat Anicia Juliana will serve as our 'control subject'. While there are many from which to choose, Juliana offers several advantages. First and perhaps most practically, there is considerably more information about her life and activities than many elite women. Indeed, we know more about her than many of her female imperial contemporaries. We therefore can speak to a greater range of activities than we might with others.

Second, her ambiguous status was almost unique: although the daughter of an emperor and descended from the Theodosian dynasty (as well as claiming lateral descent from Constantine),[4] Anicia never lived in an imperial household, nor ever became an Augusta, whether or not she possessed any such ambitions to either. As we shall discuss, her position in Constantinople and the empire was directly related to the circumstances by which her father achieved the western throne.

Third, Anicia's life and activities offer a rare look at the behaviour and behavioural limitations for women of the imperial family. That she remained outside the imperial court permitted Juliana a prominence and freedom that serves to better illuminate what such women could do or be. This chapter therefore will consider Anicia's public life and persona, highlighting both similarities and divergences with her counterparts in the fourth through sixth centuries.

A Biographical Overview

Anicia Juliana has received considerable attention for over a century. This scholarship is extensive, and includes work by von Premerstein, Mango, Speck, Capizzi, Kiilerich, Bardill, and Angelova.[5] Much of this research has focused on either her building projects in Constantinople or her portrait

---

[4] This may have been a continuation of Theodosian rulers associating themselves with the Constantinian dynasty; see Brubaker and Tobler 2000.
[5] Von Premerstein 1903. Mango and Ševčenko 1961. Speck 1991. Capizzi 1997. Kiilerich 2001. Bardill 2006. Angelova 2015.

found in the Vienna Dioscurides Codex (fig. 3). Occasionally, some studies have been more comprehensive.[6] My own assessments have suggested that her acts of self-promotion were to give credence to an imperial pedigree and intentions.[7]

A brief synopsis of her life is useful.[8] Juliana was born in 462 in Constantinople to the *inlustris* Anicius Olybrius, and the younger daughter of Valentinian III, Placidia.[9] Olybrius later reigned as the western emperor in 472, but did not live long enough either to consolidate his claim or bring his family west.[10] Anicia lived in the eastern capital for her entire life and would inherit considerable wealth and properties; she was perhaps the richest private citizen in the empire.[11]

Her father's brief imperial career had garnered her the title *nobilissima* (grk. *epiphanestate*) reserved for the children and occasionally siblings of an emperor. Although an imperial honorific, it presumed no claim on the throne.[12] In Anicia's case, it was also apparently a tacit acceptance of her father's ambiguous legitimacy (his unintended stewardship of the West having been engineered by the *magister militum* Ricimer).[13] Had he not died soon after his appointment, his tenure might not have been recognized in Constantinople.[14] Nevertheless, the title remained or was awarded. At some later date, Anicia was also granted a patriciate, apparently in her own name.[15] That was another high honour without any explicit political implications.

These titles were probably granted to serve imperial policy. When she was 17 or 18, fatherless and technically still a minor,[16] the emperor

---

[6] Notably Capizzi 1997.
[7] Nathan 2006. 2011.
[8] For a fuller account of Anicia's family, see Begass 2018, 353–62 and generally 351–80.
[9] Placidia remained separated from her husband as a hostage of the Vandals until 461, making a birth in 462 more feasible. See Joh. Malal. 14.31.
[10] Olybrius and Placidia were themselves westerners.
[11] See Brubaker 2002, 210.
[12] Alternatively, the source of Anicia's status may have come from her mother, who was also *nobilissima*: *Coll. Avell.* 62 (a. 478) and Vict. Vit. 2.3. Cf. however, one contemporary example of the title's significance: Justinian remained a *nobilissimus* until being made Augustus shortly before Justin's death in 527; see Croke 2007.
[13] The manner of appointment is not entirely clear. John Malalas suggests that Ricimer placed Olybrius on the throne after Anthemius' assassination (*Chron.* 373–75), but John of Antioch claims he was appointed in opposition to Anthemius (*fr.* 209.1–2).
[14] On Olybrius: *PLRE* 2 (Anicius Olybrius 6), 796–98. On his family: Mommaerts and Kelley 1992.
[15] Her husband, Areobindus, never received the title, implying that Anicia was honoured for her own status; see *PLRE* (Anicia Iuliana 3), 635.
[16] Technically, most women were perpetually minors in the sense they needed a male guardian, but there were degrees of adulthood. The age of marriage for women was

Zeno offered her hand in marriage to Theodoric Amal; but the union failed to materialize.[17] Shortly thereafter, she was married to another 'barbarian', Flavius Areobindus, who came from a long line of military elite in service to Rome. At some point in the 480s, Anicia bore one son, Flavius Olybrius,[18] who gained the consulship in 491 – the first juvenile to do so since Valentinian III. In 512, a revolt against Anastasius resulted in rebels offering her husband the throne. Areobindus fled (subsequently disappearing from the historical record), but the end of the affair may have included the marriage of Anicia's son to the niece of the childless ruler.[19] Fl. Olybrius might well have been the next emperor. Instead, Justin succeeded in 518, eclipsing the Theodosian line permanently. It was during the new sovereign's reign, however, that Juliana completed a massive reconstruction of the church of St. Polyeuktos.[20] She was still alive at the beginning of Justinian's reign, if we are to believe an anecdote of their meeting (see final section below).[21] Anicia must have died shortly thereafter, since eunuchs from her household travelled to Jerusalem seeking entrance into the Great Lavra of Sabas in 528.[22]

Her life raises several questions. First, how were women tools of imperial dynasties? Did they have choice in the matter of matches and how were marriages used to forward the interests of the ruling house? Second, how were they honoured and commemorated? Was this a passive exercise or was it incumbent upon the recipient to hold a certain status or perform certain activities either before or after some honour was bestowed? And lastly, how much agency did such women possess, unofficial or otherwise, and to what degree was it recognized?

Imperial Women and Marriage

"Imperial princesses [...] were destined to be diplomatic pawns".[23] This is a truism: women of all classes were often used to forge links between families. Although Christianity permitted women the option of virginity in

---

set at 12 (*CJ* 5.4.24. *Dig.* 23.1.9). For full control over property, both men and women entered their majorities at 25, although women at 18 could petition for legal adulthood (*CTh* 2.17.1a).

[17] Malch. *fr.* 16.
[18] *PLRE* 2 (Anicius Olybrius 3), 795. See Al. Cameron 1984, 162.
[19] On the *trishagion* controversy, see Meier 2007b; see also Haarer 2006, 149–62 (esp. 156–57).
[20] The beginning of this project is debated – see, e.g., Bardill 2004, 111–16 and Begass 2018, 368–70 and 378–79 – but all agree a completion date in the 520s.
[21] Gregory of Tours, *Gl. Mar.* 102–103.
[22] Cyr. Scyth., *Vit. Sabae* 69.
[23] Garland and Rapp 2006, 91–92.

some cases, for elite women this was uncommon. Even in a Christianized society, the religion reinforced Roman traditions of lawful and seemly unions.[24] The example of Melania the Younger is instructive: despite her strong desire to remain a virgin and take up an ascetic life, she was forced to marry and bear children.[25] Social convention and biology commonly trumped personal preference.

Imperial matches had obvious dynastic implications. Such marriages, particularly those between an emperor and a consort, could ensure a dynasty in producing heirs, but might also shape a ruler's future reign. Ariadne's hippodrome speech in 491 after her nuptials, for example, presaged a policy of compromise that characterized Anastasius' reign.[26] Women from the imperial household might also legitimize a new emperor's political status. Marcian's Josephite marriage to Pulcheria in 450 exemplifies what would become a recognized practice of succession through matrimony.[27] It is worth noting that sons, nephews, and grandsons were also betrothed to further familial ambitions, but this was not a defining characteristic of men's status.

It is unsurprising, then, that Anicia is first mentioned in her proposed marriage to Theodoric the Amal. Zeno and probably Pulcheria had negotiated Juliana's match, clearly taking a *de facto* familial interest in her nuptials.[28] The purpose, mentioned above, was one of political self-interest: a series of diplomatic blunders had resulted in alienating the Ostrogoth. Zeno attempted to bribe the general with both gold and the *nobilissima*. Theodoric declined; the crisis abated. Anicia remained unwed.[29]

Her marriage to Areobindus was also political and undoubtedly engineered by Zeno. The circumstances for this match are more opaque. He descended from a family of generals who had served Rome for generations, including Aspar and Ardabur.[30] But he was young; the rationale for the union can only be surmised. It is possible that the turbulent 480s had

---

[24] For a discussion of elites, see Vuolanto 2015.

[25] *Vit. Mel.* 1–4. On problems with its hagiographic tradition, see Nathan 2000, 91–92.

[26] *De cer.* 1.92. On Ariadne, see Haarer 2006, 1–5.

[27] On the significance of linking dynasties, see Nathan 2021. Such marriages were not always successful. Petronius Maximus tried to claim the western throne by marrying Licinia Eudoxia, Valentinian's widow; see Clover 1978. See also Busch 2015, 214–17.

[28] Pulcheria died ca. 484 (*PLRE* 2, 587). That she and Zeno later worked together on petitioning the Vandals to permit the appointment of a Catholic bishop of Carthage ca. 480 (Vict. Vit 2.2–3) suggests motherly involvement.

[29] Malch. *fr.* 16 (*FHG*⁴, 123). She is described as one of several suitable *feminae illustres* in the capital: καὶ γάμον αὐτῷ δώσειν τῆς Ὀλυβρίου παιδὸς ἢ ἄλλης τῶν ἐνδόξων γυναικῶν ἐν τῇ πόλει. As she is specifically mentioned, she was probably considered the most eminent.

[30] On Areobindus' family, see McEvoy 2016b.

induced Zeno to make an alliance with a promising military man; and in fact, Areobindus would later garner considerable success against Persia in 504–505. It may be that he was being groomed as a potential imperial candidate; his great-uncle had briefly been named Caesar thanks to a similar match.[31] That twenty or so years later, rebels in 512 would offer him the emperorship reinforces the possibility.

The third marriage of significance is that of Anicia's son to Irene, the niece of Anastasius. The date of the marriage is unknown; given his age, it would not have been before 500 CE. It may have come after Areobindus' consulship in 506. As already mentioned, it might have also come after the 512 rebellion, where an end to the event would have been sealed with an alliance between ruler and would-be ruler. Regardless, Anicia would have likely arranged the match and her son was a contender for the throne.[32] It is significant that Fl. Olybrius probably received his own patriciate in the 510s.[33]

These marriage scenarios are instructive. The first two fit into normative patterns of young women having little agency in their choice of spouse in first marriages. Anicia never remarried (assuming she was eventually widowed), so we cannot speak of greater agency as an older woman. Her son's nuptials also exhibit a familiar feature: that mothers traditionally negotiated marriages for their children.[34] Lastly, each episode was completely political in nature – and in at least the first case, specifically proposed to settle a crisis.

Church Politics and Femininity

How women participated in church matters is a second area of consideration. Patronage of clerics and specific churches were common activities, as were charitable endeavours.[35] Since the days of Helena, imperial women had increasingly forwarded certain clerical favourites and occasionally pushed religious agendas. Aelia Eudoxia apparently financed anti-Arian demonstrations in Constantinople,[36] and – if we are to believe her detractors

---

[31] Patricius had been briefly wed to Leontia, Leo I's daughter. Although there were occasional matches between imperial family members and Germanic military officers – most notably Stilicho to Serena – Patricius was the first to get an imperial title; see Marc. Comes s.a. 471, *Vit. S. Marcelli* 34, and Vict. Ton. 470.
[32] A contemporary prophecy claimed an "Olibus" would reign in the East; see Alexander 1967, 20–21. Alexander suggests this should be emended to Olybrius; 112, n. 50 and 126, n. 15.
[33] Joh. Malal. 18.80.
[34] Treggiari 1993, ch. 4 *passim*; Nathan 2000, 152–57. See Washington, this volume.
[35] Brown 2012, 25–30 and 273–88.
[36] Socrates, *Hist. eccl.* 6.8 and 8.8.

– engineered John Chrysostom's exile.[37] Her daughter Pulcheria was probably the prime mover of anti-Jewish legislation during her brother's minority.[38] And of course, Theodora's involvement in church affairs is well attested.[39] Although common, such activities were not always welcomed: women's roles in helping exiled clerics, for example, was often criticized.[40]

Imperial women also took interest in theological disputes. In the fifth and sixth centuries, those predominantly focused on disagreements over Christ's nature. The Chalcedonian Creed – which stated that Christ had two *physes*, human and divine, hypostatically joined into one person – was officially orthodox. In contrast, Miaphysites argued for a nature essentially divine, minimizing or even denying Christ's humanity. Between 484 and 519, eastern and western Christendom officially split over this issue and that of papal authority. The Acacian Schism became the context for this doctrinal conflict.[41]

The already discussed rebellion in November 512 exemplifies the potential ramifications of such disputes. A proponent of theological compromise, Anastasius had pushed for a modified liturgy and exchanged the capital's patriarch for one who would favour the new formula. The replacement pleased few Chalcedonians or Miaphysites. When the emperor replaced a second bishop, mob violence broke out in Constantinople, resulting in the murder of monks thought to favour the new policy, an open rejection of the ruler, and the search for a replacement in Areobindus. Even after the matter was settled, the *comes* Vitalian rebelled in Thrace, claiming he was championing orthodoxy.[42]

The end of the Acacian Schism under Justin in 519 was arguably the most important religious moment of the age: Christendom was restored, Chalcedon reconfirmed, and the state recommitted to papal supremacy.[43] But reunification proved not as simple as an imperial imprimatur. Although Justin sought to end the split, the sees of Antioch and Alexandria initially refused to condemn the advocates of compromise. Both secular and religious parties had to coordinate and agree to several conditions, reject

---

[37] Ps.-Martyrius, *Orat. Fun.* 121. On Ps.-Martryrius: Barnes 2001. Barry 2016. See also Zos. 5.23.2.
[38] *CTh* 16.8.18; 21–27. On Pulcheria's influence: Holum 1982, 98. Busch 2015, 110–35. Millar 2007, *passim* and 140–56.
[39] See Potter 2015, 157–78. Evans 2002, 67–84.
[40] Hillner 2019b.
[41] For the Acacian Schism: Schwartz 1934. Blaudeau 2012. Kötter 2013.
[42] Theoph. Conf. AM 6005. Marc. Comes s.a. 514. *Coll. Avell.* 116. Vitalian was still *comes* and not *magister militum* of Thrace when he first rebelled: *PLRE* 2 (Fl. Vitalianus 2), 1117–73.
[43] Valentinian III had *de facto* recognized the supreme authority of the Roman bishop: *N.Val.* 17.

certain precedents, and set new ones.[44] While the schism formally ended in 519, matters took several years to settle. Anicia had over her life commissioned church structures (see next section), supported and patronized monastic missions, and done charity work in the capital;[45] such enterprises had been common amongst elite women for almost two centuries. But the circumstances of reunification also provided an opportunity for Anicia to participate in the process.

The minutiae of diplomatic manoeuvring need not directly concern us, but several prominent women were involved in facilitating the schism's end. In addition to Juliana, the new empress Euphemia, the *patrikia* Anastasia (wife of Pompeius, the nephew of the previous emperor), and an otherwise unknown Palmatia all wrote to and/or received letters from Pope Hormisdas.[46] Like Anicia, Anastasia was a fierce Chalcedonian, was apparently her friend, and was likewise disenfranchised by Justin's accession.[47] We have then at least three women with close familial connections to the imperial house.

But there are two distinctive differences in their respective involvement. First, in the cases of the three other women, the Pope urges them to advocate for the papal delegation and mission with those who had the authority to act – what Andrew Gillett terms "lateral communication",[48] exerting unofficial (i.e., female) influence. In contrast, the surviving correspondence with Anicia makes clear that Hormisdas is not only asking her to use her considerable influence, but is also taking advice from the patrician.[49] In her letter from April 519, Anicia urges the Pope to keep his papal delegates in Constantinople – some of whom she was apparently housing –until matters were finalized.[50] Even more interesting is her fragmentary letter sarcastically praising the Roman bishop: it has an unctuous tone to it, suggesting that he needs to be more aggressive in his defence of the faith and piquantly offering to point him in the right direction![51]

Second, in contrast to the other involved women, there seems to have been a more extensive but unattested correspondence between Anicia and the Roman bishop.[52] The contents are unknown, but there was a degree of

---

[44] See Allen 2017.
[45] Cyr. Scyth., *Vit. Sabae* 53 and 69.
[46] Gillett 2012 suggests that Palmatia might be the unnamed wife of Vitalian.
[47] On her orthodoxy: Theoph. Conf. AM 6005; on her friendship: Cyr. Scyth., *Vit. Sabae* 53.
[48] Gillett 2012. But cf. *Coll. Avell.* 170, dated to July 519, which claims that Euphemia participates in decision-making. Gillett 2012, 267 n. 33.
[49] See *Coll. Avell.* 164. 179. 198.
[50] *Coll. Avell.* 164.
[51] *Coll. Avell.* 198.2.
[52] In *Coll. Avell.* 179:1, Hormisdas refers to Anicia's multiple letters.

participation not matched by any of the other women; given the surviving epistles, this may have included more advice-giving and matters of strategy. Why Anicia was more involved than other elite women is not entirely clear, but her prominence made her one of the papacy's most influential advocates.[53] She may have also been a more willing participant; Euphemia in contrast offered only one short response to the Pope's exhortations and remained politely non-committal.[54]

While we could never call Anicia's role in the reunification crucial, we nevertheless have a degree of involvement in religious affairs not seen since Pulcheria's regency of Theodosius II.[55] Her ability to do so must have been predicated on her own sense of importance as a defender of Chalcedonianism, her lineage, and the knowledge that her efforts could not be censured by the new regime.[56] It may have also provided a precedent that later empresses would follow.

Imperial Builders

"Constantinople was dedicated through stripping bare almost every city founded before Byzantium [of their art and public monuments]."[57] Jerome believed the new capital was created and shaped by Constantine's imperial vision; and commissioning the construction of monumental architecture was the most conspicuous display of the emperor's wealth and prestige. Urban elites also sought and were encouraged to leave their marks on the built environment. Anicia's palace in modern Saraçhane is a case in point: it stood almost equidistant between the imperial palace and the Church of the Apostles along the triumphal processional route, symbolizing a continuity and connection that would be reinforced by some of her own building projects. Like the palaces of the elite near the hippodrome, hers was undoubtedly self-aggrandizing, and exemplified a competition among an aristocracy seeking to define the capital's urban topography.[58]

In terms of public structures, the commissioning of churches and other religious buildings became the most popular form of euergetism and the most visible indication of ostensible piety. If Jerome saw an imperial purpose, Eusebius saw a religious one: turning Constantinople into a

---

[53] See Capizzi 1997, 78–91, for Anicia's correspondence.
[54] *Coll. Avell.* 194.
[55] Although Viermann 2022, 219, suggests that Anicia was a "driving force" in ending the schism.
[56] See Croke 2007.
[57] Jer. *Chron.* 330: *Dedicatur Constantinopolis omnium paene urbium nuditate.*
[58] Basset 2004, 33–36.

Christian Rome and by extension turning Rome into a Christian empire.[59] These structures often served as visual narratives of the controversies and struggles of the age.[60]

That said, although gender and religious space have occupied academic interest,[61] trying to find commissioned structures exclusive to imperial women is a problematic task. In looking at specific projects, there seems nothing distinctive or unique in their choices or methods, although elite women did like building in Jerusalem and Palestine.[62] Accordingly, when we look at Anicia's projects, we must understand her choices within a less clearly gendered activity and more in terms of class. Imperial women did fund the construction of many churches as sole patrons, including Anicia's mother and grandmother.[63] But others were less active: in twenty-three years of marriage, Theodora is known to have commissioned only one building in Constantinople, the monastery of Metanoia, in her own name.[64]

Although Juliana probably funded multiple projects, including some outside of the capital,[65] only three are specifically attested: a church to Mary in the unidentified Honoratae district, one to St. Euphemia in the Olybrian district (along the northern Mese in *Regio* XI, a neighbourhood probably named for her father),[66] and her great reconstruction of St. Polyeuktos in the Constantinianae district. Each of these projects articulated contemporary politics and the religious struggles between elites, played out in an urban landscape.

The church dedicated to Mary is notable for several reasons. First, it is the only structure which Anicia apparently built new; her two other building projects were refurbishments of existing churches. Second, the *Theotokos* had become important as a special protectress of the capital:[67] Pulcheria supposedly commissioned three churches to her at Chalkoprateia, Blachernai, and Hodegetria.[68] Third, we have a rough date of its

---

[59] Euseb. *Vit. Const.* 3.4. See Odahl 2004.
[60] Wharton 1995, 148–62.
[61] See, e.g., Fischer 2000, Beger 2011, and Bogdanović 2018.
[62] Dirschlmayer 2015, 39–43 and 146–53. Klein 2014.
[63] Explicitly stated in the dedication to St. Euphemia: *Anth. Gr.* 1.12.1: Εἰμὶ δόμος Τριάδος, τρισσὴ δέ με τεῦξε γενέθλη – "I am the home of the Trinity, and a trinity gave birth to me."
[64] Procop. *Aed.* 1.9.5–10. But see Unterweger 2014.
[65] Outside of the capital: Cyr. Scyth., *Vit. Sabae* 68–69. For within: Pargoire 1903. Capizzi 1997.
[66] See Magdalino 2001.
[67] Av. Cameron 1978.
[68] Theod. Lect. *Ep. fr.* 363. See Twardowska 2017. Note that Justin I is also credited with commissioning Blachernai; see Mango 1998.

construction and dedication – either 512 or shortly thereafter.[69] It is only known through literary sources, primarily in a manuscript dedication to Anicia (see next section).

The church's construction indicates specific political and religious purposes. The *Theotokos* cult implied the Chalcedonian formula of Christ's nature, rejecting the irenic *Henotikon*. As such, it was a public declaration of orthodoxy. That it was constructed around 512 also meant that it was built in the wake of that year's rebellion. Anicia's commitment to orthodoxy, in contrast to Anastasian conciliation and compromise, was literally set in stone. It was also the declaration of a re-ascendant imperial house.

The church dedicated to St. Euphemia has not been definitively located, but it is in part described through portions of preserved inscriptions from the building itself.[70] We also know that it was located just west of the *Philadelphion*.[71] As I will argue elsewhere, it is probably to be identified with Beyazit A, a religious structure whose foundations were discovered, surveyed, and then buried once again in the 1940s.[72]

Like the *Theotokos* herself, the church was an expression of orthodoxy. Euphemia's renown was partly based on the Miracle of the Tome: at the Council of Chalcedon, opposing credos of Christ's nature were supposedly placed in the tomb of the martyr; three days later she was found holding the Dyophysite formula to her breast while the Monophysite one laid beneath her feet.[73] This was divine sanction of Christ's dual nature and Euphemia became a favoured saint amongst the orthodox in the decades that followed.[74] Admittedly, the tale may be a later fabrication;[75] but regardless of the story's origins, Chalcedon's sessions were held in the saint's *martyrion*-church and invited the association between Euphemia and orthodoxy.[76] It is significant that four other structures dedicated to her were built in Constantinople the decades following the council, starting with the original church built by Anicia's grandmother.[77]

It is thus unsurprising that Anicia should celebrate the martyr as an articulation of her own orthodoxy. Renovating and enlarging a church

---

[69] Theoph. Conf. AM 6005. Theod. Lect. *Epit.* 504.
[70] *Anth. Gr.* 1.12–17.
[71] *De cer.* 1.5.50. On the *Philadelphion*: Janin 1964, 410–11. Mango 1990a, 28–30.
[72] Nathan (forthcoming). On Beyazit A: Mathews 1971, 67–76. 1976, 28–33. Its demolition was part of a construction project for the University of Istanbul.
[73] Recounted in the *Synaxarion*; see Jordan 2000, 71–72.
[74] Cf. Al. Cameron 1972, 145–46.
[75] The earliest full description of the 'miracle' is found in the *Syn. Eccl. Cons.* cols. 811–13 (Delahaye 1902). See Mango 1999.
[76] A surviving inscription calls Euphemia the patron of the church: *Anth. Gr.* 1.16.1–2.
[77] For an overview: Janin 1932.

her female forebears created moreover implied imperial continuity and prestige.[78] We might even deduce that it was a construction that must have been started while Anastasius still lived: it would not only have stressed their religious differences, but in doing so also legitimized Anicia's standing as a future Augusta.[79] Once Justin had come to the throne and the Acacian Schism ended, the need to proclaim Chalcedonian loyalties would have possessed diminished political and religious currency.

The construction of the church may have also impacted the new dynasty: it is perhaps not coincidental the empress was given the regnal name Euphemia.[80] Just as Anicia had attempted to coopt orthodoxy from Anastasius, Justin had coopted religious and imperial authority. He and his renamed consort might have also tried to eclipse Anicia, a woman a bit too influential in her own right.[81] This is admittedly speculative, but consistent with all the available facts.

Third is the church of St. Polyeuktos, a structure commanding the most scholarly interest.[82] All agree that it was mostly completed in the 520s[83] and that it took three years to complete.[84] Dedicated to a martyred soldier, the renovation would be Anicia's greatest project and, for a few years, also the largest church in the world. It was purportedly modelled on Solomon's Temple, as mentioned in preserved epigrams and corroborated by the church's excavation.[85] Its remains and description all indicate that it was lavishly decorated, including narrative mosaics of Constantine's conversion and his Persian campaign. Towards the end of the project, she had the entire ceiling gilded – inestimably costly and apparently requiring Anicia to liquidate much of her personal wealth to achieve (see next section).

---

[78] Nathan 2006, 438–39. Dirschlmayer 2015, 168–69.
[79] Bardill 2004, 133–34, argues for a beginning date of 508.
[80] Her original name had been Lupicina (*PLRE* 2, 423).
[81] Note that the church to Sts. Sergius and Bacchus may have been a response to Anicia; see Shahîd 2003.
[82] Bardill 2006. 2011. Connor 1999. Fowden 1994. Harrison and Hayes 1986. Harrison 1989. Mango and Ševčenko 1961. Milner 1994. Pizzone 2003. Speck 1991. Strube 1984.
[83] The general consensus is that it was constructed between 524 and 527: see Harrison and Hayes 1986, I 278–80; coin 153 in the catalogue intimates a completion date of 527. Again, Bardill 2004, 111–16, theorizes multiple phases of construction, although accepting Polyeuktos' completion in the 520s. See also Begass 2018, 368–70.
[84] The *Palatinus* manuscript of the *Greek Anthology* includes a *marginalium* at 1.10.46–47, stating the length of construction.
[85] *Anth. Gr.* 1.10.47–50. Note that Milner 1994 argued that Polyeuktos was modelled on Ezekiel's spiritual temple, but the specifications seem closer to Solomon's; see Harrison and Hayes 1986, I 410–11. See also Bardill 2006, 342. Viermann 2022 argues that the evocation of Solomon was meant to connect Anicia to Old Testament kings.

Its *raison d'être* is much debated. Anicia herself claimed that it was an act of piety to exalt herself, her ancestors, and descendants.[86] Harrison has suggested that this was the grandiose response of a failed contender to the throne; McClanan has argued that Anicia was exercising imperial prerogatives, if not imperial authority; Bardill has seen it in almost eschatological terms.[87] I have tied its construction to the power of the saint himself: Polyeuktos purportedly had the power to make good vows, and Anicia built the church as a votive for the promise of future *imperium*.[88] Whatever the rationale, its impact affected future building in Constantinople; Justinian's claim that he had surpassed Solomon at the dedication of Hagia Sophia has been convincingly argued to refer to Anicia's church.[89]

Three observations about Polyeuktos need concern us. First, like Anicia's other churches, the timing of construction was undoubtedly tied to current political and religious events. The project must be understood in the context of a reunified Church and a ruling *parvenu* dynasty.[90] Second, it was a construction that must also be tied directly to her personal prestige: the surviving epigrams sang her personal praises and made explicit reference to an imperial pedigree;[91] the Constantine mosaics fused *pietas* and *imperium*.[92] Finally, these same epigrams not only compare the church to the First Temple, but specifically compare Anicia to her male forebears, Constantine and Theodosius I – and surpassing the rest of her glorious ancestors.[93]

Cumulatively, her building regimen presents a complex picture: on the one hand, her projects suggest they are consistent with her station and emphasized continuity with her Theodosian (and orthodox) female ancestors. On the other, the grandiosity of Polyeuktos and perhaps her other churches explicitly invited comparisons to the greatest Christian emperors. As I shall discuss below, this sort of ambiguity extended to Anicia herself.

---

[86] *Anth. Gr.* 1.10.34–38.
[87] Harrison 1989, 36–40. McClanan 1996. Bardill 2006.
[88] Nathan 2006.
[89] Harrison 1989.
[90] Although the current prevailing opinion is that Polyeuktos was a multi-decade project, with at least one break during its construction (most recently Effenberger 2019), its completion must be understood as having greater significance than its inception. In that sense, its *raison d'être* must be contextualized in the political and religious environment of the 520s.
[91] *Anth. Gr.* 1.10.7–13.
[92] See Fowden 1994. Milner 1994.
[93] *Anth. Gr.* 1.10.42–49.

Representing the Imperial Woman

It is lastly worth considering Anicia Juliana's representation in art. The treatment and representation of imperial women in literature is a discussion unto itself, and deserves more space than allotted here. That said, visual depictions of elite women are valuable for our purposes. First, there is a clear record of female portraiture over time, allowing us to trace the development of certain symbolic and stylistic qualities. Second, most surviving portrayals were 'authorized' – commissioned and offered as idealized depictions of the subject. Finally, the variety and context of imagery permits a broader reading of what it meant to be female and imperial. It is important to understand art was not static and continued to evolve over the centuries. But emperor and empress by the fifth century came to be presented as a unified whole, whose union ensured victory and religious success. Empresses were commonly depicted with family and usually in explicit religious contexts.[94] And there was a confluence of three features: the development of a distinctive female imperial dress, an emphasis on marriage and family, and the expression of Christian triumphalism.

This is visible in different contexts. Byzantine imperial portraiture in churches focused on cohesion and dynasty: women appear prominently in imperial garb, doing so in the company of spouses and children.[95] Justinian and Theodora's portraits in San Vitale's Basilica are the most opulent example. In coinage (the most numerous form of representation), women's depiction was standardized: obverse portraits, bareheaded and by 500 with full regalia, and either Nike holding the cross or the cross framed by laurels on the reverse.[96] The two ivory portraits from a diptych (originally a polyptych), probably of Ariadne, one standing and one enthroned, offer a third idealization: the empress bearing a *globus cruciger* and sceptre under a baldachin, wearing a dalmatic and chlamys and a crown with elaborate *pendilia*. A portrait of her husband (Zeno or Anastasius) appears on her outer garb. Empire and faith are fully expressed (figs. 5 and 7).[97]

Two portraits of Anicia survive, although one must be deeply suspect (fig. 18). A bust in the New York Metropolitan Museum of Art of an aristocratic woman was once considered Anicia, but its provenance is uncertain.[98]

---

[94] Wainwright 2018, 187–92.

[95] Carile 2018, 75–76.

[96] Gkantzios Drápelová, this volume. After Ariadne's death in 515, however, women do not appear on coinage again until Sophia in the late 560s; see Wainwright 2018, 165–67.

[97] Angelova 2004 discusses the importance of partnership and co-rule.

[98] Personal correspondence with Dr. Helen C. Evans, curator at the NYMMA, has confirmed unclear provenance. The museum has removed the identification.

It is clearly a female of status, who may be a patrician. She does possess a weak chin, a feature of many Theodosians. But this hardly confirms her identity. More securely, there is a surviving dedicatory miniature of Anicia in the *Materia Medica* manuscript, often called the Vienna Dioscurides, appearing on the sixth folio *verso* (fig. 3) and produced between 512 and 515.[99] Compared to other imperial portraits, Anicia's bears some similarities to those found on the coinage and the above-described ivories. Like most official portraiture of the late fifth and sixth centuries, she is presented face forward. Juliana is also richly dressed and sitting on a curule chair. She wears a crown not unlike Ariadne's. The intertwined gold roping framing the centre and surrounding images serves as a *de facto* baldachin. And while the image shows no visual sign of her faith, the accompanying inscription thanks her for building the church to the *Theotokos*. She is presented as an individual of status and piety.

But there are distinctive qualities that differentiate Anicia's portrait from those of her counterparts. The paraphernalia rejects the imperial feminine: she does not wear a chlamys and her jewellery is less ostentatious than contemporaries'.[100] She bears no sceptre or globus, the latter found on almost all coinage depicting empresses from the sixth century forward. Absent, too, are any references to her husband – she is described as a member of the Anician *genos*. Moreover, she distributes money with her right hand and holds a codicil in her left. Offering wealth in this manner is a motif found among consular portraits, including her own husband's (fig. 19).[101] Lastly, the *suppedaneum* and vaulted chair legs resemble those found in Areobindus' diptych. The portrait's format and content bear much closer resemblance to Late Antique diptychs depicting men.

The image also possesses imperial qualities.[102] In terms of composition, Constantius II's portrait in the *Chronography* of 354 is perhaps the closest analogue.[103] Anicia wears a gold-striated purple trabea instead of the consular *trabea triumphalis*, an explicit reference to imperial status. There are also several accompanying anthropomorphized virtues, suggesting that the artist – and presumably Anicia – presented the *patrikia* in terms of male imperial qualities. These include *Megalopsychia* (Magnanimity), *Phronesis* (Prudence), and *Pothos tes Philoktistou* (The Desire of the Love of Building).[104]

---

[99] See Von Premerstein 1903.
[100] On the representation of women: Métraux 2008.
[101] Al. Cameron 2013. 2015.
[102] Kiilerich 2001. Nathan 2011.
[103] Romanus 1 ms., Barb. lat. 2154, fol. 13r.: https://digi.vatlib.it/view/MSS_Barb.lat.2154.pt.B (last accessed 15 November 2023). See also Salzman 1990, fig. 13.
[104] On *megalopsychia*: Patlagean 1992. *Philanthropia* would be the more 'feminine' quality of generosity: McClanan 1996. McClanan notes Anicia's *megalopsychia* in the miniature, but her *philanthropia* in commissioning St. Polyeuktos (54–55).

Moreover, *Eucharistia teknon* (Gratitude of the Arts) performs *proskynesis* before Anicia, an act with distinct imperial overtones. That the portrait was made just after the settlement of 512 undoubtedly invited the comparison.[105] In sum, while there are features of the miniature that articulate imperial femininity, it partakes more of male qualities, both imperial and non-imperial. These ambiguities were clearly intentional, reflecting Anicia Juliana's own ambiguous station in Constantinople at the time.

Towards an Imperial Understanding?

This discussion of Anicia Juliana as a near-imperial has highlighted both the similarities to and discontinuities with her contemporaries. It is important to note that the following observations are relevant primarily to Late Antiquity (ca. 300–600 CE), although the place and power of such women must be understood in a continuum over a much longer time. It is also worth stating that Anicia's life must be placed in the context of empresses specifically; for the most part, it can shed little light on imperial women who were not imperial consorts. She had more in common with Ariadne and Euphemia than she did with other *nobilissimae* who never became empresses.

That said, in some respects, Anicia's life and activities parallel those in the palace and elite women more generally. Status and honours were determined by birth; authority and agency came with age. They were independently wealthy and commanded large *koubikulariai*.[106] Public identities were commonly constructed through the medium of religion, Christianity allowing them forms of notoriety not available to earlier Roman matrons. Its primacy gave such women opportunity to exercise visible forms of authority under the guise of piety. This was true for imperial men, but their agency came within different and less circumscribed venues. Military and political offices afforded them legal authority in addition to social status. Elite and imperial women negotiated the strictures of gender that precluded them from the empire's magistracies or deliberative clerical offices.

Moreover, Anicia's life paralleled those women whose station could provide imperial prestige to *arriviste* emperors. Just as Theodosius I, Marcian, Zeno, Anthemius, and others all took imperial wives to legitimize their rules, Areobindus' marriage to Anicia made him a suitable alternative to Anastasius. Women's ability to provide legitimacy, however, should not be mistaken for their power to do so. Yes, they could have considerable say

---

[105] Viermann, 2022, 222–24, notes an analogous imperial language used in the dedicatory inscriptions at St. Polyeuktos.

[106] For a general overview, see Gettings 2003.

in these affairs, especially if they were *porphyrogenitai* or Augustae, but in every case their acquiescence to matrimony came after candidates had been already forwarded by men. Nor was there any guarantee of their impact: Leo I's daughter, Leontia, for example, could not secure the emperorship for her first husband. They might also negotiate the next generation's ruler by virtue of their status: Sophia did so with Tiberius II and Anicia tried to do so with her own son. Despite that influence, imperial women acted as conduits of authority: they had no intrinsic rights to make emperors themselves.

This is best epitomized by the anecdote found in Gregory of Tours mentioned above (*Gl. Mart.* 102–103). Justinian as a new emperor demanded most of Anicia's fortune, claiming he needed it to cover the costs of his accession. The elderly patrician had in response sold most of her property, trading it for gold and affixing this wealth to the ceiling of St. Polyeuktos. Realizing he had been outmanoeuvred, the emperor started to leave when Anicia removed an emerald ring from her finger and gave it him, saying "Accept, most sacred emperor, this tiny ring from my hand, for it is considered to be more valuable than this gold above."[107] Apocryphal or not, the story must have circulated in the decades after her death, and its implications were clear. Her approval was key to legitimizing the young ruler. But ultimately Anicia plays an intermediary here, her 'gift' a face-saving but not strictly necessary endorsement.

All this said, how can Anicia speak to the institutionalized power an emperor's consort might possess? Her dedicatory portrait had assumed symbols of male imperial authority and largely minimized female ones. In contrast, empresses were portrayed with gender-specific symbols of rule and religiosity, their regalia and accoutrements of power well established. The Anicia found in her miniature and the woman described in the epigrams found in Sts. Euphemia and Polyeuktos were not duplicated in representations of her imperial sisters.

Anicia's building projects and her forays into political and religious affairs moreover were indications of an independent actor in her own right and were activities that evoked direct imperial responses. True, there were also concrete examples of empresses exercising authority: Theodora, for example, famously participated in the emperor's *boule* during the Nika revolt and apparently controlled judicial appointments over some *dikasteria*; Aelia Sophia was *de facto* ruler as her husband's mental health deteriorated.[108]

---

[107] Gregory of Tours, *Gl. Mar.* 103: *Accipe, imperator sanctissime, hoc munisculum de manu mea, quod supra pretium huius auri valere censetur.*

[108] Theodora: Procop. *Bell.* 1.24.32–37; *Anecd.* 19–23. Aelia Sophia: Evagr. *Hist. eccl.* 5.12–13. Theoph. Conf. AM 6071. On Aelia Sophia, see Roggo and Dagnall, both this volume.

But these examples and others do not indicate any inherent institutional powers of an Augusta or *basilissa*. In contrast, Anicia Juliana's imperial self-promotion demonstrates that much of her life's work exceeded what an imperial consort would be willing to do or indeed could do. An empress' symbols of authority were not guarantors of authority.

This overview of Anicia Juliana's life ultimately raises an important and not fully answerable question: can we create a typology of the Byzantine imperial woman? Other contributors here have implicitly asked this question, but I would make three observations. First, that while imperial women by virtue of birth or marriage might provide legitimacy to a future claimant, that should not be mistaken for any intrinsic power. Second, any powers or authority such women might possess were predicated on circumstances and not any constitutional basis. Often, the latitude granted by an emperor (or his quiescence; e.g., Pulcheria during her brother's reign) dictated their range of actions. That said, tradition – especially for imperial consorts – assured them certain prerogatives that were not easily abrogated by the emperor, the court, or the Church.

It is worth noting in closing that Anicia Juliana never became an Augusta. That, in itself, was not remarkable; that she managed to survive and thrive with no great harm to herself, her family, or her legacy, was. Her churches served as stations along imperial processions; her descendants married into the houses of Anastasius and Justinian.[109] The best way to summarize her life is to paraphrase the quote from Tacitus at the beginning of this chapter. *Capax imperii cum non imperasset*: "Anicia Juliana was thought capable of ruling since she never ruled."

---

[109] Olybrius' daughter Proba married a probable relative of Anastasius. Anicia's great-granddaughter and namesake, Juliana, married another. And her great-great granddaughter Proba married a relative of Theodora. See *PLRE* 3a (Iuliana 2), 728, and (Proba 1 and 2), 1058.

10

Antonina *Patricia*: Theodora's Fixer at the Female Court and the Politics of Gender in Procopius

Christopher Lillington-Martin

> Her [sc. Antonina's] fury lurked like a scorpion in the shadows.
> ἦν γὰρ σκορπιώδης τε καὶ ὀργὴν σκοτεινή.
>
> *Anekdota* 1.26[1]

> Yet she [sc. Theodora] was in the habit of constantly lashing out viciously, like a scorpion, against her fellow actresses, for she was mad with envy.
> ἦν γὰρ τοῖς ὁρῶσιν ἄλλως τε καὶ ἀρχομένης ἡμέρας βλάσφημος οἰωνός.
> ἐς μέντοι τὰς συνθεατρίας ἀγριώτατα εἰώθει ἐς ἀεὶ σκορπιαίνεσθαι·
> βασκανίᾳ γὰρ πολλῇ εἴχετο.
>
> *Anekdota* 9.26[2]

These epigraphs demonstrate how Procopius falls into established tropes, insulting these women by reference to the same scorpion metaphor for both, in stereotyped and misogynistic ways. Moreover, they elaborate on the symmetry between their careers. This chapter examines the portrayal of Antonina's involvement in religious, political, and dynastic affairs and how she aims at her own advancement and that of Joannina,[3] her youngest daughter, while fixing things for Theodora. Procopius' narrative, our main

---

[1] Translations, with adaptations, of Procopius' *Anekdota (Secret History)* and *Wars*: Dewing 1935 and 1914, respectively; Kaldellis 2010 and Dewing and Kaldellis 2014, respectively; *Persian Wars*: Greatrex 2022a. 2022b. "*Secret History*" derives from the Latin translation, *Historia arcana*, by Niccol Alamanni, 1623. *Anekdota* is used throughout this chapter. Footnotes use *Anecd.* for *Anekdota* and *Bell.* for *Wars*.
[2] Procopius associates Theodora with the scorpion regarding her ferocity (Iliopoulos/ Ηλιόπουλος 2021, 91, n. 166 and 78, n. 102), comparable to Procop. *Anecd.* 1.13, below.
[3] *PLRE* 3a (Ioannina), 712.

and sometimes only source, is heavily influenced by earlier Greek historiography and indeed other classical genres.[4] His classicizing presentation of events often reflects established literary and cultural patterns, even where it records real historical events. The discrepancies between Procopius' accounts in the secret *Anekdota* and the publicly disseminated *Wars* are examples of this.[5] Yet rather than enumerate the ways his representations of women fall into recognisable tropes, this chapter aims to reveal the ways female agency was expressed by Procopius by looking at Antonina's relationship with Theodora, as exposed by *Anekdota* and *Wars*. What is new about this treatment of Procopius' evidence is precisely the recognition that Procopius regularly exploits tropes, stereotypes, and literary parallels in characterizing Antonina. Antonina sometimes acts on behalf of Theodora, projecting the latter's power, as an instrument, agent, or 'fixer'; but I will argue that Antonina acted almost exclusively in her own self-interest while doing Theodora's dirty work. Procopius' presentation of Antonina is hostile in his *Anekdota*, yet positive, sometimes ambiguous, in his *Wars*. Perhaps that reveals how something of the real Antonina shines through Procopius' ambiguous and dual portrait. Procopius' two interpretations are supplemented by the *Liber Pontificalis* (*Lib. Pont.*), which gives us another view of Antonina's agency.

Antonina's background and her relationship with Theodora in *Wars* and *Anekdota*, and her portrayal as adulteress and murderer will be considered first. Then her role as Theodora's 'fixer' in the *Liber Pontificalis* will be evaluated since it describes something which Procopius promises (but fails) to explain. Finally, I shall expand, in chronological order, on Antonina's agency in interactions with individuals instigated by herself or Theodora or enabled by Belisarius (i.e. with Constantinus, Photius, John the Cappadocian and John, Nephew of Vitalian, Joannina, and Anastasius).

Antonina's Background Portrayal by Procopius

Antonina was the daughter of a prostitute and a chariot-racer.[6] Her meteoric ascent from the entertainment classes of society, amongst the factions of the hippodrome, to its elite echelons (as Theodora also soared) in early sixth-century Constantinople, is highlighted by Procopius.[7] This

---

[4] For classicism in Procopius: Av. Cameron 1985, 33–46; 135–36; 216–19. Kaldellis 2004, 17–61; 71–80; 125; 149; 180; 194–95. Kaldellis 2022, 339–54. Brodka 2022, 194–211. Mecella 2022, 178–79 with n. 6–10.

[5] Procopius may have composed *Anekdota* (partly) in case Antonina and Belisarius, along with Justinian, fell victim to a plot in 549/50, to distance himself from the regime; see Börm 2015b, 305–46, esp. 321. A comic version of Joannina's plight and Belisarius' household could have strengthened Procopius' position if the plot had succeeded.

[6] Procop. *Anecd.* 1.11, discussed below under 'Joannina and Anastasius'.

[7] Procop. *Anecd.* 1.11–12.

seems to have been achieved, partly, via an advantageous first marriage (again like Theodora). However, nothing is known of her first anonymous husband, apart from his having fathered Photius (ca. 519–80, Antonina's sole biological son), and at least one anonymous daughter.[8]

In *Anekdota*, Procopius introduces Antonina thus: "Belisarius had a wife, whom I have had occasion to mention in the previous books..." and he then refers to her as "this female", "wife", "mother", "adulteress", and "woman" before finally revealing her name to be Antonina.[9] This seems intentionally condescending – if not utterly sarcastic – because it foregrounds her roles over her individual personality or identity. This aligns with Procopius' more general misogyny, which extends not only to women but also men: he has Belisarius say to Photius: "bear in mind that the sins of women do not fall on their husbands alone...".[10] Furthermore, he alleges that, on marrying Belisarius, Antonina "straightaway decided upon being an adulteress from the very start...".[11] Procopius' only example of her adultery is a nine-year affair with Theodosius (ca. 517–42),[12] starting on the voyage to Africa from late June 533.[13] This may hint that Antonina's marriage to Belisarius took place shortly before.[14] Belisarius and Antonina had just adopted Theodosius and so Procopius is alleging what we might call 'adoptive incest' since Antonina both adopted Theodosius and had an affair with him.[15] In his *Wars*, Procopius' frequent description of Antonina as a wife and mother has the effect of defining her by her social role almost to the point of excess.[16] Unsurprisingly, in his *Anekdota*, he labours his point by describing Antonina in terms of her roles as wife and (bad) mother. Then he adds other roles such as prostitute's daughter, grandmother, adulteress, sorceress, and murderer.[17] Nevertheless, Procopius goes beyond roles to give

---

[8] Procop. *Bell.* 5.5.5 and 4.8.24; 6.7.15. *PLRE* 3b (Photius 2), 1037–39.

[9] Procop. *Anecd.* 1.11: Ἦν τῷ Βελισαρίῳ γυνή, ἧς δὴ ἐν τοῖς ἔμπροσθεν λόγοις ἐμνήσθην; 1.12: αὕτη, γυνὴ, μήτηρ; 1.13: μοιχεύτρια; 1.16: γυναικὶ and Ἀντωνίνα.

[10] Procop. *Anecd.* 2.10: ἐνθυμοῦ τε ὡς αἱ τῶν γυναικῶν ἁμαρτάδες οὐκ ἐπὶ τοὺς ἄνδρας ἵενται μόνον...

[11] Procop. *Anecd.* 1.13: εὐθὺς μὲν οὖν ἠξίου μοιχεύτρια τὸ ἐξ ἀρχῆς εἶναι...

[12] *PLRE* 3b (Theodosius 8), 1292.

[13] Procop. *Anecd.* 1.12–13. 1.15–22. 2.3–17. 3.3–20.

[14] Possibly after the Nika riots of 532 when those close to Justinian and Theodora were thrown together even more closely than before, but the precise date of Belisarius and Antonina's marriage is unknown.

[15] Procop. *Anecd.* 1.16. Cf. *Dig.* 1.7.23; cf. *Inst.* 1.10.1 and Silvio Roggo's chapter section in this volume on 'The Adoption of Tiberios', 106–8.

[16] Procop. *Bell.* 1.25.11–13. 3.12.2. 3.13.24. 3.19.11. 3.20.1. 4.8.24. 5.5.5. 5.18.43. 6.4.6. 7.19.7. 7.19.30. 7.28.4. 7.30.2–3. 7.30.25 (wife) and 5.5.5. 5.18.18. 4.8.24. 6.7.15 (mother).

[17] Procop. *Anecd.* 1.11–12. 1.35. 5.33 (wife). 1.12. 1.31–34 (bad mother). 1.11 (prostitute's daughter). 5.33 (grandmother). 1.13. 1.16–20. 1.35–36. 1.42. 2.5 (adulteress). 1.12–13. 1.26. 2.2. 3.2 (sorceress). 1.27–28 (murderer).

agency to Antonina in many circumstances, in both *Wars* and *Anekdota*, as does the *Liber Pontificalis*.

Antonina's Relationship with Theodora

How Antonina and Theodora met is unknown. However, given their similar backgrounds, they may have been acquainted before either married, or developed a relationship at court. An eleventh-century source suggests that Antonina was understood to have been a tremendously close and significant associate of Theodora; this is suggested by a reference to her by the title of "girded-lady of Theodora" (ζωστή... Θεοδώρας).[18] Procopius has Theodora address Antonina as "dearest patrician" (φιλτάτη πατρικία), indicative of familiarity, and the rank she ascended to is confirmed by other sixth-century sources.[19] Antonina's closeness to Theodora may well have provided her with the opportunity to secure her second, much more advantageous, marriage to Belisarius, Justinian's most trusted general, by June 533.[20] Antonina's relationship with Theodora, is illustrated in the following stemma.

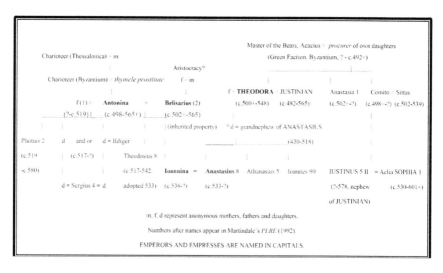

Stemma 1: Antonina's relationship with Theodora, within the context of family ties.

---

[18] *Patria Constantinopolitana* 3.117; cf. *PLRE* 3a (Antonina 1), 91–93. This was associated, anachronistically, with the ninth-century title "girded/ing lady-patrician" (ζωστή πατρικία) – a status only second in importance to empresses: for which see Guilland 1971, 272–73, Oikonomides 1972, 293 with n. 33, and Kazhdan 1991, 2231.
[19] Procop. *Anecd.* 3.16. *Lib. Pont.* 60. Liberatus, *Brev.* 22. Vict. Tun. *Chronicle* s.a. 542; cf. *PLRE* 3a (Antonina 1), 92.
[20] Procop. *Bell.* 3.12.2.

Procopius characterizes Antonina's close relationship with Theodora extensively in his *Anekdota*. Sometimes it is tumultuous: "… she dreaded the punishment the Empress might inflict. For Theodora used to rage at her savagely and, as they say, to bare her teeth at her."[21] For Procopius to exaggerate this, it would only need to have occurred once, if at all, perhaps before Antonina married Belisarius, when she was some kind of lady-in-waiting (ζωστή… Θεοδώρας or ζωστὴ πατρικία, or similar). But Antonina

> …managed to tame Theodora by serving her whenever there was a crisis, first by getting rid of Pope Silverius [537] in the way that I will describe *in a later book*,[22] and then by plotting the downfall of John the Cappadocian [Praetorian Prefect, 541], which I have described in an earlier book. After that she had no fear left at all and no longer even bothered to conceal all the crimes that she committed.[23]

"Tame" suggests comparison to animals (such as scorpions as cited at the head of this chapter), which is dehumanizing. Furthermore, this suggests Antonina committed her "crimes" openly from 537, including Antonina's vindictive execution of Constantinus in 538, considered below. Although he never delivers the promised details about Silverius, Procopius shows that Antonina's entrapment of John the Cappadocian (see below) reinforces her usefulness to Theodora.[24] As regards conducting her crime of an affair with her adopted son, Procopius accuses her of pursuing it flamboyantly from 533 onwards,[25] and of murdering witnesses of it, in Sicily, ca. 536.[26] This suggests Procopius sometimes got carried away with exaggerating his invective leading to a slip in the chronological consistency within his narrative.

Procopius lists several ways in which Theodora recompensed Antonina for having disposed of Silverius, and especially John. After entrapping John,

---

[21] Procop. *Anecd.* 1.13: …ἀλλὰ τὴν ἐκ τῆς βασιλίδος ὑποπτεύουσα τίσιν. λίαν γὰρ ἐς αὐτὴν ἡ Θεοδώρα ἠγριαίνετό τε καὶ ἐσεσήρει (alluding to Aristophanes, *Peace* 620).
[22] See below, "Antonina: fixer in the *Liber Pontificalis*".
[23] Procop. *Anecd.* 1.14: ἐπεὶ δὲ αὐτὴν ἐν τοῖς ἀναγκαιοτάτοις ὑπουργήσασα χειροήθη πεποίηται, πρῶτα μὲν Σιλβέριον διαχρησαμένη τρόπῳ ᾧπερ ἐν τοῖς ὄπισθεν λόγοις εἰρήσεται, ὕστερον δὲ Ἰωάννην κατεργασαμένη τὸν Καππαδόκην, ὥσπερ μοι ἐν τοῖς ἔμπροσθεν λόγοις ἐρρήθη, ἐνταῦθα δὴ ἀδεέστερόν τε καὶ οὐκέτι ἀποκρυπτομένη ἅπαντα ἐξαμαρτάνειν οὐδαμῇ ἀπηξίου.
[24] *PLRE* 3a (Ioannes 11), 627–35.
[25] Procop. *Anecd.* 1.18–20. When Procopius has Belisarius catch Antonina and Theodosius *in flagrante delicto* with the latter's trousers (τὰς ἀναξυρίδας) loosened, he uses exactly the same vocabulary as he does to describe the racing factionists' trousers (7.14), probably intentionally, to reconnect Antonina with her hippodrome heritage.
[26] Procop. *Anecd.* 1.26–27.

Procopius characterizes Antonina as feeling "a much greater confidence in the friendship of the Empress"[27] and later in 541, he has Theodora hear of Antonina's arrest by Belisarius on the eastern frontier for adultery, and summon the couple to Byzantium.[28] Then, "Whereas Antonina had just recently entrapped only one enemy, the Cappadocian, and betrayed him to her, Theodora rounded up an entire throng of men and, without formally charging them, turned them over to Antonina to be destroyed."[29] Procopius thereby indicates an even closer alliance between Antonina and Theodora. He reinforces this alliance by having Theodora oblige Belisarius to reconcile with Antonina and torture Photius and hide Theodosius (Antonina's adopted son and lover) in her palace. Theodora invites Antonina to see Theodosius, euphemized as a "pearl" (μάργαρον), there, and Procopius has Antonina reciprocate with extreme flattery.[30] This leads to Procopius' partially repetitive comment that, "Now it happened that Antonina, as I explained, was estranged from her husband but was on excellent terms with the empress, who regarded her as an indispensable instrument given that she had recently ruined John the Cappadocian."[31] This culminates in a note purportedly written by Theodora to Belisarius in which she states that "I, for my part, owe so much to your wife."[32] So Procopius mentions four times Theodora's close support for, and relationship with, Antonina because of her role in bringing down John. The famous mosaic of Theodora (figs. 20–21) illustrates close relationships with attendants. While their identities are unknown, they represent elite women comparable to Antonina.

Much less is made of Silverius, which suggests that John's demise (described fully in *Wars*,[33] as well as referred to in the *Anekdota*) was more important to Theodora than that of the Pope. This is not surprising considering that John was Praetorian Prefect in Constantinople and had direct influence over Justinian. It may partly explain why, in *Wars*, Procopius elaborates on John's downfall (in Constantinople, 541), but offers minimal details about that of Silverius (Rome, 537) and never expands on Antonina's involvement in deposing Silverius even in the *Anekdota*. However, those details are offered by the contemporary yet anonymous *Lib. Pont.* 60, discussed below.

---

[27] Procop. *Anecd.* 2.17: ...πολλῷ ἔτι μᾶλλον ἐπὶ τῇ τῆς βασιλίδος θαρροῦσα φιλίᾳ.

[28] Procop. *Anecd.* 3.1–4.

[29] Procop. *Anecd.* 3.7: Ἀντωνίνα μὲν γὰρ ἕνα οἱ ἔναγχος τὸν Καππαδόκην ἐχθρὸν ἐνεδρεύσασα προὔδωκεν, αὐτὴ δὲ πλῆθος ἐκείνῃ ἐγχειρίσασα ἀνδρῶν ἀνεγκλήτως ἀνῄρηκε.

[30] Procop. *Anecd.* 3.12–18.

[31] Procop. *Anecd.* 4.18: ἐτύγχανε δὲ ἡ Ἀντωνίνα, ὥς μοι εἴρηται, τῷ μὲν ἀνδρὶ διάφορος γεγενημένη, τῇ δὲ βασιλίδι φιλτάτη καὶ ἀναγκαιοτάτη οὖσα ἐν τοῖς μάλιστα ἅτε Ἰωάννην ἔναγχος κατεργασαμένη τὸν Καππαδόκην.

[32] Procop. *Anecd.* 4.27: ἐγὼ δὲ τὰ πολλὰ ὀφείλουσα τῇ σῇ γυναικί.

[33] Procop. *Bell.* 1.25.12–25.

Procopius' Antonina, in *Wars* and *Anekdota*

In *Wars*, Procopius has Antonina demonstrate her agency through intelligence, forethought, and planning skills. She preserves drinking water in Belisarius' flagship en route to Africa in 533. In 537, she persuades Belisarius to eat after the first skirmish outside Rome (March), manages logistics co-operatively with Procopius, contra Parnell 2023, 110, at Naples (October), and assists in transferring provisions from Ostia to Rome (December). She famously entraps John the Cappadocian in Constantinople, before departing to meet Belisarius on the eastern frontier in spring 541. She goes on a mission to Constantinople to request resources for the Italian war, in June 548, and (on learning of Theodora's death) requests Belisarius' recall from Italy.[34] However, in his *Anekdota*, while allocating more agency to Antonina, Procopius presents the negative side of her aforementioned skills. These include her alleged adulterous intentions on marrying Belisarius, conducting a love affair with Theodosius from 533 to 542, and murdering witnesses (Macedonia and two slaves) in 536. Moreover, she deposes Pope Silverius in March 537, insists on the execution of Constantinus in 538, and drives her biological son, Photius, from Italy, ca. 538. From 541, she delays in Constantinople to rendezvous with Theodosius and entrap John the Cappadocian, schemes to destroy Photius, and collaborates more closely with Theodora, reconciling with Belisarius yet continuing her affair with Theodosius. Then she purportedly: blocks Belisarius' reappointment to the East, ca. 543; oversees her granddaughter being courted by Sergius in 546;[35] instigates fear in John, nephew of Vitalian, 544–548;[36] dissolves Joannina's marriage to Anastasius (Theodora's grandson)[37] in 548; and dominates Belisarius until 549.[38] Patterns emerge in the analysis of the following cases: Antonina's affair with Theodosius (leading to her revenge on Constantinus and Photius), her part in deposing Pope Silverius in 537 (*Lib. Pont.* 60), and her role in unseating John the Cappadocian in 541. Her attempted ruin of John, nephew of Vitalian, in 546–548 (explained in *Anekdota* and alluded to in *Wars*), will be evaluated because it possibly led to the breakdown in Theodora and Antonina's relationship, centred on Joannina.

---

[34] Procop. *Bell.* 3.13.23–24. 5.18.43. 6.4.20. 6.7.4*ff.* 1.25.13*ff.* 1.25.23. 7.30.3. 7.30.25.
[35] *PLRE* 3b (Sergius 4), 1124–28.
[36] Ioannes 46, the nephew of Vitalian: *PLRE* 3a, 652–61.
[37] *PLRE* 3a (Anastasius 8), 63.
[38] Procop. *Anecd.* 1.13. 1.14. 1.16–17. 1.18–20. 1.25. 1.27. 1.28–29. 1.31–34. 1.35. 1.42. 2.1. 2.14. 2.16. 3.7. 3.16. 2.3–4. 2.14, 2.17. 3.12. 4.19-31. 3.15–18. 4.18–19. 4.38. 5.33. 5.14. 5.20. 5.23. 5.27.

Antonina: Adulteress and Murderer

Procopius portrays Antonina and Theodosius as lovers, notwithstanding her being his adoptive mother and about twice his age. They are repeatedly separated by circumstances, despite their boundless passion for one another, from 533 to 542 (as in "ancient romance novels").[39] This is reminiscent of Greek and Latin comedy. New Comedy included love affairs and the rapes of maidens, featuring stock characters such as servants, soldiers, courtesans, angry or avaricious old men, and young men in love,[40] all of which feature in *Anekdota*. Latin comedy included love affairs and Plautus' plot in *Truculentus* "shows the triumph of an utterly amoral and manipulative prostitute". In several of Plautus' plays "the male head of the household… comes off worst",[41] as Belisarius does. However, the fundamentals of the affair are plausible, and its inclusion binds many strands of *Anekdota* together, as well as adding meaning to parts of *Wars*.

Kaldellis argues that there is probably subtle humour in Procopius' account of Antonina and Theodosius' affair. Only Theodosius is presented as a member of the heretical Christian sect: the Eunomians. Theodosius is baptized and adopted by Belisarius, making Antonina his mother.[42] The fourth-century heretic Eunomius contended that God the Son was of a different nature and inferior to God the Father, "whereas the Orthodox believed not only in the equality but the identicalness of their natures". After Theodosius' conversion and baptism, he "the son" unquestionably appropriates the position of Belisarius, his "father", in Antonina's bed. Thus, "he had truly embraced the Orthodox position".[43] This is another indication of subtlety and literariness in Procopius' account.

Procopius presents Theodora as having the power to procure and host Theodosius.[44] One wonders whether Procopius wants his careful readers to contemplate that she had been involved in arranging his adoption, to please Antonina and destabilize Belisarius' household. Or that Theodora's own name inspired the Christian name which he was given when adopted by Belisarius.[45] This Theodosius is never explicitly identified in *Wars*. It is possible that he is identical with the soldier at *Wars* 3.1.2. There is sufficient ambiguity in Procopius' accounts for this to be the same person. This ambiguity may even extend to allow Theodosius, the son and lover, to be

---

[39] Kaldellis 2010, xxxii.
[40] Hornblower and Spawforth, 2004, 188–89.
[41] Hornblower and Spawforth, 2004, 544.
[42] Procop. *Anecd.* 1.15–16; Kaldellis 2014, 171 n. 345.
[43] Kaldellis 2010, xl.
[44] Procop. *Anecd.* 3.16–19.
[45] Procop. *Bell.* 3.12.2 and *Anecd.* 1.16.

the same person as Theodosius, chief of Belisarius' household.[46] Antonina is given agency in instigating and conducting this affair. The circumstances are enabled indirectly by Belisarius (adopting Theodosius and failing to prevent or end the affair) and directly by Theodora (hiding Theodosius in her palace and encouraging it). Talk of the affair leads to alleged drastic consequences.

On Sicily in 536, a slave-girl, Macedonia, informs Belisarius of his wife's affair with Theodosius, who then escapes Belisarius' assassins. Constantinus sympathises with Belisarius and comments, "I would sooner have done away with the wife than with the young man."[47] Procopius has Antonina hear of this and bide her time to get revenge, remarking, "Her fury lurked like a scorpion in the shadows".[48] Meanwhile:

> Not long afterward she persuaded her husband, by using magic charms or soothing flatteries, that the slave's accusation was not sound. And so he immediately recalled Theodosius and even consented to turn Macedonia and the slave-boys over to his wife. They say that first she cut out all their tongues, then cut their bodies into little pieces, which she put into sacks and threw into the sea without the slightest hesitation. In this whole horrid business, she was assisted by one of her creatures named Eugenius, who also carried out the outrage against Silverius.[49]

Once again, Procopius characterizes Antonina as a capable plotter, murdering witnesses and patiently waiting to commit her vengeful crime against Constantinus. Before she achieves her revenge at Rome in 538, she is commissioned to get rid of Pope Silverius in March 537, on Theodora's orders.[50] Eugenius is used to link the murders of the slaves with the "outrage against Silverius".

---

[46] *PLRE* 3b (Theodosius 4), 1291 is chief of Belisarius' household, at Ravenna (Procop. *Bell.* 6.28.8). *PLRE* 3b. Theodosius 8 manages the palace of Ravenna (Procop. *Anecd.* 1.33).
[47] Procop. *Anecd.* 1.24: Ἔγωγε θᾶσσον ἂν τὴν γυναῖκα ἢ τὸν νεανίαν κατειργασάμην.
[48] Procop. *Anecd.* 1.26, cited at the head of this chapter.
[49] Procop. *Anecd.* 1.26–27: οὐ πολλῷ δὲ ὕστερον ἢ μαγγανεύσασα ἢ θωπεύσασα πείθει τὸν ἄνδρα ὡς οὐχ ὑγιὲς τὸ κατηγόρημα τὸ ταύτης γένοιτο· καὶ ὃς Θεοδόσιον μὲν μελλήσει οὐδεμιᾷ μετεπέμψατο, Μακεδονίαν δὲ καὶ τὰ παιδία τῇ γυναικὶ ἐκδοῦναι ὑπέστη. [27] οὓς δὴ ἅπαντας πρῶτα τὰς γλώττας, ὥσπερ λέγουσιν, ἀποτεμοῦσα, εἶτα κατὰ βραχὺ κρεουργήσασα καὶ θυλακίοις ἐμβεβλημένη ἐς τὴν θάλατταν ὀκνήσει οὐδεμιᾷ ἔρριψε, τῶν τινος οἰκετῶν Εὐγενίου ὄνομα ὑπουργήσαντός οἱ ἐς ἅπαν τὸ ἄγος, ᾧ δὴ καὶ τὸ ἐς Σιλβέριον εἴργασται μίασμα.
[50] Procop. *Anecd.* 1.14.

Antonina: Fixer in the *Liber Pontificalis*

Lib. Pont. 60 provides the details about Antonina's part in getting rid of Pope Silverius, which Procopius promises, but fails, to deliver. However, the description in the *Lib. Pont.* does read like a demonstration of hubris and arrogance, perhaps suggesting a classically influenced author. Antonina is portrayed as having power and agency, with Belisarius in a subordinate position.[51] Or perhaps the scene is concocted to surprise readers, as Antonina seems to be holding court from a couch at the *Domus Pinciana* in Rome (Belisarius' seat of political power in 537–38).[52] After Belisarius instigates proceedings, Antonina seems dominant:

> He [sc. Belisarius] had the blessed pope Silverius come to him at the Pincian Palace, and he made all the clergy wait at the first and second curtains. On Silverius' entry with Vigilius alone into the inner chamber, the patrician Antonina was lying on a couch and the patrician Belisarius was sitting at her feet.[53]

The body language in this scene, so expressive of her power over Belisarius, is startling. Antonina's alleged involvement in this situation may have been exaggerated by the compiler of *Lib. Pont.* 60 but it is likely that an elite woman, married to the plenipotentiary commander (στρατηγὸς αὐτοκράτωρ)[54] could easily have been present at such an event. The *Lib. Pont.* continues by showing Antonina's authority, assigning agency to her by having her accuse Silverius of traitorous relations with the Goths besieging Rome in March 537, and deposing him instantly:

> When Antonina saw him she said to him: 'Tell us, lord pope Silverius, what have we done to you and the Romans to make you want to betray us into the hands of the Goths?' While she was still speaking, John, regionary subdeacon of the first region, came in, took the *pallium* from his neck and led him into a side room. He stripped him, dressed him in a monk's habit and hid him away.[55]

---

[51] Cf. Procop. *Anecd.* 5.27.
[52] *Lib. Pont.* 60; cf. Procop. *Bell.* 6.8.10; 6.9.5. Jolivet and Sotinel 2011, 147.
[53] *Lib. Pont.* 60.8.1–2: *tunc fecit beatum Silverium papam venire ad se in palatium Pineis et ad primum et secundum velum retenuit omnem clerum. Quo ingresso Silverius cum Vigilio soli in musileo, Antonina patricia iacebat in lecto et Vilisarius patricius sedebat ad pedes eius* (trans. Davis 2010).
[54] Procop. *Bell.* 5.5.4.
[55] *Lib. Pont.* 60.8.3–5: *et dum eum vidisset Antonina dixit ad eum: 'Dic, domne Silveri papa, quid fecimus tibi et Romanis, ut tu vellis nos in manus Gothorum tradere?' Adhuc ea loquente, ingressus Iohhanis, subdiaconus regionarius primae regionis, tulit pallium de collo eius et duxit*

Davis argues that the second editor of the *Lib. Pont.* composed his entry on Silverius before 546, precisely when Procopius was composing his *Wars* and *Anekdota*. That the *Lib. Pont.* fulfils Procopius' promise to describe how Antonina deposed Silverius, in the same decade that Procopius was writing, may simply be an astonishing coincidence. Alternatively, Procopius may have had a hand in its composition. There are stylistic parallels between *Lib. Pont.* and *Anekdota*, characterizing Antonina as a protagonist, with Belisarius seeming to be submissive to her, and the multiple use of direct speech (four times in *Lib. Pont.* 60.6–8 but very rare earlier in it, yet common in *Anekdota*). Procopius' full understanding regarding Antonina's deposition of Silverius does not survive from the East, not even in the secret *Anekdota*, but the *Lib. Pont.* records the story in Rome. It may be a coincidence that both accounts were written in the late 540s, in Greek and Latin respectively, in Constantinople and Rome (and perhaps Procopius did not feel the need to provide the promised details of Silverius' deposition). Alternatively, there may have been a connection between Procopius and Rome. Procopius may have written up and supplied these details which were somehow conveyed into the *Lib. Pont.* (in line with his promises to describe Silverius' fall "in a later book" and to write more about Justinian: "for his treatment of the priests will be described in my subsequent books").[56] These details could have been conveyed either directly or via a possible work which Procopius alludes to writing but, if written, has not survived.[57] Because Procopius promised to write more about Silverius, it is conceivable that *Lib. Pont.* 60 contains just such a work or draft thereof. Although speculative, this is an important possibility that has not previously been noted, and it seems to be a more likely scenario than that the composition of these two accounts of Silverius' deposition were written concurrently by coincidence.

Antonina: Constantinus, Photius, John the Cappadocian (Ioannes 11), and John, Nephew of Vitalian (Ioannes 46)

Returning to Procopius' *Wars* and *Anekdota*, we can consider Antonina's other alleged "crimes" in chronological order. General Constantinus is described as having attempted to assassinate Belisarius, early in 538. In *Wars*,[58] Procopius avoids linking Antonina to the execution of Constantinus. However, Procopius lays the blame squarely at Antonina's

---

in cubiculum; expolians eum induit eum vestem monachicam et abscondit eum (trans. Davis 2010).
[56] Procop. *Anecd.* 1.14, cited above, and 26.18: τὰ γὰρ ἀμφὶ τοῖς ἱερεῦσιν αὐτῷ πεπραγμένα ἐν τοῖς ὄπισθεν λόγοις λελέξεται.
[57] See Kaldellis 2009.
[58] Procop. *Bell.* 6.8.1–18.

door in *Anekdota*: "Not long afterward, Belisarius executed Constantinus at his wife's instigation... Even though the man would surely have been acquitted, Antonina did not relent until he had been punished for the remark that I just mentioned",[59] referring to *Anekdota* 1.24, cited above.

Soon after this, Procopius makes Antonina turn on Photius, her biological son, to facilitate her affair with Theodosius. Procopius characterizes Photius positively as discreet and of strong character.[60] Photius is mistreated by Antonina: she sets traps for him until she forces him to leave Italy and then Theodosius re-joins her there.[61] She enjoys his company, in Italy and then Constantinople, before and after her next directive from Theodora: achieving the downfall of John (the Cappadocian).

Procopius' account of the downfall of John in *Wars*, opens with his very first, publicly disseminated, mention and characterization of Antonina: "Antonina, the wife of Belisarius, was the most capable person of all mankind to contrive the uncontrivable."[62] This seemingly positive comment in *Wars* is sufficiently ambiguous to align with his viciously negative comments in *Anekdota*. Instead of placing his comprehensive account of the scheme against John chronologically,[63] at the end of *Wars* 2.14 (or confining it to the *Anekdota*), Procopius inserts this detailed penultimate chapter at *Wars* 1.25 (arguably in 546).[64] This chapter is out of chronological order and its insertion brings Procopius' characterization of Antonina forward, near the start of *Wars*, in a striking manner (just as it is near to the start of *Anekdota*).[65] Antonina's method of entrapping John is to manipulate Euphemia, John's young daughter,[66] by proposing a "false conspiracy" against the imperial family, ostensibly on behalf of Belisarius (who was on the eastern frontier).[67] Procopius has Antonina propose a secret meeting with John, and has Theodora's witnesses hidden to hear him utter treasonous words. He is arrested, after initially escaping.[68] In *Anekdota*, Procopius adds the detail of

---

[59] Procop. *Anecd.* 1.28–29: καὶ Κωνσταντῖνον δὲ οὐ πολλῷ ὕστερον Βελισάριος τῇ γυναικὶ ἀναπεισθεὶς κτείνει... μέλλοντος γὰρ τοῦ ἀνθρώπου ἀφίεσθαι, οὐ πρότερον ἀνῆκεν ἡ Ἀντωνίνα, ἕως αὐτὸν τοῦ λόγου ἐτίσατο, οὗπερ ἐγὼ ἀρτίως ἐμνήσθην (referring to 1.24).
[60] Procop. *Bell.* 5.5.5. *Anecd.*1.32.
[61] Procop. *Anecd.* 1.31–34.
[62] Procop. *Bell.* 1.25.13: Ἀντωνίνα δὲ ἡ Βελισαρίου γυνὴ ἦν γὰρ ἱκανωτάτη ἀνθρώπων ἁπάντων μηχανᾶσθαι τὰ ἀμήχανά.
[63] Procop. *Bell.* 1.25.11–30.
[64] Greatrex 1995, 2; 5. Procopius links it to the *Nika* riots of 532 (*Bell.* 1.24).
[65] Procop. *Anecd.* 1.11–30.
[66] *PLRE* 3a (Euphemia 2), 463. Similarly, Theodora manipulates Joannina, Antonina's youngest daughter, regarding Anastasius in 547/48.
[67] Antonina's entrapment of John on behalf of Theodora permits Procopius' characterization of Antonina and Belisarius as potential rebels.
[68] Greatrex 1995, 1–13.

Antonina having sworn Christian oaths to convince John and Euphemia of her sincerity.[69] This could not appear in *Wars* as it would have put Antonina's reputation, and therefore Procopius, at risk.

As soon as she completes this commission, in spring 541, Antonina schemes to remove Photius, when he is on the eastern frontier, so as to continue her affair with Theodosius. She even persuades some of Belisarius' men to harass Photius, and she libels him.[70] Antonina does nothing to stop Theodora having Photius arrested, tortured, and imprisoned but he escapes and flees to Jerusalem.[71] The Syriac text of John of Ephesus' *Ecclesiastical History* seems to corroborate Procopius' account of Antonina's moves against her son. An entire chapter, hostile to Photius, opens with:

> So this one [Photius], after having been in the army and become experienced in warfare together with Belisarius, left in the end for some reason and assumed the tonsure and the monastic dress.[72]

John of Ephesus' "some reason" is guardedly vague and aligns with Procopius' account, which gives Photius good reason not to enter into the details (of his dysfunctional family and of his escape from Theodora's prison) as to why he became a monk in Jerusalem. Photius never returned to Antonina and Belisarius,[73] preferring to maintain a significant distance from them and Constantinople. Photius is recorded as visiting the capital in 571,[74] six years after Belisarius' death, and perhaps on Antonina's (date unknown). Antonina's relations with Theodora could not have been closer after the arrest of Photius. However, a less obvious case may have led to the breakdown of Antonina's relationship with Theodora. Antonina failed to bring down another John, the nephew of Vitalian.[75] This may have contributed to Procopius' final Theodoran deed and Antonina's extremely self-interested response in *Anekdota*. We may compare the deeds of this John, the nephew of Vitalian, in *Wars* and *Anekdota*. In both, he is portrayed as an insubordinate general under Belisarius' command in Italy. In *Wars*, John is sent to Byzantium in 545 to seek reinforcements but spends time negotiating with Germanus (Justinian's cousin)[76] to marry his daughter, Justina.[77] He returns in 546 to meet Belisarius in Epidamnus/

---

[69] Procop. *Anecd.* 2.16.
[70] Procop. *Anecd.* 2.3–4.
[71] Procop. *Anecd.* 3.12. 3.22–29.
[72] Joh. Eph. *Hist. eccl.* 3.1.32 (trans. Payne Smith 1860, rev. Silvio Roggo).
[73] Procop. *Anecd.* 5.27.
[74] Joh. Eph. *Hist. eccl.* 3.1.31. 3.5.3.
[75] *PLRE* 3a (Ioannes 46), 652–61.
[76] *PLRE* 2 (Germanus 4), 505–507.
[77] *PLRE* 3a (Iustina 1), 742–43.

Dyrrachium (when Antonina is in Ravenna) but disobeys Belisarius' orders.[78] Significantly, Procopius refers to suspicion between John and Belisarius in a speech attributed to Totila, the king of the Goths, which prevents them from coordinating military operations effectively.[79] In *Anekdota*, it transpires that the suspicion is effectively between John and Antonina, because John's life is threatened by Theodora for marrying Justina,[80] and "Because of this, when John returned to Italy he did not dare to contact Belisarius, fearing the plotting of Antonina, at least until she returned to Byzantium. For one might quite reasonably suspect that the empress would commission her to arrange his murder."[81] Therefore this John, as son-in-law to Germanus, apparently survived by avoiding Antonina, whose previous deeds inspired fear in a Roman general to the extent that he avoided Belisarius' summons merely because Antonina was with him in Italy. Therefore, Antonina's relationship with Theodora allegedly gave her the power to: influence the execution of a general; cause the effective exile of her biological son (another general); depose the Praetorian Prefect; and frighten a third general into disobeying her own husband's orders. So Procopius is laying blame at the feet of his two nominated "scorpions".

Joannina and Anastasius

Procopius' final Theodoran deed may relate in part to Antonina's failure to destroy John, the nephew of Vitalian. In 547, Theodora supposedly hatched a plan: the premature cohabitation and marriage between Joannina, Antonina's underaged daughter, and the empress' grandson, Anastasius. Joannina has only been considered in passing by scholars,[82] but Procopius deploys her to embellish the relationships between Belisarius, Antonina, and Theodora, within a "Theodoran scheme" for Anastasius to inherit Belisarius' wealth,[83] although it may have been a suitable alliance between the families. Theodora may have wanted to remove Joannina from the marriage market lest her parents arrange a better match. Joannina's betrothal occurs months

---

[78] Procop. *Bell.* 7.18.1–29.
[79] Procop. *Bell.* 7.25.22.
[80] Procop. *Anecd.* 5.7. 5.9–10. 5.12–13.
[81] Procop. *Anecd.* 5.13–14: καὶ ἀπ' αὐτοῦ Ἰωάννης αὖθις ἐς Ἰταλίαν σταλεὶς οὐδαμῇ ξυμμῖξαι Βελισαρίῳ ἐτόλμησε, τὴν ἐξ Ἀντωνίνης ἐπιβουλὴν δείσας, ἕως Ἀντωνίνα ἐς Βυζάντιον ἦλθε. τήν τε γὰρ βασιλίδα ταύτῃ ἐπιστεῖλαι τὸν αὐτοῦ φόνον οὐκ ἄπο τοῦ εἰκότος ἄν τις ὑπώπτευσε.
[82] Fisher 1978, 269. Al. Cameron 1978, 270. Av. Cameron 1985, 72 and 80. Martindale 1992, *PLRE* 3a (Ioannina), 712. Andreescu-Treadgold and Treadgold 1997, 720. Parnell 2023. Evans 2011, *passim*.
[83] Procop. *Anecd.* 4.36.

after the imprisonment of Photius and death of Theodosius (both events occurred in Theodora's palace, 542/43).[84] Having been a potential heir to Belisarius' fortune, Theodosius' death suits Theodora.

Procopius names "Joannina, Belisarius' daughter, the only one of whom he was father"[85] just once, when she was betrothed to Anastasius. Procopius' phraseology may emphasize that Joannina was indeed Belisarius' only child, or it might be a case of over-emphasis to hint at the possibility of an alternative biological father for Joannina (by a rumour that Procopius was either repeating or trying to create). Her age on marriage and her year of birth are important. Herrin suggests that elite daughters were expected to marry at around 15, but there were exceptions, and some girls were married underage. An extremely unusual example, centuries later, is Simonis Paleologina, who was married at the age of 8.[86] In Roman law an *impubes* could consent to a betrothal from the age of 7 to puberty (12 for girls, 14 for boys).[87] Joannina was betrothed to Anastasius in ca. 543, but not married then. She should have been over 7 and born by 536 (possibly in Sicily).[88] Had Joannina been old enough to marry by 544, Theodora could have pressurized her parents to celebrate a marriage before departing for Italy. That this did not happen suggests that Joannina was significantly under 12 at the time, because it is very unlikely that Theodora would have accepted a betrothal if a marriage had been legally possible by 544.[89] Therefore, it is probable that Theodora settled for a betrothal because Joannina was too young for marriage by 544. This in turn suggests the likelihood of Joannina's conception after June 533 and thereby raises the possibility that her biological father may have been Antonina's son and lover, Theodosius.

Late in 547, Theodora forces Joannina (still possibly 11) to cohabit with Anastasius. Procopius presents Joannina's exploitation by Theodora as a misfortune for Belisarius' household comparable to the misfortunes that Italy suffers concurrently.[90] Antonina's manipulation of Euphemia had led to worse misfortune for her father. Joannina, Belisarius' sole, yet now unnamed, "heiress" (ἐπίκληρον) is referred to in ways which hint at her young age: daughter (παιδός); child (κόρην); daughter (παῖδα); child (γόνου); a very young underage girl (παιδίσκην); girl (κόρη).[91] Procopius

[84] Procop. *Anecd.* 3.20–22.
[85] Procop. *Anecd.* 4.37: Ἰωαννίνα τε ἡ Βελισαρίου θυγάτηρ, ἧσπερ μόνης ἐγεγόνει πατὴρ.
[86] Herrin 2000, 28 and 35.
[87] Watson 1998, I xx.
[88] Procop. *Bell.* 5.5.17–19. 4.14.4. *Anecd.* 1.21.
[89] Even though Roman law stipulated that a broken betrothal would result in substantial financial penalties (*CTh* 3.5.10–11).
[90] Procop. *Anecd.* 5.1–17. *Bell.* 7.35.1.
[91] Procop. *Anecd.* 5.18–20.

portrays Theodora as predatory yet endowed with implausible foresight regarding her distrust of Antonina's intention to fulfil the betrothal. This foreshadows *Anekdota* 5.23–24 when Antonina breaks up the couple shortly after Theodora's death (in June 548). Procopius proposes that distrust motivated the empress to explain her forcing things as Theodora:

> ...performed an **unholy** deed. For she caused the **underage girl** [παιδίσκην] to live with the **boy** [μειρακίῳ] without any sanction of law. And they say that secretly she actually forced her to offer herself, much against her will, and thus, after the **girl** [κόρῃ] had lost her virginity, she arranged the wedding for her, to the end that the Emperor might not put a stop to her machinations.[92]

The diminutive form, παιδίσκην,[93] used by Procopius in relation to Joannina, can refer to very young underage girls or prostitutes (typical characters in Greek comedy).[94] Procopius deploys παιδίσκην in a court environment as a particularly pointed sting, as tropes and caricatures probably persisted in the theatre environments in which Theodora and Antonina grew up, where the mime genre was prevalent.[95] Procopius' phrase "without any sanction of law" may refer to Joannina initially becoming an underage concubine,[96] or to a lack of parental consent, or both.[97] Perhaps considering "A girl who was less than twelve years old when she married will not be a lawful wife until she reaches that age while living with her husband",[98] Theodora celebrates their marriage soon afterwards to evade inconvenient legal issues. The narrative continues to suggest a low age: "Still, when the deed had been accomplished, Anastasius and the **child bride** (παῖς) found themselves held by an ardent love for one another, and a space of no less than eight months was passed in this way."[99] Citing Augustine (discussing the rape of Lucretia), Balberg and Muehlberger note that, "a woman (whether a virgin

---

[92] Procop. *Anecd.* 5.20–21: ...ἐργάζεται *ἀνόσιον* ἔργον. τῷ γὰρ *μειρακίῳ* τὴν *παιδίσκην* ξυνοικίζει οὐδενὶ νόμῳ. φασὶ δὲ ὡς καὶ πλησιάσαι οὔτι ἑκουσίαν ἠνάγκασε κρύβδην, οὕτω τε διαπεπαρθενευμένῃ τὸν ὑμέναιον τῇ *κόρῃ* ξυστῆναι, τοῦ μὴ βασιλέα τὰ πρασσόμενα διακωλῦσαι (my emphasis).
[93] *LSJ*: Diminutive of παῖς (ἡ), young girl, maiden, Xen. *An.* 4.3.11, Anaxil. 22.26, Men. 102, etc., or prostitute, Hdt. 1.93, Is. 6.19, Plut. *Vit. Per.* 24, *Cat. Ma.* 24, etc.
[94] Hornblower and Spawforth 2004, 185–90.
[95] Stehlíková 1993. Webb 2008.
[96] *Dig.* 23.2.4. *Pomponius 3 ad sab.*.
[97] *Inst. Iust.* 1.10.0 (*de nuptiis*).
[98] *Dig.* 23.2.4. *Pomponius 3 ad sab.*: Minorem annis duodecim nuptam tunc legitimam uxorem fore, cum apud virum explesset duodecim annos (trans. Watson 1998, II 199).
[99] Procop. *Anecd.* 5.22: τοῦ μέντοι ἔργου ἐξειργασμένου ἔρωτι ἀλλήλοιν διαπύρῳ τινὶ ὅ τε Ἀναστάσιος καὶ ἡ *παῖς* εἴχοντο, καὶ χρόνος σφίσιν οὐχ ἧσσον ἢ ὀκτὼ μηνῶν ἐν ταύτῃ τῇ διαίτῃ ἐτρίβη.

or married) who was forced into a non-marital sexual act against her will bears no moral responsibility whatsoever and should not suffer any negative consequences as a result".[100] Joannina found herself in such a situation but Procopius certainly envisages negative consequences for her:

> But when Antonina, after the Empress' death,[101] came to Byzantium,[102] she purposely forgot the benefits which the Empress *recently* had conferred upon her, and paying no attention whatever to the fact that if the **child [παῖς]** should marry anyone else, her previous record would be that of a **prostitute [πεπορνευμένη]**, she spurned the alliance with the offspring of Theodora and forced the **girl [παῖδα]**, entirely against her will, to abandon her beloved.[103]

To emphasize the result, Procopius uses πεπορνευμένη (prostitute) for the second and final time in his *Anekdota*. Initially, Procopius deploys it to epitomize Antonina: "... and her mother was one of the prostitutes (πεπορνευμένων) attached to the thymele".[104] Procopius deploys this vocabulary to link Joannina's reputation to that of her maternal grandmother. He tells us nothing more about Joannina, but the entire episode from betrothal to marriage and separation is the opposite of an appropriate alliance between two families. Here concord turns into discord, and is possibly intended to be comical. Evans suggests that divorce law did not support a separation and that Joannina and Anastasius would have resumed their marriage,[105] but Antonina may have separated the couple before Joannina became 12, thus nullifying it. In any case, Procopius is clear that Belisarius confirmed the separation the following year and so they had not resumed their marriage by 549, which suggests the marriage had probably ended.

Procopius uses the finale of the Joannina episode (the separation) to criticize Antonina (and Belisarius) through invective (ψόγος) and comedy

---

[100] August. *De civ. D.* 1.18, in Balberg and Muehlberger 2018, 302.
[101] June 548.
[102] From Otranto, Summer 548; cf. Procop. *Bell.* 7.30.25.
[103] Procop. *Anecd.* 5.23: ἡνίκα δὲ Ἀντωνίνα τῆς βασιλίδος ἀπογενομένης ἐς Βυζάντιον ἦλθεν, ἐπελάθετο μὲν ἐθελουσία ὧν ἐκείνη *ἔναγχος* εἰς αὐτὴν εἴργαστο, ὡς ἥκιστα δὲ ὑπολογισαμένη ὡς, ἤν τῳ ἑτέρῳ ἡ *παῖς* αὐτῇ ξυνοικίζοιτο, *πεπορνευμένη* τὰ πρότερα ἔσται, τὸν Θεοδώρας ἔκγονον κηδεστὴν ἀτιμάζει, τήν τε *παῖδα* ὡς μάλιστα ἀκουσίαν βιασαμένη ἀνδρὸς τοῦ ἐρωμένου ἀπέστησε.
[104] Procop. *Anecd.* 1.11: ...μητρὸς δὲ τῶν τινος ἐν θυμέλῃ *πεπορνευμένων* (my emphasis). Dewing, 1935, 8, explains that the contemptuous term "thymelic performers" denoted a lower class than stage actors (such as Theodora).
[105] Evans 2011, 199–200.

(κωμῳδία):[106] "And from this act she won a great reputation for ingratitude among all mankind, yet when her husband arrived, she had no difficulty in persuading him to share with her in this unholy business."[107] This echoes *Anekdota* 5.20 where Procopius gives Theodora foresight in distrusting Antonina, who is portrayed as simultaneously discounting her youngest daughter's wishes, disregarding Theodora's legacy and Anastasius, and being ungrateful by forgetting all that the empress had "recently" (ἔναγχος) done for her (procuring Theodosius, then arranging a reconciliation with Belisarius in 542–43).[108] Procopius may be introducing comic elements inspired by Greek and Latin comedy or contemporary mime into the episode: Theodora manoeuvres Belisarius into agreeing to the betrothal, and Joannina into a sexual union before marriage. Stereotypically, Procopius indicates the rape of Joannina as maiden, by Anastasius, but drags Theodora into the violation by accusing her of initiating the crime as a joint enterprise. He has the episode develop into a "love affair". Procopius characterizes Theodora and Antonina as both parasites and bawds. However, Joannina is the innocent maiden at risk of being seen as a prostitute; Belisarius is the angry or avaricious old man (and soldier); and Anastasius is the young man in love, an emotion purportedly later shared by Joannina. Procopius gives Antonina the agency, independent of Belisarius, to dismantle an alliance with Theodora's family, unilaterally cancelling the empress' plans, "knowing that Theodora dead was no use to her".[109] This highlights the end of Theodora's influence on her death; Justinian's lack of interest in supporting Anastasius; and Belisarius being dominated. Procopius' invective is therefore a reflection of actual power relations, some of which are linked to the Joannina episode, even though comedy or mime seems a more direct point of comparison to it.

Conclusion

Antonina surpassed Theodora by outliving her: she was her 'fixer' on occasion (deposing Silverius and John the Cappadocian) but Antonina's capacity to unravel Theodora's marital scheme (between Joannina and Anastasius) suggests Antonina was, ultimately, fixing things in her own self-interest all along. Procopius' presentation of Antonina is clearly hostile in *Anekdota* and ostensibly positive, yet sometimes ambiguous, in *Wars*.

---

[106] *Suda*, Π 2479 (Adler). Pfeilschifter 2022, 130.
[107] Procop. *Anecd.* 5.24: μεγάλην τε ἀγνωμοσύνης ἐκ τοῦ ἔργου τούτου ἀπηνέγκατο δόξαν εἰς **πάντας ἀνθρώπους**, ἥκοντά τε οὐδενὶ πόνῳ ἀναπείθει τὸν ἄνδρα τοῦ ἄγους αὐτῇ μεταλαχεῖν τοῦδε (my emphasis).
[108] Procop. *Anecd.* 3.16–17. 4.19–29.
[109] Av. Cameron 1985, 74.

Procopius allocates agency to Antonina in *Wars* when he can (her felling John the Cappadocian and her managing logistics). However, where he leaves Antonina out of *Wars*, he gives her agency in *Anekdota*, characterizing her as the troublemaker in many episodes. This makes *Anekdota* a platform for allocating greater agency to Antonina than *Wars*. Sometimes Antonina wields power autonomously; sometimes it seems contingent upon Theodora or Belisarius. From 533 to 548, Antonina accompanied Belisarius on campaigns (from Africa to Italy, Syria, and back to Italy), and exercised her own power, between Constantinople, Carthage, Rome, and Ravenna.[110] Indeed, in the seventh-century Burgundian *Chronicle of Fredegar*, Justinian's empress is named "Antonia", not Theodora.[111] This confusion suggests that, in parts of the West, Antonina was received as having been a very powerful woman, but also that one powerful woman is more or less replaceable with any other, and it is yet another equation of Theodora and Antonina as parallels, just as Procopius' scorpion metaphor links them.

Antonina was extraordinary (like Theodora), as Procopius highlights, because she rose from the entertainment classes of society and attained, via marriage to Belisarius, great power, which she exerted in religious, political, and dynastic affairs for her own advancement. Belisarius' loyalty to Justinian enabled Antonina's route to power, yet it was the main obstacle to achieving ultimate supremacy. The fact the couple survived politically, and never rebelled, suggests that either Procopius' characterization of her control over Belisarius is greatly exaggerated or that Antonina did not wish to pursue that route to imperial power. Marriage into Justinian's family may have been what Antonina, and Belisarius, hoped to fix for Joannina. However, they were not as well placed as relatives of Theodora, whose niece, Sophia, married the heir-to-be Justin II (see Stemma 1, above).

---

[110] Av. Cameron 1985, 69–80.
[111] Fredegar, *Chron.* 2.62, in Grau and Febrer 2020, 786.

11

Matasuintha: From Gothic Queen to Imperial Woman

Marco Cristini

Sixth-century imperial women often had unusual backgrounds. Lupicina, the wife of Justin I, was of barbarian origin and a former slave, Theodora was an actress of questionable virtue, and Anastasia (whose original name was Ino) had been the wife of a quartermaster before marrying the future emperor Tiberius II. Members of the imperial household or leading generals frequently chose as wife a woman who was neither 'born in the purple' nor part of Constantinople's aristocracy.[1] However, the choice of Germanus, cousin of Emperor Justinian, who was seen as potential heir to the throne, was unusual even for sixth-century standards, since he married a former Gothic queen who had been taken prisoner after the fall of Ravenna (540), namely Matasuintha.[2]

Very few Late Antique women could claim to have been both the queen of a post-Roman kingdom and the wife of a candidate to the imperial throne, yet Matasuintha has received little attention from modern scholarship,[3] although the works of Cassiodorus, Jordanes, Procopius of Caesarea, and the continuator of Marcellinus Comes enable us to examine quite well the pivotal moments of her life. Thanks to recent works on Ostrogothic Italy, the age of Justinian, and Procopius, it is now possible to assess the role played by Matasuintha at both Ravenna and Constantinople much better than only a couple of decades ago, while her two marriages

---

[1] For an introduction to sixth-century imperial women, see Garland 1999, 11–72.
[2] Justinian is called uncle of Germanus by Procop. *Bell.* 7.40.5 (ἡνίκα Ἰουστινιανὸς ὁ Γερμανοῦ θεῖος), but the reading Ἰουστινιανὸς is a modern conjecture, since all manuscripts have Ἰουστῖνος, which should be accepted. Germanus is therefore Justin's nephew and Justinian's cousin; see *PLRE* 2 (Germanus 4), 505.
[3] Grierson 1959 focuses on a coin wrongly attributed to her; Magnani 2015 on her dealings with general John. A brief biographical overview is provided by *PLRE* 3b (Matasuentha), 851–52. Krautschick 2001. Wolfram 2009a.

provide invaluable insights into the political strategies of King Vitigis and Emperor Justinian.

Regia puella: An Unmarried Gothic Princess at the Court of Ravenna

Royal women played an important role in the Gothic Kingdom. Theoderic's female relatives were part of his system of alliances with neighbouring sovereigns, and his own daughter, Amalasuintha, ruled Italy as regent during the minority of her son Athalaric.[4] After his sudden death, she tried to remain in power by appointing her cousin Theodahad as co-regent, on condition that she herself would hold power no less than before. Her murder by Theodahad destabilized the kingdom, and Justinian used it as an excuse to invade Italy. Incapable of resisting the East Roman troops, Theodahad was killed by Vitigis, an ambitious general who immediately married Matasuintha, daughter of Amalasuintha and granddaughter of Theoderic.[5]

Matasuintha was born between 515 and 522, possibly in 519–520, since she was of marriageable age in late 536.[6] Jordanes reports twice that Amalasuintha gave birth (in this order) to Athalaric and Matasuintha,[7] from which we can infer that Matasuintha was younger than her brother, who in all likelihood was born in 518.[8] Both Jordanes and Procopius mention her young age when reporting her marriage with Vitigis: the former calls her *puella* (girl), whereas the latter uses the words παρθένος (girl/virgin) and ὡραία (young/ready for marriage).[9]

We do not know Matasuintha's birthplace, but she surely grew up at the court of Ravenna. There is no information concerning her education in surviving sources, since the fragments of Cassiodorus' panegyric celebrating her marriage mostly deal with her beauty, jewels, and palace, although it is likely that her education was mentioned too, as we find a similar praise for Amalasuintha and Amalaberga. Matasuintha's mother could speak fluently Gothic, Latin, and Greek, and had a remarkable knowledge of literature. Her cousin Amalaberga was well versed in literature too, as well as in *mores*, a term that includes all skills necessary for a sixth-century princess. Amal royal women were educated to play an active political role in the royal family they married into, as is shown by Amalafrida, Amalaberga's mother,

---

[4] Vitiello 2017.
[5] For an outline of Theodahad's reign, see Vitiello 2014.
[6] Vitiello 2017, 57, prefers 518.
[7] Jord. *Get.* 81, 251.
[8] Cristini 2020.
[9] Jord. *Rom.* 373, and Procop. *Bell.* 5.11.27.

who was supposed to give advice to her second husband, the Vandal king Thrasamund.[10]

It is likely that Matasuintha received a similar education. In his panegyric, Cassiodorus briefly mentions her wisdom in connection with her eloquence,[11] from which we can infer that, like her mother, she had been taught to speak fluently in public. However, this does not necessarily mean that her relatives intended to give her in marriage to a foreign king or a member of the Gothic nobility. The fact that Matasuintha was still unmarried (and, as far as we know, un-betrothed) in late 536 is difficult to explain. Matasuintha was a girl of marriageable age[12] and the Gothic Kingdom was faced with unprecedented challenges since the death of Athalaric (534) and the outbreak of the Gothic War (535). A marriage alliance with a neighbouring people (for instance the Franks) would have been expedient, especially since Theodahad was negotiating with the heirs of Clovis to obtain their neutrality or even support shortly before Vitigis' coup.[13] The presence at the court of Ravenna of an unmarried "royal girl" (*regia puella*)[14] who was the last direct heir of Theoderic the Great represented a valuable asset, which could be used to save the kingdom from a situation that seemed hopeless, yet neither Amalasuintha nor Theodahad took action. To understand the reasons for this hesitance, it is necessary to take a closer look at Matasuintha's first marriage, which was contracted soon afterwards.

---

[10] Amalasuintha: Cassiod. *Var.* 11.1.6–7 (trans. Barnish 1992, 146): "She is fluent in the splendour of Greek oratory; she shines in the glory of Roman eloquence; the flow of her ancestral speech brings her glory [...] To this is added, as it were a glorious diadem, the priceless knowledge of literature, through which she learns the wisdom of the ancients, and the royal dignity is constantly increased" (*Atticae facundiae claritate diserta est: Romani eloquii pompa resplendet: nativi sermonis ubertate gloriatur.* [...] *Iungitur his rebus quasi diadema eximium inpretiabilis notitia litterarum, per quam, dum veterum prudentia discitur, regalis dignitas semper augetur*). Amalaberga: Cassiod. *Var.* 4.1.2 (trans. Barnish 1992, 74): "learned in letters, schooled in moral character, glorious not only for her lineage, but equally for her feminine dignity" (*litteris doctam, moribus eruditam, decoram non solum genere, quantum et feminea dignitate*). Amalafrida: Cassiod. *Var.* 5.43, with the comments by Cristini 2022b, 91–92. On the education of Ostrogothic royal women, see Vitiello 2006 and Fauvinet-Ranson 2018.
[11] Cassiod. *Or. fr.* p. 480 Tr.; see the appendix.
[12] See Cooper 2016, 306: "at her brother's death in 534 she was between eleven and seventeen, the peak age of marriageability".
[13] Procop. *Bell.* 5.13.14–15. See Vitiello 2014, 151–52.
[14] Jord. *Rom.* 373.

Socia in regno: The Marriage with Vitigis – Between Coercion and Expediency

When Vitigis usurped the throne in late 536, his chances of success (not to say survival) were slim. The Goths had been ruled by the Amal family for almost a century, and, even after the murder of Theodahad and the capture of his son, there were several candidates more illustrious than him.[15] As Vitigis was in dire need of strengthening his legitimacy, he immediately set off for Ravenna to marry Matasuintha, thereby abandoning Rome to the troops of Justinian.

Interestingly, all sources agree that Matasuintha was forced to marry Vitigis against her will, a situation that was not uncommon in Late Antique royal families but is rarely mentioned by ancient authors. Jordanes and the anonymous continuator of Marcellinus Comes report that the king married her "more with violence than love",[16] Procopius that the wedding took place against her will and with violence,[17] and even Cassiodorus cannot conceal completely her unwillingness. In his panegyric, he allusively states that she was somewhat forced to get married and that her birth could be regarded as an impediment (since she was the granddaughter of Theoderic, and Vitigis an obscure general), but concludes by saying that she could not make excuses and use the king's (lack of) courage as a pretext for refusing, because he is a brave man.[18] Cassiodorus and those who heard the panegyric were well aware of Matasuintha's opposition to the wedding, which must have given rise to a considerable scandal, and could not simply ignore it; hence, he tried to justify and at the same time downplay her recalcitrance. If Cassiodorus' account is to be trusted, the princess possibly argued that Vitigis was not a prominent member of a foreign royal family or the Gothic nobility, and that he still had to prove his courage by fighting against Belisarius.

The fact that Matasuintha was far from happy during her wedding is also revealed by Cassiodorus' praise of the traditional virtues of a Roman woman. According to him, "temperance should soothe (*sereno*) her gaze", an ambiguous expression, which could refer to the eyes either as a vehicle of *voluptas* (as would be quite conventional for a speech delivered on the occasion of a wedding) or anger. The latter reconstruction is supported by the choice of the verb *sereno*, which is used by both Virgil and Cassiodorus

---

[15] Vitiello 2014, 157–58.
[16] Jord. *Rom.* 373, and Marc. Comes *auct.* s.a. 536.7: *plus vi quam amore*. Both *Lib. Pont.* 60.2 (*cum vim*) and Paul. Diac. *Hist. Rom.* 16.15 (*per vim*) possibly derive from either of them.
[17] Procop. *Goth.* 5.11.27 (οὔτι ἐθελούσιον); 2.10.11 (βίᾳ).
[18] Cassiod. *Or.* fr. p. 480 Tr.; see the appendix.

himself [in his *Variae*] to describe a transition from clouds/sadness to a clear sky/joy.[19]

Matasuintha's unwillingness to marry Vitigis has usually been explained by referring to his humble origins or a possible role in the murder of Amalasuintha.[20] However, a careful reading of the panegyric could indicate that the girl intended to choose (or had already chosen) to lead a religious life, which would explain her hostility towards marriage. In fact, Cassiodorus exhorts "quiet modesty to put aside/allay her pious gait" (*gressus religiosos modestia tranquilla componat*). The meaning of this sentence is at first glance unclear, since Cassiodorus almost always associates the adjective *religiosus* with religious practices or inclinations.[21] Of course, it is possible that he intended to portray Matasuintha as a perfect Christian virgin, but such a praise would have been more suitable for an abbess or saint. We should not dismiss the hypothesis that the young princess had decided to embrace some form of contemplative life and had been forced to marry Vitigis in spite of her vocation or vows.[22] If this reconstruction is correct, then the expression "pious gait" (*gressus religiosos*) refers to the attitudes of a woman consecrated to God, which were ill-suited to a queen. This conjecture can find confirmation in Cassiodorus' description of her jewels, which mirrors a letter written by St. Jerome in praise of Demetrias, a Roman noblewoman of the *gens Anicia* who had been betrothed by her mother and grandmother but chose to forego marriage in order to take the veil. Jerome lists the same gems mentioned by Cassiodorus, namely pearls (*margaritae*), emeralds (*smaragdi*; in Cassiodorus *prasini*), rubies (*cerauni*; in Cassiodorus *lychnites*) and sapphires (in both *hyacinthi*). The fact that Jerome and Cassiodorus are both referring to a young woman who was unwilling to get married, and that they both list the same precious stones, which are almost never mentioned in the same passage by other authors, strongly suggests the existence of an intertextual relationship between them.[23]

---

[19] Verg. *Aen.* 1.255. 4.477. Cassiod. *Var.* 3.16.3 (the only occurrence of *sereno* within the *Variae*): "Let all the sadness deriving from misfortune disappear; let a gloomy countenance finally brighten" (*Abscedat omnis de calamitate tristitia: serenetur tandem nubilus vultus*).

[20] See, e.g., Wolfram 2009a. Cooper 2016, 307. Vitiello 2017, 99.

[21] The expression *mens religiosa* ("religious mind/attitude") occurs with this meaning in *Var.* 4.41.1. 8.8.1. *In Psalm.* 7.8. 44.10. 96.8. 110.10. 142.9. Similarly, *pectora religiosa* ("religious hearts") in *In Psalm.* 131.3, 14.

[22] Radegund made the same choice a few years later; see Huber-Rebenich 2009 for an overview of her biography.

[23] See the appendix and Jer. *Ep.* 130.7 (trans. Fremantle 1893, 265): "When you were in the world you loved the things of the world. You rubbed your cheeks with rouge and used whitelead to improve your complexion. You dressed your hair and built up a tower on your head with tresses not your own. I shall say nothing of your costly earrings,

Whatever the reasons for Matasuintha's unwillingness, Vitigis was able to overcome it, and the marriage took place. However, the position of the king remained precarious. The validity of his union with Matasuintha was questionable, since he was already married, and many Goths were in all likelihood reluctant to accept as their sovereign a man who did not belong to the Amal family.[24] Vitigis tried to increase his legitimacy by emphasizing the role of his wife and, surprisingly enough, downplaying his authority. In a letter he sent to Justinian immediately after his accession to the throne, he sued for peace portraying himself as the man who had killed Theodahad and restored Matasuintha to the throne that was hers by right of birth.[25] In a letter he sent to the Goths, he styled himself as king,[26] but he was more cautious in the epistle addressed to the emperor: apart from the *inscriptio*, he never used the term *rex* for himself, although he called Theodahad king, and Amalasuintha queen. Vitigis knew that Justinian would hesitate to recognize as the new ruler of Italy a man of humble origins who had come to power after a bloody coup, therefore he preferred to depict himself as a kind of protector of Matasuintha, who was considered as the rightful queen of the Goths.

We find a trace of this strategy of legitimization in the continuator of Marcellinus Comes, who wrote his work at Constantinople, and therefore was not directly influenced by the political communication of Ravenna's

---

your glistening pearls from the depths of the Red Sea, your bright green emeralds, your flashing onyxes, your liquid sapphires - tones which turn the heads of matrons" (*Quando eras in saeculo, ea quae erant saeculi diligebas. Polire faciem purpurisso et cerussa ora depingere; ornare crinem, et alienis capillis turritum verticem struere, ut taceam de inaurium pretiis, candore margaritarum Rubri maris profunda testantium, smaragdorum virore, cerauniorum flammis, hyacinthorum pelago, ad quae ardent et insaniunt studia matronarum*). On *cerauni/ lychnites*, see also *Coll. Avell.* 244.24. For a more detailed analysis of this passage, see Cristini 2022d, 35–37. On Demetrias, see *PChBE* 2, 544–47.

[24] The first marriage of Vitigis is attested by Jord. *Rom.* 373. Cassiod. *Var.* 10.31 (trans. Barnish 1992, 143), a letter written in the name of Vitigis to announce to all Goths his accession to the throne, lingers on his respect for (and proposed imitation of) Theoderic, stating that "he who can imitate his deeds should be thought of as his kinsman" (*parens illius debet credi, qui eius facta potuerit imitari*). Such a great emphasis on Theoderic can only be explained if the lack of kinship with him was considered as problematic by the majority of the Goths.

[25] Cassiod. *Var.* 10.32.2 (trans. Barnish 1992, 143–44): "For if vengeance on king Theodahad is sought, I deserve your love. If you have before your eyes respect for Queen Amalasuintha of divine memory, you should think on her daughter, whom the efforts of all your men should have brought to her kingdom" (*Nam si vindicta regis Theodahadi quaeritur, mereor diligi: si commendatio divae memoriae Amalasuinthae reginae prae oculis habetur, eius debet filia cogitari, quam nisus vestrorum omnium perducere decuisset ad regnum*).

[26] Cassiod. *Var.* 10.31.

court.[27] He reports that Vitigis married Matasuintha and made her "partner in the realm" (*socia in regno*). Such a wording recalls the short-lived pact between Amalasuintha and her cousin Theodahad, according to which "while the name of king was to be bestowed upon him, she herself would in fact hold power no less than before".[28] According to two letters sent by Amalasuintha and Theodahad, they were *consortes regni* ("partners in the realm").[29]

It is possible that Vitigis used a similar concept (or perhaps the very same wording) when describing to Justinian his relationship with Matasuintha. Of course, this does not mean that he intended to leave all real power to her, quite the contrary, but it was advisable to let the emperor think that the granddaughter of Theoderic co-ruled Italy, so that her husband's authority could be accepted more easily. Interestingly, the expression *socius/socia in regno* is highly unusual,[30] and it thus seems that the continuator of Marcellinus was at pains to describe what happened in Italy. Instead of simply writing that Vitigis married Matasuintha, he added the words *socia in regno*, which may be a paraphrase of *consors regni*, replacing *consors* with the more easily understandable *socius*.[31]

In late 536/early 537, a fictitious *consortium regni* would have been the best option to avoid a civil war. The former supporters of Amalasuintha were surely happy that Theodahad had been deposed, and the Gothic nobility felt reassured upon seeing that the crown had gone to an Amal woman. Vitigis had to fight against Belisarius and was in no position to strengthen his power by either eliminating or winning over his opponents. Thus, he preferred to downplay his authority for the time being. The Goths needed above all a man who could lead their army in battle, and a victory would have provided him with the prestige that was necessary to openly

---

[27] Croke 2001, 226.
[28] Procop. *Bell.* 5.4.8: ἐς Θευδάτον μὲν τὸ τῆς ἀρχῆς ὄνομα ἄγοιτο, αὐτὴ δὲ τῷ ἔργῳ τὸ κράτος οὐκ ἔλασσον ἢ πρότερον ἔχοι.
[29] Cassiod. *Var.* 10.3.2. 10.4.1.
[30] There is seemingly only another occurrence in works written before the end of the sixth century, namely Martin of Braga, *De correctione rusticorum* 19: *Oramus autem ipsius domini clementiam, ut vos ab omni malo custodiat et dignos sanctorum angelorum suorum socios in regno suo perficiat* ("We pray the mercy of the Lord Himself, that He keep you from all harm and make you worthy companions of His holy angels in His kingdom"), but the context is entirely different.
[31] See Marc. Comes *auct.* s.a. 536.7 (trans. Croke 1995, 46): *Ravennamque ingressus Matesuentham nepotem Theodorici sibi sociam in regno plus vi copulat quam amore* ("After entering Ravenna, he joined to himself as a partner in the kingdom Matasuintha, the niece of Theodoric, through duress rather than affection"). The wording *Matesuentham nepotem Theodorici sibi plus vi copulat quam amore* would have been perfectly normal given the circumstances.

bear the title of king in front of both subjects and neighbouring peoples. Unfortunately for him, such victory never materialized.

The events of 537/38 vindicated the low esteem in which previous sovereigns had held Vitigis, as well as Cassiodorus' remarks on his courage, since the king proved himself to be a valiant warrior, but a poor strategist. Instead of attacking southern Italy or raiding the Balkan provinces of the empire, he allowed Belisarius to wear down the Gothic army during the siege of Rome, losing thousands of his best soldiers without any tangible gain. When the general understood that the Goths had lost much of their strength, he ordered John, the nephew of former consul (and rebel) Vitalianus, to lay waste to Picenum.[32] John defeated the few Goths who were guarding the province, advanced quickly, and took Rimini, a mere 50 km from Ravenna.[33] Upon learning this disturbing news, Vitigis decided to raise the siege of Rome, but Matasuintha, who was at Ravenna, did not wait for her husband to return, and opened negotiations with John.

Procopius reports that they discussed "marriage and the betrayal (of Ravenna)" and based on this some scholars have argued that she asked the general to marry her.[34] Yet this reconstruction is untenable. While it is true that John belonged to a distinguished family possibly of Gothic descent, he was neither an Amal nor a member of a royal family, and thus in no way a good match for Matasuintha. Moreover, his marriage to a Gothic princess without the authorization of Justinian would have been regarded as a rebellion and cost him his position in the East Roman army (and possibly more). On the other hand, the Goths would hardly have accepted as husband of Theoderic's granddaughter a man who had been slaughtering their soldiers for months. Procopius' mention of marriage (γάμου) is more likely to refer to her union with Vitigis, which could be declared void because he already had a wife, and Matasuintha had been forced to marry him. If the passage of the *Gothic War* relates actual negotiations and not idle gossip, it may concern an agreement that possibly provided for the surrender of Ravenna, the annulment of Matasuintha's marriage, and the restoration of all power over the Goths to her.

However, the talks were unsuccessful, and the war went on. A year later, Procopius reports that, while Ravenna was under siege, Belisarius bribed an inhabitant to set fire to the warehouses where a large amount of grain was stored. Some Goths suspected that Matasuintha was responsible, but this is a mere rumour which only confirms the mistrust between the queen

---

[32] *PLRE* 3a (Ioannes 46), 652–61.
[33] Procop. *Bell.* 6.10.1–5.
[34] Procop. *Bell.* 6.10.11: γάμου τε καὶ προδοσίας πέρι. See Beck 1986, 53. Wolfram 2009b, 347. Magnani 2015.

and her husband.[35] It is likely that Matasuintha sided with those Goths who were unsatisfied with the rule of Vitigis, and this faction prevailed over the hard-liners during the spring of 540. From Procopius' account, it seems that the king was side-lined by a group of unnamed leading Goths, who started to deal directly with Belisarius.[36] But this is not the place to dwell on the negotiations which led to the fall of the city.[37] It is sufficient to note that the East Roman general took as captives both Vitigis and his wife, and brought them to Constantinople, where Justinian treated them honourably.[38] According to Jordanes, Vitigis and the emperor became friends, and the former king was appointed as patrician before his death in 542/43.[39] At the time, it must have looked likely that Matasuintha would soon be forgotten, like many ancient and modern exiled sovereigns. However, this proved not to be the case.

Patricia ordinaria: Germanus, Matasuintha, and Justinian's Succession

In late 540, the Gothic War seemed to be over. Ravenna was in the hands of the empire, Vitigis and Matasuintha had been exiled to Constantinople, and the few surviving pockets of Gothic resistance were more inclined towards fratricidal struggles than a desperate last stand.[40] However, an ambitious leader named Baduila (mostly called Totila by eastern authors) was able to reverse the situation. In a few years, he reconquered most of Italy, laid siege to Rome, and occupied it in December 546. He then sent an embassy to Justinian, trying to open peace talks, but the emperor refused to negotiate with him, since he considered Baduila a rebel. East Roman troops were able to reoccupy Rome a few months later but lost it again in January 550.[41]

---

[35] Procop. *Bell.* 6.28.25–26.
[36] Procop. *Bell.* 6.29.17–18.
[37] See Cristini 2021.
[38] Procop. *Bell.* 7.1.2.
[39] Jord. *Get.* 313: *perductum Vitigis Constantinopolim patricii honore donavit. Ubi plus biennio demoratus imperatorisque in affectu coniunctus rebus excessit humanis* (trans. Van Nuffelen and Van Hoof 2020, 368: "Taking Vitigis in captivity to Constantinople, he gave him the rank of patrician. He died having stayed there for more than two years, bound to the emperor by affection"). The appointment to the patriciate implies that Vitigis either was Catholic or converted to Catholicism, since Procopius reports that the emperor was unable to bestow the patriciate on the former Vandal king Gelimer, because he was unwilling to convert from Arianism to Catholicism; see Procop. *Bell.* 4.9.14.
[40] Wolfram 2009b, 349–52.
[41] On Baduila's reign, see Cristini 2022a.

The late 540s saw not only a bitter war that devastated most of Italy, but also a propaganda struggle between Baduila, who tried to portray himself as legitimate king and rightful heir of Theoderic, and Justinian, who sought to convince the surviving Goths to surrender.[42] Matasuintha soon came to play a prominent role in Justinian's strategy of political communication.

In 549, the emperor planned to send an expedition to Italy under the command of his cousin Germanus, and arranged the latter's marriage to Matasuintha.[43] It is likely that the wedding took place in the second half of 549, since, according to Procopius, the news had reached Italy and thrown the Goths into disarray well before the death of Germanus in summer 550.[44] Matasuintha bore Germanus a child, Germanus iunior, in late 550.[45] The marriage is reported only by Procopius and Jordanes. Although they both wrote their works in Constantinople and circulated them in the same period (550/51), their outlook was quite different and should be discussed briefly before addressing their accounts.

Procopius did not hide his sympathies for Germanus, and after narrating his death he praised him with words that are reminiscent of an imperial panegyric: "in war he was not only a most able general, but was also resourceful and independent in action, while in peace and prosperity he understood well how to uphold the laws with firmness and the order of the state".[46] Juan Signes Codoñer has convincingly established a connection between the *Secret History* and the political circumstances of the years 548–49, when Theodora died and many hoped for a transfer of power to Justinian's cousin.[47] Procopius' pamphlet, which could be compared with Seneca's *Apocolocyntosis*, was likely a kind of political satire aimed at winning the favour of a new ruler by slandering his hated predecessor.[48] It

---

[42] On the second phase of the Gothic War, see most recently Mi. Whitby 2021, 234–54. On Baduila's political communication, see Cristini 2022a, 186–94.

[43] Procopius' account of the appointment of Germanus (*PLRE* 2 [Germanus 4], 505–507) is not straightforward. It seems that Justinian first planned to give the command to Germanus, then chose Liberius, and finally appointed Germanus again; see *Bell.* 3.37.24–27. 3.39.11–28. On Germanus and his relationship with Justinian, see Cosentino 2016.

[44] Procop. *Bell.* 7.39.21.

[45] *PLRE* 3a (Germanus 3), 528.

[46] Procop. *Bell.* 7.40.9 (trans. Dewing and Kaldellis 2014, 460): ἐξ ἀνθρώπων ἠφάνιστο, ἀνὴρ ἀνδρεῖός τε καὶ δραστήριος ἐς τὰ μάλιστα, ἐν μὲν τῷ πολέμῳ στρατηγός τε ἄριστος καὶ αὐτουργὸς δεξιός, ἐν δὲ εἰρήνῃ καὶ ἀγαθοῖς πράγμασι τά τε νόμιμα καὶ τὸν τῆς πολιτείας κόσμον βεβαιότατα φυλάσσειν ἐξεπιστάμενος.

[47] Signes Codoñer 2003, followed by Börm 2015b.

[48] The date, genesis, and audience of the *Secret History* have been much discussed during the last decades. For a summary of the scholarship, see most recently Pfeilschifter 2022. An overview of the main aspects of this work is offered by Av. Cameron 1985, 49–66, but see also Kaldellis 2009.

seems therefore that Procopius was (or hoped to become) part of Germanus' circle in the late 540s.

On the other hand, Jordanes is often considered as part of a circle which included prominent exiled Italians, such as Cassiodorus. Still, this view has recently been challenged, since his relations with Cassiodorus was more strained than usually thought.[49] He did not merely abridge the latter's *Gothic History*, but reshaped and integrated it with other sources in an attempt to participate in the debate about the Goths and their future that took place at Constantinople around the year 550.[50] For instance, he seemingly knew (and tried to confute) a few passages of Procopius' works, arguing against the alleged necessity to expel Theoderic's people from the territories ruled by the empire.[51] Jordanes did not pay any special attention to Germanus, whom he mentions almost solely in connection with his wife,[52] whereas Matasuintha is a pivotal figure in the *Getica*.[53] On this basis, it is possible to conjecture that Jordanes was part of (or close to) a social circle including the exiled Amal queen, hence the emphasis on her and her child, who is described as the hope of the Anician and Amal families, possibly because the mother (or father) of Germanus senior was an Anician.[54]

---

[49] Van Hoof and Van Nuffelen 2017. Cristini 2022c.

[50] See again Van Hoof and Van Nuffelen 2017, as well as Ford 2020.

[51] Kasperski 2018.

[52] The only exception is Jord. *Rom.* 376: *Ubi Germanus patricius cum Iustino filio suo eodemque consule postquam ab Africana provincia remeasset, dum adventum Parthorum obviare nequit, relicta urbe ad partes secessit Ciliciae* (trans. Van Hoof and Van Nuffelen 2020, 213–14: "The patrician Germanus with Justin, his son and also consul, returned from the province of Africa, but could not halt the advance of the Parthians. He then abandoned the city and withdrew to the region of Cilicia").

[53] Her marriage is described three times, in Jord. *Get.* 81, 251, and 314. See also Goffart 1988, 68–75.

[54] Jord. *Get.* 314: *In quo coniuncta Aniciorum genus cum Amala stirpe spem adhuc utriusque generi domino praestante promittit* (trans. Van Nuffelen and Van Hoof 2020, 368: "In him, the family of the Anicii joined to the descendants of the Amals, still holds out hope for both families, if the Lord permits"). Momigliano 1955 has famously argued that this passage comes from Cassiodorus, who continued to update his *Gothic History* until 550, but modern scholarship has shown that his view cannot be maintained; see most recently Van Nuffelen and Van Hoof 2020, 36–37. The exact meaning of *Get.* 314 has been under discussion for almost two centuries. The most reasonable explanation is still that formulated by Mommsen 1882, 146: "Germani, Iustiniani fratris filii, parentum cum nomina ignorentur, fieri potest, ut mater Anicia fuerit vel ad Anicios aliqua ratione pertinuerit, filia fortasse Aniciae Iulianae". See also Signes Codoñer 2003, 74. However, Cosentino 2016, 117, considers this reconstruction unlikely and puts forward the possibility of a marriage between one of Germanus' sons and a woman belonging to the Anician family, although it is difficult to understand why Jordanes would have given much emphasis to such a weak relationship. On the issue of Germanus' Anician ancestry, see also Wagner 1967, 54–57, and Al. Cameron 2012, 160–61.

Turning back to Matasuintha's second marriage, Procopius attributes the idea solely to Germanus. According to him, it was the first move of an ambitious plan aimed at defeating once and for all the Goths.[55] His goal is stated quite clearly: "he hoped that, if the woman was with him in the army, the Goths would probably be ashamed to take up arms against her".[56] On the other hand, Jordanes reports that "the emperor joined Matasuintha, former wife of Vitigis, to his cousin, the patrician Germanus",[57] thereby stressing the active role played by Justinian.

The latter's account is more convincing, since a member of the imperial household could hardly have married a former Gothic queen without Justinian's approval, especially a year after being involved (allegedly against his will) in a plot to overthrow the emperor.[58] The immediate aim of Justinian and Germanus is clear, namely to win over as many Goths as possible, and only the untimely death of the latter prevented it from coming to fruition. However, we should not neglect the issue of Justinian's succession, which was on everybody's mind in late 549.

Since the death of Theodora (548), whose hostility towards Germanus was well known, the latter had become the most likely candidate to the throne. Interestingly, Procopius reports that the empress had hindered every attempt by members of Germanus' family to contract a marriage, as if she feared that it could strengthen their designs for the emperorship.[59] We do not know Justinian's stance on this issue, but he was willing to entrust Germanus with a powerful army and the task of conquering Italy a year after his alleged involvement in a plot, which makes it likely that he trusted him. One could argue that the marriage with Matasuintha was aimed at establishing a new dynasty in Italy, which should have been ruled

---

[55] Procop. *Bell.* 7.39.14.
[56] Procop. *Bell.* 7.39.15: ἤλπιζε γάρ, ἢν ξὺν αὐτῷ ἐν τῷ στρατοπέδῳ ἡ γυνὴ εἴη, αἰσχύνεσθαι, ὡς τὸ εἰκός, Γότθους ὅπλα ἐπ' αὐτὴν ἀνελέσθαι.
[57] Jord. *Get.* 314: *Mathesuentham vero iugalem eius fratri suo Germano patricio coniunxit imperator* (trans. Van Nuffelen and Van Hoof 2020, 368: "His spouse Matasuintha, however, was joined by the emperor to his brother, Germanus the patrician"). See also *Rom.* 383: *Germanus patricius [...] Mathesuentham Theodorici regis neptem et a Vitigis mortuo derelictam, tradente sibi principe in matrimonio sumptam [...] relinquens uxorem gravidam* (trans. Van Nuffelen and Van Hoof 2020, 217: "Germanus left behind his pregnant wife, Matasuintha, the granddaughter of king Theoderic and widowed by the death of Vitigis, whom he had taken in marriage as a gift from the emperor").
[58] Procop. *Bell.* 7.32; see Stewart 2020, 163–92.
[59] Procop. *Anecd.* 5.8. See Signes Codoñer 2003, 58–68. The *Secret History* should have been circulated after Justinian's death, or his removal from power, and read by people who were well acquainted with matters concerning the imperial family. It is therefore unlikely that Procopius invented or grossly exaggerated Theodora's hostility towards Germanus since many of his readers could have exposed his fabrication.

by Germanus and his heirs,[60] but there is no evidence of the existence of this plan. Even supposing, for the sake of argument, that Justinian did think about it, Germanus' move to Italy would not have prevented him from claiming the throne of Constantinople with the support of thousands of Gothic warriors after the death of the emperor, a circumstance which few could have been unaware of. On the contrary, the choice of Matasuintha can be seen as an implicit appointment of Germanus as Justinian's successor.[61] Matasuintha was the granddaughter of one of the most illustrious western kings, and, more importantly, she might have convinced the Goths to abandon their resistance and become soldiers of the empire. If Germanus was to become emperor, having a former Gothic queen as his wife would have enabled him to control Italy more easily and at the same time enlist many Goths, who could have been deployed also on the eastern front, in the Balkans or in Africa.

Jordanes reports that Germanus made Matasuintha "ordinary patrician" (*patricia ordinaria*) upon marrying her, an expression which is without parallel,[62] since the adjective *ordinarius* is usually used for ordinary consuls to distinguish them from honorary consuls. For instance, Jordanes calls Belisarius "former ordinary consul and patrician".[63] The meaning of *patricia ordinaria* is still under dispute. Since the wife of a patrician usually bore the title of *patricia*, Martindale conjectures that "perhaps Germanus had the title specially conferred on Matasuintha, so that she bore it in her own right, and not merely as his wife",[64] yet Van Hoof and Van Nuffelen argue that "we should not attribute a particular legal meaning" to this expression.[65] However, Jordanes wrote his works a few months after the marriage, possibly belonged to the circle of Matasuintha, and was quite precise when dealing with titles, as were most Late Antique writers with a legal background (he had been *notarius*), therefore it is conceivable that *patricia ordinaria* was not an invention or mistake, but an actual title.[66]

Matasuintha was already a patrician in 549, since she was the widow of Vitigis, who had been patrician himself, but she may have received the title

---

[60] See Stein 1949, 596. Stewart 2020, 189–90.
[61] Germanus was widely regarded as the most likely successor to Justinian, see, e.g., Procop. *Bell.* 7.32.10–40. Justinian never openly designated him as such, but both his marriage with Matasuintha and his being in command of the expedition against Baduila are meaningful clues.
[62] Jord. *Get.* 81.
[63] Jord. *Get.* 171: *exconsul ordinarius atque patricius*.
[64] *PLRE* 3b (Matasuentha), 851.
[65] Van Nuffelen and Van Hoof 2020, 261 n. 324.
[66] See also the chapter by Geoffrey Nathan in this volume, as well as *PLRE* 2 (Anicia Iuliana 3), 635–36. In all likelihood, Anicia Juliana also had a patriciate conferred upon her in her own right, as her husband never achieved this title.

of *patricia ordinaria* as a wedding gift. In other words, the emperor (the only person entitled to confer such honour) appointed her as a patrician in her own right, as argued by Martindale. Late Antique men (and women) were very mindful of titles and precedence, and the patriciate was an honour even superior to the consulate under Justinian.[67] The title of Matasuintha is another clue that her marriage was part of a political strategy that went beyond the war against the Goths, possibly involving Justinian's succession. By conferring upon Matasuintha a title that was second only to the imperial one, the emperor was conveying a precise political message, since more than two decades earlier he had awarded the same dignity to Theodora shortly before marrying her.[68] It seems therefore that he was ready to recognize Matasuintha as a new Theodora, and Germanus as his heir.

However, Justinian's plans were frustrated by the sudden death of his cousin. Matasuintha bore him a posthumous child, Germanus iunior, who was still seen as a possible successor of Justinian in late 551, but Constantinople could ill afford a child emperor and thus the boy and his mother played no further role in Justinian's policies. The last information we have on Matasuintha is her decision to remain a widow after the death of Germanus,[69] a choice that may hint at the reality of a religious vow she had taken (or intended to take) twenty-five years earlier at the court of Ravenna.

Conclusion

The life of Matasuintha was exceptional in several aspects, from her open opposition to the marriage with Vitigis to her title of "partner in the realm", and later *patricia ordinaria*. Her portrait evolved over time from that of a pious Christian virgin similar to Demetrias and Radegund to that of a would-be empress not unlike Theodora, thereby showing the existence of meaningful similarities in education and behaviour between Late Antique (East) Roman and Germanic elite women. She also played a role of paramount importance in the dynastic policy of the Gothic Kingdom and the empire, strengthening the authority of both of her husbands; it is likely that she had her own political agency, although the sources are often silent about it.

Regrettably, the uncertainty surrounding the periods she spent at the court of Ravenna and Constantinople makes it difficult to understand

---

[67] *NovJust* 62.2.1 (a. 537): *inter proceres nostros moris est patriciatus infulas consulari fastigio anteponi* (trans. Miller and Sarris 2018, 474: "it is customary for the patriciate's bands of rank to have precedence among our dignitaries above the high rank of consular").
[68] Procop. *Anecd.* 3.16. 9.30. Since Theodora became patrician before marrying Justinian, it is likely that she bore the title of *patricia ordinaria* too.
[69] Jord. *Get.* 81.

her aims. For instance, if she chose to lead a religious life well before the murder of her mother, then it is easier to argue that she actually intended to devote herself entirely to God. If, however, she took this decision after her mother's death and Theodahad's accession to the throne, then her move could have been an attempt to avoid the schemes of a faction of the Gothic nobility that had brought about the downfall of Amalasuintha. A few years later, her hostility towards Vitigis and her attempt to open negotiations with Constantinople could be regarded either as a way to prevent (or put an end to) a marriage she never accepted, or as proof of her desire to claim her inheritance and rule over the Goths as her mother had done before her. This fundamental ambiguity is mirrored in the *Getica*, since Jordanes' final comment on Germanus iunior could derive from Jordanes' wish to ingratiate himself with the former queen, or from his being part of a social circle led by Matasuintha and fostering the accession to the imperial throne of Theoderic's great-grandson.

Given the fragmentary nature of the evidence, any conjecture must necessarily remain speculative. However, it is clear that Matasuintha was no mere pawn in a power play that she could not hope to control. On the contrary, she tried to exercise agency before her first marriage and possibly after her second marriage too, although her actual aims cannot be reconstructed with a good degree of accuracy. The only certainty is that she ultimately never became empress, but Jordanes indicates that few would have been surprised if it had happened.

Appendix: A Translation of Cassiodorus' Praise of Matasuintha

Only a few fragments of Cassiodorus' *Panegyrics* have survived. They derive from a sixth-century manuscript from Bobbio, whose pages were split up and re-used, possibly in the fifteenth century. They are now at the Biblioteca Ambrosiana of Milan and the Bibliothèques de Nancy, whereas the fragments of the Biblioteca Nazionale Universitaria of Turin were destroyed by a fire in 1904.[70] In all likelihood, the fragments belong to two panegyrics, one in honour of Theoderic (written in 519) and the other in honour of Vitigis and Matasuintha (written in early 537). The first critical edition of all fragments is that of Traube, which was published in 1894 as an appendix to Mommsen's edition of the *Variae* (*MGH, AA* 12). To date, there is no complete English translation of Cassiodorus' *Panegyrics*. Part of the second panegyric (fol. 1–2 Ambr. = pp. 479–82 Tr. and fol. 6 Taur. = pp. 483–84 Tr.) includes a praise of Matasuintha, which represents the most detailed source on her life.[71] In the following pages, I offer an English translation of Cassiodorus' praise of the queen.[72]

Translation

[479 Tr., Ambr. 1ʳ] Let us return, then, to the fortunate lady. She *is impelled towards* something *great and only* her birth *opposes it, but* | [480 Tr., Ambr. 1ᵛ] she could not use the king's courage as a pretext for refusing, for she recognizes that she is the wife of a strong man. Therefore, gather yourselves here, in the palace chambers, most honoured sisters; gather yourselves here together with the highest grace that can adorn you. Let heavenly chastity first set the face, then rosy modesty colour the cheeks, moderate temperance

---

[70] The Turin fragments (once labelled A II.2**) were edited in Traube 1894, 465–74, 477–78, and 483–84 (they are hence called Taur.); the Nancy fragment (ms 356 [*olim* 317]) in Traube 1894, 475–76; the Milanese fragments (ms. G58 sup.) in Traube 1894, 479–82 (they are hence called Ambr.). However, the surviving fragments of the panegyric of Vitigis and Matasuintha suffer from several lacunae. Traube was often unable to reconstruct the original text, and his attempts to fill some of the lacunae yielded questionable results at times. For a more detailed analysis of these passages and Cassiodorus' panegyric of Vitigis and Matasuintha in general, see Cristini 2022d and Cristini (forthcoming).

[71] Traube convincingly argued that both fragments belong to the panegyric of Matasuintha; *contra* Vitiello 2017, 243 n. 131, who thinks that the latter deals with Amalasuintha.

[72] The following conventions are used: *** = the preceding or following page is missing; * = a few letters or words have been erased or are no longer legible; words written in italics derive from textual emendations or conjectures. The translation is based upon the Latin text I published in Cristini 2022d and Cristini (forthcoming).

soothe the gaze of the shining eyes, mild piety rule the noble heart, honest wisdom grant a suitable speech, quiet modesty allay her pious gait. The descendant of such illustrious kings deserves to have such a wedding procession of virtues.

But you, emeralds, cloud over; you, rubies, become pale; you, sapphires, whiten; you, pearls, darken. You do not devour royal riches because of unbridled greed here. She who proves to be adorned by herself receives your price from you. It is said that the attractive Venus, who is praised throughout the world, turned her gaze with squinting eyes | [481 Tr., Ambr. 2ʳ] among countless pearls and the purple with its dark colour worthy of respect, but she is even more resplendent for her placid countenance, which surpasses all her ornaments, although she is placed in the midst of gems.

Here is a resplendent throne, which rich India might admire, bejewelled Persia exalt, and noble Spain gaze upon with wonder, a throne on which we see rosy and winged virgins with shining feathers, as befits solemn Victories. Nay, crowns of pearls as white as milk, arranged on willowy necklaces of gold, close in a magnificent roundness: thus in your appearance seems to have been placed what fortune alone deserves as a prize.

You can also see the sapphires, sparkling with dark light and spurting out black glints mixed with flickers of white light, the emeralds play with a green radiance, the rubies pour out flames of icy light, the obsidian emits a bloody colour, and a single arrangement of your jewels creates as many diadems | [482 Tr., Ambr. 2ᵛ] as would be *enough to adorn* all queens of the world *with great pomp*.

A kind of starry *mirror* * perennial * that before not * not superior to summer * beauty * costumes the wealth of patrimony * a strong sweetness * have deserved the looks * you know, cease. True * represents * the sun covered the law * abandon * you sum * always in those what was always praised *. For we see * shining in their cloaks with ample***

*** [483 Tr., Taur. 6ʳ] surpasses all kingdoms, you are recognized as the master of yourself. Already, if you are compared with your own manner, you are easily surpassed by that illustrious part of the soul, you who conquer all that is mortal with the beauty of your body.

You have also made, my lady, a palace that would show your glory in an obvious way even to foreigners, because from a magnificent dwelling you can see the greatness of those who live in it. A marble cladding of the same colour as the gems shines, the gold scattered in the stone slabs glitters, minute mosaics frame the stones that make up the vaults of the rooms, and where paintings made with wax are absent, everything is embellished with metallic colours.

It is said that queen Semiramis built the walls of Babylon by mixing bitumen, sulphur and iron. But why should we be surprised? Being accessible to iron, it was impossible to escape from weapons. It is narrated that the palace of the Persian king Cyrus was built of various kinds of stone held together by gold, | **[484 Tr., Taur. 6ᵛ]** and the palace of Susa was also ***.

Imperial Women after Curtains

Julia Hillner

On 25 August 386, Gregory of Nyssa held an oration on Pulcheria, daughter of Theodosius I. She had passed away at the age of 7 or 8 and had been buried in Constantinople the day before.[1] Gregory described the devastating effect of the death of the girl – a sacred, sparkling flower not yet opened and the good fortune of the imperial house – on the imperial family and the urban population at large who had attended her funeral.[2] A few weeks later, Theodosius was hit by another bereavement, for Pulcheria's mother, Flaccilla, also died. Gregory delivered the eulogy at her funeral in Constantinople as well. Towards the end, he returned to Pulcheria's death, praising Flaccilla for having left her sons as inheritance to their father, "so they would become the bulwark of empire", while taking her daughter with her. This, to Gregory, was an act of conjugal love.[3]

Gregory's words about Flaccilla underscored her supreme virtues of fertility and motherhood, which guaranteed the security and continuity of empire through imperial sons. Yet his simultaneous praise of Pulcheria as an imperial asset, able to cement Theodosian legitimacy in the minds of Constantinople's population, and of Pulcheria's death as something her mother could be almost lauded for, should make us pause. For it reveals the ambiguity around female members of the imperial family. They played important roles in the self-representation of the imperial household as harmonious and otherworldly, reflecting in its splendour, order, and natural beauty the heavenly realm.[4] Nonetheless, these images also imbued imperial women with a magnetic attractiveness as bearers of imperial authority, which could turn into a dangerous problem for imperial men. This was especially so for women on the dynastic fringes: daughters, sisters,

---

[1] Gregory of Nyssa, *In Pulcheriam*, ed. Spira 1992, 461–72. Also see Leppin 2000b, 487–506. McEvoy 2021, 117–41.
[2] Gregory of Nyssa, *In Pulcheriam*, 462.16–17.
[3] Gregory of Nyssa, *In Flacillam*, ed. Spira 1992, 475–90, at 488.15–489.3. Also see Chiriatti 2021, 46–63.
[4] As shown by Angelova 2015, esp. 183–202.

and widows, many of whom appear on the pages of this book.[5] Pulcheria's brothers, Arcadius and Honorius, may have counted themselves lucky, then, that their sister was now an imperial interlocutor with the divine, instead of an earthly woman whose physical and symbolic ability to reproduce needed to be closely guarded.

From this perspective, several themes emerge from these chapters that deserve further investigation. The first set of themes regard the consequences, including for imperial women themselves, of the rise of the imperial consort's representation as the emperor's 'partner in reign', in addition to, or instead of, a mother of heirs. This concept is most visible in sixth-century iconography, such as on the coinage of Justin II discussed by Pavla Gkantzios Drápelová in this volume, which regularly shows his wife Sophia enthroned next to him, holding sceptre or globe, taking the place that had previously been reserved for co-emperors or Caesars. As Gkantzios Drápelová argues, this image of co-rulership was a significant development from earlier coinage that had featured Augustae alone, or at most – in the fifth century – scenes of marriage. It may be linked to Sophia's unusual position at Justin's court, detailed in this volume by Lewis Dagnall and Silvio Roggo, but the wider iconographic context also suggests a larger development. For, as Liz James has already shown, Sophia's coinage can be compared to the appearance of double portraits of the imperial couple in many other media and spaces in the sixth century. Among these we find the 'Ariadne' diptychs discussed by Anja Wieber here, but also consular diptychs, such as the diptych of the consul Justinus in 540, a mosaic on the Chalke gate in Constantinople, which featured Justinian and Theodora observing a triumph, or the sixth-century Rossano Gospels, which contain an illustration of a court scene with the effigies of the imperial couple.[6] Significantly, then, the imperial consort appears in spheres which so far had been the prerogative of men: the appointment of officials, jurisdiction, military victory. The idea of co-rulership (*koinōnia*) is also reflected in the words of urban acclamations and courtly orators, which seem to predate the appearance of physical images articulating it by some decades and may therefore have driven its development.[7] As is well known, Gregory of Nyssa described Flaccilla as sharing in the *archē*

---

[5] On imperial women's 'dynastic potential' see Busch 2015, 214–17.

[6] James 2001b, 133–35; on the Rossano Gospels, 41–42. For imperial images, in this case of two emperors, being placed behind a judge as a sign of authority, see also the diptych of the *vicarius urbis Romae* Rufius Probianus, discussed by Chastagnol 1960, 382.

[7] For the dynamics between text and image, see Roberts 1989, 66–121. Cf., however, the early fourth-century double portrait of Galerius and Valeria on the so-called small arch of Galerius mentioned by Anja Wieber in this volume, 27, which suggests that we may perhaps miss earlier double images.

of her husband Theodosius, and Claudian described Honorius' wife Maria as his *consors imperii*.[8] The Theodosian dynasty, with its focus on correct Christian behaviour as a source of imperial legitimacy, measurable in both men and women, has been rightly seen as a watershed moment in this representation of imperial women.[9] Another cultural change that may have influenced it was the phasing out of divorce and remarriage, even in case of childlessness (no emperor between Honorius and Heraclius remarried and no emperor after Valentinian I divorced). This made the imperial consort appear irreplaceable, which, here as elsewhere in late Roman society, led to the emphasis of horizontal connection through marriage, rather than the vertical line between father and children.[10]

What is less clear is whether the concept of power-sharing translated into actual rulership of imperial women, or at least into heightened opportunities to influence government decisions. The optimism of Kenneth Holum, especially with regard to the importance of Pulcheria, sister of Theodosius II, is now met with scepticism, and has to some extent been reduced to the religious sphere.[11] An important and understudied area in this regard is the presence of imperial women at court and their relations to ceremonial and governmental spaces. It is, in fact, very difficult to establish whether imperial consorts took part in the rituals by which the emperor from the fifth century predominantly communicated his persona, such as the daily *adoratio*, banquets, the reception of foreign embassies, the reading of laws, trials, or the attendance at circus games. We also know little about whether she took part in the emperor's consistorium with his advisors.[12] Interestingly, in terms of the emperor's public appearances, we can mostly place the empress together with the emperor at church, and even here she sat on a separate gallery.[13] As Mads Ortving Lindholmer shows in this volume, Theodora may have been the first imperial consort who appeared at the *adoratio*, and even this evidence, coming as it does from Procopius, is problematic.[14] Incidentally, all of this may mean that imperial women were not even present during the delivery of speeches or letters addressing them. Rather, from the sources we gain the impression of their physical segregation. As Anja Wieber has shown elsewhere, during ceremonies this segregation could come via the strategic use of curtains, a practice also

---

[8] Gregory of Nyssa, *In Flacillam*, 488.7–9. Claud. *Epithal.* 277.
[9] Holum 1982. Busch 2015.
[10] On this development see Cooper 2007b.
[11] See Harries 2013.
[12] For these activities of the emperor see McCormick 2001, 156–60.
[13] Evagr. *Hist. eccl.* 4.31.
[14] Theodora is also the first empress recorded as having given a speech in the consistorium, during the Nika riot, also by Procop. *Bell.* 1.24.32–39.

alluded to by Gregory of Nyssa with regard to Flaccilla.[15] Yet, from at least the time of Marcian, it was also institutionalized, with the imperial consort being awarded her own *cubiculum*, with separate staff, from the *praepositus sacri cubiculi* to eunuchs, *cubiculariae*, and ushers (*silentiarii*).[16] As is well known, Theodora lived away from her husband Justinian for most of the year.[17]

This development seems to mirror that of the iconography of co-rulership, which also shows the imperial couple side by side, rather than connected. Did spatial segregation therefore lead to more or to less power? There is evidence that the former is true, for, as Lindholmer also shows, it is well established that imperial women not only lived separately, but also held separate audiences from the emperor (which could include imperial rituals, like the *proskynesis*). In addition, as Wieber has argued, segregation was not limited to imperial women, but also the emperor employed techniques of secrecy and revelation, which increased his aura of sacrality.[18] In concomitance with the image of co-rulership, spatial segregation therefore may have aided the establishment, at least in subjects' minds, of imperial women as a separate route to air grievances or lodge appeal, which must have given them many opportunities to hear concerns first, and in a different form (although we need more research on the contexts in which such messages were then passed on).[19] The concept of segregation may also be useful to approach anew the role of imperial women in the fourth century or of imperial women who did not carry the title of Augusta. It is indeed also important to ask where imperial women were situated physically and whether they participated in imperial ceremonial during times when the imperial court was itinerant, such as during most of the fourth century and into the early fifth century – that is, in times and spaces in which imperial women were awarded the title of Augusta more rarely.[20] It appears that such women also, more often than not, lived apart from the emperor, who was in any case frequently on campaign. While this requires more systematic investigation, as examples here may suffice the many imperial women who visited the city of Rome on their own in this period.[21] If we take such segregation as a dynamic that made imperial women more distinctive in the eyes of subjects, it may be the case that being itinerant themselves and

---

[15] Wieber 2000. Cf. Gregory of Nyssa, *In Flacillam*, 483–84.
[16] Noethlichs 1998, 23. McCormick 2001, 141.
[17] Procop. *Anecd.* 15.36.
[18] Wieber 2000, 101.
[19] According to Busch 2015, 207, textual and visual discourses around co-rulership changed how subjects perceived the imperial consort and augmented their authority.
[20] Kolb 2010a, 23–35, and James 2001b, 120–22, provide lists of Augustae, although they do not entirely overlap.
[21] See list in Hillner 2017, 90–91.

on their own also gave them more opportunities to act in response to local concerns. The example of Antonina, described by Christopher Lillington-Martin in this volume, serves as a reminder of how mobility allowed women to increase their networks and therefore exercise their 'matronage' more effectively, which may also be true for imperial women of the fourth century.[22] It is indeed striking that some of the most obvious female appropriations of imperial ritual derive from the fourth century and/or from the Roman West, including Eusebia, the wife of Constantius II, being granted an imperial-style adventus in the city of Rome, or Serena, sister of Honorius, holding audiences in Rome while sitting on a golden throne.[23]

A second set of themes that emerges from these chapters is the perception of imperial women as vessels of dynastic legitimacy, with consequences for their role during regime change; precisely what Gregory of Nyssa, in the case of little Pulcheria, might have been concerned about. The understanding of Theodosian women having 'dynastic potential' has been well established by Anja Busch, who has also shown that the foundations laid during the early fifth century had repercussions for many decades to come.[24] In the second half of the fifth century, we see many men aspiring to the imperial purple attaching themselves to the 'left-over' women of previous dynasties, with varying success. Mostly, such 'attachment' meant marriage, as happened in the case of Marcian and Pulcheria, surviving sister of Theodosius II, or of Petronius Maximus and Licinia Eudoxia, widow of Valentinian III.[25] But it could also mean calling upon imperial women for public endorsement of imperial aspirations, as happened with Verina, widow of Leo I, twice enlisted to endorse an usurper, and, famously, Ariadne, daughter of Leo I and widow of Zeno, who was formally approached by the senate and the people to choose a new emperor, Anastasius (whom she, however, also married).[26] Yet there are also many questions unanswered about this development, its nature and its origins, especially if we turn our gaze backwards into the fourth century. As Belinda Washington shows in this volume, already in the fourth century, imperial women were sought-after assets of those vying for imperial power: we see this, for example, in the marriage of Magnentius to Justina, a member of the Constantinian family, in 350/51, in the endorsement of Vetranio's election by Constantina, sister of Constantius II, in 350, and in the parading of Faustina and Constantia, widow and daughter of Constantius II respectively, in front of the people of Constantinople and the army by Procopius in 366/67. Again, marriage

---

[22] For the concept of 'matronage' see Wieber, this volume.
[23] Eusebia: Julian. *Or.* 3.129C. Serena: Gerontius, *Vit. Mel.* 12.
[24] See n. 5 above.
[25] *PLRE* 2 (Aelia Pulcheria), 929–30, and (Licinia Eudoxia 2), 410–12.
[26] Verina: Vallejo Girvès 2017; Ariadne: Meier 2010.

was only one way of creating a link to a previous or rival dynasty through women; simple public validation also features. To these cases, we may add that of Valeria, daughter of Diocletian and widow of Galerius, who in 311–314, according to Lactantius, rejected marriage proposals from both Maximinus Daza and Licinius who were competing for control over Galerius's former territory.[27]

The case of Valeria suggests that the origins of 'dynastic potential' are likely much older than the Theodosian dynasty, although the heightened publicity around imperial women and their promotion as 'co-rulers' described above will have accelerated understandings of this potential. Another issue that needs investigation in this regard is imperial demography. It is well known that late Roman emperors did not produce many sons (no son of an emperor lived to adulthood between the death of Arcadius in 408 and the ascent of Maurice in 582). Where they did, this often led to conflict, especially in the context of the imperial colleges in the fourth century, where we see the extinction of tetrarchic lines by 313 and then of the Constantinian family by 363, despite an abundancy of male progeny in both cases. By contrast, there were many imperial daughters, many of whom did live to adulthood. For example, Constantine and Valens had two daughters, Valentinian I had three, and Arcadius had four; other emperors, including Constantius II, Theodosius II, Valentinian III, Marcian, Leo I, and Justin II, only had surviving daughters.[28] This again must have increased women's visibility, but also their reputation as carriers of institutional memory. The fear of the 'dynastic potential' of imperial daughters or sisters led both to endogamic marriage patterns within the imperial family (with women marrying their cousins, such as Constantina and Helena in the fourth century, Licinia Eudoxia in the fifth, and Sophia in the sixth) and to daughters not marrying at all, such as Theodosius II's daughters and two of Valentinian III's sisters.[29] Some of them were therefore extremely long-living 'palace veterans', like Pulcheria or Ariadne, who at the ascent of Marcian and Leo had been living in the imperial palace for over fifty and thirty years respectively and as such must have had an institutional memory only rivalled by some eunuchs.[30]

Imperial women therefore provided a precious link to the past for more than one reason. Nonetheless, more research is needed into what exactly their 'dynastic potential' consisted of. Was it just their symbolic

---

[27] Lactant. *De mort. pers.* 39; 50.
[28] See *PLRE* 1 stemmata 2 and 4; *PLRE* 2 stemmata 1, 3, 5, and 7; and *PLRE* 3b stemma 1.
[29] This as a reason for female imperial asceticism; see McEvoy 2019.
[30] On this point, and the relations between imperial women and eunuchs, see also McCormick 2001, 151–53.

association with a previous imperial house that could be exploited for an emperor's acceptance by ever-changing constituencies?[31] Was it their precious knowledge of and networks within palace environments that would have made a new emperor's government much easier? Or were women in possession of the tangible insignia needed to prove the legitimacy of an imperial claim? Regarding the last, it is interesting to note that already in the case of Valeria, Lactantius – a contemporary – couches the link she could provide to Galerius in the language of 'inheritance', a legalistic claim we find repeated elsewhere.[32] Other women are described as being in possession of actual emblems interpreted as conferring imperial power or were suspected of having access to these. A famous example is that of Honoria, sister of Valentinian III, to whom, according to Priscus, the Hunnic leader Attila thought belonged the imperial sceptre, but again we find similar ideas already in the fourth century.[33] In 360, Julian's soldiers allegedly tried to crown him with the diadem of his wife Helena, the daughter of Constantine, while at the funeral of Valentinian II, Ambrose of Milan went to great lengths to persuade his listeners that Valentinian's consecrated sisters had not been given any imperial regalia, surely to discourage any potential suitors.[34] In none of these cases did such items actually confer imperial power, but it is significant that at least some contemporaries thought or feared they did. Over time, and with the increasing iconography of imperial women in full regalia, they actually might have done. Sophia, at least, was recorded as refusing to hand over her jewellery to the next imperial consort, Tiberius's wife Anastasia, in order to hang onto her imperial authority, which suggests that, by this point, there may have been an institutionalized transmission of insignia via women from one dynasty to the next.[35]

This book also encourages us to ask another set of questions about the 'dynastic potential' of imperial women, namely, how contingent it was on other factors, and whether the idea was taken up elsewhere, most notably in the post-Roman kingdoms. Geoffrey Nathan's study of Anicia Juliana shows that it was not self-evident that women's imperial descendance was sought after by power-minded men, nor did it always translate easily

---

[31] For the concept of social 'groups of acceptance' as foundations of imperial legitimacy and its changing composition (army, senate, clergy, etc.) see Pfeilschifter 2013. Here, a potential area to investigate is the army, which after all swore oaths to the imperial family.

[32] Lactant. *De mort. pers.* 50; SHA *Marc.* 19.9: Faustina gives the empire to Marcus Aurelius as a dowry. Paul. Diac. *Hist. Lang.* 15: Constantina conveys her father Tiberius's *imperium* to Maurice.

[33] Priscus, *fr.* 20.

[34] Julian: Amm. Marc. 20.4.17–18. Valentinian: Ambrose, *de ob. Val.* 38.

[35] Joh. Eph. *Hist. eccl.* 3.3.7.

into male relatives' political success. Although Anicia Juliana was the daughter, granddaughter, and great-granddaughter of emperors, she was refused as an imperial bride by Theodoric the Amal, and neither her husband Areobindus nor her son Olybrius succeeded to the imperial throne. Perhaps Anicia Juliana's imperial ambitions have been overstated or perhaps Theodoric, Areobindus, and Olybrius had other political priorities, or perhaps, especially during the reign of Anastasius, the prestige of the Theodosian house was waning.[36] In turn, it is suggestive that, during the Ostrogothic wars of the 540s, one of the last female remnants of the Amal dynasty and widow of an Ostrogothic king, Matasuintha, was married to a relative of the emperor. As shown by Cristini here, Matasuintha came from an environment inspired by the discourse around co-rulership of women concurrent in the sixth-century East, and our sources are quite open about her potential to legitimize imperial actions in Italy.[37] It is therefore not surprising that the imperial court both sought to safely control and to exploit her symbolic potential. The question remains how far we can see other post-Roman courts buying into this discourse and what this might tell us about the origins of medieval queenship.[38]

Finally, a third set of themes raised by this book concerns the spectre of violence surrounding imperial women. Although certain incidents of such violence have received much attention – most notably the murder of Fausta, wife of Constantine, in a Roman bath house in 326[39] – it is underappreciated how endemic it was in Late Antiquity. This is especially so if we widen our gaze from blatant physical violence such as killings or banishments to more subtle forms, including child marriage, forced celibacy, kidnapping, or house arrest.[40] We need to ask more probing questions about why this was so, but this book suggests that women's 'dynastic potential', fuelled by discourses of their co-rulership, their access to resources, and demography has at least a role to play. It heightened the visibility of imperial women, but it also made them vulnerable to be killed, or to have their agency otherwise shut down, after an imperial husband, father, or brother died. At least some of them seem to have known it. Silvia Holm astutely observes how the more puzzling actions we associate with Constantius II's wife Eusebia – her persecution of Helena, wife of her protégé Julian – can be explained if we see it in the light of the childless Eusebia's desire to create a situation that provided her with security should Constantius die before her and Julian

---

[36] Begass 2018, 351–80.
[37] On Ostrogothic ideas about co-rulership, see also La Rocca 2012, 127–43.
[38] On the medieval concept of 'consors regni', see Stafford 2001, 398–415.
[39] See Hillner 2023, 182–94.
[40] Vihervalli and Leonard 2023 give a breathtaking overview of incidents for late Roman Italy alone.

succeed him. This is not dissimilar from Sophia and her attempts, argued for here by Silvio Roggo, to create an environment conducive to letting her live autonomously after Justin II's death, in the event unsuccessfully. A similar set of considerations, if under different historical circumstances, seems to underpin Heraclius' widow Martina's actions, and especially her marriage proposals – marriage being, as observed by Nadine Viermann, "the ultimate ticket into the imperial palace".

Although such deeds have traditionally been described as 'power-grabs', they are better understood as risk assessments in the knowledge of how volatile imperial succession could be and how dangerous to new men the surviving imperial female body was perceived to be.[41] Because modern historians tend to look at late Roman imperial women on a case-by-case basis, we ignore that imperial women themselves were confronted with a genealogy of violence, often within living memory, but, through such examples, were also provided with knowledge of how to survive this violence. In fact, as the below table shows, the majority of imperial consorts who outlived their husbands between the tetrarchy and the early seventh century are recorded as being incapacitated in some way or as undertaking actions to prevent such incapacitation (the exceptions are, as far as we can tell, Albia Domnica and possibly Anastasia). In most of these cases, this is the only information we have about their experiences during widowhood. While of course there could have been more to their lives than violence, the data that we do have indicate that their fate was generally not an easy one.

Table 1: Fate of Imperial Widows, from Diocletian to Heraclius

Imperial widow	During widowhood attested as...
Prisca, widow of Diocletian	Murdered (Lactant. *DMP* 51.1–2).
Eutropia, widow of Maximian	Forced to confess adultery (*Origo Const.* 1–4).
Valeria, widow of Galerius	Murdered (Lactant. *DMP* 51.1–2).
Maximinus Daza's widow	Murdered (Lactant. *DMP* 50.6).
Constantia, widow of Licinius	Reabsorbed into Constantine's court (Rufinus, *Hist. eccl.* 10.12; Socrates, *Hist. eccl.* 1.25; Sozom. *Hist. eccl.* 2.27; Theod. *Hist. eccl.* 2.3).
Faustina, widow of Constantius II	Trophy of Procopius (Amm. Marc. 26.7.10).

[41] A particularly persistent myth around an imperial woman craving power and independent rulership surrounds Constantina's role in the election of Vetranio in 350, see, e.g., Vanderspoel 2020, 79–80.

270 *Empresses-in-Waiting*

Imperial widow	During widowhood attested as...
Charito, widow of Jovian?	"Living in fear" (according to John Chrysostom, see Washington, this volume).
Albia Domnica, widow of Valens	Defending Constantinople (Socrates, *Hist. eccl.* 5.1; Sozom. *Hist. eccl.* 7.1).
Laeta, widow of Gratian	Supported by Theodosius' imperial fisc out of "generosity", which implies some property confiscation (Zos. 5.39.4).
Justina, widow of Valentinian I	Securing elevation of her infant son and later marriage into the Theodosian dynasty through her daughter.[42]
Galla Placidia, widow of Constantius III, in 422	Banished from palace (Olymp. *fr.* 40; Philostorg. *Hist. eccl.* 12.13; Prosper Tiro s.a. 423; *Chron. Gall.* 452 no. 90).
Licinia Eudoxia, widow of Valentinian III	Forcibly married to usurper Petronius Maximus, kidnapped (see *PLRE* 2 [Licinia Eudoxia 2], 411).
Verina, widow of Leo I	Forcibly consecrated, imprisoned (see Vallejo Girvès 2017 and 2022).
Ariadne, widow of Zeno	Married next emperor (see Meier 2010).
Sophia, widow of Justin II	Confined in palace, with property confiscation (see Roggo, this volume).
Anastasia, widow of Tiberius	Buried as Augusta (Theoph. Conf. AM 6085).
Constantina, widow of Maurice	Murdered (*Chron. Pasch.* s.a. 605; Theoph. Conf. AM 6099).
Martina, widow of Heraclius	Mutilated and exiled, perhaps killed (see Viermann, this volume).

This list could be extended to imperial daughters or sisters. What it already reveals is that we might have to consider our liberal use of the term 'dowager empress' when it comes to imperial widows. The term implies a regular and official role of imperial widows at court. This might have been the case where such widows had sons elevated to emperor or where they had secured marriage to the next emperor. The above table shows,

---

[42] On Justina and her agency see Hillner 2023, 298–308, and Cooper 2023.

however, that such developments were far from certain, and were perhaps even the exception to a rule that saw imperial widows violated: a twisted confirmation of how great their 'dynastic potential' was feared to be. Where imperial widows succeeded in preserving their position – or even in simply surviving – we can sense that they worked incredibly hard for it. We get a reflection of such hard work in the figure of Justina, widow of Valentinian I, who not only managed to have her 4-year-old son elevated to Augustus in Pannonia in 375, but accomplished the survival of her family a second time, by courageously convincing Theodosius in 387 to let go of his plans to support the usurper Magnus Maximus, and to marry her daughter Galla instead. The alternative would almost certainly have been to be killed or confined, as Theodosius' subsequent treatment of Magnus Maximus' female relatives shows.[43] It is in such actions where we can locate the true agency of imperial women.

---

[43] See Ambrose, *ep.* 40.32, ed. Zelzer 1982.

Bibliography

Ajbabin, A. 2011, *Archäologie und Geschichte der Krim in byzantinischer Zeit*, Mainz.
Ajbabin, A. and Ivakin, H. 2007, (eds.) *Kiev – Cherson – Constantinople, Ukrainian Papers at the XXth International Congress of Byzantine Studies (Paris, 19–25 August 2001)*, Paris.
Alexander, P. 1967, *The Oracle of Baalbek: The Tiburtine Sibyl in Greek Dress*, Washington (DC).
Alföldi, A. 1970, *Die monarchische Repräsentation im römischen Kaiserreiche*, Darmstadt.
Alföldy, G. ²1979, *Römische Sozialgeschichte*, Wiesbaden.
Allen, P. 1981, *Evagrius Scholasticus the Church Historian*, Leuven.
Allen, P. 2013, *John Chrysostom, Homilies on Paul's Letter to the Philippians. Introduced, Translated and Annotated by Pauline Allen*, Atlanta.
Allen, P. 2017, 'Church and emperor in the letters of Hormisdas I, bishop of Rome (514–523)', in Heil and Ulrich 2017, 320–36.
Allen, P. and Mayer, W. 1999, *John Chrysostom*, London.
Alwis, A. 2011, *Celibate Marriages in Late Antique and Byzantine Hagiography: The Lives of Saints Julian and Basilissa, Andronikos and Athanasia, and Galaktion and Episteme*, London.
Ameling, W. 2014a, '2554: Greek mosaic inscription of Lady Silthus', in Ameling 2014b, 547–49.
Ameling, W. et al. 2014b, (eds.) *Corpus Inscriptionum Iudaeae/Palaestinae, Tome III: South Coast 2161–2648*, Berlin and Boston.
Amirav, H., Hoogerwerf, C., and Perczel, I. 2021, (eds.) *Christian Historiography between Empires, 4th–8th Centuries*, Leuven.
Amirav, H. and Romeny, B. ter Haar, 2007, (eds.) *From Rome to Constantinople: Studies in Honour of Averil Cameron*, Leuven.
Andreescu-Treadgold, I. and Treadgold, W. 1997, 'Procopius and the imperial panels of S. Vitale', *The Art Bulletin* 79, 708–23.
Angelidi, C. 2008, *Pulcheria. La castità al potere*, Milan.
Angelova, D. 2004, 'The ivories of Ariadne and ideas about female imperial authority in Rome and early Byzantium', *Gesta* 43, 1–15.
Angelova, D. 2015, *Sacred Founders: Women, Men, and Gods in the Discourse of Imperial Founding, Rome through Early Byzantium*, Oakland/CA.
Anokhin, V.A. 1977, *Monetnoje delo Chersonesa: (IV v. do n.e.–XII v. n.e.)*, Kyiv.

Arena, P. and Goldbeck, F. 2010, '*Salutationes* in republican and imperial Rome: development, functions and usurpations of the ritual', in Schwedler and Tounta 2010, 413–46.
Arjava, A. 1996, *Women and Law in Late Antiquity*, Oxford.
Armstrong, P. 2013, (ed.) *Authority in Byzantium*, Farnham.
Arnold, J., Shane Bjornlie, M. and Sessa, K. 2016, (eds.) *A Companion to Ostrogothic Italy*, Leiden and Boston.
Ashbrook Harvey, S. 2001, 'Theodora the "believing queen": a study in Syriac historiographical tradition', *Hugoye* 4, 209–34.
Asutay-Effenberger, N. and Daim, F. 2019, (eds.) *Sasanidische Spuren in der byzantinischen, kaukasischen und islamischen Kunst und Kultur*, Mainz.
Atkinson, M. and Robertson, A. 1907, (trans.) *Nicene and Post-Nicene Fathers, Second Series, Vol. 4: St. Athanasius. Select Works and Letters*, New York.
Aujoulat, N. 1983, 'Eusébie, Héléne et Julien II: Le témoignage des historiens', *Byzantion* 53, 421–52.
Aulbach, A. 2015, *Die Frauen der Diadochen. Eine prosopographische Studie zur weiblichen Entourage Alexanders des Großen und seiner Nachfolger*, Munich.
Avery, W. 1940, 'The "adoratio purpurae" and the importance of the imperial purple in the fourth century of the Christian era', *Memoirs of the American Academy in Rome* 17, 66–80.
Avramea, A., Laiou, A., and Chrysos, E. 2003, (eds.) *ΒΥΖΑΝΤΙΟ ΚΡΑΤΟΣ ΚΑΙ ΚΟΙΝΩΝΙΑ. ΜΝΗΜΗ ΝΙΚΟΥ ΟΙΚΟΝΟΜΙΔΗ – Byzantium, State and Society. In memory of Nikos Oikonomides*, Athens.
Azarnoush, M. 1991, 'La Mort de Julien l'apostat selon les sources Iraniennes', *Byzantion* 61, 322–29.
Badel, C. 2007, 'L'audience chez les sénateurs', in Caillet and Sot 2007, 141–64.
Baker-Brian, N. and Tougher, S. 2012, (eds.) *Emperor and Author: The Writings of Julian the Apostate*, Swansea.
Baker-Brian, N. and Tougher, S. 2020, (eds.) *The Sons of Constantine, AD 337–361: In the Shadows of Constantine and Julian*, Cham.
Balberg, M. and Muehlberger, E. 2018, 'The will of others: coercion, captivity, and choice in late antiquity', *SLA* 2, 294–315.
Baldwin, B. 1977, 'Four problems in Agathias', *BZ* 70, 295–305.
Baldwin, B. 1978, 'Menander Protector', *DOP* 32, 99–125.
Baldwin, B. 1980, 'The date of the *Cycle* of Agathias', *BZ* 73, 334–40.
Barceló, P. 1999, 'Caesar Gallus und Constantius II. Ein gescheitertes Experiment?', *ACl* 42, 23–34.
Bardill, J. 2004, *Brickstamps of Constantinople*, 2 vols., Oxford.
Bardill, J. 2006, 'A new temple for Byzantium: Anicia Iuliana, King Solomon, and the gilded ceiling of the church of St. Polyeuktos in Constantinople', in Bowden, Gutteridge, and Machado 2006, 339–70.
Bardill, J. 2011, 'Église Saint-Polyeucte. Constantinople: nouvelle solution pour l'énigme de sa reconstruction', in Spieser 2011, 77–103; 155–58.
Barker, J. 1996, *Justinian and the Later Roman Empire*, Madison.

Barlow, C. 1969, (trans.) *Iberian Fathers, Vol. 1: Martin of Braga, Paschasius of Dumium, Leander of Seville*, Washington (DC).

Barnard, A. and Spencer, J. ²2010, (eds.) *The Routledge Encyclopedia of Social and Cultural Anthropology*, London and New York.

Barnes, T. 1975, 'Publius Optatianus Porfyrius', *AJPh* 96, 173–86.

Barnes, T. 1982, *Constantine and Eusebius*, London.

Barnes, T. 1993, *Athanasius and Constantius: Theology and Politics in the Constantinian Empire*, London.

Barnes, T. 1998, *Ammianus Marcellinus and the Representation of Historical Reality*, Ithaca/NY.

Barnes, T. 2001, 'The funerary speech for John Chrysostom (BHG^3 871 = CPG 6517)', *Studia Patristica* 37, 328–45.

Barnes, T. and Bevan, G. 2013, (trans.) *The Funerary Speech for John Chrysostom*, Liverpool.

Barnish, S. 1992, (trans.) *Selected Variae of Magnus Aurelius Cassiodorus Senator*, Liverpool.

Barrett, A. 2002, *Livia: First Lady of Imperial Rome*, New Haven and London.

Barry, J. 2016, 'Diagnosing heresy: Ps-Martyrius's funerary speech for John Chrysostom', *JECS* 24, 395–418.

Bassett, S. 2004, *The Urban Image of Late Antique Constantinople*, Cambridge.

Bastien, P. 1988, *Monnaie et donativa au Bas-Empire, Numismatique romaine XVII*, Wetteren.

Battistella, F. 2019, 'Zur Datierung von Prokops Geheimgeschichte', *Byzantion* 89, 37–57.

Beaucamp, J. 1990, *Le statut de la femme à Byzance (4e–7e siècle)*, Paris.

Becher, M., Fischelmanns, A., and Gahbler, K. 2021, (eds.) *Vormoderne Macht und Herrschaft. Geschlechterdimensionen und Spannungsfelder*, Göttingen.

Becher, U.A. and Rüsen, J. 1988, (eds.) *Weiblichkeit in geschichtlicher Perspektive*, Frankfurt am Main.

Beck, H.-G. 1986, *Kaiserin Theodora und Prokop. Der Historiker und sein Opfer*, Munich.

Becker, V. 2017, 'Théodora. De la femme de l'empereur à la conseillère du prince', in Bottineau and Guelfucci 20172011, 387–401.

Bedi, T. 2016, '"Network not paperwork": political parties, the Malkin, and political matronage in Western India', *Politics & Gender* 12, 107–42.

Begass, C. 2018, *Die Senatsaristokratie des oströmischen Reiches, ca. 457–518. Prosopographische und sozialgeschichtliche Untersuchungen*, Munich.

Beger, T. 2011, *Gender Differences and the Making of Liturgical History: Lifting a Veil on Liturgy's Past*, Farnham.

Beihammer, A., Constantinou, S., and Parani, M. 2013, (eds.) *Court Ceremonies and Rituals of Power in Byzantium and the Medieval Mediterranean: Comparative Perspectives*, Leiden and Boston.

Bell, C. 1992, *Ritual Theory, Ritual Practice*, Oxford.

Bell, P. 2013, *Social Conflict in the Age of Justinian: Its Nature, Management, and Mediation*, Oxford.

Bensammar, E. 1976, 'La titulature de l'impératrice et sa signification: recherches sur les sources byzantines de la fin du VIIIe siècle à la fin du XIIe siècle', *Byzantion* 46, 243–91.

Bérat, E., Hardie, R., and Dumitrescu, I. 2021, (eds.) *Relations of Power: Women's Networks in the Middle Ages*, Göttingen.

Berdowski, P. 2007, 'Some remarks on the economic activity of women in the Roman Empire: a research problem', in Berdowski and Blahaczek 2007, 283–98.

Berdowski, P. and Blahaczek, B. 2007, (eds.) *Haec mihi in animis vestris templa. Studia Classica in Memory of Professor Leslaw Morawiecki*, Rzeszów.

Berkel, M. van, Hagesteijn, R.R., and Velde, P. van de 1986, (eds.) *Private Politics: A Multi–Disciplinary Approach to 'Big–Man' Systems*, Leiden.

Bidez, J. 1956, *Kaiser Julian. Der Untergang der heidnischen Welt*, Hamburg (French original Paris 1930).

Bielman, A. 2012, 'Female patronage in the Greek Hellenistic and Roman republican periods', in James and Dillon 2012, 238–48.

Biernath, A. 2005, *Missverstandene Gleichheit – Die Frau in der frühen Kirche zwischen Charisma und Macht*, Stuttgart.

Birk, S., Myrup Kristensen, T., and Poulsen, B. 2014, (eds.) *Using Images in Late Antiquity*, Barnsley.

Blaudeau, P. 2012, 'Between Petrine ideology and Realpolitik: The see of Constantinople and Roman geo-ecclesiology', in Grig and Kelly 2012, 364–84.

Bleckmann, B. 1994, 'Constantina, Vetranio und Gallus Caesar', *Chiron* 24, 29–68.

Bleckmann, B. 2021, *Die letzte Generation der griechischen Geschichtsschreiber: Studien zur Historiographie im ausgehenden 6. Jahrhundert*, Stuttgart.

Bleckmann, B. and M. Stein 2015, (eds.) *Philostorgios, Kirchengeschichte. Editiert, übersetzt und kommentiert. Bd. 2: Kommentar*, Paderborn.

Bliesemann de Guevara, B. and Reiber, T. 2011, (eds.) *Charisma und Herrschaft. Führung und Verführung in der Politik*, Frankfurt and New York.

Blockley, R. 1972, 'Constantius Gallus and Julian as Caesars of Constantius II', *Latomus* 31, 433–68.

Blockley, R. 1980, 'Doctors as diplomats in the sixth century A.D.', *Florilegium* 2, 89–100.

Blockley, R. 1985a, *The History of Menander the Guardsman: Introductory Essay, Text, Translation and Historiographical Notes*, Leeds.

Blockley, R. 1985b, 'Subsidies and diplomacy: Rome and Persia in Late Antiquity', *Phoenix* 39, 62–74.

Blockley, R. 1992, *East Roman Foreign Policy: Formation and Conduct from Diocletian to Anastasius*, Leeds.

Boatwright, M. 2021, *Imperial Women of Rome: Power, Gender, Context*, Oxford.

Bodel, J. and Dimitrova, N. 2015, (eds.) *Ancient Documents and Their Contexts: First North American Congress of Greek and Latin Epigraphy (2011)*, Leiden and Boston.

Bogdanović, J. 2018, (ed.) *Perceptions of the Body and Sacred Space in Late Antiquity*, London and New York.
Bolotov, V.V. 1907, K istorii imperatora Iraklija, *Vizantijskij Vremennik* 14/1, 68–124.
Boris, E., Trudgen Dawson, S., and Molony B. 2021, (eds.) *Engendering Transnational Transgressions: From the Intimate to the Global*, London.
Börm, H. 2008, '"Es war allerdings nicht so, daß sie es im Sinne eines Tributes erhielten, wie viele meinten…": Anlässe und Funktion der persischen Geldforderungen an die Römer (3. bis 6. Jh.)', *Historia* 57, 327–46.
Börm, H. 2013, 'Justinians Triumph und Belisars Erniedrigung. Überlegungen zum Verhältnis zwischen Kaiser und Militär im späten Römischen Reich', *Chiron* 43, 63–91.
Börm, H. 2015a, 'Born to be emperor: the principle of succession and the Roman monarchy', in Wienand 2015, 239–64.
Börm, H. 2015b, 'Procopius, his predecessors, and the genesis of the *Anecdota*: antimonarchic discourse in late antique historiography', in Börm 2015c, 305–46.
Börm, H. 2015c, (ed.) *Antimonarchic Discourse in Antiquity*, Stuttgart.
Börm, H. 2018, *Westrom. Von Honorius bis Justinian*, 2nd rev. ed., Stuttgart.
Booth, P. 2011, 'Shades of blues and greens in the Chronicle of John of Nikiou', *BZ* 104, 555–601.
Booth, P. 2016, 'The last years of Cyrus, Patriarch of Alexandria (†642)', in Fournet and Papaconstantinou 2016, 509–58.
Bosch, U.V. 1982, 'Fragen zum Frauenkaisertum', *JÖB* 32, 499–505.
Bose, M. 2016, (ed.) *Women, Gender and Art in Asia, c. 1500–1900*, London and New York.
Bottineau, A. and Guelfucci, M.-R. 2011, (eds.) *Conseillers et ambassadeurs dans l'Antiquité*, Besançon.
Boudignon, C. 2011, 'Darf der Kaiser seine Nicht heiraten? Ein politisch-religiöser Disput über Inzest und Ehepolitik im Byzanz des siebten Jahrhunderts', in Morgenstern, Boudignon, and Tietz 2011, 221–37.
Boudignon, C. 2021, 'Is the patriarch Pyrrhos (638–641 and 654) the author of the first part of Nicephoros' Short History (chapters 1–32)?', in Amirav, Hoogerwerf, and Perczel 2021, 21–40.
Bowden, W., Gutteridge, A., and Machado, C. 2006, (eds.) *Late Antique Archaeology 3.1: Social and Political Life in Late Antiquity*, Leiden and Boston.
Breckenridge, J.D. 1979, 'Portraiture', in Weitzmann 1979, 7–130.
Brennan, C. 2018, *Sabina Augusta: An Imperial Journal*, Oxford.
Britt, K. 2008, 'Fama et memoria: portraits of female patrons in mosaic pavements of churches in Byzantine Palestine and Arabia', *Medieval Feminist Forum: A Journal of Gender and Sexuality* 44, 119–43.
Brodka, D. 2022, 'Procopius as a Historiographer', in Meier and Montinaro 2022, 194–211.

Brøns, C. and Nosch, M.-L. 2017, (eds.) *Textiles and Cult in the Ancient Mediterranean*, Oxford and Havertown.
Brooks, E. 1923, *Lives of the Eastern Saints: John of Ephesus*, Paris.
Brooks, S. 2014, '23: Women's authority in death: the patronage of aristocratic laywomen in late Byzantium', in Theis, Mullett, and Grünbart 2014, 317–32.
Brown, P. 2001, 'Holy Men', in *CAH* XIV, Cambridge, 781–810.
Brown, P. 2012, *Through the Eye of a Needle: Wealth, the Fall of Rome, and the Making of Christianity in the West, 350–550 AD*, Princeton.
Brubaker, L. 1997, 'Memories of Helena: patterns in imperial female matronage in the fourth and fifth centuries', in James 1997, 52–75.
Brubaker, L. 2002. 'The Vienna Diokorides and Anicia Juliana', in Maguire, Wolschke-Bulmahnm, and Littlewood 2002, 189–214.
Brubaker, L. and Tobler, H. 2000, 'The gender of money: Byzantine empresses on coins (324–802)', *Gender and History*, 572–94.
Bruno, N., Filosa, M. and Marinelli, G. 2022, (eds.) *Fragmented Memory: Omission, Selection, and Loss in Ancient and Medieval Literature and History*, Berlin and Boston.
Bülow, G. von and Zabehlicky, H. 2011, (eds.) *Bruckneudorf und Gamzigrad. Spätantike Paläste und Großvillen im Donau-Balkan-Raum*, Bonn.
Burgess, R. 1993–1994, 'The accession of Marcian in the light of Chalcedonian apologetic and Monophysite polemic', *BZ* 86/87, 47–68.
Burgess, R. 2008, 'The summer of blood: the "Great Massacre" of 337 and the promotion of the sons of Constantine', *DOP* 62, 5–51.
Burgess, R. 2013, 'Morte e successione costantiniana', in *Costantino I. Enciclopedia costantiniana sulla figura e l'immagine dell'imperatore del cosiddetto editto di milano 313–2013*, Vol. 1, Rome, 89–104.
Burke, J. et al. 2006, (eds.) *Byzantine Narrative: Papers in Honour of Roger Scott*, Melbourne.
Bury, J. 1889, *A History of the Later Roman Empire: From Arcadius to Irene (395 A.D. to 800 A.D.)*, 2 vols., vol. 2, London and New York.
Bury, J. 1924, 'A misinterpreted monogram of the sixth century', in *Mélanges offerts à M. Gustave Schlumberger: à l'occasion du quatre-vingtième anniversaire de sa naissance (17 octobre 1924)*, 2 vols., vol. 2, Paris, 301–302.
Busch, A. 2015, *Die Frauen der theodosianischen Dynastie. Macht und Repräsentation kaiserlicher Frauen im 5. Jahrhundert*, Stuttgart.
Büttner-Wobst, T. 1892, 'XXXIX. Der Tod des Kaisers Julian', *Philologus* 51, 561–80.
Caillet, J. and Sot, M. 2007 (eds.) *L'audience. Rituels et cadres spatiaux dans l'Antiquité et le haut Moyen Âge*, Paris.
Cambi, N. and Marin, E. 1998, (eds.) *Actes du XIIIe congrès international d'archéologie chrétienne*, Vol. 2, Rome.
Cameron, Al. 1972, *Circus Factions*, Oxford.
Cameron, Al. 1978, 'The House of Anastasius', *GRBS* 19, 259–76.

Cameron, Al. 1984, 'Junior consuls', *Zeitschrift für Papyrologie und Epigraphik* 56, 159–72.
Cameron, Al. 2012, 'Anician myths', *JRS* 102, 133–71.
Cameron, Al. 2012, 'Nicomachus Flavianus and the Date of Ammianus' Lost Books', *Athenaeum* 100, 337–58.
Cameron, Al. 2013, 'The origin, concept and function of imperial diptychs', *JRS* 103, 174–207.
Cameron, Al. 2015, 'City personifications and consular diptychs', *JRS* 105, 250–87.
Cameron, Al., Long, J., and Sherry, L. 1993, *Barbarians and Politics at the Court of Arcadius*, Berkeley, Los Angeles, and London.
Cameron, Av. 1967, 'Notes on the Sophiae, the Sophianae and the harbour of Sophia', *Byzantion* 37, 11–20.
Cameron, Av. 1970, *Agathias*, Oxford.
Cameron, Av. 1975a, 'Corippus' poem on Justin II: a terminus of antique art?', *Annali della Scuola Normale Superiore di Pisa. Classe di Lettere e Filosofia* 3, 129–65.
Cameron, Av. 1975b, 'The Byzantine sources of Gregory of Tours', *JTS* 26, 421–26.
Cameron, Av. 1975c, 'The empress Sophia', *Byzantion* 45, 5–21.
Cameron, Av. 1976a, 'An emperor's abdication', *ByzSlav* 37, 161–67.
Cameron, Av. 1976b, *Flavius Cresconius Corippus: In laudem Iustini Augusti minoris*, London.
Cameron, Av. 1976c, 'The early religious policies of Justin II', *Studies in Church History* 13, 51–67.
Cameron, Av. 1977, 'Early Byzantine Kaiserkritik: two case histories', *BMGS* 3, 1–17.
Cameron, Av. 1978, 'The Theotokos in sixth-century Constantinople. A city finds its symbol', *JThS* 29, 79–108.
Cameron, Av. 1980a, 'The career of Corippus again', *CQ* 30, 534–39.
Cameron, Av. 1980b, 'The artistic patronage of Justin II', *Byzantion* 50, 62–84.
Cameron, Av. 1981, 'The empress and the poet', *YClSt* 27, 217–89.
Cameron, Av. 1985, *Procopius and the Sixth Century*, London.
Cameron, Av. 1987, 'The construction of court ritual: the Byzantine *Book of Ceremonies*', in Cannadine and Price 1987, 106–36.
Cameron, Av. 1988, 'Eustratius' life of the patriarch Eutychius and the fifth ecumenical council', in Chrysostomides 1988, 225–47.
Cameron, Av. 1990, 'Models of the past in the late sixth century: the life of the patriarch Eutychius', in Clarke 1990, 205–23.
Cameron, Av. 1995, (ed.) *The Byzantine and Islamic Near East, Vol. 3: States, Resources and Armies*, Princeton.
Cameron, Av. and Cameron, Al. 1966, 'The *Cycle* of Agathias', *The Journal of Hellenic Studies* 86, 6–25.

Cameron, Av. and Garnsey, P. 1996, (eds.) *The Cambridge Ancient History, Vol. 13: The Late Empire, A.D. 337–425*, Cambridge.

Cameron, Av. and Hall, S. 1999, *Eusebius. Life of Constantine. Introduction, Translations, and Commentary*, Oxford.

Cameron, Av., Ward-Perkins, B., and Whitby, Mi. 2001, (eds.) *The Cambridge Ancient History, Vol. 14: Late Antiquity: Empire and Successors, A.D. 425–600*, Cambridge.

Canepa, M. 2009, *The Two Eyes of the Earth: Art and Ritual of Kingship between Rome and Sasanian Iran*, Berkeley, Los Angeles, and London.

Cannadine, D. and Price, S. 1987, (eds.) *Rituals of Royalty: Power and Ceremonial in Traditional Societies*, Cambridge.

Capek, M. 1987, (ed.) *A Women's Thesaurus: An Index of Language Used to Describe and Locate Information by and about Women*, New York.

Capizzi, C. 1977, 'L'attività edilizia di Anicia Giuliana', *Or. Chr. An.* 204, 119–46.

Capizzi, C. 1997, *Anicia Giuliana (462 ca.–530 ca.): Ricerche sulla sua famiglia e la sua vita, Rivista di studi bizantini e neoellenici*, Milan.

Cargill-Martin, H. 2023, *Messalina: A Story of Empire, Slander and Adultery*, New York.

Carile, M. 2018, 'Imperial bodies in sacred space? Imperial family images between monumental decoration and space definition in Late Antiquity and Byzantium', in Bogdanović 2018, 59–86.

Carile, M. 2021, 'Piety, power, or presence? Strategies of monumental visualization of patronage in late antique Ravenna', *Religions* 12. https://doi.org/10.3390/rel12020098.

Carlà, F. and Gori, M. 2014a, 'Introduction' in Carlà and Gori 2014b, 7–47.

Carlà, F. and Gori, M. 2014b, (eds.) *Gift Giving and the 'Embedded' Economy in the Ancient World*, Heidelberg.

Carlà-Uhink, F. and Faber, E. (forthcoming), (eds.) *Corruption in the Graeco-Roman World: Re-Reading the Sources*, Berlin and Boston.

Carlà-Uhink, F. and Wieber, A. 2020, (eds.) *Orientalism and the Reception of Powerful Women from the Ancient World*, London.

Carney, E. 2013, *Arsinoe of Egypt and Macedon: A Royal Life*, Oxford.

Carney, E. 2019, *Eurydice and the Birth of Macedonian Power*, Oxford.

Carney, E. and S. Müller 2020, (eds.) *The Routledge Companion to Women and Monarchy in the Ancient Mediterranean World*, London and New York.

Carswell, G. and De Neve, G. 2020, 'Paperwork, patronage, and citizenship: the materiality of everyday interactions with bureaucracy in Tamil Nadu, India', *Journal of Royal Anthropology Institute* 26, 495–514.

Caseau-Chevallier, B. 2007, *Byzance: économie et société du milieu du VIIIe siècle à 1204*, Paris.

Cassia, M. 2023, *The Roman Empress Ulpia Severina*, Cham.

Castritius, H., Geuenich, D., and Werner, M. 2009, (eds.) *Die Frühzeit der Thüringer. Archäologie, Sprache, Geschichte*, Berlin and New York.

Catafygiotu Topping, E. 1978, 'On earthquakes and fires: Romanos' encomium to Justinian', *BZ* 71, 22–35.
Caviness, M. 1993, 'Patron or matron? A Capetian bride and a vade mecum for her marriage bed', *Speculum* 68, 333–62.
Cesaretti, P. 2001, *Theodora, Ascesa di una imperatrice*, Milan.
Chabot, J.B. 1901, (ed./trans.) *Chronique de Michael le Syrien*, Vol. 2, Paris.
Chabot, J.B. 1916, (ed./trans.) *Chronicon anonymi auctoris ad annum Christi 1234 pertinens*, Vol. 1, Paris.
Charles, R. 1916, *The Chronicle of John, Bishop of Nikiu, translated from Zotenberg's Ethiopic Text*, Oxford.
Chastagnol, A. 1960, *La préfecture urbaine à Rome sous le Bas-Empire*, Paris.
Chatterjee, O. 2018, 'Iconoclasm's legacy: interpreting the Trier ivory', *ArtBull* 100, 28–47.
Chausson, F. 2007, *Stemmata Aurea: Constantin, Justine, Théodose: revendications généalogiques et idéologie imperialé au IVe siècle ap. J.-C.*, Rome.
Chausson, F. and Destephen, S. 2018, (eds.) *Augusta, Regina, Basilissa. La souveraine de l'Empire romain au Moyen Âge: entre héritages et métamorphoses*, Paris.
Chiriatti, M. 2021, 'La representación literaria de la emperatriz Elia Flavia Flaccila en el βασιλικὸς λόγος de Gregorio de Nisa', in Chiriatti and Villegas Marín 2021, 46–63.
Chiriatti, M. and Villegas Marín, R. 2021, (eds.) *Mujeres imperiales, mujeres reales. Representaciones públicas y representaciones del poder en la Antigüedad tardía y Bizancio*, Leiden and Boston 2021.
Choda, K.C., Sterk de Leeuw, M., and Schulz, F. 2020, (eds.) *Gaining and Losing Imperial Favour in Late Antiquity: Representation and Reality*, Leiden and Boston.
Christie, N. 1995, *The Lombards*, Oxford.
Chrysostomides, J. 1988, (ed.) *Kathēgētria: Essays Presented to Joan Hussey for Her 80th Birthday*, Camberley.
Clark, G. 1993, *Women in Late Antiquity: Pagan and Christian Life-Styles*, Oxford.
Clarke, G. 1990, (ed.) *Reading the Past in Late Antiquity*, Rushcutters Bay.
Clayman, D. 2014, *Berenice II and the Golden Age of Ptolemaic Egypt*, Oxford.
Cohen, S. 2008, 'Augustus, Julia and the development of exile "ad insulam"', *CQ* 58, 206–17.
Clover, F. 1971, 'Flavius Merobaudes: A translation and historical commentary', *Transactions of the American Philosophical Society* n.s. 61, 1–78.
Clover, F. 1978, 'The family and early career of Anicius Olybrius', *Historia* 27, 169–96.
Connor, C. 1999, 'The epigram in the church of Hagios Polyeuktos in Constantinople and its Byzantine response', *Byzantion* 69, 479–527.
Conrad, R., Drecoll, V., and Hirbodian, S. 2019, (eds.) *Säkulare Prozessionen. Zur religiösen Grundierung von Umzügen, Einzügen und Aufmärschen*, Tübingen.

Consolino, F. and Herrin, J. 2020, (eds.) *The Early Middle Ages*, Atlanta.
Conybeare, F. 1910, 'Antiochus Strategos' account of the sack of Jerusalem in A. D. 614', *EHR* 25, 502–17.
Cooper, K. 2007a, 'Closely watched households: visibility, exposure and private power in the Roman *domus*', *P&P* 197, 3–33.
Cooper, K. 2007b, *The Fall of the Roman Household*, Cambridge.
Cooper, K. 2016, 'The heroine and the historian: Procopius of Caesarea on the troubled reign of Queen Amalasuentha', in Arnold, Shane Bjornlie and Sessa 2016, 296–315.
Cooper, K. 2023, *Queens of a Fallen World: The Lost Women of Augustine's Confessions*, London.
Cooper, K. and Wood, J. 2020, (eds.) *Social Control in Late Antiquity: the Violence of Small Worlds*, Cambridge.
Corbier M. 1995, 'Male power and legitimacy through women: the *Domus Augusta* under the Julio-Claudians', in Hawley and Levick 1995, 179–93.
Cormack, R. and Jeffreys, E. 2000, (eds.) *Through the Looking Glass: Byzantium through British Eyes. Papers from the Twenty-Ninth Spring Symposium of Byzantine Studies, London, March 1995*, Aldershot.
Cosentino, S. 2016, 'Il patrizio Germano e la famiglia imperiale nel VI secolo', in Creazzo et al. 2016, 115–30.
Cosentino, S. 2021, 'La famiglia di Eraclio, Martina e l'anno dei quattro imperatori', in Chiriatti and Marín 2021, 271–93.
Creazzo, T., Crimi, C., Gentile R., and Strano, G. 2016, (eds.) *Studi bizantini in onore di Maria Dora Spadaro*, Acireale and Rome.
Creazzo, T., Crimi, C., Gentile R., and Strano, G. 2016, (eds.) *Studi bizantini in onore di Maria Dora Spadaro*, Acireale and Rome.
Creed, J. 1984, *Lactantius. De Mortibus Persecutorum. Translated by J. L. Creed*, Oxford.
Cristini, M. 2020, 'De aetate Athalarici regis Gothorum a. 526° (Iord. *Get.* 304)', *VoxLat* 56, 475–78.
Cristini, M. 2021, 'Justinian, Vitiges and the Peace Treaty of 540 (Proc. *Bell. Goth.* 2.29.2)', *ByzZeit* 114, 1001–12.
Cristini, M. 2022a, *Baduila: Politics and Warfare at the End of Ostrogothic Italy*, Spoleto.
Cristini, M. 2022b, *Teoderico e i regni romano-germanici (489–526): rapporti politico-diplomatici e conflitti*, Spoleto.
Cristini, M. 2022c, '*Oblivio non natura nobis venit*: Cassiodorus and the lost Gothic history', in Bruno, Filosa, and Marinelli 2022, 215–32.
Cristini, M. 2022d, 'Fragmenta Ambrosiana Cassiodori laudis dictae Matasuinthae Vitigique (Cassiod. *Or.* fr. pp. 479–482 Tr.): editio critica commentariis illustrata', *Latinitas* 10, 19–43.
Cristini, M. (forthcoming), 'L'ultimo frammento delle Laudes cassiodoree (Cassiod. *Or.* fr. p. 483–484 Traube): attribuzione, testo, traduzione e commento', Hermes.

Croke, B. 1984, 'Marcellinus on Dara: A fragment of his lost *De Temporum Qualitatibus et Positionibus Locorum*', *Phoenix* 38, 77–88.
Croke, B. 1995, (trans.) Marcellinus Comes, *The Chronicle of Marcellinus*, Sidney.
Croke, B. 2001, *Count Marcellinus and His Chronicle*, Oxford.
Croke, B. 2005, 'Dynasty and ethnicity: Emperor Leo I and the eclipse of Aspar', *Chiron* 35, 147–204.
Croke, B. 2006, 'Justinian, Theodora, and the church of Saints Sergius and Bacchus', *DOP* 60, 25–63.
Croke, B. 2007, 'Justinian under Justin: reconfiguring a reign', *BZ* 100, 191–226.
Croke, B. 2010, 'Reinventing Constantinople: Theodosius I's imprint on the imperial city', in McGill, Sogno, and Watts 2010, 241–64.
Croke, B. 2015a, 'Ariadne Augusta: shaping the identity of the early Byzantine empress', in Dunn and Mayer 2015, 291–320.
Croke, B. 2015b, 'Dynasty and aristocracy in the fifth century', in Maas 2015, 98–124.
Croke, B. and Crow, J. 1983, 'Procopius and Dara', *The Journal of Roman Studies* 73, 143–59.
Curta, F. 2006, *Southeastern Europe in the Middle Ages 500–1250*, Cambridge.
Dagnall, L. (forthcoming), 'The Price of Empire? Justinian I's Use of Cash Subsidies in Foreign Policy, 527–565', PhD thesis, University of Sheffield.
Dagron, G. 1996, *Empereur et prêtre. Etude sur le «césaropapisme» byzantin*, Paris.
Dagron, G. 2007, 'From the *mappa* to the *akakia*: symbolic drift', in Amirav and Romeny 2007, 203–20.
Dagron, G. and B. Flusin 2020, *Constantini Porphyrogeniti Liber de cerimoniis*, 6 vols., Paris.
Daim, F. and Drauschke, J. 2010, (eds.) *Byzanz – Das Römerreich im Mittelalter, Vol. 1: Welt der Ideen, Welt der Dinge*, Mainz.
Davenport, C. and McEvoy, M. 2023, (eds.) *The Roman Imperial Court in the Principate and Late Antiquity*, Oxford.
Davis, R. 2010, *The Book of Pontiffs/Liber Pontificalis*, Liverpool.
De Boor, C. 1883, (ed.) *Theophanis Chronographia*, Leipzig.
Delahaye, H. 1902, *Synaxarium Ecclesiae Constantinopolitanae: Propylaeum ad AASS Novembris*, Brussels.
Delbrueck, R. 1929, *Die Consulardiptychen und verwandte Denkmäle*, 2 vols., Berlin and Leipzig.
Deliyannis, D. 2010, *Ravenna in Late Antiquity*, Cambridge.
Desnier, J.-L. 1987, 'Zosime II, 29 et la mort de Fausta', *Bulletin de l'Association Guillaume Budé* 1, 297–309.
Dewing, H. 1914, *Procopius de bellis/Wars*, London.
Dewing, H. 1935, *Procopius: Secret History. Translated by H. Dewing*, Cambridge/MA.

Dewing, H. and Kaldellis, A. 2014, Prokopios, *The Wars of Justinian. Translated by H. B. Dewing. Revised and Modernized, with an Introduction and Notes by A. Kaldellis*, Indianapolis and Cambridge.
Diamanti, D. and Vassiliou, A. 2019, (eds.) *Εν Σοφίᾳ μαθητεύσαντες. Essays in Byzantine Material Culture and Society in Honour of Sophia Kalopissi-Verti*, Oxford.
Dickey, E. 2001, 'Κypie, δεσπότα, *domine*: Greek politeness in the Roman empire', *JHS* 121, 1–11.
Dickey, E. 2002, *Latin Forms of Address: From Plautus to Apuleius*, Oxford.
Diefenbach, S. 1996, 'Frömmigkeit und Kaiserakzeptanz im frühen Byzanz', *Saeculum* 47, 35–66.
Diehl, C. 1901, *Justinien et la civilisation byzantine au VIe siècle*, Paris.
Diehl, C. 1904, *Theodora, impératrice de Byzance*, Paris.
Diehl, C. 1906–1908, *Figures byzantines*, 2 vols., Paris.
Diehl, C. 1963, *Byzantine Empresses*, New York (French original Paris 1906).
Dijkstra, H. and Raschle, C. 2020, (eds.) *Religious Violence in the Ancient World*, Cambridge.
Dirschlmayer, M. 2015, *Kirchenstiftungen römischer Kaiserinnen vom 4. bis zum 6. Jahrhundert. Die Erschließung neuer Handlungsspielräume*, Münster.
Draycott, J. 2022, *Cleopatra's Daughter: From Roman Prisoner to African Queen*, London.
Drijvers, J. 1992a, *Helena Augusta: The Mother of Constantine the Great and the Legend of Her Finding of the True Cross*, Leiden.
Drijvers, J. 1992b, 'Flavia Maxima Fausta: some remarks', *Historia* 41, 500–506.
Drijvers, J.W. and Hunt, D. 1999, (eds.) *The Late Roman World and Its Historian: Interpreting Ammianus Marcellinus*, London.
Drinkwater, J. 2000, 'The revolt and ethnic origin of the usurper Magnentius (350–353) and the rebellion of Vetranio', *Chiron* 30, 131–59.
Drinkwater, J. 2022, 'The battle of Mursa, 351: causes, course, and consequences', *JLA* 15, 28–68.
Drinkwater, J. and Elton, H. 1992, (eds.) *Fifth-Century Gaul: A Crisis of Identity?*, Cambridge.
Drobner, H.R. and Viciano, A. 2000, (eds.) *Gregory of Nyssa. Homilies on the Beatitudes. An English Version with Commentary and Supporting Studies. Proceedings of the Eighth International Colloquium on Gregory of Nyssa (Paderborn, 14–18 September 1998)*, Leiden.
Duindam, J., Artan, T., and Kunt, M. 2011, (eds.) *Royal Courts in Dynastic States and Empires: A Global Perspective*, Leiden and Boston.
Dunn, G. and Mayer, W. 2015, (eds.) *Christians Shaping Identity from the Roman Empire to Byzantium: Studies Inspired by Pauline Allen*, Leiden and Boston.
Earenfight, T. 2013, *Queenship in Medieval Europe*, Basingstoke and New York.
Eastmond, A. 2001, (ed.) *Eastern Approaches to Byzantium: Papers from the Thirty-Third Spring Symposium of Byzantine Studies, University of Warwick, Coventry, March 1999*, Aldershot.

Eastmond, A. and James, L. 2001, (eds.) *Wonderful Things: Byzantium through its Art. Papers from the Forty-Second Spring Symposium of Byzantine Studies, London, 20–22 March 2009*, London.

Edmondson, J. and Keith, A. 2008, (eds.) *Roman Dress and the Fabrics of Roman Culture*, Toronto.

Edwell, P., Fisher, G., Greatrex, G., Whateley, C., and Wood, P. 2015, 'Arabs in the conflict between Rome and Persia, AD 491–630', in Fisher 2015, 214–75.

Effenberger, A. 2019, '"Sasanidischer" Baudekor in Byzanz? Der Fall der Polyeuktoskirche in Konstantinopel', in Asutay-Effenberger and Daim 2019, 155–93.

Elias, N. 1969, *Die höfische Gesellschaft*, Frankfurt am Main (first published in English as *The Court Society*, Oxford 1983).

Ellis, L. and Kidner, F.L. 2004, (eds.) *Travel, Communication and Geography in Late Antiquity: Sacred and Profane*, Aldershot.

Entwistle, C. 2016 = 2003, (ed.) *Through a Glass Brightly: Studies in Byzantine and Medieval Art and Archaeology. Presented to David Buckton*, Oxford and Havertown.

Erdkamp, P. 2007, (ed.) *A Companion to the Roman Army*, Oxford.

Errington, R. 1996, 'The accession of Theodosius I', *Klio* 78, 438–53.

Erskine, A., Llewellyn-Jones, L., and Wallace, S. 2017, (eds.) *The Hellenistic Court: Monarchic Power and Elite Society from Alexander to Cleopatra*, Swansea.

Esders, S., Fox, Y., Hen, Y., and Sarti L. 2019, (eds.) *East and West in the Early Middle Ages: The Merovingian Kingdoms in Mediterranean Perspective*, Cambridge.

Evans, J.A. 2002, *The Empress Theodora: Partner of Justinian*, Austin/TX.

Evans, J.A. 2011, *The Power Game in Byzantium: Antonina and the Empress Theodora*, London.

Evans Grubbs, J. 2002, *Women and the Law in the Roman Empire. A Sourcebook on Marriage, Divorce and Widowhood*, London and New York.

Fagan, G. 2002, 'Messalina's folly', *CQ* 52, 566–79.

Fantham, E. 2006, *Julia Augusti*, Oxford.

Fauvinet-Ranson, V. 2018, 'Reines et princesses du royaume ostrogothique d'Italie au VIe siècle', in Chausson and Destephen 2018, 59–78.

Featherstone, M. 2005, 'The chrysotriklinos seen through *de cerimoniis*', in Monchizadeh and Hoffmann 2005, 845–52.

Featherstone, M. 2015, 'Space and ceremony in the great palace of Constantinople under the Macedonian dynasty', in *LXII Settimana di studio del CISAM. Le corti nell'alto medioevo*, Spoleto, 587–610.

Ferrary, J.-L. and Scheid, J. 2015, (eds.) *Il princeps romano: autocrate o magistrato? Fattori giuridici e fattori sociali del potere imperiale da Augusto a Commodo*, Pavia.

Fischer, B. 2000, 'Gemeinschaftsgebet in den christlichen Gemeinden und in der christlichen Familie in der alten Christenheit', in Gerhards and Heinz 2000, 1–17.

Fischler, S. 1994, 'Social stereotypes and historical analysis: the case of the imperial women at Rome', in L. Archer, S. Fischler, and M. Wyke (eds.), *Women in Ancient Societies: An Illusion of the Night*, London, 115–33.

Fisher, A. 2019, 'Money for nothing? Franks, Byzantines and Lombards in the sixth and seventh centuries', in Esders, Fox, Hen, and Sarti 2019, 108–26.

Fisher, E. 1978, 'Theodora and Antonina in the Historia Arcana: history and/or fiction?', *Arethusa* 11, 253–79.

Fisher, G. 2011, *Between Empires: Arabs, Romans and Sasanians in Late Antiquity*, Oxford.

Fisher, G. 2015, (ed.) *Arabs and Empires before Islam*, Oxford.

Flaig, E. 1992, *Den Kaiser herausfordern. Die Usurpation im Römischen Reich*, Frankfurt.

Flaig, E. ²2019, *Den Kaiser herausfordern. Die Usurpation im Römischen Reich*, Frankfurt.

Flower, H. 2006, *The Art of Forgetting: Disgrace and Oblivion in Roman Political Culture*, Chapel Hill.

Fögen, T. and Lee, M. 2009, (eds.) *Bodies and Boundaries in Graeco-Roman Antiquity*, Berlin.

Ford, R. 2020, 'From Scythian, to Getan, to Goth: the Getica of Jordanes and the classical ethnographic tradition', in Heydemann and Reimitz 2020, 95–119.

Foss, C. 2002, 'The empress Theodora', *Byzantion*, 72, 141–76.

Fournet, J.-L. and Papaconstantinou, A. 2016, (eds.) *Mélanges Jean Gascou*. Travaux et Mémoires 19, Paris.

Fowden, G. 1994, 'Constantine, Sylvester and the church of St. Polyeuktos in Constantinople', *Journal of Roman Archaeology* 7, 274–84.

Foxhall, L. and Neher, G. 2013, *Gender and the City before Modernity*. Gender and History Special Issue Book Series, Malden/MA, Oxford, and Chichester.

Frakes, R. 2006, 'The dynasty of Constantine down to 363', in Lenski 2006, 91–110.

Freisenbruch, A. 2010, *The First Ladies of Rome: The Women behind the Caesars*, London.

Fremantle, W. 1893, (trans.) *The Principal Works of St. Jerome*, New York.

Frendo, J. 1975, *Agathias: The Histories. Translated by J.D. Frendo*, Berlin.

Frier, B. 2016, (ed.) *The Codex of Justinian: A New Annotated Translation, with Parallel Latin and Greek Text Based on a Translation by Justice Fred H. Blume*, Cambridge.

Fromentin, F.V., Bertrand, E., Coltelloni-Trannoy, M., Molin, M., and Urso, G. 2016, (eds.) *Cassius Dion: nouvelles lectures*, Bordeaux.

Fuhrer, T. 2011, (ed.) *Rom und Mailand in der Spätantike*, Berlin and Boston.

Fündling, J. 2011 (Review of Kolb 2010), *BMCR* 2011.03.40. https://bmcr.brynmawr.edu/2011/2011.03.40/ (accessed 30 March 2022).
Galliker, J. 2014, 'Middle Byzantine Silk in Context: Integrating the Textual and Material Evidence', PhD thesis, University of Birmingham.
García Ruiz, M. 2015, 'Una Lectura Conjunta del Primer *Encomio A Constancio* y el *Encomio A Eusebia* de Juliano', *ExClass* 19, 155–73.
García Ruiz, M.P. 2012, 'Significado de σωφροσύνη (αὐτή) en el Encomio a Eusebia de Juliano', *Emerita* 80, 69–87.
Garland, L. 1999, *Byzantine Empresses: Women and Power in Byzantium, AD 527–1204*, London and New York.
Garland, L. 2006a, 'Imperial women and entertainment at the middle Byzantine court', in Garland 2006b, 177–91.
Garland, L. 2006b, (ed.) *Byzantine Women: Varieties of Experience AD 800–1200*, London.
Garland, L. and Rapp, S. 2006, 'Mary of "Alania": women and empresses between two worlds', in Garland 2006b, 91–122.
Garlick, B., Dixon, S., and Allen, P. 1992, (eds.) *Stereotypes of Women in Power: Historical Perspectives and Revisionist Views*, New York, Westport, and London.
Geertz, C. 1973, *The Interpretation of Cultures: Selected Essays*, New York.
Gerhards, A. and Heinz, A. 2000, (eds.) *Frömmigkeit der Kirche: Gesammelte Studien zu christlichen Spiritualität*, Bonn.
Gettings, E. 2003. 'Elite women: dignity, power, piety', in Kalavrezou 2003, 67–75.
Giessauf, J., Murauer, R., and Schennach, M.P. 2010, (eds.) *Päpste, Privilegien, Provinzen: Festschrift für Werner Maleczek zum 65. Geburtstag*, Vienna.
Gillett, A. 2012, 'Advise the emperor beneficially: lateral communication in diplomatic embassies between the post-imperial West and Byzantium', in A. Becker and N. Drocourt, *Ambassadeurs et ambassades au couer des relations diplomatique. Rome – Occident Médiéval – Byzance (VIIIe s. après J.-C.*, Metz, 257–85.
Ginkel, J. van 1995, *John of Ephesus: A Monophysite Historian in Sixth-Century Byzantium*, Groningen.
Ginkel, J. van 2020, 'Monk, missionary, and martyr: John of Ephesus, a Syriac orthodox historian in sixth century Byzantium', *Journal of the Canadian Society for Syriac Studies* 5, 35–50.
Girotti, B., Marsili, G., and Pomero, M.E. 2022, (eds.) *Il potere dell'immagine e della parola. Elementi distintivi dell'aristocrazia femminile da Roma a Bisanzio*, Spoleto.
Gizewski, C. 1997, '"Informelle Gruppenbildungen" in unmittelbarer Umgebung des Kaisers an spätantiken Höfen', in Winterling 1997b, 113–49.
Gkantzios Drápelová, P. 2016, 'Byzantine empresses on coins in the early Byzantine period (565–610): a survey of the problems of interpretation and identification', *Byzantinoslavica LXXIV*, 75–91.

Gkantzios Drápelová, P. 2019, 'The mint of Byzantine Antioch (ca 516–610 AD): some remarks on trends in provincial coinage', in Diamanti and Vassiliou 2019, 313–24.

Godoy, Y. 2004, *Gosvinta. La regina dei visigoti*, Milan.

Goetz, H., Jarnut, J., and Pohl, W. 2003, *Regna and Gentes: The Relationship between Late Antique and Early Medieval Peoples and Kingdoms in the Transformation of the Roman World*, Leiden.

Goffart, W. 1957, 'Byzantine policy in the West under Tiberius II and Maurice: the pretenders Hermenegild and Gundovald (579–585)', *Traditio* 13, 73–118.

Goffart, W. 1988, *The Narrators of Barbarian History (A.D. 550–800): Jordanes, Gregory of Tours, Bede, and Paul the Deacon*, Princeton.

Goldbeck, F. 2010, *Salutationes: Die Morgenbegrüßungen in Rom in der Republik und der frühen Kaiserzeit*, Berlin.

Goldbeck, F. and J. Wienand 2017, (eds.) *Der römische Triumph in Prinzipat und Spätantike*, Berlin.

Gordon, C. 1949, 'Subsidies in Roman imperial defence', *Phoenix* 3, 60–69.

Gordon, C. 1959, 'Procopius and Justinian's financial policies', *Phoenix* 13, 23–30.

Grau, S. and O. Febrer 2020, 'Procopius on Theodora: ancient and new biographical patterns', *BZ* 113, 769–88.

Gray, P. 2005, 'The legacy of Chalcedon', in Maas 2005, 215–38.

Greatrex, G. 1995, 'The composition of Procopius' *Persian Wars* and John the Cappadocian', *Prudentia* 27, 1–13.

Greatrex, G. 1998, *Rome and Persia at War, 502–542*, Cambridge.

Greatrex, G. 2020, 'The emperor, the people and urban violence in the fifth and sixth centuries', in Dijkstra and Raschle 2020, 389–405.

Greatrex, G. 2022a, *Procopius of Caesarea: The Persian Wars. A Historical Commentary*, Cambridge.

Greatrex, G. 2022b, *Procopius of Caesarea: The Persian Wars. Translation, with Introduction and Notes*, Cambridge.

Greatrex, G. and Janniard, S. 2018, (eds.) *Le Monde de Procope – The World of Procopius*, Paris.

Greatrex, G. and Lieu, S. 2002, *The Roman Eastern Frontier and the Persian Wars. Part 2, AD 363–630*, London.

Grierson, P. 1959, 'Matasuntha or Mastinas: a reattribution', *NC* 19, 119–30.

Grierson, P. 1982, *Byzantine Coins*, London.

Grig, L. and Kelly, G. 2012, (eds.) *Two Romes: Rome and Constantinople in Late Antiquity*, Oxford.

Grillet, B. and G. Ettlinger 1968, *Jean Chrysostome. À une jeunve veuve. Sur le mariage unique. Introduction, traduction et notes par Bernard Grillet. Texte grec établie et présenté par Gérard H. Ettlinger, SJ*, Paris.

Grünbart, M. 2014, 'Female founders – Das Konzept: Zu Stiftungshandlungen in der Byzantinischen Welt', in Theis, Mullett, and Grünbart 2014, 21–28.

Guilland, R. 1971, 'Contribution à l'histoire administrative de l'Empire byzantin: la patricienne à ceinture, ἡ ζωστὴ πατρικία', *ByzSlav* 32, 269–75.
Günther, R. 1995, *Römische Kaiserinnen zwischen Liebe, Macht und Religion*, Leipzig.
Haarer, F. 2006, *Anastasius I. Politics and Empire in the Late Roman World*, Cambridge.
Hächler, N. 2022, 'Heraclius Constantine III – emperor of Byzantium (613–641)', *BZ* 115, 69–116.
Haines-Eitzen, K. 2000, *Guardians of Letters: Literacy, Power, and the Transmitters of Early Christian Literature*, New York.
Hahn, I. 1960, 'Der ideologische Kampf um den Tod Julians des Abtrünnigen', *Klio* 38, 225–32.
Hahn, U. 1994, *Die Frauen des römischen Kaiserhauses und ihre Ehrungen im griechischen Osten anhand epigraphischer und numismatischer Zeugnisse von Livia bis Sabina*, Saarbrücken.
Hahn, W. 1978, 'The numismatic history of Cherson in early Byzantine times: a survey', *NCirc* 86, 414–15; 471–72; 521–23.
Haldon, J. 1990, *Byzantium in the Seventh Century: The Transformation of a Culture*, Cambridge.
Haldon, J. 2016, *The Empire That Would Not Die: Eastern Roman Survival, 640–740*, Cambridge/MA.
Halsall, G. 2007, *Barbarian Migration and the Roman West, 376–568*, Cambridge.
Hämmerling, R. 2019, *Zwischen dynastischem Selbstbild und literarischem Stereotyp. Königinnen der Seleukiden und der Mittelmächte Kleinasiens*, Rahden.
Harich-Schwarzbauer, H. and Späth, T. 2005, (eds.) *Gender Studies in den Altertumswissenschaften. Räume und Geschlechter in der Antike*, Trier.
Harries, J. 2013, 'Men without women: Theodosius' consistory and the business of government', in C. Kelly 2013b, 67–89.
Harries, J. 2014, 'The Empresses' Tale, AD 300–360', in C. Harrison, C. Humfress, and I. Sandwell (eds.), *Being Christian in Late Antiquity*, Oxford, 196–214.
Harrison, R. 1989, *A Temple for Byzantium: The Discovery and Excavation of Anicia Juliana's Palace Church in Istanbul*, London.
Harrison, R. and Hayes, J.W. 1986, *Excavations at Saraçhene in Istanbul*, 2 vols. Washington (DC).
Hartmann, E., Hartmann, U., and Pietzner, K. 2007, (eds.) *Geschlechterdefinitionen und Geschlechtergrenzen in der Antike*, Stuttgart.
Harvey, S. 2010, 'Theodora the "believing queen": a study in Syriac historiographical tradition', *Journal of Syriac Studies* 4, 209–34.
Hawley, R. and Levick, B. 1995, (eds.) *Women in Antiquity: New Assessments*, London.

Heather, P. 2001, 'The late Roman art of client management: imperial defence in the fourth century west', in Pohl, Wood, and Reimitz 2001, 15–68.
Heather, P. 2006, *The Fall of the Roman Empire: A New History of Rome and the Barbarians*, Oxford.
Heather, P. 2020, *Rome Resurgent: War and Empire in the Age of Justinian*, Oxford.
Heather, P. and Moncur, D. 2001, *Politics, Philosophy, and Empire in the Fourth Century: Select Orations of Themistius*, Liverpool.
Heil, U. and J. Ulrich 2017, (eds.) *Kirche und Kaiser in Antike und Spätantike. Festschift für Hanns Christof Brennecke zum 70. Geburstag*, Berlin and Boston.
Heinzelmann, M. 1994, *Gregor von Tours (538–594): 'Zehn Bücher Geschichte'*, Darmstadt.
Hekster, O. 2007, 'The Roman army and propaganda', in Erdkamp 2007, 339–58.
Hellmann-Rajanayagam, D. 2011, 'Frauen, Dynastie und Politik in Indien: Das Charisma der Sonia Gandhi', in Bliesemann de Guevara and Reiber 2011, 201–28.
Helly, D. and Reverby, S. 1992, (eds.) *Gendered Domains: Rethinking Public and Private in Women's History*, Ithaca and London.
Hemelrijk, E. 2015, *Hidden Lives, Public Personae: Women and Civic Life in the Roman West*, Oxford and New York.
Hendy, M. 1985, *Studies in the Byzantine Monetary Economy: c. 300–1450*, Cambridge.
Herrin, J. 2000, 'The imperial feminine in Byzantium', *P&P* 169, 3–35.
Herrin, J. 2001, *Women in Purple: Rulers of Medieval Byzantium*, Princeton and Oxford.
Herrin, J. 2013, *Unrivalled Influence: Women and Empire in Byzantium*, Princeton and Oxford.
Herrin, J. 2014, 'Les femmes de la cour à Byzance', in Malamut and Nicolaïdès 2014, 55–68.
Herrin, J. 2016, 'Late antique origins of the "Imperial Feminine": western and eastern empresses compared', *Byzantinoslavica* 74, 5–25.
Herrmann-Otto, E. 1998, 'Der Kaiser und die Gesellschaft des spätrömischen Reiches im Spiegel des Zeremoniells', in Kneissl and Losemann 1998, 346–69.
Heydemann, G. and Reimitz, H. 2020, (eds.) *Historiography and Identity II. Post-Roman Multiplicity and New Political Identities*, Turnhout.
Hill, B. 1999 = 2013, *Imperial Women in Byzantium 1025–1204: Power, Patronage and Ideology*, London and New York.
Hillner, J. 2015, *Prison, Punishment and Penance in Late Antiquity*, Cambridge.
Hillner, J. 2016, 'Review of Joyce E. Salisbury, Rome's Christian empress: Galla Placidia rules at the twilight of the empire', *AHB Online Reviews* 6, 121–24.

Hillner, J. 2017, 'A woman's place: imperial women in late antique Rome', *Antiquité Tardive* 25, 75–94.
Hillner, J. 2018, 'Constantina, Daughter of Constantine, Wife of Gallus Caesar, and Patron of St Agnes at Rome', in *The Oxford Classical Dictionary.* https://doi.org/10.1093/acrefore/9780199381135.013.8066.
Hillner, J. 2019a, 'Empresses, queens, and letters: finding a "female voice" in late antiquity?', *Gender & History* 31, 353–82.
Hillner, J. 2019b, 'Imperial women and clerical exile in Late Antiquity', *SLA* 3, 369–412.
Hillner, J. 2020, 'Female crime and female confinement in Late Antiquity', in Cooper and Wood 2020, 15–38.
Hillner, J. 2023, *Helena Augusta: Mother of the Empire*, Oxford.
Hillner, J. and MacCarron, M. 2021, 'Female networks and exiled bishops between late antiquity and the early middle ages: the cases of Liberius of Rome and Wilfrid of York', in Bérat, Hardie, and Dumitrescu 2021, 19–44.
Holum, K. 1982, *Theodosian Empresses: Women and Imperial Dominion in Late Antiquity*, Berkeley, Los Angeles, and London.
Holum, K. 2003, 'Review: Liz James, empresses and power in early Byzantium', *Speculum* 78, 1324–26.
Holum, K. and Vikan, G. 1979, 'The Trier Ivory, "Adventus" ceremonial, and the relics of St. Stephen', *DOP* 33, 113; 115–33.
Hornblower, S. and Spawforth, A. 2004, (eds.) *The Oxford Companion to Classical Civilization*, Oxford.
Howard-Johnston, J. 2010, *Witnesses to a World Crisis: Historians and Histories of the Middle East in the Seventh Century*, Oxford.
Howard-Johnston, J. 2021, *The Last Great War of Antiquity*, 2021.
Huber-Rebenich, G. 2009, 'Die thüringische Prinzessin Radegunde in der zeitgenössischen Überlieferung', in Castritius, Geuenich, and Werner 2009, 235–52.
Huebner, S. and Ratzan, D. 2021, (eds.) *Missing Mothers: Maternal Absence in Antiquity*, Leuven.
Humphrey, J. 1999, (ed.) *The Roman and Byzantine Near East 2: Some Recent Archaeological Research*, Portsmouth.
Humphries, M. 2000, *Communities of the Blessed: Social Environment and Religious Change in Northern Italy, AD 200–400*, Oxford.
Humphries, M. 2019a, 'Family, dynasty, and the construction of legitimacy from Augustus to the Theodosians', in Tougher 2019, 13–27.
Humphries, M. 2019b, 'The shifting importance of dynasty in Heraclian ideology', in Tougher 2019, 28–51.
Humphries, M. 2020, 'The memory of Mursa: usurpation, civil war, and contested legitimacy under the sons of Constantine', in Baker-Brian and Tougher 2020, 157–84.
Icks, M. 2017, 'Of lizards and peacocks: criticism of the princeps clausus in fourth- and fifth-century sources', *Mediterraneo Antico* 20, 457–84.

Iliopoulos / Ηλιοπουλος, Π. 2021, 'Τα ζώα στον προσβλητικό λόγο των Βυζαντινών', in *BYZANTINA SYMMEIKTA* 31. https://doi.org/10.12681/byzsym.24394.

Isaac, B. 1995, 'The army in the late Roman East. The Persian Wars and the defence of the Byzantine provinces', in Av. Cameron 1995, 125–56.

James, L. 1997, (ed.) *Women, Men and Eunuchs: Gender in Byzantium*, London and New York.

James, L. 1999, (ed.) *Desire and Denial in Byzantium*, Aldershot.

James, L. 2000, '"As the actress said to the bishop ...": the portrayal of Byzantine women in English-language fiction', in Cormack and Jeffreys 2000, 237–49.

James, L. 2001a, 'Bearing gifts from the east: imperial relic hunters abroad', in Eastmond 2001, 119–31.

James, L. 2001b, *Empresses and Power in Early Byzantium*, London and New York.

James, L. 2012, 'Is there an empress in the text? Julian's Speech of Thanks to Eusebia', in Baker-Brian and Tougher 2012, 47–59.

James, L. 2013, 'Ghosts in the machine: the lives and deaths of Constantinian imperial', in Neil and Garland 2013, 93–112.

James, L. 2014, 'Making a name: reputation and imperial founding and refounding in Constantinople', in Theis, Mullett, and Grünbart 2014, 63–72.

James, L. 2016 = 2003, 'Who's that girl? Personifications of the Byzantine empress', in Entwistle 2016 = 2003, 51–56.

James, S.L. and Dillon, S. 2012 (eds.), *A Companion to Women in the Ancient World*, Malden/MA.

Janin, R. 1932, 'Les églises Sainte-Euphémie à Constantinople', *Echos D'Orient* 3, 270–83.

Janin, R. 1964, *Constantinople byzantine: développement urbain et repertoire topographique*, Istanbul.

Jay, N. 1992, *Throughout Your Generations Forever: Sacrifice, Religion, and Paternity*, Chicago.

Jolivet, V. and Sotinel, C. 2011, 'Die *Domus Pinciana*. Eine kaiserliche Residenz in Rom', in Fuhrer 2011, 137–60.

Jones, A.H.M. 1964, *The Later Roman Empire, 284–602: A Social Economic and Administrative Survey*, 2 vols., Oxford.

Jones, A.H.M., Martindale, J.R., and Morris, J. 1971, (ed.) *Prosopography of the Later Roman Empire, Vol. 1*, London.

Jones, L. 2016a, 'Perceptions of Byzantium: Radegund of Poitiers and relics of the True Cross', in Jones 2016b, 105–24.

Jones, L. 2016b, (ed.) *Byzantine Images and Their Afterlives: Essays in Honor of Annemarie Weyl Carr*, Oxford and New York.

Jonge, P. de 1972, *Philological and Historical Commentary on Ammianus Marcellinus XV*, Groningen.

Jordan, R. 2000, (trans.) *The Synaxarion of the Monastery of the Theotokos Evergetis*, Vol. 1, Belfast.
Joska, S. 2019, '"Show them that you are Marcus's daughter": the public role of imperial daughters in second- and third-century CE Rome', in Rantala 2019, 105–29.
Jütte, R. 2008, *Contraception: A History*, Cambridge and Malden/MA.
Kaegi, W. 1981, *Byzantine Military Unrest, 471–843: An Interpretation*, Amsterdam.
Kaegi, W. 2003, *Heraclius: Emperor of Byzantium*, Cambridge.
Kahrstedt, U. 1910, 'Frauen auf antiken Münzen', *Klio* 10, 289–99.
Kalavrezou, I. 2003, (ed.) *Byzantine Women and Their World*, Cambridge/MA.
Kaldellis, A. 2004a, *Procopius of Caesarea: A Tyranny, History, and Philosophy at the End of Antiquity*, Philadelphia.
Kaldellis, A. 2004b, 'Identifying dissident circles in sixth-century Byzantium: the friendship of Prokopios and Ioannes Lydos', *Florilegium* 21, 1–17.
Kaldellis, A. 2009, 'The date and structure of Prokopios' *Secret History* and his projected work on church history', *GRBS* 49, 585–616.
Kaldellis, A. 2010, *Prokopios: The Secret History with Related Texts*, Indianapolis.
Kaldellis, A. 2015, *The Byzantine Republic: Power and People in New Rome*, Cambridge/MA.
Kaldellis, A. 2022, 'The classicism of Procopius', in Meier and Montinaro 2022, 339–54.
Kantorowicz, E. 1960, 'On the golden marriage belt and the marriage rings of the Dumbarton Oaks Collection', *DOP* 14, 1–16.
Kasperski, R. 2018, 'Jordanes versus Procopius of Caesarea: considerations concerning a certain historiographic debate on how to solve the problem of the Goths', *Viator* 49, 1–23.
Kazhdan, A. 1991, (ed.) *The Oxford Dictionary of Byzantium*, Oxford.
Kazhdan, A. 1998, 'Women at home', *DOP* 52, 1–17.
Kelleher, M. 2015, 'What do we mean by "women and power"?', *Medieval Feminist Forum* 51, 104–15.
Keller, K. 2021, *Die Kaiserin. Reich, Ritual und Dynastie*, Vienna, Cologne, and Weimar.
Kelly, B. and Hug, A. 2022, (eds.) *The Roman Emperor and His Court c. 30 BC–c. AD 300*, 2 vols., Cambridge.
Kelly, C. 2013a, 'Stooping to conquer: the power of imperial humility', in Kelly 2013b, 221–43.
Kelly C., 2013b, (ed.) *Theodosius II: Rethinking the Roman Empire in Late Antiquity*, Cambridge.
Kelly, G. 2013, 'The political crisis of AD 375–376', *Chiron* 43, 357–409.
Kemezis, A. 2016, 'The fall of Elagabalus as literary narrative and political reality: a reconsideration', *Historia* 65, 348–90.
Keser-Kayaalp, E. and Erdoğan, N. 2017, 'Recent research on Dara/Anastasiopolis', in Rizos 2017, 153–76.

Kettenhofen, E. 1979, *Die syrischen Augustae in der historischen Überlieferung. Ein Beitrag zum Problem der Orientalisierung*, Bonn.
Kienast, D., Eck, W., and Heil, M. ⁶2017, *Römische Kaisertabelle: Grundzüge einer römischen Kaiserchronologie*, Darmstadt.
Kiilerich, B. 2001, 'The image of Anicia Juliana in the Vienna Dioscurides: flattery or appropriation of imperial imagery?', *Symbolae Osloenses* 76, 169–90.
Klein, K. 2014, 'Do good in thy good pleasure unto Zion: the patronage of Aelia Eudokia in Jerusalem', in Theis, Mullett, and Grünbart 2014, 85–95.
Klein, K. 2019, 'Zur spätantiken Kaiserin als Stifterin (Review Article Dirschlmayer 2015)', *Plekos* 21, 87–115.
Klein, K. and Wienand, J. 2022, (eds.) *City of Caesar, City of God: Constantinople and Jerusalem in Late Antiquity*, Berlin and Boston.
Kneissl, P. and Losemann, V. 1998, (eds.) *Imperium Romanum: Studien zu Geschichte und Rezeption. Festschrift für Karl Christ zum 75. Geburtstag*, Stuttgart.
Köhn, S. 1999, *Ariadne auf Naxos. Rezeption und Motivgeschichte von der Antike bis 1600*, Munich.
Kolb, A. 2006, (ed.) *Herrschaftsstrukturen und Herrschaftspraxis. Konzepte, Prinzipien und Strategien der Administration im römischen Kaiserreich. Akten der Tagung an der Universität Zürich, 18.–20.10.2004*, Berlin.
Kolb, A. 2010a, 'Augustae – Zielsetzung, Definition, prosopographischer Überblick', in Kolb 2010b, 11–35.
Kolb, A. 2010b, (ed.) *Augustae. Machtbewusste Frauen am römischen Kaiserhof?*, Berlin.
Kotsis, K. 2012a, 'Mothers of the empire: empresses Zoe and Theodora on a Byzantine medallion cycle', *Medieval Feminist Forum* 48, 5–96.
Kotsis, K. 2012b, 'Defining female authority in eighth-century Byzantium: the numismatic images of the empress Irene (797–802)', *JLA* 5, 185–215.
Kötter, J.-M. 2013, *Zwischen Kaisern und Aposteln. Das Akakianische Schisma (484–519) als kirchlicher Ordnungskonflikt der Spätantike*, Stuttgart.
Krautschick, S. 2001, 'Matasuntha', *Reallexikon der germanischen Altertumskunde* 19, 432–33.
Kroll, J. and Bachrach, B. 1993, 'Justin's madness: weak-mindedness or organic psychosis?', *Journal of the History of Medicine and Allied Sciences* 48, 40–67.
Kroll, J. and Bachrach, B. 2005, *The Mystic Mind: The Psychology of Medieval Mystics and Ascetics*, London.
Kroll, J. and Pouncey, C. 2016, 'The ethics of APA's Goldwater Rule', *Journal of American Academic Psychiatry Law* 44, 226–35.
Kuefler, M. 2001, *The Manly Eunuch: Masculinity, Gender Ambiguity, and Christian Ideology in Late Antiquity*, Chicago.
Kulikowski, M. 2006, *Rome's Gothic Wars: From the Third Century to Alaric*, Cambridge.

Kunst, C. 2005, 'Frauenzimmer in der römischen "domus"', in Harich-Schwarzbauer and Späth 2005, 111–31.
Kunst, C. 2008, *Livia. Macht und Intrigen am Hof des Augustus*, Stuttgart.
Kunst, C. 2010, 'Patronage/matronage der Augustae', in Kolb 2010b, 145–61.
Kunst, C. 2013a, 'Das *Vermögen* der Frauen im Umfeld der Adoptivkaiser', in Kunst 2013c, 109–22.
Kunst, C. 2013b, 'Matronage von Herrscherfrauen. Eine Einführung', in Kunst 2013c, 7–18.
Kunst, C. 2013c, (ed.) *Matronage. Handlungsstrategien und soziale Netzwerke antiker Herrscherfrauen. Beiträge eines Kolloquiums an der Universität Osnabrück vom 22. bis 24. März 2012*, Rahden.
Kunst, C. 2021, *Basilissa – Die Königin im Hellenismus*, 2 vols., Rahden.
Kunst, C. and Riemer, U. 2000, (eds.) *Grenzen der Macht. Zur Rolle der römischen Kaiserfrauen*, Stuttgart.
Kurdock, A. 2003, *The Anician Women: Patronage and Dynastic Strategy in a Late Roman Domus, 350 CE–600 CE*, PhD thesis, University of Manchester.
Laiou, A. 1981, 'The role of women in Byzantine Society', *JBÖB* 31, 233–60.
Laiou, A. 1992a, *Mariage, amour et parenté à Byzance aux XI*-XIII* siècles*, Paris.
Laiou, A. 1992b, 'Imperial marriages and their critics in the eleventh century: the case of Skylitzes', *DOP* 46, 165–76.
Langford, J. 2013, *Maternal Megalomania: Julia Domna and the Imperial Politics of Motherhood*, Baltimore.
La Rocca, M. 2012, '*Consors regni*: a problem of gender? The consortium between Amalasuntha and Theodahad in 534', in Nelson, Reynolds, and Johns 2012, 127–43.
Leatherbury, S. 2017, '21. Textiles as gifts to God in late antiquity: Christian altar cloths as cultic objects', in Brøns and Nosch 2017, 243–57.
Lee, A. 2007, *War in Late Antiquity: A Social History*, Oxford.
Lee, A. 2013, *From Rome to Byzantium AD 363 to 565: The Transformation of Ancient Rome*, Edinburgh.
Lendon, J. 2006, 'The legitimacy of the Roman emperor: against Weberian legitimacy and imperial "strategies of legitimation"', in Kolb 2006, 53–64.
Lenski, N. 1997, '*Initium mali romano imperio*: contemporary reactions to the battle of Adrianople', *TAPA* 127, 129–68.
Lenski, N. 2000, 'The election of Jovian and the role of the late imperial guards', *Klio* 82, 492–515.
Lenski, N. 2002, *Failure of Empire: Valens and the Roman State in the Fourth Century A.D.*, London.
Lenski, N. 2004, 'Empresses in the Holy Land: the creation of a Christian utopia in Late Antique Palestine', in Ellis and Kidner 2004, 113–24.
Lenski, N. 2006, (ed.) *The Cambridge Companion to the Age of Constantine*, Cambridge.

Leonard, V. 2019, 'Galla Placidia as "human gold": consent and autonomy in the early fifth century west', *Gender and History* 31, 334–52.
Leppin, H. 2000a, 'Kaiserliche Kohabitation. Von der Normalität Theodoras', in Kunst and Riemer 2000, 75–85.
Leppin, H. 2000b, 'Das Bild der kaiserlichen Frau bei Gregor von Nyssa', in Drobner and Viciano 2000, 487–506.
Leppin, H. 2002, 'Theodora und Iustinian', in Temporini-Gräfin Vitzthum 2002, 437–81.
Lerner, G. 1975, 'Placing women in history: definitions and challenges', *Feminist Studies* 3, 5–14.
Levick, B. 2007, *Julia Domna: Syrian Empress*, Oxford.
Levick, B. 2014, *Faustina I and II: Imperial Women of the Golden Age*, Oxford.
Lewis, W. 2020, 'Constantine II and his brothers: the civil war of AD 340', in Baker-Brian and Tougher 2020, 57–92.
Lidov, A. 2016, (ed.) *Round Table: Icons of Space, Icons in Space, Iconography or Hierotopy, 23rd International Congress of Byzantine Studies*, Belgrade.
Lidova, M. 2016a, 'The adoration of the Magi: from iconic space to icon in space', in Lidov 2016, 34–38.
Lidova, M. 2016b, 'Empress, virgin, ecclesia: the icon of Santa Maria in Trastevere in the early Byzantine context', *IKON: Journal of Iconographic Studies* 9, 109–28.
Liebeschuetz, J. 1990, *Barbarians and Bishops: Army, Church, and State in the Age of Arcadius and Chrysostom*, Oxford.
Liebeschuetz, J. 2005, *Ambrose of Milan. Political Letters and Speeches. Translated by J.H.W.G. Liebeschuetz*, Liverpool.
Liebeschuetz, J. 2011, *Ambrose and John Chrysostom: Clerics between Desert and Empire*, Oxford.
Lillington-Martin, C. and Turquois, E. 2018, (eds.) *Procopius of Caesarea: Literary and Historical Interpretations*, London.
Lin, S. 2021, 'Justin under Justinian. The rise of emperor Justin II revisited', *DOP* 75, 121–42.
Lindholmer, M. 2021, *Rituals of Power: The Roman Imperial Admission from the Severans to the Fourth Century*, PhD thesis, University of St Andrews.
Llewellyn-Jones, L. and A. McAuley 2023, *Sister-Queens in the High Hellenistic Period: Kleopatra Thea and Kleopatra III*, London and New York.
Longo, K. 2009, *Donne di Potere nella Tarda Antichitá. Le Augustae attraverso Le Immagini Monetali*, Reggio Calabria.
Loseby, S. 2015, 'Gregory of Tours, Italy, and the empire', in Murray 2015, 462–97.
Louth, A. 2008, 'Justinian and his legacy (500–600)', in Shepard 2008, 99–129.
Lunn-Rockliffe, S. 2010, 'Commemorating the usurper Magnus Maximus: ekphrasis, poetry, and history in Pacatus' Panegyric of Theodosius', *JLA* 3, 316–36.

Maas, M. 2005, (ed.) *The Cambridge Companion to the Age of Justinian*, Cambridge.
MacCormack, S. 1981, *Art and Ceremony in Late Antiquity*, Berkeley.
Macrides, R. 2010, (ed.) *History as Literature in Byzantium*, Farnham.
Magdalino, P. 1994, (ed.) *New Constantines: The Rhythm of Imperial Renewal in Byzantium, 4th–13th Centuries. Papers from the Twenty-Sixth Spring Symposium of Byzantine Studies, St Andrews, March 1992*, Aldershot.
Magdalino, P. 2001, 'Aristocratic *Oikoi* in the tenth and eleventh regions of Constantinople', in Necipoğlu 2001, 53–69.
Magliaro, L. 2013, *Arianna. La garante della porpora*, Milan.
Magnani, A. 2002, *Serena. L'ultima Romana*, Milan.
Magnani, A. 2015, '"Di Nozze e di tradimento": Giovanni di Vitaliano, Belisario e Matasunta', *Studi sull'oriente cristiano* 19, 31–43.
Maguire, H., Wolschke-Bulmahnm, J., and Littlewood, A. 2002, (eds.) *Byzantine Garden Culture*, Dumbarton Oaks (DC).
Maier, F. 2019, *Palastrevolution. Der Weg zum hauptstädtischen Kaisertum im Römischen Reich des vierten Jahrhunderts*, Leiden and Boston.
Main, R. 2019, *After Justinian: Foreign Policy in the Byzantine Empire during the Reigns of Justin II and Tiberius II Constantine (565–582)*, Oxford.
Malamut, É. and Nicolaïdès, A. 2014, (eds.) *Impératrices, Princesses, Aristocrates et Saintes Souveraines. De l'Orient Chrétien et Musulman au Moyen Âge et au Début des Temps Modernes*, Aix-en-Provence.
Malmberg, S. 2014, 'Triumphal arches and gates of piety at Constantinople, Ravenna and Rome', in Birk, Myrup Kristensen, and Poulsen 2014, 150–89.
Manders, E. 2012, *Coining Images of Power: Patterns in the Representation of Roman Emperors on Imperial Coinage, A.D. 193–284*, Leiden and Boston.
Mango, C. 1985, 'Deux études sur Byzance et la Perse sassanide', *T&M* 9, 105–18.
Mango, C. 1990a, *Le Dévelopement urbain de Constantinople, IVe–VIIe siècles*, Paris.
Mango, C. 1990b, *Nikephoros, Patriarch of Constantinople: Short History*, Washington (DC).
Mango, C. 1998, 'The origins of the blachernae shrine at Constantinople', in Cambi Marin 1998, 61–76.
Mango, C. 1999, 'The relics of St. Euphemia and the Synaxarion of Constantinople', *Bollettino di Badia Greca di Grottoferrata* 53, 79–87.
Mango, C. and Scott, R. 1997, *The Chronicle of Theophanes Confessor: Byzantine and Near Eastern History AD 284–813*, Oxford.
Mango, C. and Ševčenko, I., 1961, 'Remains of the church of St. Polyeuktos in Constantinople', *DOP* 15, 243–47.
Marasco, G. 2010, (ed.) *Greek and Roman Historiography in Late Antiquity: Fourth to Sixth Century A.D*, Leiden and Boston.
Martindale, J. 1980, *Prosopography of the Later Roman Empire*, Vol. 2, Cambridge.

Martindale, J. 1992, *Prosopography of the Later Roman Empire*, Vols. 3a and 3b, Cambridge.

Martindale, J., Jones, A.H.M., and Morris, J. 1971, *Prosopography of the Later Roman Empire*, Vol. 1, Cambridge.

Martínez López, C. 2021, 'Matronage: a useful concept for understanding the involvement of women in the public sphere in ancient societies', in Boris, Trudgen Dawson, and Molony 2021, 14–29.

Maslev, S. 1966, 'Die staatsrechtliche Stellung der byzantinischen Kaiserinnen', in *ByzSlav* 27, 308–43.

Mathews, T. 1971, *The Early Churches of Constantinople: Architecture and Liturgy*, University Park.

Mathews, T. 1976. *The Byzantine Churches of Istanbul: A Photographic Survey*, University Park.

Mathisen, R. and Shanzer, D. 2011, (eds.) *Romans, Barbarians, and the Transformation of the Roman World*, Farnham.

Matthews, J. 1989, *The Roman Empire of Ammianus*, Baltimore.

McCabe, J. 1911, *The Empresses of Rome*, London.

McCabe, J. 1913, *The Empresses of Constantinople*, London.

McCail, R. 1969, 'The *Cycle* of Agathias: new identifications scrutinised', *JHS* 89, 87–96.

McCash, J.H. 1996 (ed.), *The Cultural Patronage of Medieval Women*, Atlanta.

McClanan, A. 1996, 'The empress Theodora and the tradition of women's patronage in the early Byzantine Empire', in McCash 1996, 50–72.

McClanan, A. 2002, *Representations of Early Byzantine Empresses: Image and Empire*, London and New York.

McCormick, M. 1986, *Eternal Victory: Triumphal Rulership in Late Antiquity, Byzantium and the Early Medieval West*, Cambridge.

McCormick, M., 1991, 'Empress', in *The Oxford Dictionary of Byzantium*, ed. A. Kazhdan. Vol. 1, 694–695.

McCormick, M. 2001, 'Emperor and court', in Av. Cameron, Ward-Perkins, and Mi. Whitby 2001, 135–63.

McEvoy, M. 2013, *Child Emperor Rule in the Late Roman West, AD 367–455*, Oxford.

McEvoy, M. 2016a, 'Constantia: the last Constantinian', *Antichthon* 50, 154–79.

McEvoy, M. 2016b, 'Becoming Roman? The not-so-curious case of Aspar and the Ardaburii', *JLA* 9, 483–511.

McEvoy, M. 2018, 'Dynastic dreams and visions of early Byzantine emperors (ca. 518–565 AD)', in Neil and Anagnostou-Laoutides 2018, 99–177.

McEvoy, M. 2019, 'Celibacy and survival in court politics in the fifth century AD', in Tougher 2019, 115–34.

McEvoy, M. 2021, 'Orations for the first generation of Theodosian imperial women', *JLA* 14, 117–41.

McGill, S., Sogno, C., and Watts, E. 2010, (eds.) *From the Tetrarchs to the Theodosians: Later Roman History and Culture, 284–450 CE*, Cambridge.

McLynn, N. 1994, *Ambrose of Milan: Church and Court in a Christian Capital*, Berkeley.
McLynn, N. 2019, 'Imperial piety in action: the Theodosians in church', *T&M* 22, 315–40.
McMahon, K. 2016, *Celestial Women: Imperial Wives and Concubines in China from Song to Qing*, Lanham et al.
Mecella, L. 2022, 'Procopius' sources', in Meier and Montinaro 2022, 178–93.
Meier, M. 2004, 'Zur Funktion der Theodora-Rede im Geschichtswerk Prokops (BP 1, 24, 33–37)', *RhM* 147, 88–104.
Meier, M. 2007a, 'Die Demut des Kaisers. Aspekte der religiösen Selbstinszenierung bei Theodosius II (408–450 n. Chr.)', in Pecar and Trampedach 2007, 135–58.
Meier, M. 2007b, 'Staurotheis di'hemas. Der Aufstand gegen Anastasios im Jahr 512', *Millennium-Jahrbuch* 4, 157–238.
Meier, M. 2010, 'Ariadne. Der "rote Faden" des Kaisertums', in Kolb 2010b, 277–92.
Meier, M. 2017, 'Der Monarch auf der Suche nach seinem Platz. Kaiserherrschaft im frühen Byzanz (5. bis 7. Jahrhundert n. Chr.)', in Rebenich 2017, 509–44.
Meier, M. 2019a, *Geschichte der Völkerwanderung. Europa, Asien und Afrika vom 3. bis zum 8. Jahrhundert n. Chr.*, Munich.
Meier, M. 2019b, 'Der "Triumph Belisars" 534 n. Chr.', in Conrad, Drecoll, and Hirbodian 1999, 43–61.
Meier, M. and Montinaro, F. 2022, (eds.) *A Companion to Procopius of Caesarea*, Leiden and Boston.
Menze, V. 2008, *Justinian and the Making of the Syrian Orthodox Church*, Oxford.
Métraux, G. 2008, 'Prudery and *chic* in Late Antique clothing', in Edmondson and Keith 2008, 271–93.
Meyer, M. 2014, 'Visibility of female founders: the case of ancient Greece', in Theis, Mullett, and Grünbart 2014, 29–41.
Meyers, C. 2013, *Rediscovering Eve: Ancient Israelite Women in Context*, New York and Oxford.
Meyers, R. 2012, 'Female portraiture and female patronage in the high imperial period', in James and Dillon 2012, 453–66.
Millar, F. 1977, *The Emperor in the Roman World (31 BC–AD 337)*, London.
Millar, F. 2007, *A Greek Roman Empire: Power and Belief under Theodosius II (408–450)*, Berkeley.
Miller, D. and Sarris, P. 2018, (trans.) *The Novels of Justinian: A Complete Annotated English Translation*, 2 vols., Cambridge.
Milner, C. 1994. 'The image of the rightful ruler: Anicia Juliana's Constantine mosaic in the church of Hagios Polyeuktos', in Magdalino 1994, 73–81.
Milnor, K. 2013, 'Public and private', in Tulluch 2013, 105–24.
Mitchel, J. 2010, 'Patrons and clients', in Barnard and Spencer [2]2010, 528–30.

Modesti, A. 2013, 'The self-fashioning of a female "prince": the cultural matronage of Vittoria della Revere', in O'Brien 2013, 253–97.
Momigliano, A. 1955, 'Cassiodorus and Italian culture of his time', *PBA* 41, 207–45.
Mommaerts T. and Kelley, D.H. 1992, 'The Anicii of Gaul and Rome', in Drinkwater and Elton 1992, 112–21.
Mommsen, T. ²1877, *Römisches Staatsrecht*, 2. Bd. II. Abt., Leipzig.
Mommsen, T. 1882, (ed.) Iordanis *Romana et Getica*, Berlin.
Mommsen, T. 1894, (ed.) Cassiodori Senatoris *Variae*, Berlin.
Monchizadeh, A. and Hoffmann, L.M. 2005, (eds.) *Zwischen Polis, Provinz und Peripherie. Beiträge zur byzantinischen Geschichte und Kultur*, Mainz.
Moore, K. 2021, 'Octavia Minor and patronage', in Carney and Müller 2020, 375–87.
Moore, S. and Myerhoff, B. 1977, (eds.) *Secular Ritual*, Amsterdam.
Morelli, P. and Saulle, S. 1998, *Anna Comnena. La poetessa epica*, Milan.
Morgenstern, M., Boudignon, C., and Tietz, C. 2011, (eds.) *'Männlich und weiblich schuf Er sie'. Studien zur Genderkonstruktion und zum Eherecht in den Mittelmeerreligionen*, Göttingen.
Morrisson, C. 1997, 'Débat. L'Augusta sur le monnaies d'Héraclius, Eudocie ou Martine?', *RN* 152, 453–56.
Morrisson, C. 2012, 'Imperial generosity and its monetary expression: the rise and decline of the "largesses"', in Spieser and Yota 2012, 25–46.
Morrisson, C. 2013, 'Displaying the emperor's authority and kharaktèr on the marketplace', in Armstrong 2013, 65–80.
Mratschek, S. 2007, '"Männliche Frauen". Außenseiterinnen in Philosophenmantel und Melote', in Hartmann, Hartmann, and Pietzner 2007, 211–27.
Mullett, M. 2014, 'Female founders – in conclusion: the gynamics of foundation', in Theis, Mullett, and Grünbart 2014, 417–28.
Murray, A. 2015, (ed.) *A Companion to Gregory of Tours*, Leiden.
Myerhoff, B. 1977, 'We don't wrap herring in a printed page: fusion, fiction and continuity in secular ritual', in Moore and Myerhoff 1977, 199–226.
Näf, B. 2015, 'Das Charisma des Herrschers. Antike und Zeitgeschichte in der ersten Hälfte des 20. Jahrhunderts', in D. Boschung and J. Hammerstaedt (eds.), *Das Charisma des Herrschers*, Paderborn, 11–50.
Nathan, G. 2000, *The Family in Late Antiquity: The Rise of Christianity and the Endurance of Tradition*, London and New York.
Nathan, G. 2006, '"*Pothos tes Philoktistou*": Anicia Juliana's architectural narratology', in Burke 2006, 433–43.
Nathan, G. 2011, 'The *Vienna Dioscurides' dedicatio* to Anicia Juliana: a usurpation of imperial heritage?', in Nathan and Garland 2011, 95–102.
Nathan, G. 2021, 'Fact, fiction and family: stepmothers in Valentinian-Theodosian dynasty', in Huebner and Ratzan 2021, 127–39.
Nathan, G. (forthcoming), *The Shadow Empress: Studies on Anicia Juliana*.

Nathan, G. and Garland, L. 2011, (eds.) *Basileia: Essays on* Imperium *and Culture. In Honor of Elizabeth and Michael Jeffreys*, Brisbane.
Nechaeva, E. 2014, *Embassies – Negotiations – Gifts: Systems of East Roman Diplomacy in Late Antiquity*, Stuttgart.
Necipoğlu, N. 2001, (ed.) *Byzantine Constantinople: Monuments, Topography and Everyday Life*, Leiden and Boston.
Neil, B. and Anagnostou-Laoutides, E. 2018, (eds.) *Dreams, Memory and Imagination in Byzantium*, Leiden and Boston.
Neil, B. and Garland, L. 2013, (eds.) *Questions of Gender in Byzantine Society*, Farnham.
Nelson, J. and Linehan, P. 2001, (eds.) *The Medieval World*, London.
Nelson, J., Reynolds, S., and Johns, S.M. 2012, (eds.), *Gender and Historiography: Studies in the Earlier Middle Ages in Honour of Pauline Stafford*, London.
Neville, L. 2016, *Anna Komnene: The Life and Work of a Medieval Historian*, Oxford.
Nicholson, O. 1985, 'Two notes on Dara', *AJA* 89, 663–71.
Nikolaou, G. 1999, 'Οι Αυγούστες στα χαλκά βυζαντινά νομίσματα του 6ου και 7ου αι.', in Α' Συνάντηση των Βυζαντινολόγων της Ελλάδος και της Κύπρου 1998, Ioannina, 23–124.
Nikšić, G. 2011, 'Diocletian's palace – design and construction', in von Bülow Zabehlicky 2011, 187–202.
Noethlichs, K. 1998, 'Strukturen und Funktionen des spätantiken Kaiserhofes', in Winterling 1998, 13–49.
O'Brien, E. 2013, (ed.) *Representing Women's Authority in the Early Modern World*, Rome.
O'Flynn, J. 1983, *Generalissimos of the Western Roman Empire*, Edmonton.
Odahl, C. 1986, 'Constantinian coin motifs in ancient literary sources', *JRMMRA* 7, 1–15.
Odahl, C. 2004, *Constantine and the Christian Empire*, Abingdon and New York.
Oikonomides, N. 1972, *Les listes de préséance byzantines des IXe et Xe siècles*, Paris.
Olster, D.M. 1982, 'The dynastic iconography – Heraclius dynasty', *JÖB* 32, 99–408.
Olster, D.M. 1993, *The Politics of Usurpation in the Seventh Century: Rhetoric and Revolution in Byzantium*, Amsterdam.
Omissi, A. 2018, *Emperors and Usurpers in the Later Roman Empire: Civil War, Panegyric, and the Construction of Legitimacy*, Oxford.
Omissi, A. and Ross, A. 2020, (eds.) *Imperial Panegyric from Diocletian to Honorius*, Liverpool.
Oost, I. 1968, *Galla Placidia Augusta: A Biographical Essay*, Chicago.
Opitz-Belakhal, C. 2021, 'Macht und Geschlecht in der Vormoderne. Forschungsergebnisse und -desiderate einer Geschlechtergeschichte des Politischen', in Becher, Fischelmanns, and Gahbler 2021, 13–31.

Parani, M. 2018, 'Mediating presence: curtains in middle and late Byzantine imperial ceremonial and portraiture', *BMGS* 42, 1–25.
Pargoire, J. 1903, 'Constructions des Juliana Anicia', *BZ* 12, 486–90.
Parnell, D. 2023, *Belisarius and Antonina: Love and War in the Age of Justinian*, Oxford.
Paterson, J. 2007, 'Friends in high places: the creation of the court of the Roman emperor', in Spawforth 2007b, 121–56.
Patlagean, E. 1992, 'De la chasse et du souverain', *DOP* 46, 257–63.
Paton, W. 1916–1927, *The Greek Anthology. In Five Volumes*, London.
Payne, R. 2013, 'Cosmology and the expansion of the Iranian Empire, 502–628 CE', *P&P* 220, 3–33.
Payne Smith, R. 1860, *The Third Part of the Ecclesiastical History of John, Bishop of Ephesus*, Oxford.
Pazdernik, C. 1994, '"Our most pious consort given us by God": dissident reactions to the partnership of Justinian and Theodora, A.D. 525–548', *ClAnt* 13, 256–81.
Pazdernik, C. 2009, 'Paying attention to the man behind the curtain: disclosing and withholding the imperial presence in Justinianic Constantinople', in Fögen and Lee 2009, 63–86.
Pearce, J. 1934, 'Notes on some Aes of Valentinian II and Theodosius', *Numismatic Chronicle and Journal of the Royal Numismatic Society* 14, 114–30.
Pecar, A. and Trampedach, K. 2007, (eds.) *Die Bibel als politisches Argument. Voraussetzungen und Folgen biblizistischer Herrschaftslegitimation in der Vormoderne*, Munich.
Pelttari, A. 2022, 'Speaking from the margins: paratexts in Greek and Latin poetry', in Verhelst and Scheijnen 2022, 69–88.
Pfeilschifter, R. 2013, *Der Kaiser und Konstantinopel. Kommunikation und Konfliktaustrag in einer spätantiken Metropole*, Berlin and Boston.
Pfeilschifter, R. 2022, 'The secret history', in Meier and Montinaro 2022, 121–36.
Pistellato, A. 2015, '*Augustae ominee honorare*: il ruolo delle Augustae fra "Staatsrecht" e prassi politica', in Ferrary and Scheid 2015, 393–427.
Pizzone, M. 2003, 'Da Melitene a Costantinopoli: S. Polieucto nella politica dinastica di Giuliana Anicia: alcune osservazione in margine ad A.P. I 10', *Maia* 55, 107–32.
Pohl, W. ²2018, *The Avars: A Steppe Empire in Central Europe, 567–822*, Ithaca.
Pohl, W., Wood, I., and Reimitz, H. 2001, (eds.) *The Transformation of Frontiers from Late Antiquity to the Carolingians*, Leiden.
Pohlsander, H. 1984, 'Crispus: brilliant career and tragic end', *Historia* 33, 79–106.
Pohlsander, H. 1995, *Helena: Empress and Saint*, Chicago.
Potter, D. 2013, *Constantine the Emperor*, Oxford.
Potter, D. 2015, *Theodora: Actress, Empress, Saint*, Oxford.
Pottier, H. 1997, 'À propos de l'*Augusta* des *folles* d'Héraclius', *RN 152*, 467–72.
Price, R. 2009, *The Acts of the Council of Constantinople of 553*, Liverpool.

Priwitzer, S. 2009, *Faustina minor – Ehefrau eines Idealkaisers und Mutter eines Tyrannen. Quellenkritische Untersuchungen zum dynastischen Potential, zur Darstellung und zu Handlungsspielräumen von Kaiserfrauen im Prinzipat*, Bonn.

Puliatti, S. 1991, *Ricerche sulle novelle di Giustino II*, Milan.

Rantala, J. 2019, (ed.) *Gender, Memory, and Identity in the Roman World*, Amsterdam.

Raum, T. 2021, *Szenen eines Überlebenskampfes. Akteure und Handlungsspielräume im Imperium Romanum 610–630*, Stuttgart.

Ravegnani, G. 2016, *Teodora*, Roma.

Rebenich, S. 2017, (ed.) *Monarchische Herrschaft im Altertum*, Berlin and Boston.

Reimitz, H. 2019, '*Pax inter utramque Gentem*: The Merovingians, Byzantium and the history of Frankish identity', in Esders, Fox, Hen, and Sarti 2019, 45–64.

Reverby, S. and Helly, D. 1992, 'Introduction: converging on history', in Helly and Reverby 1992, 1–24.

Ringrose, K. M 2008, 'Women and power at the Byzantine court', in Walthall 2008b, 65–80.

Rizos, E. 2017, (ed.) *New Cities in Late Antiquity: Documents and Archaeology*, Turnhout.

Roberto, U. 2010, 'The circus factions and the death of the tyrant: John of Antioch on the fate of the emperor Phocas', in Daim and Drauschke 2010, 55–77.

Roberts, M. 1989, *The Jeweled Style: Poetry and Poetics in Late Antiquity*, Ithaca/ NY and London.

Rogge, J. 2015, 'Mächtige Frauen? Königinnen und Fürstinnen im europäischen Mittelalter (11.–14. Jahrhundert) – Zusammenfassung', in Zey 2015, 437–57.

Roggo, S. 2019, 'The deposition of patriarch Eutychius of Constantinople in 565 and the Aphthartodocetic Edict of Justinian', *Byzantion* 89, 433–46.

Roller, D. 2012, *Cleopatra: A Biography*, Oxford.

Roller, D. 2021, *Cleopatra's Daughter and Other Royal Women of the Augustan Era*, Oxford.

Rollinger, C. 2020, 'The importance of being splendid: competition, ceremonial, and the semiotics of status at the court of the late Roman emperors (4th–6th centuries)', in Choda, Sterk de Leeuw, and Schulz 2020, 36–72.

Rollinger, C. 2023, 'Another heaven: imperial audiences and the aesthetics of ideology in Late Antique ceremonial', *DOP* 77, 85–129.

Rollinger, C. 2024, *Zeremoniell und Herrschaft in der Spätantike. Die Rituale des Kaiserhofs in Konstantinopel*, Stuttgart.

Rollinger, C. (forthcoming a), 'Balkan promises: sixth-century diplomacy and the "corrupion" of the Justinianic state', in Carlà-Uhink and Faber (forthcoming).

Rollinger, C. (forthcoming b), 'Put a crown on it: imperial coronations in the seventh century', in Viermann and Wienand (forthcoming).
Roth, D. 1978/1994, *Matronage: Patterns in Women's Organizations, Atlanta, Georgia, 1890–1940*, New York (originally PhD diss., George Washington University, 1978).
Rousseau, V. 2004, 'Emblem of an empire: the development of the Byzantine empress's crown', *Al–Masaq. Islam and the Medieval Mediterranean* 16, 5–15.
Rubery, E. 2013, 'The Vienna "Empress" ivory and its companion in Florence: crowned in different glories?', in Eastmond and James 2001, 99–114.
Rubin, B. 1960, *Das Zeitalter Iustinians*. Vol. 1, Berlin.
Rubin, Z. 1986, 'The Mediterranean and the dilemma of the Roman Empire in Late Antiquity', *Mediterranean Historical Review* 1, 13–62.
Ruprecht, S. 2021, *Unter Freunden: Nähe und Distanz in sozialen Netzwerken der Spätantike*, Munich.
Sabbah, G. 2010, 'Ammianus Marcellinus', in Marasco 2010, 43–84.
Sághy, M. and Schoolmann, E.M. 2017, (eds.) *Pagans and Christians in the Late Roman Empire: New Evidence, New Approaches (4th–8th Centuries)*, Budapest.
Salisbury, J. 2015, *Rome's Christian Empress: Galla Placidia Rules at the Twilight of the Empire*, Baltimore.
Saller, R. 1982, *Personal Patronage under the Early Empire*, Cambridge.
Saller, R. 1999, '*Pater familias, mater familias*, and the gendered semantics of the Roman household', *CPh* 94, 182–97.
Salzman, M. 1990, *On Roman Time: The Codex Calendar of 354 and the Rhythms of Urban Life in Late Antiquity*, Berkeley and Los Angeles.
Santoro L'Hoir, F. 1994, 'Tacitus and women's usurpation of power', *CW* 88, 5–25.
Sarantis, A. 2016, *Justinian's Balkan Wars: Campaigning, Diplomacy and Development in Illyricum, Thrace and the Northern World, A.D. 527–65*, Prenton.
Sarantis, A. 2018, 'Diplomatic relations between the eastern Roman empire and the "barbarian" successor states, 527–565', *History Compass* 16, 1–14.
Sarris, P. 2006, *Economy and Society in the Age of Justinian*, Cambridge.
Sarris, P. 2011, *Empires of Faith: The Fall of Rome to the Rise of Islam, 500–700*, Oxford.
Scarfo, B. 2020, *Pregnancy, Childbirth, and Primary Care-Givers in Ancient Rome*, Hamilton.
Schade, K. 2003, *Frauen in der Spätantike – Status und Repräsentation. Eine Untersuchung zur römischen und frühbyzantinischen Bildniskunst*, Mainz.
Schäfer, C. 2006, *Kleopatra*, Darmstadt.
Scheer, T. 2011, *Griechische Geschlechtergeschichte*, Munich.
Schlinkert, D., 1996, 'Vom Haus zum Hof. Aspekte höfischer Herrschaft in der Spätantike', *Klio* 78, 454–82.
Schmitt Pantel, P. 1994, (ed.) *History of Women in the West, Vol. 1: From Ancient Goddesses to Christian Saints*, Cambridge.

Scholten, H. 1995, *Der Eunuch in Kaisernähe: zur politischen und sozialen Bedeutung des praepositus sacri cubiculi im 4. und 5. Jahrhundert n. Chr.*, Frankfurt am Main.
Scholten, H. 1998, 'Der oberste Hofeunuch. Die politische Effizienz eines gesellschaftlich Diskriminierten', in Winterling 1998, 51–74.
Schreiner, P. 2010, 'Gregor von Tours und Byzanz', in Giessauf, Murauer, and Schennach 2010, 403–18.
Schrijver, F. 2018, 'The court of women in early Palaiologan Byzantium (ca.1260–1350)', *BMGS* 42, 219–36.
Schrijvers, J. 1986, 'Make your son a king: political power through matronage and motherhood', in van Berkel, Hagesteijn, and van de Velde 1986, 13–32.
Schwartz, E. 1934, *Publizistische Sammlungen zum Acacianischen Schisma*, Munich.
Schwedler, G. and Tounta, E. 2010 (eds.), *State, Power, Violence*, Vol. 3, Wiesbaden.
Scott, R. 2010, 'From propaganda to history and literature: the Byzantine stories of Theodosius' apple and Marcian's eagles', in Macrides 2010, 115–31.
Shahîd, I. 2003, 'The church of Sts Sergios and Bakchos in Constantinople: some new perspectives', in Avramea, Laiou, and Chrysos, 2003, 467–80.
Shepard, J. 2008, (ed.) *The Cambridge History of the Byzantine Empire c. 500–1492*, Cambridge.
Shepardson, C. 2009, 'Rewriting Julian's legacy: John Chrysostom's On Babylas and Libanius' Oration 24', *JLA* 2, 99–115.
Sidorenko, V. 2007, 'The copper coinage of Byzantine Bosporos (ca. 590–659), in Ajbabin and Ivakin 2007, 77–105.
Signes Codoñer, J. 2000, (trans.) *Procopio de Cesarea: Historia Secreta*, Madrid.
Signes Codoñer, J. 2003, 'Prokops Anekdota und Justinians Nachfolge', *JÖB* 53, 47–82.
Sion-Jenkis, M. 2016, 'Frauenfiguren bei Cassius Dio: der Fall der Livia', in Fromentin, Bertrand, Coltelloni-Trannoy, Molin, and Urso 2016, 725–40.
Sirago, V.A. 1996, *Galla Placidia. La nobilissma*, Milan.
Sirago, V.A. 1999, *Amalasunta la regina*, Milan.
Sivan, H. 2011, *Galla Placidia: The Last Roman Empress*, Oxford.
Smith, J. 2000, 'Did women have a transformation of the Roman world?', *Gender & History* 12, 552–71.
Smith, R. 2007, 'The imperial court of the late Roman empire, c. AD 300–c. AD 450', in Spawforth 2007b, 157–232.
Smith, R. 2011, 'Measures of difference: the fourth-century transformation of the Roman imperial court', *AJPh* 132, 125–51.
Sokolova, I. 1983, *Monety I pechati vizantijskovo Chersona*, Leningrad.
Sowers, B. 2008, *Eudocia: The Making of a Homeric Christian*, PhD thesis, University of Cincinnati.

Sowers, B. 2020, *In Her Own Words: The Life and Poetry of Aelia Eudocia*, Cambridge (MA).
Späth, T. 1994, *Männlichkeit und Weiblichkeit bei Tacitus. Zur Konstruktion der Geschlechter in der römischen Kaiserzeit*, Frankfurt am Main and New York.
Spawforth, A. 2007a, 'Introduction', in Spawforth 2007b, 2–16.
Spawforth, A. 2007b, (ed.) *The Court and Court Society in Ancient Monarchies*, Cambridge.
Speck, P. 1988, *Das geteilte Dossier. Beobachtungen zu den Nachrichten über die Regierung des Kaisers Herakleios und die seiner Söhne bei Theophanes und Nikephoros*, Bonn.
Speck, P. 1991, 'Julia Anicia, Konstantine der Grosse und die Polyeuktoskirche in Konstantinopel', *Poikila Byzantina* 11, 133–47.
Speck, P. 1997, 'Epiphania et Martine sur les monnaies d'Héraclius', *RN* 152, 457–65.
Spieser, J.-M. 2002, 'Impératrice romaines et chrétiennes', *T&M* 14 (Mélanges Gilbert Dagron), 593–604.
Spieser J.-M. 2011, (ed.) *Architecture Paléochrétienne*, Gollion.
Spieser, J.-M. and Yota, E. 2012, (eds.) *Donation et donateurs dans le monde byzantine. Actes du colloque international de l'Université de Fribourg, 13–15 mars 2008*, Paris.
Spira, A. 1992, (ed.) *Gregorii Nysseni Sermones*, Vol. 9.1, Leiden.
Stafford, P. 2001, 'Powerful women in the early Middle Ages: queens and abbesses', in Nelson and Linehan 2001, 398–415.
Stehlíková, E. 1993, 'Drama in Late Antiquity', *LF* 116, 1–9.
Stein, E. 1919, *Studien zur Geschichte des Byzantinischen Reiches, vornehmlich unter den Kaisern Justinus II und Tiberius Constantinus*, Stuttgart.
Stein, E. 1949, *Historie du Bas-Empire*, trans. J.R. Palanque, Vol. 2, Paris.
Steinicke, M. and Weinfurter, S. 2005, (eds.) *Investitur- und Krönungsrituale: Herrschaftseinsetzungen im kulturellen Vergleich*, Cologne.
Stewart, M. 2016, *The Soldier's Life: Martial Virtues and Manly Romanitas in the Early Byzantine Empire*, Leeds.
Stewart, M. 2020, *Masculinity, Identity, and Power: Politics in the Age of Justinian. A Study of Procopius*, Amsterdam.
Stöcklin-Kaldewey, S. 2015, 'Kaiser Julian, An den Senat und das Volk der Athener. Einleitung, Übersetzung und Kommentar', *Klio* 97, 687–725.
Stolte, B. 1999, 'Desires denied: marriage, adultery, and divorce in early Byzantine law', in James 1999, 77–86.
Stratos, A. 1968, *Byzantium in the Seventh Century, Vol. 1: 602–634*, Amsterdam.
Stratos, A. 1972, *Byzantium in the Seventh Century, Vol. 2: 634–641*, Amsterdam.
Stratos, A. 1975, *Byzantium in the Seventh Century, Vol. 3: 642–668*, Amsterdam.
Strobel, H. 2011, *The Artistic Matronage of Queen Charlotte (1744–1818): How a Queen Promoted Both Art and Female Artists in English Society*, Lewiston/NY.

Strootman, R. 2014, *Courts and Elites in the Hellenistic Empires: The Near East after the Achaemenids, c. 330 to 30 BCE*, Edinburgh.
Strube, C. 1984, *Polyeuktoskirche und Hagia Sophia: Umbildung und Auflösung antiker Formen, Entstehung des Kämpferkapitells*, Munich.
Szidat, J. 1977, *Historischer Kommentar zu Ammianus Marcellinus Buch XX–XXI, Teil I. Die Erhebung Julians*, Wiesbaden.
Szidat, J. 2013, 'Zur Rolle des Patriarchen von Konstantinopel bei der Erhebung eines Kaisers im 5. und 6. Jahrhundert', *GFA* 16, 51–61.
Talbot, A.-M. 2001, 'Building activity in Constantinople under Andronikos II: the role of women patrons in the construction and restoration of the monasteries', in Necipoğlu 2001, 329–43.
Taylor, C. 2018, *Late Antique Images of the Virgin Annunciate Spinning: Allotting the Scarlet and the Purple*, Leiden and Boston.
Temporini-Gräfin Vitzthum, H. 1979, *Die Frauen am Hofe Trajans. Ein Beitrag zur Stellung der Augustae im Principat*, Berlin.
Temporini-Gräfin Vitzthum, H. 2002, (ed.) *Die Kaiserinnen Roms. Von Livia bis Theodora*, Munich.
Theis, L., Mullett, M., and Grünbart, M. 2014, (eds.) *Female Founders in Byzantium and Beyond*, Vienna, Cologne, and Weimar.
Thomas, Y. 1994, 'The division of the sexes in Roman law', in Schmitt Pantel 1994, 83–137.
Thompson, E. 1947, *The Historical Work of Ammianus Marcellinus*, Cambridge.
Thomson, R. and Howard-Johnston, J. 1999, *The Armenian History Attributed to Sebeos*, 2 vols., Liverpool.
Thorpe, L. 1974, *Gregory of Tours: The History of the Frank. Translated by L. Thorpe*, London.
Tougher, S. 1998a, 'In praise of an empress: Julian's Speech of Thanks to Eusebia', in Ma. Whitby 1998, 103–23.
Tougher, S. 1998b, 'The advocacy of an empress: Julian and Eusebia', *CQ* 48, 595–99.
Tougher, S. 1999, 'Ammianus and the eunuchs', in Drijvers and Hunt 1999, 64–73.
Tougher, S. 2000, 'Ammianus Marcellinus on the empress Eusebia: a split personality?', *G&R* 47, 94–101.
Tougher, S. 2019, (ed.) *The Emperor in the Byzantine World: Papers from the Forty-Seventh Spring Symposium of Byzantine Studies*, London and New York.
Tougher, S. 2020, 'Eusebia and Eusebius: the roles and significance of Constantinian imperial women and court eunuchs', in Baker-Brian and Tougher 2020, 185–220.
Tougher, S. 2021, *The Roman Castrati: Eunuchs in the Roman Empire*, London.
Trampedach, K. 2005, 'Kaiserwechsel und Krönungsritual im Konstantinopel des 5.–6. Jahrhunderts', in Steinicke and Weinfurter 2005, 275–90.
Traube, L. 1894, (ed.) 'Cassiodori *Orationum Reliquiae*', in Mommsen 1894, 457–84.

Treadgold, W. 1990, 'A note on Byzantium's year of four emperors (641)', *BZ* 83, 431–33.
Treadgold, W. 2007, *The Early Byzantine Historians*, Basingstoke.
Treggiari, S. 1991, *Roman Marriage: Iusti Coniuges from the Time of Cicero to the Time of Ulpian*, Oxford.
Trout, D. 2015, 'Vergil and Ovid at the Tomb of Agnes: Constantina, epigraphy, and the genesis of Christian poetry', in Bodel and Dimitrova 2015, 263–82.
Tulluch, J.H. 2013, (ed.) *A Cultural History of Women in Antiquity*, London and New York.
Tuori, K. 2016, 'Judge Julia Domna? A historical mystery and the emergence of imperial legal administration', *The Journal of Legal History* 37, 180–97.
Turtledove, H. 1977, *The Immediate Successor of Justinian: A Study of the Persian Problem and of Continuity and Change in Internal Secular Affairs in the Later Roman Empire during the Reigns of Justin II and Tiberius II Constantine (AD 565–582)*, Michigan.
Turtledove, H. 1983, 'Justin II's observance of Justinian's Persian treaty of 562', *BZ* 76, 292–301.
Twardowska, K. 2017, 'The church foundations of Empress Pulcheria in Constantinople according to Theodore Lector's Church History and other contemporary sources', *Res Gestae* 5, 83–94.
Unterweger, U. 2014, 'The image of the empress Theodora as patron', in Theis, Mullett, and Grünbart 2014, 97–108.
Vallejo Girvès, M. 2017, 'Empress Verina among the pagans', in Sághy and Schoolmann 2017, 43–58.
Vallejo Girvès, M. 2022, 'Augusta Verina's symbols of power in the context of Leontius' usurpation of Zeno', in Girotti, Marsili, and Pomero 2022, 75–93.
Van Bremen, R. 1996, *The Limits of Participation: Women and Civic Life in the Greek East in the Hellenistic and Roman Periods*, Amsterdam.
Van Dieten, J. 1972, *Geschichte der Patriarchen von Sergios I. bis Johannes VI. (610–715)*, Amsterdam.
Van Hoof, L. and Van Nuffelen, P. 2017, 'The historiography of crisis: Jordanes, Cassiodorus and Justinian in mid-sixth-century Constantinople', *JRS* 107, 275–300.
Van Nuffelen, P. and Van Hoof, L. 2020, (trans.) *Jordanes*: Romana *and* Getica, Liverpool.
Vanderspoel, J. 2020, 'From the tetrarchy to the Constantinian dynasty: a narrative introduction', in Baker-Brian and Tougher 2020, 23–55.
Varner, E. 2001, 'Portraits, plots, and politics: "damnatio memoriae" and the images of imperial women', *Memoirs of the American Academy in Rome* 46, 41–93.
Vatsend, K. 2000, *Die Rede Julians auf Kaiserin Eusebia: Abfassungszeit, Gattungszugehörigkeit, panegyrische Topoi und Vergleiche, Zweck*, Oslo.

Veh, O. 2005, *Prokop: Anekdota. Geheimgeschichte des Kaiserhofs von Byzanz. Übersetzt von O. Veh*, Düsseldorf.
Veh, O. and G. Wirth ²1997, *Ammianus Marcellinus. Das römische Weltreich vor dem Untergang. Sämtliche erhaltene Bücher übersetzt von Otto Veh, eingeleitet und erläutert von Gerhard Wirth*, Amsterdam.
Veikou, M. 2016, 'Space in texts and space as text: a new approach to Byzantine spatial notions', *Scandinavian Journal of Byzantine and Modern Greek Studies* 2, 143–75.
Ven, P. van den 1965, 'L'accession de Jean le Scholastique au siège patriarcal de Constantinople en 565', *Byzantion* 35, 320–52.
Verhelst, B. and Scheijnen, T. 2022, (eds.) *Greek and Latin Poetry of Late Antiquity: Form, Tradition, and Context*, Cambridge and New York.
Viermann, N. 2021, *Herakleios, der schwitzende Kaiser: Die oströmische Monarchie in der ausgehenden Spätantike*, Berlin and Boston.
Viermann, N. 2022, 'Surpassing Solomon: church-building and political discourse in Late Antique Constantinople', in Klein and Wienand 2022, Berlin and Boston, 217–41.
Viermann, N. and Wienand, J. (forthcoming), (eds.) *Reading the Late Roman Monarchy*, Stuttgart.
Vihervalli, U. and Leonard, V. 2023, 'Elite women and gender-based violence in Late Roman Italy', in Wijndendaele 2023, 201–22.
Vitiello, M. 2006, '"Nourished at the breast of Rome": the queens of Ostrogothic Italy and the education of Roman elite', *RhM* 149, 398–412.
Vitiello, M. 2014, *Theodahad: A Platonic King at the Collapse of Ostrogothic Italy*, Toronto, Buffalo, and London.
Vitiello, M. 2017, *Amalasuintha: The Transformation of Queenship in the Post-Roman World*, Philadelphia.
Volkmann, H. 1972, 'Princeps' *DKP* 4, 1135–40.
Von Premerstein, A. 1903, 'Anicia Iuliana im Weiner Dioskorides-Kodex', *Jahrbuch der Kunsthistorischen Sammlungen des ah. Kaiserhauses* 24, 105–24.
Vukašinović, M. 2017, 'Great is the imperial dignity. Voices, *adventus*, and power of the first Macedonian empresses', *ByzSlav* 75, 99–115.
Vuolanto, V. 2015, *Children and Asceticism in Late Antiquity: Continuity, Family Dynamics and the Rise of Christianity*, Aldershot.
Vuolanto, V. 2019, 'Public agency of women in the later Roman world', in Rantala 2019, 41–61.
Wagner, N. 1967, *Getica. Untersuchungen zum Leben des Jordanes und zur frühen Geschichte der Goten*, Berlin.
Wagner-Hasel, B. 1988, '"Das Private wird politisch". Die Perspektive "Geschlecht" in der Altertumswissenschaft', in Becher and Rüsen 1988, 11–50.

Wagner-Hasel, B. 2020a, *The Fabric of Gifts: Culture and Politics of Giving and Exchange in Archaic Greece* (= rev. ed. of *Der Stoff der Gaben. Kultur und Politik des Schenkens und Tauschens im archaischen Griechenland*, Frankfurt and New York 2000), Lincoln/ NE.

Wagner-Hasel, B. 2020b, 'Instead of a conclusion: gynaecocracy in the Orient, Oriental seclusion in the Occident', in Carlà-Uhink and Wieber 2020, 200–209.

Wagner-Hasel, B. and Nosch, M.-L. 2019, (eds.) *Gaben, Waren und Tribute. Stoffkreisläufe und Antike Textilökonomie. Akten eines Symposiums (9./10. Juni 2016 in Hannover)*, Stuttgart.

Wainwright, L.A. 2018, *Portraits of Power: The Representations of Imperial Women in the Byzantine Empire*, Birmingham.

Wallace-Hadrill, A. 1981, 'The Emperor and his virtues', *Historia* 30, 298–320.

Wallace-Hadrill, A. 1996, 'The imperial court', in Av. Cameron and Garnsey 1996, 283–308.

Wallace-Hadrill, A. 2011, 'The Roman imperial court: seen and unseen in the performance of power', in Duindam, Artan, and Kunt 2011, 91–102.

Walthall, A. 2008a, 'Introducing palace women', in Walthall 2008b, 1–21.

Walthall, A. 2008b, (ed.) *Servants of the Dynasty: Palace Women in World History*, Berkeley, Los Angeles, and London.

Washington, B. 2016, *Roles of Imperial Women in the Later Roman Empire (AD 306–455)*, Edinburgh.

Washington, B. 2020, 'Playing with conventions in Julian's 'Encomium to Eusebia': does gender make a difference?', in Omissi and Ross 2020, 93–116.

Watson, A. 1998, (ed. and trans.) *The Digest of Justinian*, 2 vols., Philadelphia.

Webb, R. 2008, *Demons and Dancers: Performance in Late Antiquity*, London.

Weber, M. ²1966, *Staatssoziologie. Soziologie der rationalen Staatsanstalt und der modernen politischen Parteien und Parlamente. Mit einer Einführung und Erläuterungen herausgegeben von Johannes Winckelmann*, Berlin.

Weitzmann, K. 1979, (ed.) *Age of Spirituality: Late Antique and Early Christian Art, Third to Seventh Century*, New York.

Westbrook, N. 2020, *The Great Palace in Constantinople*, Turnhout.

Wharton, A. 1995, *Refiguring the Post-Classical City: Dura Europos, Jerash, Jerusalem and Ravenna*, Cambridge.

Whately, C. 2016, *Battles and Generals: Combat, Culture, and Didacticism in Procopius' Wars*, Leiden and Boston.

Whitby, Ma. 1998, (ed.), *The Propaganda of Power: The Role of Panegyric in Late Antiquity*, Leiden.

Whitby, Ma. and Whitby, Mi. 1989, *Chronicon Paschale 284–628 AD*, Liverpool.

Whitby, Mi. 1988, *The Emperor Maurice and His Historian: Theophylact Simocatta on Persian and Balkan Warfare*, Oxford.

Whitby, Mi. 1994, 'Images for emperors in late antiquity: a search for New Constantine', in Magdalino 1994, 83–93.
Whitby, Mi. 1998, 'Evagrius on patriarchs and emperors', in Ma. Whitby 1998, 321–44.
Whitby, Mi. 2001, 'The successors of Justinian', in Av. Cameron, Ward-Perkins, and Mi. Whitby 2001, 86–111.
Whitby, Mi. 2021, *The Wars of Justinian*, Barnsley and Philadelphia.
Whiting, M. 2022, 'From the city of Caesar to the city of God: routes, networks, and connectivity between Constantinople and Jerusalem', in Klein and Wienand 2022, 111–38.
Wickham, C. 1981, *Early Medieval Italy, Central Power and Local Society 400–1000*, London.
Wieber, A. 2000, 'Vorhang zur Macht – Herrschaftsteilhabe der weiblichen Mitglieder des spätantiken Kaiserhofs', in Kunst and Riemer 2000, 97–112.
Wieber, A. 2006, 'Women rulers', in *Brill's New Pauly*, eds. H. Cancik and H. Schneider, English edition by Christine F. Salazar. http://dx.doi.org/10.1163/1574-9347_bnp_e12222600 (last accessed 3 November 2023).
Wieber, A. 2010, 'Eine Kaiserin von Gewicht? Julians Rede auf Eusebia zwischen Geschlechtsspezifik, höfischer Repräsentation und Matronage', in Kolb 2010b, 253–75.
Wieber, A. 2013, 'Von dickflorigen Teppichen und mancherlei Geschenken. Strategien spätantiker Matronage', in Kunst 2013c, 123–36.
Wieber, A. 2019, 'Abgabe, Bestechung oder Geschenk? Textilien für die spätantike Obrigkeit', in Wagner-Hasel and Nosch 2019, 137–60.
Wieber-Scariot, A. 1998, 'Im Zentrum der Macht: zur Rolle der Kaiserin an spätantiken Kaiserhöfen am Beispiel der Eusebia in den *Res gestae* des Ammianus Marcellinus', in Winterling 1998, 103–31.
Wieber-Scariot, A. 1999, *Zwischen Polemik und Panegyrik. Frauen des Kaiserhauses und Herrscherinnen des Ostens in den* Res gestae *des Ammianus Marcellinus*, Trier.
Wienand, J. 2015, (ed.) *Contested Monarchy: Integrating the Roman Empire in the 4th Century AD*, Oxford.
Wijndendaele, J. 2023, (ed.), *Late Roman Italy: Imperium to Regnum*, Edinburgh.
Williamson, G. and Sarris, P. 2007, *Procopius: The Secret History. Translation by G. Williamson and P. Sarris*, London.
Winterling, A. 1997a, '"Hof". Versuch einer idealtypischen Bestimmung anhand der mittelalterlichen und frühneuzeitlichen Geschichte', in Winterling 1997b, 11–25.
Winterling, A. 1997b, (ed.) *Zwischen 'Haus' und 'Staat'. Antike Höfe im Vergleich*, Munich.
Winterling, A. 1998, (ed.) *Comitatus. Beiträge zur Erforschung des spätantiken Kaiserhofes*, Berlin.

Winterling, A. 1999, *Aula Caesaris: Studien zur Institutionalisierung des römischen Kaiserhofes in der Zeit von Augustus bis Commodus (31 v. Chr.–192 n. Chr.)*, Munich.

Winterling, A. 2009, *Politics and Society in Imperial Rome*, Malden/MA, Oxford and Chichester.

Winterling, A. 2011a, 'Zu Theorie und Methode einer neuen Römischen Kaisergeschichte', in Winterling 2011b, 1–11.

Winterling, A. 2011b, (ed.) *Zwischen Strukturgeschichte und Biographie. Probleme und Perspektiven einer neuen Römischen Kaisergeschichte zur Zeit von Augustus bis Commodus*, Munich.

Wolfram, H. 2009a, 'Matasunta', *Dizionario Biografico degli Italiani* 72, 108–109.

Wolfram, H. 2009b, *Die Goten. Von den Anfängen bis zur Mitte des sechsten Jahrhunderts. Entwurf einer historischen Ethnographie*, Munich.

Wood, I. 1994, *The Merovingian Kingdoms: 450–751*, London.

Woodacre, E. 2018, (ed.) *A Companion to Global Queenship*, Leeds.

Woodacre, E. 2021, *Queens and Queenship*, Leeds.

Woods, D. 1996, 'The Saracen defenders of Constantinople in 378', *Greek, Roman and Byzantine Studies* 37, 259–79.

Woods, D. 1998, 'On the death of the empress Fausta', *G&R* 45, 70–86.

Woods, D. 2004, 'The Constantinian origin of Justina (Themistius, Or. 3.43b)', *CQ* 54, 325–27.

Woods, D. 2006, 'Valentinian, Severa, Marina and Justina', *Classica et Mediaevalia* 57, 173–87.

Woods, D. 2015, 'Gregory of Nazianzus on the death of Julian the Apostate (Or. 5.13)', *Mnemosyne* 68, 297–303.

Zacharopoulou, E. 2016, 'Justinian and Theodora: rivals or partners in the Christianisation of Nubia? A critical approach to the account of John of Ephesus', *Journal of Early Christian History* 6, 67–85.

Zacos, G. and Veglery, A. 1959, 'An unknown *solidus* of Anastasios I', *NCirc* 67, 154–55.

Zanichelli, G. 2020, 'Early medieval iconography of the Virgin Mary between East and West', in Consolino and Herrin 2020, 167–204.

Zelzer, M. 1982, *Sancti Ambrosi opera, pars X. Epistulae et acta, tom. III: Epistularum liber decimus, Epistulae extra collectionem, Gesta concili Aquileiensis (CSEL 82,3)*, Vienna.

Zey, C. 2015, (ed.) *Mächtige Frauen? Königinnen und Fürstinnen im europäischen Mittelalter (11.– 14. Jahrhundert)*, Ostfildern.

Zuckerman, C. 1995, 'La petite Augusta et le Turc. Epiphania-Eudocie sur les monnaies d'Héraclius', *RN* 150, 113–26.

Zuckerman, C. 1997, 'Au sujet de la petite *augusta* sur les monnaies d'Héraclius', *RN* 152, 473–78.

Zuckerman, C. 2010, 'On the titles and office of the Byzantine Βασιλευς', *Mélanges Cécile Morrisson, T&M* 16, 865–90.

Zuckerman, C. 2013a, 'Heraclius and the return of the Holy Cross', in Zuckerman 2013b, 197–218.
Zuckerman, C. 2013b, *Constructing the Seventh Century. Travaux et Mémoires 17*, Paris.

Fig. 1: Trier Adventus Ivory (date uncertain). © Ann Münchow / Hohe Domkirche Trier

Fig. 2: Steelyard weight with bust of an empress (fifth century). © New York Metropolitan Museum of Art, Accession Number 19840.416.a, b

Fig. 3: Vienna Dioscurides, Portrait of Anicia Juliana. © Österreichische Nationalbibliothek Wien, *Codex (Vindobonensis) medicus Graecus 1*, fol. 6v

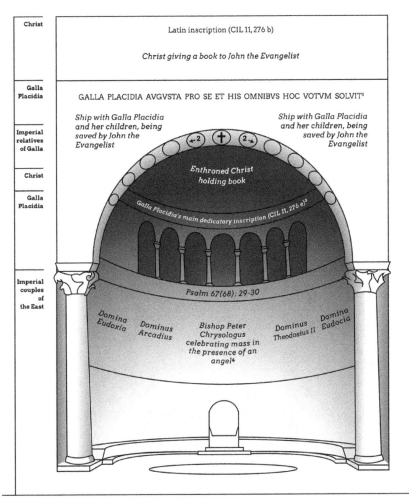

[1] „Galla Placidia Augusta fulfilled this vow in her name and the name of all of these." (CIL 11, 276 b; trans. AW)
[2] Bust medallions of male imperial relatives of Galla: Constantinian, Valentinian and Theodosian lineage.
[3] CIL 11, 276 e: Galla's reason for founding the church – the rescue from a storm.
[4] Imperial couples of the East (Galla's half-brother Arcadius, his wife, their son and daughter in-law or Licinia Eudoxia and Arcadius as children of Theodius and Eudocia), above the clergy's bench.

Fig. 4: San Giovanni Evangelista, reconstruction (based on Deliyannis 2010, fig. 13, 69). © Cambridge University Press 2010, reproduced with permission of The Licensor through PLSclear, annotations by Anja Wieber

Fig. 5: Diptych of Ariadne (fifth/sixth century). © Kunsthistorisches Museum Wien / Antikensammung X 39

Fig. 6: Diptych of Ariadne (fifth/sixth century). © Museo Nazionale del Bargello / Collezioni Riccardi, Florence, inv. 24C and 5a

Fig. 7: Detail of the Florentine diptych of Ariadne (fig. 6)

Fig. 8: Justin II and Sophia, Constantinople, *follis*, 568/69. *MIBEc* 43a. © Classical Numismatics Group, LLC. E-auction 281, Lot: 477 / www.cngcoins.com

Fig. 9: Justin II and Sophia, Constantinople, *follis*, 572/73. *MIBEc* 73. © Classical Numismatics Group, LLC. Feature auction 100, Lot: 1984 / www.cngcoins.com

Fig. 10: Justin II, Cyzicus, *pentanummium*, 565/66–577/78. *MIBEc* 53. © Classical Numismatics Group, LLC. E-auction 379, Lot: 611 / www.cngcoins.com

Fig. 11: Tiberius II and Anastasia, Thessalonica, half-*follis*, 580/81. *MIBEc* 65. © Classical Numismatics Group, LLC. E-auction 259, Lot: 431 / www.cngcoins.com

Fig. 12: Maurice, Constantina, and Theodosius, Cherson, *follis*, 582–602. *MIBEc* 157. © Classical Numismatics Group, LLC. Triton XIII – Session Three – Roman Imperial Coinage Part II through World Coinage Part I, Lot: 918 / www.cngcoins.com

Fig. 13: Theodosius, Maurice, and Constantina, Carthage, silver half-*siliqua*, 590–592. *MIBEc* 59a–b. © Classical Numismatics Group, LLC. Feature auction 88, Lot: 1572 / www.cngcoins.com

Fig. 14: Phocas and Leontia, Antioch, *follis*, 602/603. *MIBEc* 83a. © Classical Numismatics Group, LLC. Feature auction 76, Lot: 1681 / www.cngcoins.com

Fig. 15: Heraclius, Heraclius Constantine, and Martina, Constantinople, *follis*, 618/19. *MIB* III 161. © Classical Numismatics Group, LLC. E-auction 351, Lot: 708 / www.cngcoins.com

Fig. 16: Heraclius, Heraclius Constantine, and Martina, Rome, half-*follis*, 624/25. *MIB* III 244. © Classical Numismatics Group, LLC. E-auction 382, Lot: 480 / www.cngcoins.com

Fig. 17: Heraclius, Heraclius Constantine, and Martina, Carthage, third *siliqua*, 617–641 (?). *MIB* III 149. © Classical Numismatics Group, LLC. E-auction 481, Lot: 647 / www.cngcoins.com

Fig. 18: Marble Portrait Bust of a Woman with Scroll, formerly identified as Anicia Juliana (fifth century). © New York Metropolitan Museum of Art / The Cloisters Collection, 1966 (66.25)

Fig. 19: Diptych of Flavius Areobindus Dagalaifus, 506. © Musée de Cluny / Musée national du Moyen Âge (Cl. 13135)

Fig. 20: Theodora and her Entourage, including (possibly) Antonina (sixth century). San Vitale, Ravenna. © Opera di Religione della Diocesi di Ravenna

Fig. 21: Detail of the Theodora mosaic panel in Ravenna (fig. 20): Theodora's ladies-in-waiting, including (possibly) Antonina. © Opera di Religione della Diocesi di Ravenna

Indices

Index of Names

Adamantia 60
Albia Domnica 269–70
Amalaberga 244
Amalafrida 244
Amalasuintha 4, 6, 244, 247–49, 257
Ambrose of Milan 74, 89, 91, 165, 267
Anastasia (niece-in-law to Anastasius) 212
Anastasia, Aelia (formerly Ino, wife of Tiberius II), 134, 184, 192, 234, 267, 270
Anastasius (grandson of Theodora) 229, 236–40
Anastasius I 12, 63, 141, 170n65, 178, 208–9, 211, 216, 218, 220, 222, 224
Anicia Juliana 6, 12, 32, 35, 205–9, 212, 214, 218–22, 267–68
Anicius Olybrius 207
Antonina Patricia 6, 12, 223–41, 265
Arabia (daughter of Justin II and Sophia) 97, 106, 108
Arcadius 8, 67, 70–71, 74, 84, 87n76, 88, 90–95, 147–48, 183, 262, 266
Areobindus, Flavius 208–11, 219–20, 268
Ariadne (wife of Anastasius) 4, 36–37, 63, 99, 141, 170n65, 178, 209, 218–20, 262, 265–66, 270
Aristaenetus, 61–62
Aspar 141, 209

Athalaric 244–45
Attila 151, 267

Baduila 251–52
Belisarius 12, 167–72, 224–41, 246, 249–51, 255

Cassiodorus 243–47, 250, 253, 258
Charito (widow of Jovian), 73, 270
Constans I 71–72, 78, 80, 84
Constans II 138, 145–47, 149, 151–52
Constantia (daughter of Constantius II) 63, 74–77, 85–86, 265
Constantina (daughter of Constantine) 19, 23, 43, 51, 61–62, 77–79, 81, 83–85, 88, 265–66
Constantina (wife of Maurice) 106, 141, 184, 192–93, 197, 270
Constantine I 19, 34, 43, 56, 62–63, 79–82, 86, 88, 92, 159–60, 164–65, 177, 183, 206, 213, 216–17, 266–68
Constantius II 10–11, 19, 43–64, 70–73, 70–73, 76–81, 83–85, 219, 265–66, 268
Constantius III 87, 94
Cyrus (patriarch of Alexandria) 147–48

David (son of Heraclius) 149
David, "the Translator" 150–52
Demetrias 247, 256

329

Diocletian 23, 43, 63, 80, 266
Domentzia (daughter of Phocas) 142
Domnica (wife of Valens) 71, 76, 92, 269

Epiphania (daughter of Heraclius) 140, 142–43, 190–92
Eudocia, Aelia 4, 5, 35, 84, 87–88
Eudocia (first wife of Heraclius) 139–40, 191
Eudoxia, Aelia 8, 68, 74, 79, 86, 88–95, 210
Eudoxia, Licinia 27, 35, 37, 151, 265–66, 270
Euphemia (empress) 212–13, 216, 220
Euphemia, Saint 35, 214–15, 221
Eusebia (wife of Constantius II) 11, 15–16, 24, 30, 43–64, 265, 268
Eusebius (brother of Eusebia) 44, 51–52, 59–60, 62
Eutherius (praepositus sacri cubiculi) 48, 58–59
Eutropia (daughter of Constantius I) 77–83, 88, 269
Eutychios (patriarch of Constantinople) 108–11

Faustina (wife of Constantius II) 63, 71, 76–77, 85, 265, 269
Flaccilla, Aelia Flavia 36

Galeria Valeria (daughter of Diocletian) 27, 63–64, 80, 86, 266–67, 269
Galerius 27, 63–64, 80, 86, 267
Galla (wife of Theodosius I) 87, 92, 271
Galla Placidia 4, 34, 82, 87, 94–95, 192, 270
Gelimer 119, 167–68
Germanus 12, 235–36, 243, 251–57
Gorgonia 60
Gratian 63, 70–71, 73–74, 76–77, 86, 92

Gregoria (daughter of Niketas) 142

Helena (daughter of Constantine, wife of Julian) 11, 43, 50–58, 62, 73n23, 266–68
Helena (mother of Constantine) 4, 31, 36, 63, 82, 92, 153, 165, 183, 210
Heraclius 6, 10–11, 138–51, 153, 169, 187–92, 194, 198, 263, 269
Heraclius Constantine 138, 140–50, 154, 189–91
Heraclonas 138, 143–46, 148–54
Honoria 34, 151, 267
Honorius 31, 81, 87, 90, 92, 95, 160, 164, 262–63, 265
Hypatius 44, 60

Ino *see* Aelia Anastasia

Jerome 213, 247
Joannina (daughter of Antonina) 12, 223–24, 229, 236–41
John (nephew of Vitalian) 224, 229, 233, 235–36, 250
John Chrysostom 10, 11, 67, 211
John of Ephesus 97–98, 100–8, 110–12, 118, 121–22, 125, 129, 132
John Scholastikos 104, 109–10
John the Cappadocian 224, 227–29, 233–36, 240–41
Jordanes 243–44, 246, 251–57
Jovian 71–73, 270
Julia Domna 3, 162–64
Julian 11, 15, 19, 24, 30, 43–64, 71–72, 159, 164, 267–68
Justin I 12, 101, 149, 167, 180–82, 208, 211–12, 216, 243
Justin II 10–11, 97–104, 106–9, 111–13, 115–36, 143, 178–85, 190, 193, 194, 196, 241, 262, 266, 269, 270
Justina 71–74, 77, 79, 81–82, 84–86, 88–89, 91, 265, 270–71

Justinian I 106, 109, 111–36, 153, 157–61, 164, 166–75, 180–83, 208, 217–18, 221–22, 226, 228, 233, 240–41, 243–44, 246–48, 256, 262, 264

Kubrat 150–51

Lactantius 64, 266–67
Laeta 76, 270
Leo I 63, 140–41, 221, 265–66
Leo II 140, 194
Leontia (daughter of Leo I) 141, 221
Leontia (wife of Phocas) 186, 194, 198
Leontius (bishop of Tripolis ad Maenandrum) 58, 61
Licinia Eudoxia 27, 35, 37, 151, 265–66, 270
Licinius 63, 80, 88, 266
Livia 13, 162–64

Magnentius 19, 62, 72, 77–85, 265
Magnus Maximus 71, 271
Marcellus (magister equitum per Gallias) 47–48, 55, 58
Marcian 141, 209, 220, 264–66
Maria (wife of Honorius) 90, 263
Marina Severa 74, 86–86
Martina 6, 11–13, 137–54, 169, 190–92, 269–70
Mary Theotokos 214–15, 219
Matasuintha 12, 243–59, 268
Maurice 10, 97, 103, 106, 112, 116–17, 134, 136, 140–41, 144, 149, 152, 184–86, 190, 193–95, 266–67
Maximian 43, 79
Maximinus Daza 64, 80, 86, 266, 269
Maximinus Daza's wife 80, 269
Maximus Confessor 148
Melania the Elder 30
Melania the Younger 209

Nepotianus 77–80, 83
Nicetas 142

Olybrius (son of Anicia Iuliana) 207–8, 210, 268

Patricius (son of Aspar) 141, 210n31
Petronius Maximus 151, 265, 270
Philagrius 146–47
Phocas 139, 141–142, 149, 152, 186–87, 194
Photius (son of Antonina) 224–25, 228–29, 233–35, 237
Polyeuktos, Saint 35, 208, 214, 216, 217, 221
Prisca (wife of Diocletian) 80, 86, 269
Priscus 142, 149
Procopius (usurper) 63, 76–77, 85–87, 265, 269
Procopius of Caesarea 8, 10, 12, 16–17, 33, 118–20, 153, 157–62, 166, 168–70, 173–74, 223–41, 243–44, 246, 250–54, 263
Pulcheria (daughter of Theodosius I) 261, 265
Pulcheria (sister of Theodosius II) 4, 23, 35, 84, 87–88, 95, 141, 153, 192, 209, 211, 213–14, 222, 263, 265–66
Pyrrhus (patriarch of Constantinople) 145–46, 148–50, 154

Salutius (praefectus praetorio Orientis) 47–48
Serena 4, 31, 81, 92, 265
Shahrbaraz 142
Silverius (bishop of Rome) 227–33
Sophia (wife of Justin II) 6, 10–11, 97–13, 115–36, 143, 178–83, 186, 193–94, 196–97, 221, 241, 262, 266–67, 270

Theodahad 244–46, 248–49, 257
Theodora 1–4, 6, 8, 10, 12–13, 15–17, 25, 31, 33, 79, 84, 98, 105, 116–21, 135–36, 153, 157–62, 166–76, 181, 193, 205, 211, 214, 218, 221–31, 234–41, 243, 252, 254, 256, 262–64
Theodoric the Amal 208–9, 268
Theodosius (adopted son of Antonina and Belisarius) 225
Theodosius (son of Maurice) 140, 185–86
Theodosius I 36, 70–71, 73–74, 76, 87–88, 92, 94, 144, 217, 220, 261
Theodosius II 8, 84, 87–88, 92, 140–41, 153, 160, 164–65, 183, 213, 228–35, 237, 240, 263, 265–66

Tiberius II 10, 86, 116–17, 126, 130–36, 141, 144, 183–85, 193–94, 221, 243, 267

Valens 71, 76, 85–86, 89, 92, 266
Valentinian I 63, 70–74, 77, 81, 84–86, 263, 266, 271
Valentinian II 70–74, 76–77, 88–89, 91–92, 267
Valentinian III 87, 94, 151, 207–8, 265, 266–67
Valentinus 148–54
Verina 36, 63, 265, 270
Vetranio 19, 62, 77, 78, 81, 83, 85, 87, 265
Vitalian 211, 224, 229, 233, 235–36, 250
Vitigis 12, 244–51, 254–58

Zeno 12, 63, 141, 160, 208–10, 210, 220, 265

Index of Places

Antioch 23, 60, 62, 67, 179–84, 187, 194, 196, 198, 211

Carthage 179–81, 184–86, 188, 189–90, 194–99, 241
Cherson 179, 181, 184–90, 194–95, 197, 199
Constantinople 6, 10, 12–13, 21, 23, 35, 49, 67–69, 74–76, 80, 84–85, 87–88, 90–95, 97, 100, 104, 108–9, 111, 127, 130, 134–35, 138–54, 161, 169, 179, 183–90, 196, 198, 206–7, 211–17, 220, 224, 228–29, 233–35, 241, 243, 248, 251–57, 261–62, 265
Cyprus 148, 188, 199
Cyzicus 179–80, 187–88, 192, 196, 198–99

Nicomedia 21, 62, 179–80, 187–88, 192, 196, 198

Ravenna 1, 25, 31, 180, 188–89, 199, 236, 241, 243–46, 248, 250–51, 256
Rome 12–13, 24, 28, 46, 49, 52–54, 56, 58, 61, 78–80, 88, 115, 122, 126–27, 144, 162, 180–81, 188–89, 199, 208–9, 214, 228–29, 231–33, 241, 246, 250–51, 264–65

Thessalonica / Thessaloniki 27, 179–80, 184, 187–88, 196–98

General Index

Acacian Schism 211, 216
Adoption 102–3, 106–8, 225, 227–38, 230–31
Agency 2, 4, 6, 7, 10–13, 18, 25, 28, 43, 98, 100–1, 105, 112, 116, 136, 146, 206, 208, 210, 220, 224, 226, 229, 231–32, 240–41, 256–57, 268, 271

Basileia *see* Rulership

Celibacy 268
Ceremonies / imperial ceremonial 6–7, 9–10, 22, 24, 33, 61, 141, 160–61, 166–75, 163–64
    Accession 47, 55, 77, 89–90, 89, 100–1, 112–13, 115, 117, 123, 132, 145, 167, 169–71, 172, 212, 221, 248, 257
    Adoratio 10, 158, 160, 164–66, 263
    Adventus 24–25, 46, 265
    Audience 8, 27, 30, 123, 131, 136, 169–70, 264–65
    On the move 21, 24
    Salutatio 158–60
    Triumph 101, 118, 167–74, 213, 262
Chalcedon
    Council 104, 215
    Creed 35, 148, 211, 215
Comes excubitorum 101, 117, 131–32, 149, 151
Consistory / consistorium 160, 170, 263
Costume 259
    Imperial costume 24
    Mappa 31, 34, 37
    Paludamentum / chlamys 24, 34, 37, 179, 189, 218–19
    Tablion 37

Court
    Court ceremonies *see* Ceremonies / imperial ceremonial
    Court studies 7
    Female court / court of women / gynaikonitis 1, 6, 8, 9, 21–23, 223
    Gender segregation 21–22, 263–64
    Imperial court 1, 6, 7, 9, 10–11, 13, 51, 55, 67, 79, 88–89, 100, 103, 117, 132, 206, 264, 268

Demography 266, 268
Divorce 83, 97–98, 106–8, 110–11, 239, 263
Dynasty 4, 8, 25, 34, 36, 43–44, 47, 53–54, 57, 62, 64, 67, 71, 74–76, 78, 81–82, 84, 86–88, 126–27, 137–45, 153, 177, 193–94, 206, 209, 216–18, 254, 263, 266–68
    Dynastic potential 18n25, 262n5, 265–68, 271
    Dynastic prestige 18–19

Emperor
    Imperial couple 11, 27, 44, 49, 57, 61, 101–2, 104–5, 123, 158, 160–61, 172–73, 175, 179–87, 193–94, 262, 264
Empress
    Dowager e. 27, 45, 63, 82–83, 146–47, 154, 270
    E.'s household 8–9, 12, 20, 60, 208,
Eunuchs 1, 7, 22–23, 51, 59–60, 208, 264, 266

Family networks 142
Follis (pl. folles) 99, 180–81, 184–85, 187–89, 196

Gender / Gender roles 5, 13, 16,
   18–21, 25, 27–30, 34, 37–39, 48,
   105–6, 112, 125, 135, 174, 205,
   214, 220–21, 223
Guards 62, 149

Henotikon 215

Insignia, imperial / regalia 9, 37, 181,
   185, 218, 221, 267
Investiture, imperial 59, 109–11

Marriage 2, 6, 11–12, 26–27, 43–45,
   50–51, 63, 68, 79, 84, 88, 97–100,
   105–12, 138–39, 141–44, 151,
   154, 157, 177, 189–90, 208–10,
   214, 218, 220, 22, 225–26, 229,
   236–41, 243–57, 262–70
   Remarriage 97, 210, 263
Matronage 10–11, 15, 25–45, 49, 265
   Matrona 26–28
Mental illness 102, 116, 129, 221
Miaphysites / monophysites 104–5,
   108, 110, 121, 148, 211, 215
Midwife / obstetrix 53–56
Mint 88, 179–99
Mobility 265

Palace physicians 55, 131
Patrician / patricius/a 30, 32, 133–34,
   159, 170, 173, 207, 210, 212, 219,
   221, 223, 226, 232, 251, 254,
   255–56
Private vs. public 8, 17, 19, 45, 51,
   16, 169

Queenship, medieval 4, 268

Ritual 10, 24, 157–75, 263–65
Rulership 28, 171, 174, 263
   Arche 20, 262
   Basileia 20, 24
   Co-rulership 262, 264, 268

Silentiarii 9, 264
Siliqua (pl. siliquae) 180, 186, 190,
   196–99
Solidus 99, 129, 132, 134, 180, 183
Succession, imperial 132, 138–39,
   141–41, 144–45, 149, 154, 194,
   209, 251, 254, 256, 269

Tetrarchy 63, 144, 266, 269
Title, imperial 20, 28, 36, 44,
   63, 92–94, 106, 116, 134, 179,
   182–83, 191, 205, 207, 226, 250,
   255, 256, 264

Usurpation / usurper 19, 43–44, 52,
   62–63, 67, 71–72, 76–81, 83–86,
   94, 109, 246, 265, 270–71

Violence 76, 80–82, 88, 94, 194
   Kidnapping 268, 270

Widow / widowhood 10–11, 38,
   67–69, 71, 73–76, 80–82, 84–88,
   92–93, 97, 108, 110, 112, 141, 146,
   169, 210, 255–56, 262, 265–66,
   268–71